CLYMER®
MANUALS

HONDA

CRF230F, CRF230L & CRF230M • 2003-2013

WHAT'S IN YOUR TOOLBOX?

More information available at Clymer.com
Phone: 805-498-6703

Haynes Publishing Group
Sparkford Nr Yeovil
Somerset BA22 7JJ England

Haynes North America, Inc
861 Lawrence Drive
Newbury Park
California 91320 USA

ISBN 10: 1-59969-680-0
ISBN-13: 978-1-59969-680-5
Library of Congress: 2014933649

Common spark plug conditions

NORMAL
Symptoms: Brown to grayish-tan color and slight electrode wear. Correct heat range for engine and operating conditions.
Recommendation: When new spark plugs are installed, replace with plugs of the same heat range.

WORN
Symptoms: Rounded electrodes with a small amount of deposits on the firing end. Normal color. Causes hard starting in damp or cold weather and poor fuel economy.
Recommendation: Plugs have been left in the engine too long. Replace with new plugs of the same heat range. Follow the recommended maintenance schedule.

CARBON DEPOSITS
Symptoms: Dry sooty deposits indicate a rich mixture or weak ignition. Causes misfiring, hard starting and hesitation.
Recommendation: Make sure the plug has the correct heat range. Check for a clogged air filter or problem in the fuel system or engine management system. Also check for ignition system problems.

ASH DEPOSITS
Symptoms: Light brown deposits encrusted on the side or center electrodes or both. Derived from oil and/or fuel additives. Excessive amounts may mask the spark, causing misfiring and hesitation during acceleration.
Recommendation: If excessive deposits accumulate over a short time or low mileage, install new valve guide seals to prevent seepage of oil into the combustion chambers. Also try changing gasoline brands.

OIL DEPOSITS
Symptoms: Oily coating caused by poor oil control. Oil is leaking past worn valve guides or piston rings into the combustion chamber. Causes hard starting, misfiring and hesitation.
Recommendation: Correct the mechanical condition with necessary repairs and install new plugs.

GAP BRIDGING
Symptoms: Combustion deposits lodge between the electrodes. Heavy deposits accumulate and bridge the electrode gap. The plug ceases to fire, resulting in a dead cylinder.
Recommendation: Locate the faulty plug and remove the deposits from between the electrodes.

TOO HOT
Symptoms: Blistered, white insulator, eroded electrode and absence of deposits. Results in shortened plug life.
Recommendation: Check for the correct plug heat range, over-advanced ignition timing, lean fuel mixture, intake manifold vacuum leaks, sticking valves and insufficient engine cooling.

PREIGNITION
Symptoms: Melted electrodes. Insulators are white, but may be dirty due to misfiring or flying debris in the combustion chamber. Can lead to engine damage.
Recommendation: Check for the correct plug heat range, over-advanced ignition timing, lean fuel mixture, insufficient engine cooling and lack of lubrication.

HIGH SPEED GLAZING
Symptoms: Insulator has yellowish, glazed appearance. Indicates that combustion chamber temperatures have risen suddenly during hard acceleration. Normal deposits melt to form a conductive coating. Causes misfiring at high speeds.
Recommendation: Install new plugs. Consider using a colder plug if driving habits warrant.

DETONATION
Symptoms: Insulators may be cracked or chipped. Improper gap setting techniques can also result in a fractured insulator tip. Can lead to piston damage.
Recommendation: Make sure the fuel anti-knock values meet engine requirements. Use care when setting the gaps on new plugs. Avoid lugging the engine.

MECHANICAL DAMAGE
Symptoms: May be caused by a foreign object in the combustion chamber or the piston striking an incorrect reach (too long) plug. Causes a dead cylinder and could result in piston damage.
Recommendation: Repair the mechanical damage. Remove the foreign object from the engine and/or install the correct reach plug.

CONTENTS

QUICK REFERENCE DATA

MODEL: _____   YEAR: _____

VIN NUMBER: _____

ENGINE SERIAL NUMBER: _____

THROTTLE BODY SERIAL NUMBER OR I.D. MARK: _____

TIRE INFLATION PRESSURE

	kPa (psi)
CRF230F models	
Front and rear tires	100 (15)
CRF230L models	
Front	125 (18)
Rear	150 (22)
CRF230M models	
Front and rear tires	200 (29)

RECOMMENDED LUBRICANTS AND FUEL

Air filter	Foam air filter oil
Brake fluid	DOT 4
Engine oil	
Grade	API SG or higher/JASO MA*
Viscosity	SAE10W-30*
Fork oil	Pro Honda Suspension Fluid SS-8
Fuel	
CRF230F models	Octane rating of 91 or higher
CRF230L and CRF230M models	Octane rating of 86 or higher
Steering and suspension lubricant	Multipurpose grease

*See text for additional information.

ENGINE OIL CAPACITY

	Liters	Quarts
Oil change only	1.0	1.1
After engine disassembly	1.2	1.3

CLUTCH, BRAKE AND THROTTLE ADJUSTMENTS

Clutch lever free play	10-20 mm (3/8-3/4 in.)
Rear brake master cylinder pushrod height	
(CRF230L and CRF230M models)	69.5 mm (7.74 in.)
Rear brake pedal free play (CRF230F models)	20-30 mm (3/4-1 1/4 in.)
Throttle grip free play	2-6 mm (1/8-1/4 in.)

DRIVE CHAIN AND SLIDER SPECIFICATIONS

Drive chain	
CRF230F models	DID 520V6 (110 links)
	RK520MOZ2 (110 links)
CRF230L models	DID 520VC5 (100 links)
	RK520MOZ9 (100 links)
CRF230M models	DID 520V (100 links)
	RK520MOZ9 (100 links)
Drive chain slack	
CRF230F models	20-30 mm (3/4-1 1/4 in.)
CRF230L and CRF230M models	25-35 mm (1.0-1 3/8 in.)
Drive chain roller diameter (CRF230F models)	18 mm (0.7 in.) min.

SPARK PLUG SPECIFICATIONS

Spark plug gap	0.8-0.9 mm (0.03-0.04 in.)
Spark plug type	
Standard	NGK DPR8EA-9 or Denso X24EPR-U9
Cold weather operation*	NGK DP7EA-9 or Denso X22EP-U9

*Below 41° F (4° C).

IDLE SPEED SPECIFICATION

Engine idle speed	1300-1500 rpm

Table 10 ENGINE COMPRESSION AND VALVE CLEARANCE SPECIFICATIONS

Engine compression	1294 kPa (187 psi) @ 450 rpm
Valve clearance	
CRF230L and CRF230M models	
Intake and exhaust	0.08-0.12 mm (0.003-0.005 in.)
CRF230F models	
Intake and exhaust	0.10 mm (0.004 in.)

Table 11 MAINTENANCE TORQUE SPECIFICATIONS

	N•m	in.-lb.	ft.-lb.
Clutch lever pivot bolt			
2004-on CRF230F models	1	9	–
Clutch lever pivot nut			
2004-on CRF230F models	6	53	–
Crankshaft hole cap	8	71	–
Drive chain cover stay screw	6.0	53	–
Drive chain slider screw			
CRF230F models	4	35	–
CRF230L and CRF230M models	4.2	37	–
Engine mounting plate bolts			
8-mm	34	–	25
10-mm	59	–	44
Gearshift lever pinch bolt			
CRF230F models	12	106	–
CRF230L and CRF230M models	16	–	12
Oil centrifugal filter rotor cover screws	5	44	–
Oil drain cap	15	–	11
Rear axle nut			
CRF230F models	108	–	80
CRF230L and CRF230M models	93	–	69
Rear brake pedal locknut	17.2	–	13
Spark arrestor bolts			
CRF230F models	14	–	10
CRF230L and CRF230M models*	6.35	56	–
Spark plug			
New		Refer to text	
Used	18	–	13
Timing hole cap			
CRF230F models	6	53	–
CRF230L and CRF230M models	10	89	–
Valve adjuster cover	15	–	11
Valve adjuster locknut	14	–	10
Wheel rim locknut	13	115	–
Wheel spokes	4	35	–

* Apply molybdenum-disulfide grease to bolt threads.

CHAPTER ONE

GENERAL INFORMATION

This detailed and comprehensive manual covers 2003-2013 Honda CRF230F models and 2008-2009 CRF230L and CRF230M models.

The text provides complete information on maintenance, tune-up, repair and overhaul. Hundreds of photos and drawings guide the reader through every job. All procedures are in step-by-step format and designed for the reader who may be working on the motorcycle for the first time.

MANUAL ORGANIZATION

A shop manual is a reference tool and, as in all Clymer manuals, the chapters are thumb-tabbed for easy reference. Important items are indexed at the end of the manual. Frequently-used specifications and capacities from individual chapters are summarized in the *Quick Reference Data* section at the front of the manual.

During some of the procedures there will be references to headings in other chapters or sections of the manual. When a specific heading is called out in a step, it is italicized as it appears in the manual. If a sub-heading is indicated as being "in this section", it is located within the same main heading. For example, the sub-heading *Handling Gasoline Safely* is located within the SAFETY main heading.

This chapter provides general information on shop safety, tool use, service fundamentals and shop supplies. **Tables 1-10** at the end of the chapter provide general motorcycle specifications, mechanical data and shop information.

Chapter Two provides methods for quick and accurate diagnoses of problems. Troubleshooting procedures present typical symptoms and logical methods to pinpoint and repair a problem.

Chapter Three explains all routine maintenance.

Subsequent chapters describe specific systems, such as engine, clutch, transmission, fuel system, electrical system, wheels, tires, drive chain, suspension, brakes and body components.

Specification tables, when applicable, are located at the end of each chapter.

WARNINGS, CAUTIONS AND NOTES

The terms WARNING, CAUTION and NOTE each have specific meanings in this manual.

A WARNING emphasizes areas where injury or even death could result from negligence. Mechanical damage may also occur. WARNINGS are to be taken seriously.

A CAUTION emphasizes areas where equipment damage could result. Disregarding a CAUTION could cause permanent mechanical damage, though injury is unlikely.

A NOTE provides additional information to make a step or procedure easier or clearer. Disregarding a NOTE could cause inconvenience, but would not cause equipment damage or injury.

SAFETY

Professional mechanics can work for years and never sustain a serious injury or mishap. Follow these guidelines and practice common sense to safely service the motorcycle:

1. Do not operate the motorcycle in an enclosed area. The exhaust gases contain carbon monoxide, an odorless, colorless and tasteless poisonous gas. Carbon monoxide levels build quickly in small enclosed areas and can cause unconsciousness and death in a short time. Make sure the work area is properly ventilated, or operate the motorcycle outside.

2. Never use gasoline or any flammable liquid to clean parts. Refer to *Handling Gasoline Safely* and *Cleaning Parts* in this section.

3. Never smoke or use a torch in the vicinity of flammable liquids, such as gasoline or cleaning solvent.

4. Avoid contact with engine oil and other chemicals. Most are known carcinogens. Wash your hands thoroughly after coming in contact with engine oil. If possible, wear a pair of disposable gloves.

5. If welding or brazing on the motorcycle, remove the fuel tank and shocks to a safe distance at least 15 m (50 ft.) away.

6. Use the correct types and sizes of tools to avoid damaging fasteners.

7. Keep tools clean and in good condition. Replace or repair worn or damaged equipment.

8. When loosening a tight fastener, be guided by what would happen if the tool slips.

9. When replacing fasteners, make sure the new fasteners are the same size and strength as the originals.

10. Keep the work area clean and organized.

11. Wear eye protection any time the safety of your eyes is in question. This includes procedures involving drilling, grinding, hammering, compressed air and chemicals.

12. Wear the correct clothing for the job. Tie up or cover long hair so it can not catch in moving equipment.

13. Do not carry sharp tools in clothing pockets.

14. Always have an approved fire extinguisher available. Make sure it is rated for gasoline (Class B) and electrical (Class C) fires.

15. Do not use compressed air to clean clothes, the motorcycle or the work area. Debris may be blown into the eyes or skin. Never direct compressed air at anyone. Do not allow children to use or play with any compressed air equipment.

16. When using compressed air to dry rotating parts, hold the part so it cannot rotate. Do not allow the force of the air to spin the part. The air jet is capable of rotating parts at extreme speeds. The part may be damaged or disintegrate, causing serious injury.

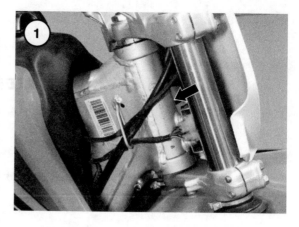

17. Do not inhale the dust created by brake pad and clutch wear. These particles may contain asbestos. In addition, some types of insulating materials and gaskets may contain asbestos. Inhaling asbestos particles is hazardous to health.

18. Never work on the motorcycle while someone is working under it.

19. When placing the motorcycle on a stand or overhead lift, make sure it is secure before walking away.

Handling Gasoline Safely

Gasoline is a volatile, flammable liquid and is one of the most dangerous items in the shop. Because gasoline is used so often, many people forget that it is hazardous. Only use gasoline as fuel for gas internal combustion engines. Keep in mind when working on a motorcycle, gasoline is always present in the fuel tank, fuel line and carburetor. To avoid an accident when working around the fuel system, carefully observe the following precautions:

1. Never use gasoline to clean parts. Refer to *Cleaning Parts* (this section).

2. When working on the fuel system, work outside or in a well-ventilated area.

3. Do not add fuel to the fuel tank or service the fuel system while the motorcycle is near open flames, sparks or where someone is smoking. Gasoline vapor is heavier than air, collects in low areas and is more easily ignited than liquid gasoline.

4. Allow the engine to cool completely before working on any fuel system component.

5. Do not store gasoline in glass containers. If the glass breaks, an explosion or fire may occur.

6. Immediately wipe up spilled gasoline with rags. Store the rags in a metal container with a lid until they can be properly disposed of, or place them outside in a safe place for the fuel to evaporate.

7. Do not pour water onto a gasoline fire. Water spreads the fire and makes it more difficult to put

6. Wear a vapor respirator if the instructions call for it.

7. Wash hands and arms thoroughly after cleaning parts.

8. Keep chemicals, especially coolant, away from children and pets,. Animals are attracted to anti-freeze.

9. Thoroughly clean all oil, grease and cleaner residue from any part that must be heated.

10. Use a nylon brush when cleaning parts. Metal brushes may cause a spark.

11. When using a parts washer, only use the solvent recommended by the manufacturer. Make sure the parts washer is equipped with a metal lid that will lower in case of fire.

Warning Labels

Most manufacturers attach information and warning labels to the motorcycle. These labels contain instructions that are important to safety when operating, servicing, transporting and storing the motorcycle. Refer to the owner's manual for the description and location of labels. Order replacement labels from the manufacturer if they are missing or damaged.

SERIAL NUMBERS

Serial numbers are stamped in various locations on the frame, engine and carburetor. Record these numbers in the *Quick Reference Data* section in the front of this manual. Have these numbers available when ordering parts.

The VIN number (**Figure 1**) is stamped on the right side of the steering head.

The engine serial number (**Figure 2**) is stamped on the lower, left surface of the crankcase.

The carburetor serial number is located on the side of the carburetor body above the float bowl. On CRF230F models, the serial number (**Figure 3**) appears on the right side. On CRF230L and CRF230M models, the serial number appears on the left side.

FASTENERS

WARNING
Do not install fasteners with a strength classification lower than what was originally installed by the manufacturer. Doing so may cause equipment failure and/or damage.

Proper fastener selection and installation is important to ensure the motorcycle operates as designed and can be serviced efficiently. Make sure replace-

out. Use a class B, BC or ABC fire extinguisher to extinguish the fire.

8. Always turn off the engine before refueling. Do not spill fuel onto the engine or exhaust system. Do not overfill the fuel tank. Leave air space at the top of the tank to allow room for the fuel to expand due to temperature fluctuations.

Cleaning Parts

Cleaning parts is one of the more tedious and difficult service jobs performed in the home garage. Many types of chemical cleaners and solvents are available for shop use. Most are poisonous and extremely flammable. To prevent chemical exposure, vapor buildup, fire and injury, observe each product's warning label and note the following:

1. Read and observe the entire product label before using any chemical. Always know what type of chemical is being used and whether it is poisonous and/or flammable.

2. Do not use more than one type of cleaning solvent at a time. If mixing chemicals is required, measure the proper amounts according to the manufacturer.

3. Work in a well-ventilated area.

4. Wear chemical-resistant gloves.

5. Wear safety glasses.

ment fasteners meet the original manufacturer's requirements.

Threaded Fasteners

Threaded fasteners secure most of the components on the motorcycle. Most are tightened by turning them clockwise (right-hand threads). If the normal rotation of the component being tightened would loosen the fastener, it may have left-hand threads. If a left-hand threaded fastener is used, it is noted in the text.

Two dimensions are required to match the thread size of the fastener: the number of threads in a given distance and the outside diameter of the threads.

Two systems are currently used to specify threaded fastener dimensions: the U.S. Standard system and the metric system (**Figure 4**). Pay particular attention when working with unidentified fasteners; mismatching thread types can damage threads.

To ensure the fastener threads are not mismatched or cross-threaded, start all fasteners by hand. If a fastener is difficult to start or turn, determine the cause before tightening with a wrench.

Match fasteners by their length (L, **Figure 5**), diameter (D) and pitch (T), or distance between thread crests. A typical metric bolt may be identified by the numbers, 8-1.25 × 130. This indicates the bolt has a diameter of 8 mm, the distance between thread crests is 1.25 mm and the length is 130 mm. Always measure bolt length as shown in L, **Figure 5** to avoid installing replacements of the wrong lengths.

If a number is located on the top of a metric fastener (**Figure 5**), this indicates the strength. The higher the number, the stronger the fastener. Typically, unnumbered fasteners are the weakest.

Many screws, bolts and studs are combined with nuts to secure particular components. To indicate the size of a nut, manufacturers specify the internal diameter and thread pitch.

The measurement across two flats on a nut or bolt indicates the wrench size.

Torque Specifications

The materials used in the manufacture of the motorcycle may be subjected to uneven stresses if fasteners are not installed and tightened correctly. Improperly-installed fasteners or ones that worked loose can cause extensive damage. It is essential to use an accurate torque wrench, as described in this chapter, with the torque specifications in this manual.

Specifications for torque are provided in Newton-meters (N•m), foot-pounds (ft.-lb.) and inch-pounds (in.-lb.). Refer to **Table 7** for general torque recom-

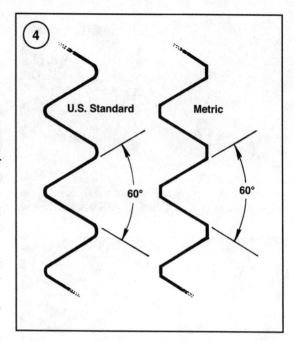

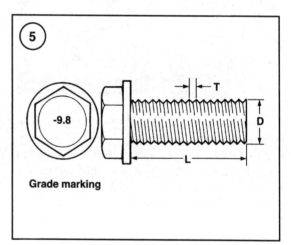

mendations. To use **Table 7**, first determine the size of the fastener as described in this section. Torque specifications for specific components are located at the end of the appropriate chapters. Torque wrenches are covered in *Tools* (this chapter).

Self-Locking Fasteners

Several types of bolts, screws and nuts incorporate a system that creates interference between the two fasteners. Interference is achieved in various ways. The most common types used are the nylon insert nut, and application of a dry adhesive coating on the threads of a bolt.

Self-locking fasteners offer greater holding strength than standard fasteners, which improves their resistance to vibration. Self-locking fasteners cannot be reused. The materials used to form the lock become

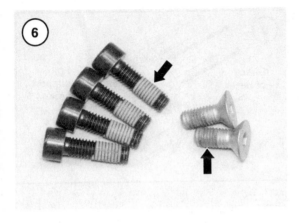

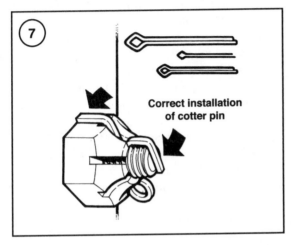

Correct installation of cotter pin

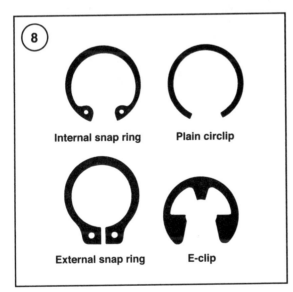

Internal snap ring   Plain circlip

External snap ring   E-clip

fasteners, remove the threadlock residue from the threads. Then, apply a new coating of the threadlock specified in the text.

Washers

The two basic types of washers are flat washers and lockwashers. Flat washers are simple discs with a hole to fit a screw or bolt. Lockwashers are used to prevent a fastener from working loose. Washers can be used as spacers and seals or to help distribute fastener load and prevent the fastener from damaging the component.

As with fasteners, when replacing washers make sure the replacements meet the manufacturer's original specifications.

Cotter Pins

A cotter pin is a split metal pin inserted into a hole or slot to prevent a fastener from loosening. In certain applications, such as the rear axle, the fastener must be secured in this way. For these applications, a cotter pin and castellated (slotted) nut is used.

To use a cotter pin, first make sure the diameter is correct for the hole in the fastener. After correctly tightening the fastener and aligning the holes, insert the cotter pin through the hole and bend the ends over the fastener (**Figure 7**). Unless instructed to do so, never loosen a tightened fastener to align the holes. If the holes do not align, tighten the fastener just enough to achieve alignment.

Cotter pins are available in various diameters and lengths. Measure length from the bottom of the head to the tip of the shortest pin.

Snap Rings and E-clips

Snap rings (**Figure 8**) are circular-shaped metal retaining clips. They are required to secure parts and gears in place on parts such as shafts, pins or rods. External-type snap rings are used to retain items on shafts. Internal-type snap rings secure parts within housing bores. In some applications, in addition to securing the component(s), snap rings of varying thicknesses also determine endplay. These are usually called selective snap rings.

The two basic types of snap rings are machined and stamped snap rings. Machined snap rings (**Figure 9**) can be installed in either direction because both faces have sharp edges. Stamped snap rings (**Figure 10**) are manufactured with a sharp edge and round edge. When installing a stamped snap ring in a thrust application, install the sharp edge facing away from the part producing the thrust.

distorted after the initial installation and removal. Do not replace self-locking fasteners with standard fasteners.

Some fasteners are equipped with threadlock (**Figure 6**) preapplied to the fastener threads. When replacing these fasteners, do not apply additional threadlock. When it is necessary to reuse one of these

E-clips are used when it is not practical to use a snap ring. Remove E-clips with a flat-bladed screwdriver by prying between the shaft and E-clip. To install an E-clip, center it over the shaft groove and push or tap it into place.

Observe the following when installing snap rings:
1. Remove and install snap rings with snap ring pliers. Refer to *Tools* (this chapter).
2. In some applications, it may be necessary to replace snap rings after removing them.
3. Compress or expand snap rings just enough to install them. If overly expanded, they lose their retaining ability.
4. After installing a snap ring, make sure it seats completely.
5. Wear eye protection when removing and installing snap rings.
6. If you're installing a snap ring on a splined shaft, align the snap ring gap with a groove, not with one of the splines **(Figure 9)**.

SHOP SUPPLIES

Lubricants and Fluids

Periodic lubrication helps ensure a long service life for any type of equipment. Using the correct type of lubricant is as important as performing the lubrication service, although in an emergency the wrong lubricant type is better than not using one. The following section describes the types of lubricants most often required. Make sure to follow the manufacturer's recommendations.

Engine oils

Engine oil for a four-stroke motorcycle engine use is classified by three standards: the American Petroleum Institute (API) service classification, the Society of Automotive Engineers (SAE) viscosity rating and the Japanese Automobile Standards Organization (JASO) T 903 certification standard.

The JASO certification specifies the oil has passed requirements specified by Japanese motorcycle manufacturers.

The API and SAE information is found on all oil container labels. The JASO information is found on oil containers sold by the oil manufacturer specifically for motorcycle use. Two letters indicate the API service classification. The number or sequence of numbers and letter (10W-40 for example) is the oil's viscosity rating. The API service classification and the SAE viscosity index are not indications of oil quality.

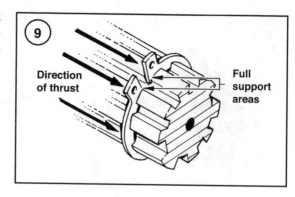

Direction of thrust — Full support areas

The API service classification indicates that the oil meets specific lubrication standards. The first letter in the classification S indicates that the oil is for gasoline engines. The second letter indicates which standard the oil satisfies.

The JASO certification label identifies two separate oil classifications and includes a registration number to ensure the oil has passed all JASO certification standards for use in four-stroke motorcycle engines. The classifications are: MA (high friction applications) and MB (low friction applications). The JASO standards indicate that the oil is suitable for use in wet-type motorcycle clutches. Do not use automotive oils that include friction modifiers. These can cause clutch slippage.

Viscosity is an indication of the oil's thickness. Thin oils have a lower number while thick oils have a higher number. Engine oils fall into the 5- to 50-weight range for single-grade oils.

Most manufacturers recommend multi-grade oil. These oils perform efficiently across a wide range of operating conditions. Multi-grade oils are identified by a W after the first number, which indicates the low-temperature viscosity.

Engine oils are most commonly mineral (petroleum-based); however, synthetic and semi-synthetic types are being used more frequently. Always use oil with a classification recommended by the manufacturer (Chapter Three). Using oil with a different classification can cause engine damage.

Greases

Grease is lubricating oil with thickening agents added to it. The National Lubricating Grease Institute (NLGI) grades grease. Grades range from No. 000 to No. 6, with No. 6 being the thickest. Typical multipurpose grease is NLGI No. 2. For specific applications, manufacturers may recommend a water-resistant type grease, or one with an additive such as molybdenum-disulfide (MoS_2).

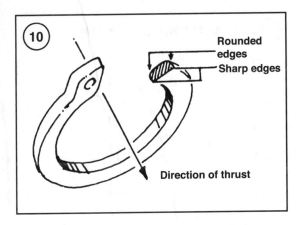

Rounded edges
Sharp edges
Direction of thrust

Brake fluid

WARNING
Never put a mineral (petroleum-based) oil into the brake system. Mineral oil causes rubber parts in the system to swell and break apart, resulting in complete brake failure.

Brake fluid is the hydraulic fluid used to transmit hydraulic pressure (force) to the wheel brakes. Brake fluid is classified by the Department of Transportation (DOT). Current designations for brake fluid are DOT 3, DOT 4 and DOT 5. This classification appears on the fluid container. The models covered in this manual require DOT 4 brake fluid.

Each type of brake fluid has its own definite characteristics. Do not intermix different types of brake fluid; this may cause brake system failure. DOT 5 brake fluid is silicone-based. DOT 5 is not compatible with other brake fluids or in systems for which it was not designed. Mixing DOT 5 fluid with other fluids may cause brake system failure. When adding brake fluid, only use DOT 4 brake fluid.

Brake fluid damages any plastic, painted or plated surface it contacts. Use extreme care when working with brake fluid, and remove any spills immediately with soap and water.

Hydraulic brake systems require clean and moisture-free brake fluid. Never reuse brake fluid. Keep containers and reservoirs properly sealed.

Cleaners, Degreasers and Solvents

Many chemicals are available to remove oil, grease and other residue from the motorcycle. Before using cleaning solvents, consider their uses and disposal methods, particularly if they are not water-soluble. Local ordinances may require special procedures for the disposal of many types of cleaning chemicals. Refer to *Safety* and *Cleaning Parts* in this chapter for more information on their uses.

Use brake parts cleaner to clean brake system components when contact with petroleum-based products will damage seals. Brake parts cleaner leaves no residue. Use electrical contact cleaner to clean electrical connections and components without leaving any residue. Carburetor cleaner is a powerful solvent used to remove fuel deposits and varnish from fuel system components. Use this cleaner carefully as it may damage finishes.

Generally, degreasers are strong cleaners used to remove heavy accumulations of grease from engine and frame components.

Most solvents are designed to be used with a parts washing cabinet for individual component cleaning. For safety, use only nonflammable solvents or those with a high flash point.

Gasket Sealant

Sealants are most often used in combination with a gasket or seal. Occasionally, they are used alone. Use extreme care when choosing a sealant different from the type originally recommended. Choose sealants based on their resistance to heat, various fluids and their sealing capabilities.

One of the most common sealants is RTV, or room temperature vulcanizing, sealant. This sealant cures at room temperature over a specific time period. This allows the repositioning of components without damaging gaskets.

Moisture in the air causes the RTV sealant to cure. Always install the tube cap as soon as possible after applying RTV sealant. RTV sealant has a limited shelf life and will not cure properly if the shelf life has expired. Keep partial tubes sealed and discard them if they have surpassed the expiration date. If there is no expiration date on a sealant tube, use a permanent marker and write the date on the tube when it is first opened. Manufacturers usually specify a shelf life of one year after a container is opened, though it is recommended to contact the sealant manufacturer to confirm shelf life.

Removing RTV sealant

Silicone sealant is used on many engine gasket surfaces. When cleaning parts after disassembly, a razor blade or gasket scraper is required to remove the silicone residue that cannot be pulled off by hand from the gasket surfaces. To avoid damaging gasket surfaces, use silicone stripper (Permatex part No. 80647), or an equivalent, to help soften the residue before scraping.

Applying RTV sealant

Clean all old sealant residue from the mating surfaces. Then, inspect the mating surfaces for damage. Remove all sealant material from blind threaded holes; it can cause inaccurate bolt torque. Spray the mating surfaces with aerosol parts cleaner, and then wipe with a lint-free cloth. Because gasket surfaces must be dry and oil-free for the sealant to adhere, be thorough when cleaning and drying the parts.

Apply RTV sealant in a continuous bead 2-3 mm (0.08-0.12 in.) thick. Circle all the fastener holes unless otherwise specified. Do not allow any sealant to enter these holes. Drawings in specific chapters show how to apply the sealer to specific gasket surfaces. Assemble and tighten the fasteners to the specified torque within the time frame recommended by the RTV sealant manufacturer.

Gasket Remover

Aerosol gasket remover can help remove stubborn gaskets. This product can speed up the removal process and prevent damage to the mating surface that may be caused by using a scraping tool. Most of these types of products are very caustic. Follow the gasket remover manufacturer's instructions for use.

Threadlock

> *CAUTION*
> *Threadlock is anaerobic and damages most plastic parts and surfaces. Use caution when using this product in areas where plastic components are located.*

Threadlock is a fluid applied to the threads of fasteners. After tightening the fastener, the fluid dries and becomes a solid filler between the threads. This makes it difficult for the fastener to work loose from vibration or heat expansion and contraction. Some threadlock formulas compounds also provide a seal against fluid leaks.

Before applying threadlock, remove any old threadlock residue from both thread areas and clean them with aerosol parts cleaner. Use the threadlock sparingly. Excess fluid can run into adjoining parts.

Threadlock is are available in various strengths, temperatures and repair applications.

TOOLS

Most of the procedures in this manual can be carried out with hand tools and test equipment already

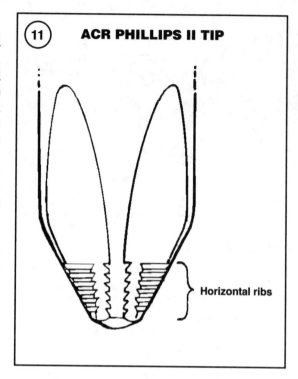

familiar to the home mechanic. Always use the correct tools for the job. Keep tools organized and clean. Store them in a tool chest with related tools organized together.

Quality tools are essential. The best are constructed of high-strength alloy steel. These tools are light, easy-to-use and resistant to wear. Their working surfaces are devoid of sharp edges and the tools are carefully polished. They have an easy-to-clean finish and are comfortable to use. Quality tools are a good investment.

When purchasing tools to perform the procedures covered in this manual, consider the tool's potential frequency of use. If a tool kit is just now being started, consider purchasing a tool set from a quality tool supplier. These sets are available in many tool combinations and offer substantial savings when compared to individually-purchased tools. As work experience grows and tasks become more complicated, specialized tools can be added.

Some of the procedures in this manual specify special tools. In most cases, the tool is illustrated in use. In some case it may be possible to substitute similar tools or fabricate a suitable replacement. However, at times, the specialized equipment or expertise required may make it impractical for the home mechanic to perform the procedure. When necessary, such operations are identified in the text with the recommendation to have a dealership or specialist perform the task.

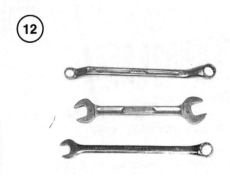

panies offer ACR Phillips II screwdrivers in different tip sizes and interchangeable bits to fit screwdriver bit holders.

Another way to prevent camout and increase the grip of a Phillips screwdriver is to apply valve grinding compound or Permatex Screw & Socket Gripper onto the screwdriver tip. After loosening/tightening the screw, clean the screw recess to prevent possible contamination.

Wrenches

Box-end, open-end and combination wrenches (**Figure 12**) are available in a variety of types and sizes.

The number stamped on the wrench refers to the distance between the work areas gripping the fastener. This size must match the size of the fastener head.

The box-end wrench is an excellent tool because it grips the fastener on all sides. This reduces the chance of the tool slipping. The box-end wrench is designed with either a 6- or 12-point opening. For stubborn or damaged fasteners, the 6-point provides superior holding ability by contacting the fastener across a wider area at all six edges. For general use, the 12-point works well. It allows the wrench to be removed and reinstalled without moving the handle over such a wide arc.

An open-end wrench is fast and works best in areas with limited overhead access. It contacts the fastener at only two points, and is subject to slipping under heavy force or if the tool or fastener is worn. A box-end wrench is preferred in most instances, especially when breaking loose and applying the final tightening force to a fastener.

The combination wrench has a box-end on one end, and an open-end on the other. This combination makes it a convenient tool.

Adjustable Wrenches

An adjustable wrench (**Figure 13**) can fit nearly any nut or bolt head that has clear access around its entire perimeter.

However, adjustable wrenches contact the fastener at only two points, which makes them more subject to slipping off the fastener. One jaw is adjustable and may loosen, which increases this possibility. Make certain the solid jaw is the one transmitting the force.

However, adjustable wrenches are typically used to prevent a large nut or bolt from turning while the other end is being loosened or tightened with a box-end or socket wrench.

Screwdrivers

The two basic types of screwdrivers are the slotted tip (flat-bladed) and the Phillips tip. These are available in sets that often include an assortment of tip sizes and shaft lengths.

As with all tools, use the correct screwdriver. Make sure the size of the tip conforms to the size and shape of the fastener. Use them only for driving screws. Never use a screwdriver for prying or chiseling. Repair or replace worn or damaged screwdrivers. A worn tip may damage the fastener, making it difficult to remove.

Phillips-head screws are often damaged by incorrectly fitting screwdrivers. Poor quality or damaged Phillips screwdrivers can back out and round over the screw head (camout). Compounding the problem of using poor quality screwdrivers are Phillips-head screws made from weak or soft materials and screws initially installed with air tools.

The best type of screwdriver to use on Phillips screws is the ACR Phillips II screwdriver, which has horizontal anti-camout ribs found on the driving faces or flutes of the screwdrivers tip (**Figure 11**). ACR Phillips II screwdrivers are to be used with ACR Phillips II screws, but they also work well on all common Phillips screws. A number of tool com-

Socket Wrenches, Ratchets and Handles

> *WARNING*
> *Do not use hand sockets with air or impact tools; they may shatter and cause injury. Always wear eye protection when using impact or air tools.*

Sockets (**Figure 14**) that attach to a ratchet handle are available with 6-point (A, **Figure 15**) or 12-point (B) openings. Sockets also come in different drive sizes. The drive size indicates the size of the square hole that accepts the ratchet handle. The number stamped on the socket is the size of the work area gripping the fasteners and must match the fastener head.

As with wrenches, a 6-point socket provides superior-holding ability, while a 12-point socket needs to be moved only half as far to reposition it on the fastener.

Sockets are designated for either hand tool or impact tool use. Impact sockets are made of a thicker material for more durability. Compare the size and wall thickness of a 19-mm hand socket (A, **Figure 16**) and the 19-mm impact socket (B). Use impact sockets when using an impact driver or air tool. Use hand sockets with hand-driven attachments.

Various handles are available for sockets. The speed handle is used for fast operation. Flexible ratchet heads in varying lengths allow the socket to be turned with varying force and at odd angles. Extension bars allow the socket setup to reach difficult areas. The ratchet is the most versatile. It allows the user to install or remove the nut without removing the socket.

Sockets, combined with any number of drivers make them undoubtedly the fastest, safest and most convenient tool for fastener removal and installation.

Impact Driver

> *WARNING*
> *Do not use hand sockets with air or impact tools because they may shatter and cause injury. Always wear eye protection when using impact or air tools.*

An impact driver provides extra force for removing fasteners by converting the impact of a hammer into a turning motion. This makes it possible to remove stubborn fasteners without damaging them. Impact drivers and interchangeable bits (**Figure 17**) are available from most tool suppliers. When using a socket with an impact driver make sure the socket is designed for impact use. Refer to *Socket Wrenches, Ratchets and Handles* (this section).

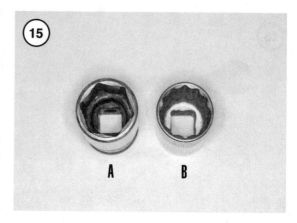

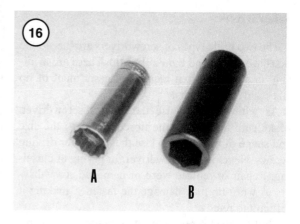

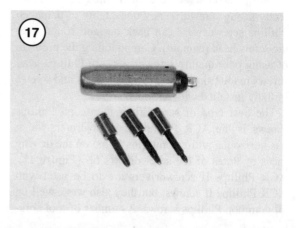

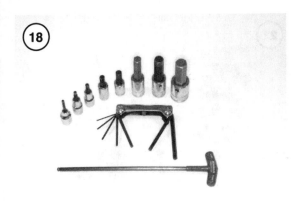

Allen Wrenches

Allen, or setscrew wrenches (**Figure 18**), are used on fasteners with hexagonal recesses in the fastener head. These wrenches are available in L-shaped bar, socket and T-handle types. Allen bolts are sometimes called socket bolts.

Torx Fasteners

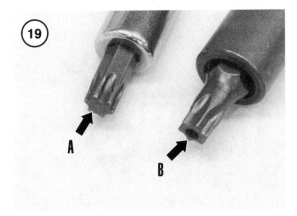

A Torx fastener head has a 6-point, star-shaped pattern (A, **Figure 19**). Torx fasteners are identified with a T and a number indicating their drive size; T25 for example. Torx drivers are available in L-shaped bars, sockets and T-handles. Tamper-resistant Torx fasteners are also used and have a round shaft in the center of the fastener head. Tamper-resistant Torx fasteners require a Torx bit with a hole in the center of the bit (B, **Figure 19**).

Torque Wrenches

A torque wrench (**Figure 20**) is used with a socket and torque adapter, or similar extension, to tighten a fastener to a measured torque. Torque wrenches come in several drive sizes (1/4, 3/8, 1/2 and 3/4) and use various methods of displaying the torque value. The drive size indicates the size of the square drive that accepts the socket, adapter or extension. Common methods of displaying the torque value are the reflecting beam, the dial indicator and the audible click. When choosing a torque wrench, consider the torque range, drive size and accuracy. The torque specifications in this manual provide an indication of the range required. A torque wrench is a precision tool that must be properly cared for to remain accurate. Store torque wrenches in cases or separate padded drawers within a toolbox. Follow the tool manufacturer's instructions for their care and calibration.

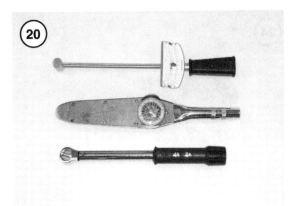

Torque Adapters

Torque adapters (**Figure 21**), or extensions, extend or reduce the reach of a torque wrench. Specific adapters are required to perform some of the procedures in this manual. These are available from the motorcycle manufacturer or can be fabricated by welding a socket (A, **Figure 22**) that matches the fastener onto a metal plate (B). Use another socket or extension (C, **Figure 22**) welded to the plate to attach to the torque wrench drive (**Figure 23**). The adapter shown (**Figure 24**) is used to tighten a fastener while preventing another fastener on the same shaft from turning.

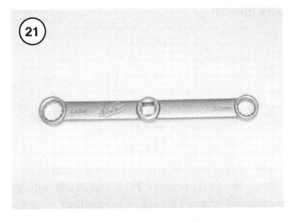

If a torque adapter changes the effective lever length, the torque reading on the wrench will not equal the actual torque applied to the fastener. It is necessary to recalibrate the torque setting on the wrench to compensate for the change of lever length. When a torque adapter is used at a right angle to the drive head, calibration is not required because the lever length has not changed.

To recalculate a torque reading when using a torque adapter, use the following formula, and refer to **Figure 25**.

$$TW = \frac{TA \times L}{L + A}$$

TW is the torque setting or dial reading on the wrench.

TA is the torque specification and the actual amount of torque that will be applied to the fastener.

A is the amount the adapter increases (or in some cases reduces) the effective lever length as measured along the centerline of the torque wrench.

L is the lever length of the wrench as measured from the center of the drive to the center of the grip.

The effective lever length is the sum of L and A.

Example:

TA = 20 ft.-lb.

A = 3 in.

L = 14 in.

$$TW = \frac{20 \times 14}{14 + 3} = \frac{280}{17} = 16.5 \text{ ft.-lb.}$$

In this example, the torque wrench would be set to the recalculated torque value (TW = 16.5 ft.-lb.). When using a beam-type wrench, tighten the fastener until the pointer aligns with 16.5 ft.-lb. In this example, although the torque wrench is pre-set to 16.5 ft.-lb., the actual torque applied is 20 ft.-lb.

Pliers

Pliers come in a wide range of types and sizes. Pliers are useful for holding, cutting, bending, and crimping. Do not use them to turn fasteners unless they are designed to do so. **Figure 26** and **Figure 27** show several types of pliers. Each design has a specialized function. Slip-joint pliers are general-purpose pliers used for gripping and bending. Diagonal cutting pliers are needed to cut wire and can be used to remove cotter pins. Needlenose pliers are used to hold or bend small objects. Locking pliers (**Figure 27**), sometimes called Vise Grips, hold objects tightly. They have many uses ranging from holding two parts together, to gripping the end of a broken stud. Use caution when using locking pliers; the sharp jaws will damage the objects they hold.

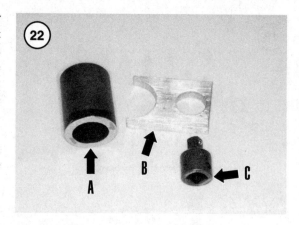

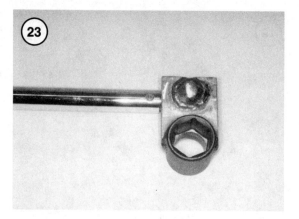

Snap Ring Pliers

WARNING
Snap rings can slip and fly off when removing and installing them. In addition, the snap ring pliers tips may break. Always wear eye protection when using snap ring pliers.

Snap ring pliers are specialized pliers with tips that fit into the ends of snap rings to remove and install them.

Snap ring pliers (**Figure 28**) are available with a fixed action (either internal or external) or the pli-

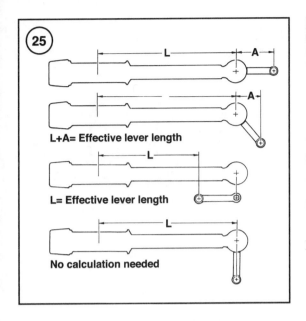

L+A= Effective lever length

L= Effective lever length

No calculation needed

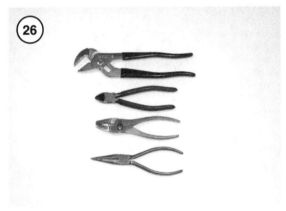

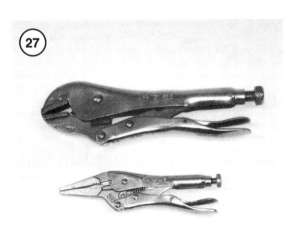

Hammers

WARNING
Always wear eye protection when using
hammers. Make sure the hammer face
is in good condition and the handle is
not cracked. Select the correct hammer
for the job and make sure to strike the
object squarely. Do not use the handle
or the side of the hammer to strike an
object.

Various types of hammers are available to fit a number of applications. A ball-peen hammer is used to strike another tool, such as a punch or chisel. Soft-faced hammers are required when a metal object must be struck without damaging it. Never use a metal-faced hammer on engine and suspension components; damage will occur in most cases.

Ignition Grounding Tool

Some test procedures in this manual require turning the engine over without starting it. Do not remove the spark plug cap(s) and crank the engine without grounding the plug cap(s). Doing so will damage the ignition system.

An effective way to ground the system is to fabricate the tool shown in **Figure 29** from a No. 6 screw, two washers and a length of wire with an alligator clip soldered on one end. To use the tool, insert it into the spark plug cap and attach the alligator clip to a known engine ground. A separate grounding tool is required for each spark plug cap.

This tool is safer than a spark plug or spark tester because there is no spark firing across the end of the plug/tester to potentially ignite fuel vapor spraying from an open spark plug hole or leaking fuel component.

ers are convertible (one tool works on both internal and external snap rings). They may have fixed tips or interchangeable ones of various sizes and angles. For general use, select convertible type pliers with interchangeable tips.

MEASURING TOOLS

The ability to accurately measure components is essential to successfully service many components. Equipment is manufactured to close tolerances, and obtaining consistently accurate measurements is essential.

Each type of measuring instrument is designed to measure a dimension with a certain degree of accuracy and within a certain range. When selecting the measuring tool, make sure it is applicable to the task.

As with all tools, measuring tools provide the best results if cared for properly. Improper use can damage the tool and cause inaccurate results. If any measurement is questionable, verify the measurement using another tool. A standard gauge is usually provided with measuring tools to check accuracy and calibrate the tool if necessary.

Accurate measurements are only possible if the mechanic possesses a good feel for using the tool. Heavy-handed use of measuring tools produces less accurate results. Hold the tool gently by the fingertips so the point at which the tool contacts the object is easily felt. This feel for the equipment will produce more accurate measurements and reduce the risk of damaging the tool or component. Refer to the following sections for specific measuring tools.

Feeler Gauge

The feeler, or thickness gauge (**Figure 30**), is used for measuring the distance between two surfaces.

A feeler gauge set consists of an assortment of steel strips of graduated thicknesses. Each blade is marked with its thickness. Blades can be of various lengths and angles for different procedures.

A common use for a feeler gauge is to measure valve clearance. Wire (round) type gauges are used to measure spark plug gap.

Calipers

Calipers (**Figure 31**) are excellent tools for obtaining inside, outside and depth measurements. Although not as precise as a micrometer, they allow reasonable precision, typically to within 0.05 mm (0.001 in.). Most calipers have a range up to 150 mm (6 in.).

Calipers are available in dial, vernier or digital versions. Dial calipers have a dial readout that provides convenient reading. Vernier calipers have marked scales that must be compared to determine the measurement. The digital caliper uses a LCD to show the measurement.

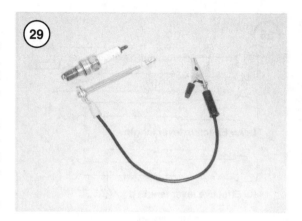

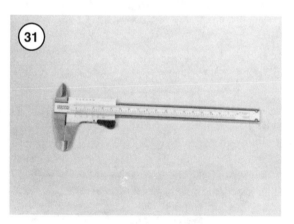

Properly maintain the measuring surfaces of the caliper. There must not be any dirt or burrs between the tool and the object being measured. Never force the caliper closed around an object; close the caliper around the highest point so it can be removed with a slight drag. Some calipers require calibration. Always refer to the tool manufacturer's instructions when using a new or unfamiliar caliper.

To read a vernier caliper, refer to **Figure 32**. The fixed scale is marked in 1 mm increments. Ten individual lines on the fixed scale equal 1 cm. The moveable scale is marked in 0.05 mm (hundredth) increments. To obtain a reading, establish the first

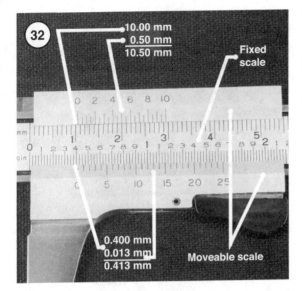

al sizes are 0-25 mm (0-1 in.), 25-50 mm (1-2 in.), 50-75 mm (2-3 in.) and 75-100 mm (3-4 in.).

Micrometers that cover a wider range of measurements are available. These use a large frame with interchangeable anvils of various lengths. This type of micrometer offers a cost savings; however, its overall size may make it less convenient.

Adjustment

Before using a micrometer, check its adjustment as follows.

1. Clean the anvil and spindle faces.
2A. To check a 0-25 mm or 0-1 in. micrometer:
  a. Turn the thimble until the spindle contacts the anvil. If the micrometer has a ratchet stop, use it to ensure the proper amount of pressure is applied.
  b. If the adjustment is correct, the 0 mark on the thimble will align exactly with the 0 mark on the sleeve line. If the marks do not align, the micrometer is out of adjustment.
  c. Follow the tool manufacturer's instructions to adjust the micrometer.
2B. To check a micrometer larger than 25 mm or 1 in., use the standard gauge supplied by the manufacturer. A standard gauge is a steel block, disc or rod that is machined to an exact size.
  a. Place the standard gauge between the spindle and anvil and measure its outside diameter or length. If the micrometer has a ratchet stop, use it to ensure the proper amount of pressure is applied.
  b. If the adjustment is correct, the 0 mark on the thimble will align exactly with the 0 mark on the sleeve line. If the marks do not align, the micrometer is out of adjustment.
  c. Follow the tool manufacturer's instructions to adjust the micrometer.

Care

Micrometers are precision instruments. They must be used and maintained with great care. Note the following:

1. Store micrometers in protective cases or separate padded drawers in a toolbox.
2. When in storage, make sure the spindle and anvil faces do not contact each other or another object. If they do, temperature changes and corrosion may damage the contact faces.
3. Do not clean a micrometer with compressed air. Dirt forced into the tool causes wear.
4. Lubricate micrometers to prevent corrosion.

number by the location of the 0 line on the moveable scale in relation to the first line to the left on the fixed scale. In this example, the number is 10 mm. To determine the next number, note which of the lines on the movable scale align with a mark on the fixed scale. A number of lines will seem close, but only one will align exactly. In this case, 0.50 mm is the reading to add to the first number. The result of adding 10 mm and 0.50 mm is a measurement of 10.50 mm.

Micrometers

A micrometer (**Figure 33**) is an instrument designed for linear measurement using the decimal divisions of the inch or meter. While there are many types and styles of micrometers, most of the procedures in this manual call for an outside micrometer. The outside micrometer is used to measure the outside diameter of cylindrical forms and the thicknesses of materials.

A micrometer's size indicates the minimum and maximum size of a part that it can measure. The usu-

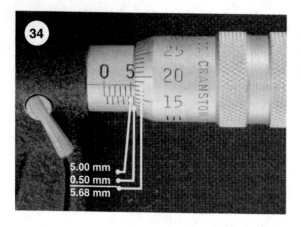

5.00 mm
0.50 mm
5.68 mm

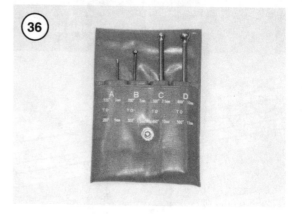

Reading

When reading a micrometer, numbers are taken from different scales and added together.

For accurate results, properly maintain the measuring surfaces of the micrometer. There cannot be any dirt or burrs between the tool and the measured object. Never force the micrometer closed around an object. Close the micrometer around the highest point so it can be removed with a slight drag.

The standard metric micrometer is accurate to one one-hundredth of a millimeter (0.01 mm). The sleeve line is graduated in millimeter and half millimeter increments. The marks on the upper half of the sleeve line equal 1.00 mm. Each fifth mark above the sleeve line is identified with a number. The number sequence depends on the size of the micrometer. A 0-25 mm micrometer, for example, will have sleeve marks numbered 0 through 25 in 5 mm increments. This numbering sequence continues with larger micrometers. On all metric micrometers, each mark on the lower half of the sleeve equals 0.50 mm.

The tapered end of the thimble has 50 lines marked around it. Each mark equals 0.01 mm. One complete turn of the thimble aligns its 0 mark with the first line on the lower half of the sleeve line, or 0.50 mm.

When reading a metric micrometer, add the number of millimeters and half-millimeters on the sleeve line to the number of one one-hundredth millimeters on the thimble. Perform the following steps while referring to **Figure 34**.

1. Read the upper half of the sleeve line and count the number of lines visible. Each upper line equals 1 mm.

2. See if the half-millimeter line is visible on the lower sleeve line. If so, add 0.50 mm to the reading in Step 1.

3. Read the thimble mark that aligns with the sleeve line. Each thimble mark equals 0.01 mm.

4. If a thimble mark does not align exactly with the sleeve line, estimate the amount between the lines. For more accurate readings in two-thousandths of a millimeter (0.002 mm), use a metric vernier micrometer.

5. Add the readings to determine the final measurement.

Telescoping and Small Hole Gauges

Use telescoping gauges (**Figure 35**) and small hole gauges (**Figure 36**) to measure bores. Neither gauge has a scale for direct readings. An outside micrometer must be used to determine the reading.

To use a telescoping gauge, select the correct size gauge for the bore. Compress the moveable post and carefully insert the gauge into the bore. Carefully move the gauge in the bore to make sure it is centered. Tighten the knurled end of the gauge to hold the moveable post in position. Remove the gauge and measure the length of the posts. Telescoping gauges are typically used to measure cylinder bores.

To use a small hole gauge, select the correct size gauge for the bore. Carefully insert the gauge into the bore. Tighten the knurled end of the gauge to carefully expand the gauge fingers to the limit within the bore. Do not overtighten the gauge; there is no built-in release. Excessive tightening can damage the bore surface and tool. Remove the gauge and measure the outside

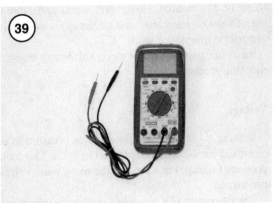

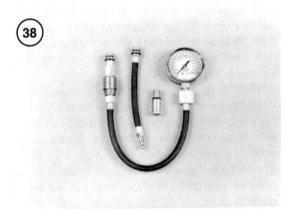

dimension with a micrometer (**Figure 33**). Small hole gauges are typically used to measure valve guides.

Dial Indicator

A dial indicator (**Figure 37**) is a gauge with a dial face and needle used to measure variations in dimensions and movements. Measuring brake rotor runout is a typical use for a dial indicator.

Dial indicators are available in various ranges and graduations and have three types of mounting bases: magnetic, clamp or screw-in stud.

Cylinder Bore Gauge

A cylinder bore gauge is similar to a dial indicator. These typically consist of a dial indicator, handle and different length adapters (anvils) to fit the gauge to various bore sizes. The bore gauge is used to measure bore size, taper and out-of-round. When using a bore gauge, follow the tool manufacturer's instructions.

Compression Gauge

A compression gauge (**Figure 38**) measures combustion chamber (cylinder) pressure, usually in kg/cm^2 or psi. The gauge adapter is either inserted and held in place or screwed into the spark plug hole to obtain the reading. Disable the engine so it will not start and hold the throttle in the wide-open position when performing a compression test. An engine that does not have adequate compression cannot be properly tuned. Refer to Chapter Three for compression test procedures.

Multimeter

A multimeter (**Figure 39**) is an essential tool for electrical system diagnosis. The voltage function indicates the voltage applied or available to various electrical components. The ohmmeter function tests circuits for continuity, or lack of continuity, and measures the resistance of a circuit.

Some manufacturers' specifications for electrical components are based on results using a specific test meter. Results may vary if using a meter not recommend by the manufacturer. Such meter requirements are noted when applicable.

Ohmmeter (analog) calibration

Each time an analog ohmmeter is used or the scale is changed, the ohmmeter must be calibrated.

Digital ohmmeters do not require calibration.

1. Make sure the meter battery is in good condition.
2. Make sure the meter probes are in good condition.
3. Touch the two probes together and observe the needle location on the ohms scale. The needle must align with the 0 mark to obtain accurate measurements.
4. If necessary, rotate the meter ohms adjust knob until the needle and 0 mark align.

ELECTRICAL SYSTEM FUNDAMENTALS

A thorough study of the many types of electrical systems used in today's motorcycles is beyond the scope of this manual. However, a basic understanding of voltage, resistance and amperage is necessary to perform diagnostic tests.

Refer to Chapter Two for electrical system troubleshooting procedures.

Voltage

Voltage is the electrical potential or pressure in an electrical circuit and is expressed in volts. The more pressure (voltage) in a circuit, the more work can be performed.

Direct current (DC) voltage means the electricity flows in one direction. All circuits powered by a battery are DC circuits.

Alternating current (AC) means the electricity flows in one direction momentarily, and then switches to the opposite direction. Alternator output is an example of AC voltage. This voltage must be changed or rectified to direct current to operate in a battery-powered system.

Resistance

Resistance is the opposition to the flow of electricity within a circuit or component and is measured in ohms. Resistance causes a reduction in available current and voltage.

Resistance is measured in an inactive circuit with an ohmmeter. The ohmmeter sends a small amount of current into the circuit and measures how difficult it is to push the current through the circuit.

An ohmmeter, although useful, is not always a good indicator of a circuit's actual ability under operating conditions. This is due to the low voltage (6-9 volts) that the meter uses to test the circuit. The voltage in an ignition coil secondary winding can be several thousand volts. Such high voltage can cause the coil to malfunction, even though it tests acceptable during a resistance test.

Resistance generally increases with temperature. Perform all testing with the component or circuit at room temperature. Resistance tests performed at high temperatures may indicate false resistance readings and cause the unnecessary replacement of a component.

Amperage

Amperage is the unit of measure for the amount of current within a circuit. Current is the actual flow of electricity. The higher the current, the more work can be performed up to a given point. If the current flow exceeds the circuit or component capacity, the system will be damaged.

SERVICE METHODS

Many of the procedures in this manual are straightforward and can be performed by anyone reasonably competent with tools. However, consider previous experience carefully before performing any operation involving complicated procedures.

1. Front, in this manual, refers to the front of the motorcycle. The front of any component is the end closest to the front of the motorcycle. The left and right sides refer to the position of the parts as viewed by the rider sitting on the seat facing forward.

2. When servicing the motorcycle, secure it upright in a safe manner.

3. Whenever possible, photograph the location of all related parts before removing them. Label all similar parts for location and mark all mating parts for position. Note or draw the number and thickness of any shim as it is removed.

4. Identify parts by placing them in sealed and labeled plastic bags. It is possible for carefully laid out parts to become disturbed, making it difficult to reassemble the components correctly without a diagram or other means of idenitifcation.

5. Label disconnected wires and connectors with masking tape and a marking pen. Do not rely on memory alone.

6. Protect finished surfaces from physical damage or corrosion. Keep gasoline and other chemicals off painted surfaces.

7. Use penetrating oil on frozen or tight bolts. Avoid using heat where possible. Heat can warp, melt or affect the temper of parts. Heat also damages the finish of paint and plastics. Refer to *Heating Components* (this section).

8. When a part is a press fit or requires a special tool for removal, the information or type of tool is identified in the text. Otherwise, if a part is difficult to remove or install, determine the cause before proceeding.

9. To prevent objects or debris from falling into the engine, cover all openings.

10. Read each procedure thoroughly and compare the figures to the actual components before starting the procedure. Perform the procedure in sequence as written.

11. Recommendations are occasionally made to refer service to a dealership or specialist. In these cases, the work can be performed more economically by the specialist than by the home mechanic.

12. The term replace means to discard a defective part and replace it with a new part. Overhaul means to remove, disassemble, inspect, measure, repair and/or replace parts as required to recondition an assembly.

13. Some operations require the use of a hydraulic press. If a press is not available, have these operations performed by a shop equipped with the necessary equipment.

14. Repairs are much faster and easier if the motorcycle is clean before starting work. Degrease the motorcycle with a commercial degreaser; follow the directions on the container for the best results. Clean all parts with cleaning solvent.

15. Do not use makeshift equipment that may damage the motorcycle. Do not direct high-pressure water at steering bearings, fuel body hoses, wheel bearings, suspension and electrical components. The water forces the grease out of the bearings and could damage the seals.

16. If special tools are required, have them available before starting the procedure. When special tools are required, they will be described at the beginning of the procedure.

17. Make sure all shims and washers are reinstalled in the same location and position as noted during removal.

18. Whenever rotating parts contact a stationary part, look for a shim or washer.

19. Use new gaskets if there is any doubt about the condition of old ones.

20. If self-locking fasteners are used, replace them. Do not install standard fasteners in place of self-locking ones.

21. Use grease to hold small parts in place if they tend to fall out during assembly. Do not apply grease to electrical or brake components.

Heating Components

WARNING
Wear protective gloves to prevent burns and injury when heating parts.

CAUTION
Do not use a welding torch when heating parts. A welding torch applies excessive heat to a small area very quickly, which can damage parts.

A heat gun or propane torch is required to disassemble, assemble, remove and install many parts and components in this manual. Read the safety and operating information supplied by the manufacturer of the heat gun or propane torch while also noting the following:

1. The work area should be clean and dry. Remove all combustible components and materials from the work area. Wipe up all grease, oil and other fluids from parts. Check for leaking or damaged fuel sys-tem components. Repair or remove these parts before beginning work.

2. Never use a flame near the battery, fuel tank, fuel lines or other flammable materials.

3. When using a heat gun, remember that the temperature can be in excess of 540° C (1000° F).

4. Have a fire extinguisher near the job.

5. Always wear protective goggles and gloves when heating parts.

6. Before heating a part installed on the motorcycle, check areas around the part and those hidden that could be damaged or possibly ignite. Do not heat surfaces than can be damaged by heat. Shield materials like cables and wiring harnesses near the part or area to be heated.

7. Before heating a part, read the entire procedure to make sure the required tools are available. This allows quick work while the part is at its optimum temperature.

8. The amount of heat recommended to remove or install a part is typically listed in the procedure. However, before heating parts without a specific recommendation, consider the possible effects and damage that can occur. To avoid damaging a part, monitor the temperature with heat sticks or an infrared thermometer, if possible. Another way, though not as accurate, is to place tiny drops of water on the part. When the water starts to sizzle, the part is hot enough. Keep the heat in motion to prevent overheating.

Removing Frozen Fasteners

If a fastener cannot be removed, several methods may be used to loosen it. First, liberally apply penetrating oil, and let it penetrate for 10-15 minutes. Rap the fastener several times with a small hammer. Do not hit it hard enough to cause damage. Reapply the penetrating oil, if necessary.

For frozen screws, apply penetrating oil as described, and then insert a screwdriver in the slot and rap the top of the screwdriver with a hammer. This loosens the rust so the screw can be removed in the normal way. If the screw head is too damaged to use this method, grip the head with locking pliers and twist it out.

If heat is required, refer to *Heating Components* (this section).

Removing Broken Fasteners

If the head breaks off a screw or bolt, several methods are available for removing the remaining portion. If a large portion of the remainder projects out, try gripping it with locking pliers. If the project-

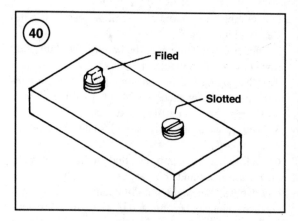

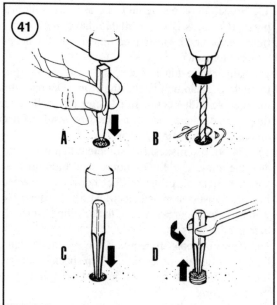

ing portion is too small, file it to fit a wrench or cut a slot in it to fit a screwdriver (**Figure 40**).

If the head breaks off flush, use a screw extractor. To do this, center punch the exact center of the screw or bolt (A, **Figure 41**), and then drill a small hole in the screw (B) and tap the extractor into the hole (C). Back the screw out with a wrench on the extractor (D, **Figure 41**).

Repairing Damaged Threads

Occasionally, threads are stripped through carelessness or impact damage. Often the threads can be repaired by running a tap (for internal threads on nuts) or die (for external threads on bolts) through the threads (**Figure 42**). To clean or repair spark plug threads, use a spark plug tap.

If an internal thread is damaged, it may be necessary to install a Helicoil or some other type of thread insert. Follow the insert manufacturer's instructions when installing it.

If it is necessary to drill and tap a hole, refer to **Table 9** for metric tap and drill sizes.

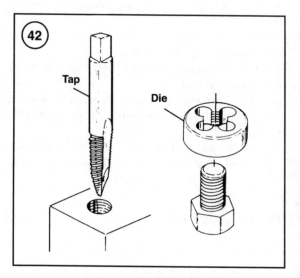

Stud Removal/Installation

A stud removal tool (**Figure 43**) is available from most tool suppliers. This tool makes the removal and installation of studs easier. If one is not available and the threads on the stud are not damaged, thread two nuts onto the stud and tighten them against each other. Remove the stud by turning the lower nut.

1. Measure the height of the stud above the surface.
2. Thread the stud removal tool onto the stud and tighten it, or thread two nuts onto the stud.
3. Remove the stud by turning the stud remover or the lower nut.
4. Remove any threadlock residue from the threaded hole. Clean the threads with an aerosol parts cleaner.
5. Install the stud removal tool onto the new stud, or thread two nuts onto the stud.

6. If recommended by the manufacturer, apply threadlock to the threads of the stud.
7. Install the stud and tighten with the stud removal tool or the top nut.
8. Install the stud to the height noted or tighten to the torque specification.
9. Remove the stud removal tool or the two nuts.

Removing Hoses

When removing stubborn hoses, do not exert excessive force on the hose or fitting. Remove the hose clamp and carefully insert a small screwdriver or similar blunt nose tool between the fitting and hose. Apply a spray lubricant under the hose and carefully twist the hose off the fitting. Clean the fitting of any corrosion or rubber hose material with a wire brush.

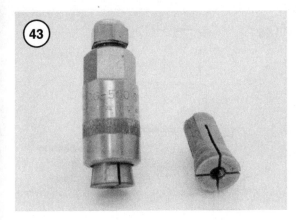

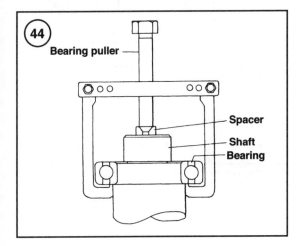

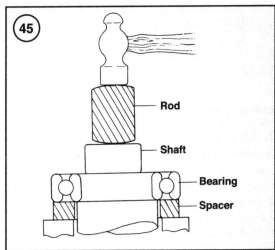

Clean the inside of the hose thoroughly. Do not use any lubricant when installing the hose (new or old). The lubricant may allow the hose to come off the fitting, even with the clamp tightened securely.

Bearings

Bearings are precision parts that must be serviced with proper lubrication and periodic maintenance. If a bearing is damaged, replace it immediately. When installing a new bearing, make sure to prevent damaging it. Bearing replacement procedures are included in the individual chapters where applicable; however, use the procedures in this section as a guideline.

Unless otherwise specified, install bearings with the manufacturer's mark or number facing outward.

Removal

While bearings are normally removed only when damaged, there may be times when it is necessary to remove a bearing that is in good condition. However, improper bearing removal will damage the bearing and possibly the shaft or case half. Note the following when removing bearings:

1. Before removing the bearings, note the following:
   a. Refer to the bearing replacement procedure in the appropriate chapter for any special instructions.
   b. Remove any seals that interfere with bearing removal. Refer to *Seal Replacement* (this section).
   c. When removing more than one bearing, identify the bearings before removing them. Refer to the numbers or marks on the bearing.
   d. Note and record the direction in which the bearing numbers face for proper installation.
   e. Remove any set plates or bearing retainers before removing the bearings.
2. When using a puller to remove a bearing from a shaft, make sure the shaft is not damaged. Always place a piece of metal between the end of the shaft and the puller screw. In addition, place the puller arms next to the inner bearing race. Refer to **Figure 44**.
3. When using a hammer to remove a bearing from a shaft, do not strike the hammer directly against the shaft. Instead, use a brass or aluminum rod between the hammer and shaft (**Figure 45**) and make sure to support both bearing races with wooden blocks as shown.
4. The ideal method of bearing removal is with a hydraulic press. Note the following when using a press:
   a. Always support the inner and outer bearing races with a suitable size wooden or aluminum ring spacer (**Figure 46**). If only the outer race is supported, pressure applied against the balls and/or the inner race will damage them.
   b. Always make sure the press ram (**Figure 46**) aligns with the center of the shaft. If the ram is not centered, it may damage the bearing and/or shaft.
   c. The moment the shaft is free of the bearing, it will drop to the floor. Secure or hold the shaft to prevent it from falling.

d. When removing bearings from a housing, support the housing with 4 × 4 in. wooden blocks to prevent damage to gasket surfaces.

5. Use a blind bearing puller to remove bearings installed in blind holes (**Figure 47**).

Installation

1. When installing a bearing in a housing, apply pressure to the outer bearing race (**Figure 48**). When installing a bearing on a shaft, apply pressure to the inner bearing race (**Figure 49**).

2. When installing a bearing as described in Step 1, a driver is required. Never strike the bearing directly with a hammer or the bearing will be damaged. When installing a bearing, use a piece of pipe or a driver with a diameter that matches the bearing race. **Figure 50** shows the correct way to use a driver and hammer to install a bearing on a shaft.

3. Step 1 describes how to install a bearing in a housing or over a shaft. However, when installing a bearing over a shaft and into the housing at the same time, a tight fit will be required for both outer and inner bearing races. In this situation, install a spacer underneath the driver tool so pressure is applied evenly across both races. Refer to **Figure 51**. If the outer race is not supported, the balls push against the outer bearing race and damage it.

Interference fit

1. Follow this procedure when installing a bearing over a shaft. When a tight fit is required, the bearing inside diameter will be smaller than the shaft. In this case, driving the bearing on the shaft using normal methods may cause bearing damage. Instead, heat the bearing before installation. Note the following:

a. Secure the shaft so it is ready for bearing installation.

b. Clean all residues from the bearing surface of the shaft. Remove burrs with a file.

c. Fill a suitable pot or beaker with clean mineral oil. Place a thermometer rated above 120° C (248° F) in the oil. Support the thermometer so it does not rest on the bottom or side of the pot.

d. Remove the bearing from its wrapper and secure it with a piece of heavy wire bent to hold it in the pot. Hang the bearing in the pot so it does not touch the bottom or sides of the pot.

e. Turn the heat on and monitor the thermometer. When the oil temperature rises to approximately 120° C (248° F), remove the bearing from the pot and quickly install it. If necessary, place a socket on the inner bearing race

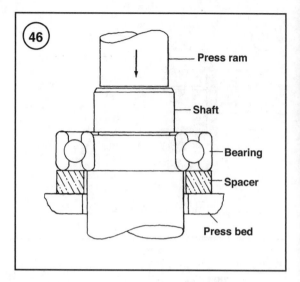

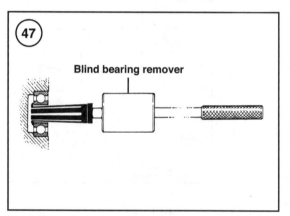

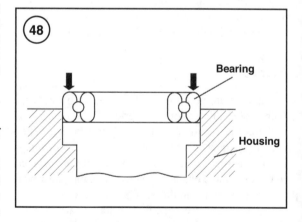

and tap the bearing into place. As the bearing chills, it tightens on the shaft, so installation must be done quickly. Make sure the bearing is installed completely.

2. Follow this step when installing a bearing in a housing. Bearings are generally installed in a housing with a slight interference fit. Driving the bearing into the housing using normal methods may damage the housing or

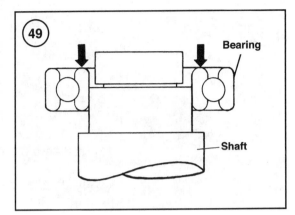

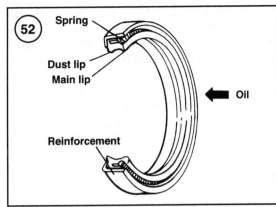

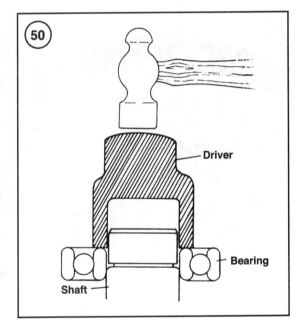

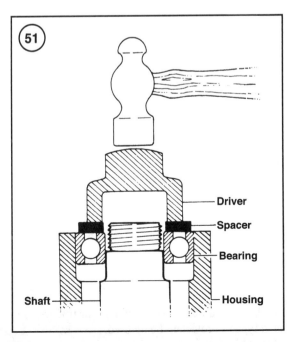

cause bearing damage. Instead, heat the housing before the bearing is installed. Note the following:

a. Before heating the housing in this procedure, wash the housing thoroughly with detergent and water. Rinse and rewash the housing as required to remove all oil and chemicals.

b. Heat the housing to approximately 100° C (212° F) with a heat gun or on a hot plate. Monitor temperature with an infrared thermometer, heat sticks or place tiny drops of water on the housing; if they sizzle and evaporate immediately, the temperature is correct. Heat only one housing at a time.

c. If a hot plate is used, remove the housing and place it on wooden blocks.

d. Hold the housing with the bearing side down and tap the bearing out with a suitable size socket and extension. Repeat for all bearings in the housing.

e. Before heating the bearing housing, place the new bearing in a freezer, if possible. Chilling a bearing slightly reduces its outside diameter while the heated bearing housing assembly is slightly larger due to heat expansion. This makes bearing installation easier.

f. While the housing is still hot, install the new bearing(s) into the housing. Install the bearings by hand, if possible. If necessary, lightly tap the bearing(s) into the housing with a socket placed on the outer bearing race (**Figure 48**). Do not install bearings by driving on the inner bearing race. Install the bearing(s) until it seats completely.

Seal Replacement

Seals are used to contain oil, water, grease or combustion gasses in a housing or shaft. Improper removal of a seal can damage the housing or shaft. Improper installation of the seal can damage the seal.

Before replacing a seal, identify it as a rubber or Teflon seal. Both types are used on the models covered in this manual. On a rubber seal (**Figure 52**), the body and sealing element will be made of the same material. The seal lip (element) will also be equipped with a garter spring. On a Teflon seal, the body and seal lip will be noticeably different. The outer part is normally made of rubber and the sealing lip, placed in the middle of the seal, is Teflon. A garter spring is not used.

Rubber seals

1. Prying is generally the easiest and most effective method of removing a seal from the housing. However, always place a rag under the pry tool (**Figure 53**) to prevent damage to the housing.
2. Before installing a typical rubber seal, pack waterproof grease in the seal lips.
3. In most cases, install seals with the manufacturer's numbers or marks face out.
4. Install seals either by hand or with tools. Center the seal in its bore and attempt to install it by hand. If necessary, install the seal with a socket or bearing driver placed on the outside of the seal as shown in **Figure 54**. Drive the seal squarely into the housing until it is flush with its mounting bore. Never install a seal by hitting against the top of the seal with a hammer.

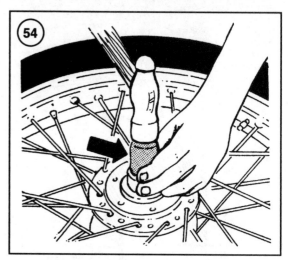

STORAGE

Several months of non-use can cause a general deterioration of the motorcycle. This is especially true in areas of extreme temperature variations. This deterioration can be minimized with careful preparation for storage. A properly stored motorcycle is much easier to return to service.

Storage Area Selection

When selecting a storage area, consider the following:
1. The storage area must be dry. A heated area is best, but not necessary. It should be insulated to minimize extreme temperature variations.
2. If the building has large window areas, mask them to keep sunlight off the motorcycle.
3. Avoid storage areas close to saltwater.
4. Consider the area's risk of fire, theft or vandalism. Check with your insurer regarding motorcycle coverage while in storage.

Preparing the Motorcycle for Storage

The amount of preparation a motorcycle should undergo before storage depends on the expected length of non-use, storage area conditions and personal preference. Consider the following list the minimum requirement:
1. Wash the motorcycle thoroughly. Make sure all dirt, mud and road debris are removed.
2. Start the engine and allow it to reach operating temperature. Drain the engine oil regardless of the riding time since the last service. Fill the engine with the recommended type and quantity of oil.
3. Fill the fuel tank completely.
4. Remove the spark plug from the cylinder head. Ground the spark plug cap to the engine. Refer to *Ignition Ground Tool* in this chapter. Pour a teaspoon (5 ml) of engine oil into the cylinders. Place a rag over the openings and slowly turn the engine over to distribute the oil. Reinstall the spark plug.
5. Remove the battery. Store it in a cool, dry location. Charge the battery once a month. Refer to *Battery* in Chapter Nine for service.
6. Cover the exhaust and intake openings.
7. Apply a protective substance to the plastic and rubber components, including the tires. Make sure to follow the product manufacturer's instructions for each type of protectant being used.

8. Rotate the front tire periodically to prevent a flat spot from developing and damaging the tire.

9. Cover the motorcycle with old bed sheets or something similar. Do not cover it with any plastic material that will trap moisture.

Returning the Motorcycle to Service

The amount of service required when returning a motorcycle to service after storage depends on the length of non-use and storage conditions. In addition to performing the reverse of the above procedure, make sure the brakes, clutch, throttle and engine stop switch work properly before operating the motorcycle. Refer to Chapter Three and evaluate the service intervals to determine which areas require additional service.

Table 1 MOTORCYCLE DIMENSIONS (CRF230F MODELS)

Footpeg height	365 mm (14.4 in.)
Ground clearance	305 mm (12.0 in.)
Overall height	
2003-2007 models	1159 mm (45.6 in.)
2008-on models	1167 mm (45.9 in.)
Overall length	2059 mm (81.1 in.)
Overall width	
2003-2007 models	812 mm (32.0 in.)
2008-on models	801 mm (31.5 in.)
Seat height	
2003-2007 models	872 mm (34.3 in.)
2008-on models	878 mm (34.6 in.)
Wheelbase	1372 mm (54.0 in.)

Table 2 MOTORCYCLE DIMENSIONS (CRF230L MODELS)

Footpeg height	300 mm (11.8 in.)
Ground clearance	243 mm (9.6 in.)
Overall height	1113 mm (43.8 in.)
Overall length	2072 mm (81.6 in.)
Overall width	848 mm (33.4 in.)
Seat height	810 mm (31.9 in.)
Wheelbase	1340 mm (52.8 in.)

Table 3 MOTORCYCLE DIMENSIONS (CRF230M MODELS)

Footpeg height	295 mm (11.6 in.)
Ground clearance	235 mm (9.3 in.)
Overall height	1080 mm (42.5 in.)
Overall length	2002 mm (78.8 in.)
Overall width	816 mm (32.1 in.)
Seat height	805 mm (31.7 in.)
Wheelbase	1336 mm (52.6 in.)

Table 4 MOTORCYCLE CURB WEIGHT

CRF230F models	
2003-2007 models	113.5 kg (250 lb.)
2008-on models	112.7 kg (248.5 lb.)
CRF230L models	121 kg (267 lb.)
CRF230M models	125 kg (276 lb.)

Table 5 FUEL TANK CAPACITY

Total (including reserve)	
CRF230F	
2003-2007	8.2 liters (2.2 gal.)
2008-on	7.0 liters (1.9 gal.)
CRF230L and CRF230M	8.7 liters (2.3 gal.)
Reserve	
CRF230F	
2003-2007	1.5 liters (0.4 gal.)
2008-on	1.3 liters (0.3 gal.)
CRF230L and CRF230M	2.7 liters (0.7 gal.)

Table 6 DECIMAL AND METRIC EQUIVALENTS

mm	in.	Nearest fraction	mm	in.	Nearest fraction
1	0.0394	1/32	26	1.0236	1 1/32
2	0.0787	3/32	27	1.0630	1 1/16
3	0.1181	1/8	28	1.1024	1 3/32
4	0.1575	5/32	29	1.1417	1 5/32
5	0.1969	3/16	30	1.1811	1 3/16
6	0.2362	1/4	31	1.2205	1 7/32
7	0.2756	9/32	32	1.2598	1 1/4
8	0.3150	5/16	33	1.2992	1 5/16
9	0.3543	11/32	34	1.3386	1 11/32
10	0.3937	13/32	35	1.3780	1 3/8
11	0.4331	7/16	36	1.4173	1 13/32
12	0.4724	15/32	37	1.4567	1 15/32
13	0.5118	1/2	38	1.4961	1 1/2
14	0.5512	9/16	39	1.5354	1 17/32
15	0.5906	19/32	40	1.5748	1 9/16
16	0.6299	5/8	41	1.6142	1 5/8
17	0.6693	21/32	42	1.6535	1 21/32
18	0.7087	23/32	43	1.6929	1 11/16
19	0.7480	3/4	44	1.7323	1 23/32
20	0.7874	25/32	45	1.7717	1 25/32
21	0.8268	13/16	46	1.8110	1 13/16
22	0.8661	7/8	47	1.8504	1 27/32
23	0.9055	29/32	48	1.8898	1 7/8
24	0.9449	15/16	49	1.9291	1 15/16
25	0.9843	31/32	50	1.9685	1 31/32

Table 7 CONVERSION TABLES

Multiply:	By:	To get the equivalent of:
Length		
Inches	25.4	Millimeter
Inches	2.54	Centimeter
Miles	1.609	Kilometer
Feet	0.3048	Meter
Millimeter	0.03937	Inches
Centimeter	0.3937	Inches
Kilometer	0.6214	Mile
Meter	3.281	Feet
Fluid volume		
U.S. quarts	0.9463	Liters
U.S. gallons	3.785	Liters

(continued)

Table 7 CONVERSION TABLES (continued)

Multiply:	By:	To get the equivalent of:
Fluid volume (continued)		
U.S. ounces	29.573529	Milliliters
Imperial gallons	4.54609	Liters
Imperial quarts	1.1365	Liters
Liters	0.2641721	U.S. gallons
Liters	1.0566882	U.S. quarts
Liters	33.814023	U.S. ounces
Liters	0.22	Imperial gallons
Liters	0.8799	Imperial quarts
Milliliters	0.033814	U.S. ounces
Milliliters	1.0	Cubic centimeters
Milliliters	0.001	Liters
Torque		
Foot-pounds	1.3558	Newton-meters
Foot-pounds	0.138255	Meters-kilograms
Inch-pounds	0.11299	Newton-meters
Newton-meters	0.7375622	Foot-pounds
Newton-meters	8.8507	Inch-pounds
Meters-kilograms	7.2330139	Foot-pounds
Volume		
Cubic inches	16.387064	Cubic centimeters
Cubic centimeters	0.0610237	Cubic inches
Temperature		
Fahrenheit	$(°F - 32) \times 0.556$	Centigrade
Centigrade	$(°C \times 1.8) + 32$	Fahrenheit
Weight		
Ounces	28.3495	Grams
Pounds	0.4535924	Kilograms
Grams	0.035274	Ounces
Kilograms	2.2046224	Pounds
Pressure		
Pounds per square inch	0.070307	Kilograms per square centimeter
Kilograms per square centimeter	14.223343	Pounds per square inch
Kilopascals	0.1450	Pounds per square inch
Pounds per square inch	6.895	Kilopascals
Speed		
Miles per hour	1.609344	Kilometers per hour
Kilometers per hour	0.6213712	Miles per hour

Table 8 GENERAL TORQUE RECOMMENDATIONS

Fastener	N•m	in.-lb.	ft.-lb.
5 mm			
Bolt and nut	5.0	44	–
Screw	4.0	35	–
6 mm			
Bolt and nut	10	88	–
Small flange bolt (8-mm head)	10	88	–
Large flange bolt (8-mm head)	12	106	–
Large flange bolt (10-mm head)	12	106	–
Screw	9	80	–
8 mm			
Bolt and nut	22	–	16
Screw	26	–	19
10 mm			
Bolt and nut	34	–	25
Flange bolt	39	–	29
12 mm			
Bolt and nut	54	–	40

Table 9 TECHNICAL ABBREVIATIONS

A	Ampere
AC	Alternating current
A.h.	Ampere hour
C	Celsius
cc	Cubic centimeter
CDI	Capacitor discharge ignition
CKP	Crankshaft position
cm	Centimeter
cu. in.	Cubic inch and cubic inches
cyl.	Cylinder
DC	Direct current
DOHC	Dual overhead camshaft
EFI	Electronic fuel injection
F	Fahrenheit
fl. oz.	Fluid ounces
ft.	Foot
ft.-lb.	Foot-pounds
gal.	Gallon and gallons
hp	Horsepower
Hz	Hertz
ICM	Ignition control module
in.	Inch and inches
in.-lb.	Inch-pounds
in. Hg	Inches of mercury
kg	Kilogram
kg/cm^2	Kilogram per square centimeter
kgm	Kilogram meter
km	Kilometer
km/h	Kilometer per hour
kPa	Kilopascals
kW	Kilowatt
L	Liter and liters
L/m	Liters per minute
lb.	Pound and pounds
lbf	Pound(s) force
m	Meter
mL	Milliliter
mm	Millimeter
mPa	Megapascal
N	Newton
N·m	Newton meter
oz.	Ounce and ounces
p	Pascal
PCV	Purge control valve
PAIR	Pulsed secondary air injection
psi	Pounds per square inch
pt.	Pint and pints
qt.	Quart and quarts
RFVC	Radial four valve combustion
rpm	Revolution per minute
SOHC	Single overhead camshaft
TDC	Top dead center
V	Volt
VAC	Alternating current voltage
VDC	Direct current voltage
W	Watt

Table 10 METRIC TAP DRILL SIZE

Metric size	Drill equivalent	Decimal fraction	Nearest fraction
3 × 0.50	No. 39	0.0995	3/32
3 × 0.60	3/32	0.0937	3/32
4 × 0.70	No. 30	0.1285	1/8
4 × 0.75	1/8	0.125	1/8
5 × 0.80	No. 19	0.166	11/64
5 × 0.90	No. 20	0.161	5/32
6 × 1.00	No. 9	0.196	13/64
7 × 1.00	16/64	0.234	15/64
8 × 1.00	J	0.277	9/32
8 × 1.25	17/64	0.265	17/64
9 × 1.00	5/16	0.3125	5/16
9 × 1.25	5/16	0.3125	5/16
10 × 1.25	11/32	0.3437	11/32
10 × 1.50	R	0.339	11/32
11 × 1.50	3/8	0.375	3/8
12 × 1.50	13/32	0.406	13/32
12 × 1.75	13/32	0.406	13/32

CHAPTER TWO

TROUBLESHOOTING

The troubleshooting procedures described in this chapter provide typical symptoms and logical methods for isolating the cause(s). There may be several ways to solve a problem, but only a systematic approach will be successful in avoiding wasted time and unnecessary parts replacement. Gather as much information as possible to aid in diagnosis. Never assume anything and do not overlook the obvious. Make sure the engine stop/run switch is in the run position and that there is fuel in the tank.

An engine needs three basics to run properly: correct air/ fuel mixture, adequate compression and a spark at the correct time. If one of these is missing, the engine will not run.

Learning to recognize symptoms makes troubleshooting easier. In most cases, expensive and complicated test equipment is not needed to determine whether repairs can be performed at home. On the other hand, be realistic and do not start procedures that are beyond the level of personal experience and specialized equipment necessary. If the motorcycle requires the attention of a professional, describe symptoms and conditions accurately and fully. The more information a technician has available, the easier it is to diagnose the problem.

STARTING THE ENGINE

When experiencing engine-starting troubles, it is easy to work out of sequence and forget basic starting procedures. The following sections describe the recommended starting procedures.

Before starting the engine, perform a pre-ride inspection (Chapter Three).

Starting Procedure

Engine is cold

1. Shift the transmission into neutral.

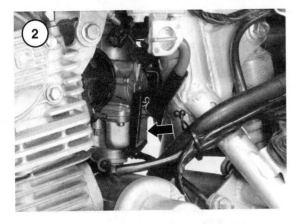

2. Turn the fuel valve on (**Figure 1**).

3A. On CRF230F models, if the air temperature is below 35° C (95° F), pull the choke lever (**Figure 2**) up all the way to richen the air/fuel mixture.

3B. On CRF230L and CRF230M models, if the air temperature is below 35° C (95° F), pull the choke lever (**Figure 3**) all the way toward the handlebar to richen the air/fuel mixture.

4. Turn the ignition switch to on, and set the engine stop switch to run (CRF230L and CRF230M models).

5. While keeping the throttle closed, pull the clutch lever fully in and press the starter button (**Figure 4**).

6. When the engine starts, use the throttle to keep the engine running until the engine warms up and the choke can be fully closed.

7. If the temperature is 10°-35° C (50°-95° F), move the choke lever to the midpoint position until the engine will operate cleanly without the choke.

Engine is warm

1. Shift the transmission into neutral.

2. Turn the fuel valve on (**Figure 1**).

3. Turn the ignition switch on, and set the engine stop switch to run (CRF230L and CRF230M models).

4. While keeping the throttle closed, pull the clutch lever fully in and press the starter button (**Figure 4**).

NOTE
If the engine is not at normal operating temperature, it may be necessary to place the choke lever at the midpoint to prevent engine stumbling.

Flooded engine

If the engine fails to start after several attempts, it is probably flooded. This occurs when too much fuel is drawn into the engine and the spark plug fails to ignite it. The smell of gasoline is often evident when the engine is flooded. Troubleshoot a flooded engine as follows:

1. Look for gasoline overflowing from the carburetor or overflow hose. If gasoline is evident, the engine is flooded and/or the float in the carburetor bowl is stuck. If the carburetor float is stuck, remove and repair the float assembly (Chapter Eight or Chapter Nine).

2. Shift the transmission into neutral.

3. Check that the choke lever (**Figure 2** or **Figure 3**) is fully open.

4. Press the engine stop button (CRF230F models) or move the engine stop switch to off (CRF230L and CRF230M models).

CAUTION
Excessive starter motor operation can damage the starter motor.

5. Hold the throttle in the fully-open position. Press the starter button (**Figure 4**) for 5 seconds. Then, release the starter button and wait 10 seconds.
6. On CRF230L and CRF230M models, set the engine switch to run before trying to restart the engine.
7. Make sure the choke is off, and then attempt to start the engine. If the engine fails to start, repeat the procedure.
8. If the engine still does not start, refer to *Engine Will Not Start* in this chapter.

ENGINE WILL NOT START

Identifying the Problem

If the engine does not start, perform the steps of this procedure in order. If the engine fails to start after performing these steps, refer to the troubleshooting procedures indicated in the steps. If the engine starts, but idles or runs roughly, refer to *Poor Engine Performance* (this chapter).
1. Refer to *Starting the Engine* (this chapter) to make sure all starting procedures are correct.
2. If the starter does not operate, refer to *Electric Starting System* (this chapter).
3. If the engine seems flooded, refer to *Starting The Engine* (this chapter). If the engine is not flooded, continue with the procedure.
4. Remove the cap from the fuel tank and make sure there is a sufficient amount of fuel to start the engine.
5. If there is sufficient fuel in the fuel tank, remove the spark plug immediately after attempting to start the engine. The plug insulator should be wet, indicating that fuel is reaching the engine. If the plug tip is dry, fuel is not reaching the engine. Refer to *Fuel System* (this chapter). If there is fuel on the spark plug and the engine will not start, the engine may not have adequate spark. Continue with the procedure.

NOTE
When examining the spark plug cap, check for the presence of water.

6. Make sure the spark plug wire is secure. Push down on the spark plug cap and slightly rotate it to clean the electrical connection between the plug and the connector. If the engine does not start the procedure.

NOTE
A cracked or damaged spark plug cap and cable can cause intermittent problems that are difficult to diagnose. If

the engine occasionally misfires or cuts out, use a spray bottle to wet the plug cap and plug cable while the engine is running. Water that enters one of these areas causes an arc through the insulating material, resulting in an engine misfire.

NOTE
Engine misfire can also be caused by water that enters through connectors. Check the connectors for loose wire ends. On waterproof connectors, check for damage where the wires enter the connector.

7. Perform a *Spark Test* (this section). If there is a strong spark, continue the procedure. If there is no spark or if the spark is very weak, refer to *Ignition System* (this chapter).
8. If the fuel and ignition systems are working correctly, perform a leakdown test (this chapter) and cylinder compression test (Chapter Three). If the leakdown test indicates a problem, or the compression is low, refer to *Low Engine Compression* (this chapter).

Spark Test

Perform a spark test to determine if the ignition system is producing adequate spark. This test should be performed with a spark tester. A spark tester looks like a spark plug with an adjustable gap between the center electrode and grounded base.

Because the voltage required to jump the spark tester gap is sufficiently larger than that of a normally-gapped spark plug, the test results are more accurate than with a spark plug. Do not assume that because a spark jumped across a spark plug gap, the ignition system is working correctly.

Perform this test when the engine it is both cold and hot, if possible. If the test results are positive

for each test, the ignition system is functioning correctly.

> *CAUTION*
> *After removing the spark plug cap and before removing the spark plug, clean the area around the spark plug with compressed air. Dirt that falls into the cylinder causes rapid engine wear.*

1. Disconnect the spark plug cap (**Figure 5**). Check for the presence of water.
2. Visually inspect the spark plug for damage.
3. Set the spark tester gap to 6 mm (0.24 in.).
4. Connect the spark tester to the spark plug cap. Ground the spark tester base (or spark plug) to a good ground (**Figure 6**). Position the spark tester or spark plug firing tip away from the spark plug hole, if open. Position the spark tester so the electrodes are visible.
5. Shift the transmission into neutral.

> *WARNING*
> *Do not hold the spark tester, spark plug or connector or a serious electrical shock may result.*

6. Make sure the ignition switch is on.
7. On CRF230L and CRF230M models, set the engine switch to run.
8. Turn the engine over with the starter. A fat blue spark must be evident between the spark tester or spark plug terminals.
9A. If the spark was weak (white or yellow) or if there was no spark, refer to *Ignition System* (this chapter).
9B. If there is a strong, blue spark, the ignition system is functioning properly. Check for one or more of the following possible malfunctions:
   a. Faulty fuel system component.
   b. Flooded engine.
   c. Engine damage (low compression).

POOR ENGINE PERFORMANCE

If the engine runs, but performance is unsatisfactory. refer to the section that best describes the symptoms.

Engine Starts but Stalls and is Hard to Restart

Check for the following:
1. Incorrect choke operation. This can be due to improper use or a stuck choke valve in the carburetor.
2. Plugged fuel tank vent hose, if so equipped.
3. Plugged fuel hose, fuel shutoff valve or fuel filter.
4. Incorrect carburetor adjustment.
5. Incorrect float level adjustment.

> *NOTE*
> *If a warm or hot engine will start with the choke on, or if a cold engine starts and runs until the choke is turned off, the pilot jet is probably plugged.*

6. Plugged carburetor jets.
7. Contaminated or stale fuel.
8. Clogged air filter.
9. Intake tube air leak.
10. Plugged exhaust system. Check the silencer or muffler, especially if the motorcycle was just returned from storage.
11. Faulty ignition system component.

Engine Backfires, Cuts Out or Misfires During Acceleration

A backfire occurs when fuel is burned or ignited in the exhaust system.
1. A lean air/fuel mixture can cause these engine performance problems. Check for the following conditions:
   a. Incorrect float level adjustment.
   b. Plugged pilot jet or pilot system.
2. Loose exhaust pipe-to-cylinder head connection.
3. Intake air leak.
4. Incorrect ignition timing or a damaged ignition system can cause these conditions. Refer to *Ignition System* (this chapter) to isolate the damaged ignition system component. Check the ignition timing as described in Chapter Three.
5. Check the following engine components:
   a. Broken valve springs.
   b. Stuck or leaking valves.
   c. Worn or damaged camshaft lobes.
   d. Incorrect valve timing due to incorrect camshaft installation or a mechanical failure.

Engine Backfires on Deceleration

If the engine backfires when the throttle is released, check the following:
1. Lean carburetor pilot system.
2. Loose exhaust pipe-to-cylinder head connection.
3. On CRF230L and CRF230M models, check for a faulty secondary air supply system.
4. Faulty ignition system component.
5. Check the following engine components:
   a. Broken valve springs.
   b. Stuck or leaking valves.
   c. Worn or damaged camshaft lobes.
   d. Incorrect valve timing due to incorrect camshaft installation or a mechanical failure.

Poor Fuel Mileage

1. Clogged fuel system.
2. Dirty or clogged air filter.
3. Incorrect ignition timing or defective ignition system components.

Engine Will Not Idle or Idles Roughly

1. Clogged air filter element.
2. Poor fuel flow resulting from a partially-clogged fuel valve, fuel filter or fuel hose.
3. Contaminated or stale fuel.
4. Incorrect carburetor adjustment.
5. Leaking head gasket.
6. Intake air leak.
7. Incorrect ignition timing or defective ignition system components.
8. Low engine compression.

Low Engine Power

1. Support the motorcycle on a stand with the rear wheel off the ground. Then, spin the rear wheel by hand. If the wheel spins freely, continue the procedure. If the wheel does not spin freely, check for the following conditions:

> *NOTE*
> *After riding the motorcycle, come to a stop on a level surface. Turn the engine off and shift the transmission into neutral. Walk or push the motorcycle forward. If the motorcycle is harder to push than normal, check for dragging brakes.*

   a. Dragging brakes. Check for this condition immediately after riding the motorcycle.
   b. Damaged or binding drive chain.

   c. Damaged wheel bearings.
2. Test ride the motorcycle and accelerate quickly from first to second gear.
3A. If the engine speed increased according to throttle position, continue the procedure.
3B. If the engine speed did not increase, check for one or more of the following problems:
   a. Slipping clutch.
   b. Warped clutch plates.
   c. Worn clutch plates.
   d. Weak or damaged clutch springs.
4. Test ride the motorcycle and accelerate lightly.
5A. If the engine speed increased according to throttle position, continue the procedure.
5B. If the engine speed did not increase, check for one or more of the following problems:
   a. Clogged air filter.
   b. Restricted fuel flow.
   c. Pinched fuel tank breather hose, if so equipped.
   d. Clogged or damaged silencer or muffler.
6. Check for retarded ignition timing (Chapter Three). A decrease in power results when the plug fires later than normal.
7. Check for one or more of the following problems:
   a. Low engine compression.
   b. Worn spark plug.
   c. Fouled spark plug.
   d. Incorrect spark plug heat range.
   e. Weak ignition coil.
   f. Incorrect ignition timing or defective ignition system component.
   g. Plugged carburetor passages.
   h. Incorrect oil level (too high or too low).
   i. Contaminated oil.
   j. Worn or damaged valve train assembly.
   k. Engine overheating.
8. If the engine knocks when it is accelerated or when running at high speed, check for one or more of the following possible malfunctions:
   a. Incorrect type of fuel.
   b. Lean fuel mixture.
   c. Over-advanced ignition timing (defective ignition control module).
   d. Excessive carbon buildup in combustion chamber.
   e. Worn pistons and/or cylinder bores.

Poor Idle or Low Speed Performance

1. Check for an incorrect pilot screw adjustment.
2. Check for damaged or loose intake pipe and air filter housing hose clamps. These conditions will cause an air leak.
3. Perform the spark test (this chapter). Note the following:

a. If the spark is good, continue the procedure.
b. If the spark is weak, perform the troubleshooting procedures in *Ignition System* (this chapter) to isolate the damaged ignition system component.
4. Check the ignition timing (Chapter Three). If ignition timing is correct, continue the procedure. If the timing is incorrect, refer to *Ignition System* (this chapter) to isolate the damaged ignition system component.
5. Check the fuel system (this chapter).

Poor High Speed Performance

1. Check ignition timing (Chapter Three). If the ignition timing is correct, perform Step 3.
2. If the timing is incorrect, refer to *Ignition System* (this chapter) to isolate the damaged ignition system component.
3. Check the fuel system (this chapter).
4. Check the valve clearance (Chapter Three). Note the following:
   a. If the valve clearance is correct, continue the procedure.
   b. If the clearance is incorrect, adjust the valves (Chapter Three).
5. Incorrect valve timing and worn or damaged valve springs can cause poor high-speed performance. If the camshaft was timed just before the motorcycle experiencing this type of problem, the cam timing may be incorrect. If the cam timing was not set or changed, and all other inspection procedures (this section) failed to locate the problem, inspect the camshaft and valve assembly.

FUEL SYSTEM

The following section isolates common fuel system problems under specific complaints. If there is a good spark, poor fuel flow may be preventing the correct amount of fuel from being supplied to the spark plug. Troubleshoot the fuel system as follows:
1. Clogged fuel tank breather hose, if so equipped.
2. Check that there is a sufficient amount of fuel in the tank.
3. After attempting to start the engine, remove the spark plug (Chapter Three) and check for fuel on the plug tip. Note the following:
   a. If there is no fuel visible on the plug, check for a clogged fuel shutoff valve, fuel filter or fuel line.

NOTE
If the motorcycle has not been used for some time, and was not properly stored, the fuel may be stale due to lighter parts of the fuel evaporating.

Depending on the condition of the fuel, a no-start condition can result.

b. If there is fuel present on the plug tip, and the engine has spark, check for an excessive intake air leak or the possibility of contaminated or stale fuel.
c. If there is an excessive amount of fuel on the plug, check for a clogged air filter or flooded carburetor.

Rich Mixture

The following conditions can cause a rich air/fuel mixture:
1. Clogged air filter.
2. Choke stuck open.
3. Float level too high.
4. Contaminated float valve seat.
5. Worn or damaged float valve and seat.
6. Leaking or damaged float.
7. Clogged carburetor jets.
8. Incorrect carburetor jetting.

Lean Mixture

The following conditions can cause a lean air/fuel mixture:
1. Intake air leak.
2. Float level too low.
3. Clogged fuel line, fuel filter or fuel shutoff valve.
4. Partially restricted fuel tank breather hose, if so equipped.
5. Plugged carburetor air vent hose.
6. Damaged float.
7. Damaged float valve.
8. Incorrect carburetor jetting.

ENGINE

Smoke

The color of engine smoke can help diagnose engine problems or operating conditions.

Black Smoke

Black smoke is an indication of a rich air/fuel mixture.

Blue Smoke

Blue smoke indicates that the engine is burning oil in the combustion chamber as it leaks past worn valve stem seals and piston rings. Excessive oil consumption is another indicator of an engine that is burning oil. Perform a compression test (Chapter Three) to isolate the problem.

White Smoke or Steam

It is normal to see white smoke or steam from the exhaust after first starting the engine in cold weather. This is actually condensed steam formed by the engine during combustion. If the motorcycle is ridden far enough, the water cannot collect in the crankcase and should not become a problem. Once the engine heats up to normal operating temperature, the water evaporates and exits the engine through the crankcase vent system. However, if the motorcycle is ridden for short trips or repeatedly started and stopped and allowed to cool off without the engine getting warm enough, water will start to collect in the crankcase. With each short run of the engine, more water collects. As this water mixes with the oil in the crankcase, sludge is produced. Sludge can eventually cause engine damage as it circulates through the lubrication system and blocks off oil passages.

Low Compression

Problems with the engine top end will affect engine performance. When the engine condition is suspect, perform a cylinder leakdown test (this chapter) and a compression test (Chapter Three). Interpret the results as described in each procedure to troubleshoot the suspect area. An engine can lose compression through the following areas:
1. Valves:
    a. Incorrect valve adjustment.
    b. Incorrect valve timing.
    c. Worn or damaged valve seat surfaces.
    d. Bent valves.
    e. Weak or broken valve springs.
2. Cylinder head:
    a. Loose spark plug or damaged spark plug hole.
    b. Damaged cylinder head gasket.
    c. Warped or cracked cylinder head.
3. Damaged decompressor assembly.

High Compression

Excessive carbon buildup in the combustion chamber.

Overheating

1. Improper spark plug heat range.
2. Low oil level.
3. Oil not circulating properly.

4. Valves leaking.
5. Heavy carbon deposits in the combustion chamber.
6. Dragging brake(s).
7. Slipping clutch.
8. Over-advanced ignition timing caused by a defective ignition system component.

Preignition

Preignition is the premature burning of fuel and is caused by hot spots in the combustion chamber. Glowing deposits in the combustion chamber, inadequate cooling or an overheated spark plug can all cause preignition. Preignition is first noticed as a power loss, but eventually causes damage to the internal parts of the engine because of the high combustion chamber temperature.

Detonation

Detonation is the violent explosion of fuel in the combustion chamber before the proper time of ignition. Using low octane gasoline is a common cause of detonation.

Even when using a high octane gasoline, detonation can still occur. Other causes are over-advanced ignition timing, lean air/fuel mixture at or near full throttle, inadequate engine cooling, or the excessive accumulation of carbon deposits in the combustion chamber.

Continued detonation can result in engine damage.

Power Loss

Refer to *Poor Engine Performance* (this chapter).

Noises

Unusual noises are often the first indication of a developing problem. Investigate any new noises as soon as possible. Something that may be a minor problem, if corrected, could prevent the possibility of more extensive damage.

Use a mechanic's stethoscope or a small section of hose held near your ear (not directly on your ear) with the other end close to the source of the noise to isolate the location. Determining the exact cause of a noise can be difficult. If this is the case, consult with a professional mechanic to determine the cause. Do not disassemble major components until all other possibilities have been eliminated.

Consider the following when troubleshooting engine noises:
1. Knocking or pinging during acceleration can be caused by using a lower octane fuel than recom-

mended. This noise may also be caused by poor fuel. Pinging can also be caused by an incorrect spark plug heat range or carbon buildup in the combustion chamber.

> *NOTE*
> *Piston slap is easier to detect when the engine is cold and before the piston has expanded. Once the engine has warmed up, piston expansion reduces piston-to-cylinder clearance.*

2. Slapping or rattling noises at low speed or during acceleration may be caused by excessive piston-to-cylinder wall clearance (piston slap).
3. Knocking or rapping while decelerating is usually caused by excessive rod bearing clearance.
4. Persistent knocking and vibration occurring every crankshaft rotation is usually caused by worn rod or main bearing(s). This noise can also be caused by broken piston rings or a damaged piston pin.
5. Rapid on-off squeal can be caused by a compression leak around cylinder head gasket or spark plug.
6. Valve train noise can be caused by the following:
   a. Excessive valve clearance.
   b. Worn or damaged camshaft.
   c. Damaged camshaft.
   d. Worn or damaged valve train components.
   e. Valve sticking in guide.
   f. Broken valve spring.
   g. Low oil pressure.
   h. Clogged cylinder oil hole or oil passage.

Engine Vibration

1. Incorrect balancer shaft timing.
2. Excessive crankshaft runout.
3. Damaged crankshaft and balancer shaft bearings.

ENGINE LUBRICATION

An improperly-operating engine lubrication system quickly leads to engine seizure. Check the engine oil level as described in Chapter Three. Oil pump service is described in Chapter Five.

High Oil Consumption or Excessive Exhaust Smoke

1. Worn valve guides.
2. Worn valve guide seals.
3. Worn or damaged piston rings.
4. Incorrect piston ring installation.

Low Oil Pressure

1. Low oil level.
2. Worn or damaged oil pump.
3. Clogged oil strainer screen.
4. Clogged oil filter.
5. Internal oil leaks.
6. Oil relief valve stuck open.
7. Incorrect type of engine oil.

High Oil Pressure

1. Oil relief valve stuck closed.
2. Clogged oil filter.
3. Clogged oil gallery or metering orifices.
4. Incorrect type of engine oil.

No Oil Pressure

1. Low oil level.
2. Oil relief valve stuck closed.
3. Damaged oil pump.
4. Incorrect oil pump installation.
5. Internal oil leaks.

Oil Level Too Low

1. Oil level not maintained at correct level.
2. Worn piston rings.
3. Worn cylinder.
4. Worn valve guides.
5. Worn valve guide seals.
6. Piston rings incorrectly installed during engine overhaul.
7. External oil leaks.

Oil Contamination

This condition can be caused when the oil and filter are not changed at specified intervals or when operating conditions demand more frequent changes.

CYLINDER LEAKDOWN TEST

A cylinder leakdown test can accurately pinpoint engine problems caused by leaks from the head gasket, cracks in the cylinder head and cylinder, or by worn valves, valve seats and piston rings. This test is performed by applying compressed air to the cylinder through a special tester, and then measuring the amount of leak as a percentage. A cylinder leakdown tester (**Figure 7**) and an air compressor are needed to perform this test.

When performing a leakdown test, the engine is first set at TDC on its compression stroke so that all the valves are closed. When the combustion chamber is pressurized, very little air should escape. However, the difficulty in performing a leakdown test on a single cylinder engine (especially on the engines described in this manual with low static engine compression) is in preventing the piston from moving as the combustion chamber starts to pressurize. Any piston movement will force the crankshaft to turn away from TDC and allow air to escape past an open valve seat.

To perform the leakdown, it will be necessary to lock the engine at TDC on its compression stroke. Follow the tester manufacturer's directions, along with the following information, when performing a cylinder leakdown test.

1. Support the motorcycle on a work stand with the rear wheel off the ground.

2. Remove the air filter assembly (Chapter Three). Open and secure the throttle so it is at its wide-open position.

3A. If the drive chain is equipped with a master link, remove the master link and slide the drive chain off the drive sprocket.

3B. If the motorcycle is equipped with an endless drive chain, loosen the rear axle nut and move the rear wheel forward to obtain as much chain slack as possible. Then, remove the drive sprocket cover and the drive sprocket as described in Chapter Twelve. Reinstall the drive sprocket without the drive chain.

4. Remove the spark plug (Chapter Three).

5. Install the threaded hose adapter from the leakdown tester tool set. Then, install the leakdown gauge onto the hose.

6. Remove the ignition timing hole cap (A, **Figure 8**) from the left crankcase cover.

7. Remove the flywheel bolt cap (B, **Figure 8**) from the left crankcase cover.

NOTE
Because the leakdown test in this section is shown performed with the cylinder head cover installed on the engine, the camshaft lobes cannot be viewed to ensure that the engine is positioned at TDC on its compression stroke.

8. To determine when the engine is approaching TDC on its compression stroke, or whether it is 360° off, observe the following two indicators to predict engine position:

   a. When aligning the index marks, listen for pressure building inside the combustion chamber, indicating that the piston is moving to TDC on its compression stroke.

   b. Then, view the gauge on the leakdown tester when turning the engine. As the piston moves toward TDC on its compression stroke,

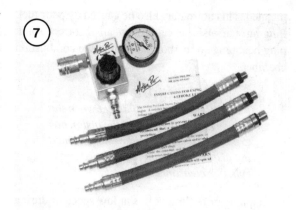

compression building inside the combustion chamber may cause the gauge needle to move slightly.

   c. If the crankshaft is 360° off, these indicators will not be present.

9. Rotate the engine using the flywheel bolt. Rotate the engine counterclockwise until the engine is at top dead center (TDC) on the compression stroke. Make sure the flywheel timing T mark aligns with the index mark on the crankcase (**Figure 9**).

WARNING
Do not attempt to lock the engine by trying to use a tool to hold the flywheel bolt on the end of the crankshaft. Once the combustion chamber becomes pressurized, any crankshaft movement can throw the tool away from the engine under considerable force. Attempting to hold the tool can cause serious injury. Engine damage may also occur to the crankshaft or left crankcase cover. Lock the engine as described in this section.

10. Perform the following to lock the transmission so the engine remains at TDC on its compression stroke when performing the leakdown test:

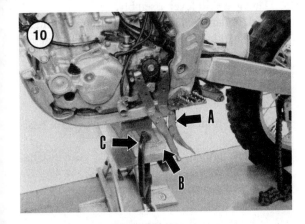

a. Turn the drive sprocket by hand and shift the transmission into top gear with the shift pedal.

b. Attach a clutch holder (A, **Figure 10**), or an equivalent holding tool, to the drive sprocket. Use a wooden block (B, **Figure 10**) and clamp (C) to secure the holding tool so it cannot move when the combustion chamber becomes pressurized.

c. Check that the TDC marks are still aligned as described in this section. If not, turn the crankshaft as required, and then relock the holding tool in position.

11. Detach the crankcase breather hose from the fitting on the rear of the crankcase.

NOTE
Because of play in the transmission gears, it is unlikely the engine will stay at TDC on the first try. If the crankshaft turns, reposition the countershaft slightly, and then relock it in position with the holding tool. Several attempts may be required to determine the amount of transmission play and which direction the countershaft should be turned and locked.

12. Perform a cylinder leakdown test by applying air pressure to the combustion chamber. Follow the tester manufacturer's instructions while reading the leak percent on the gauge. Listen for air leaking while noting the following:

NOTE
*If a large amount of air escapes from the exhaust pipe or through the carburetor, the air is leaking through an open valve. Check the index mark (**Figure 9**) to make sure the engine is at TDC on the compression stroke. If the engine is remaining at TDC but there is still a large amount of air escaping from the engine, the crankshaft is off one revolution. Turn the engine 360°, realign the TDC mark, amd then relock it as described in this section.*

a. Air leaking through the exhaust pipe indicates a leaking exhaust valve.

b. Air leaking through the carburetor indicates a leaking intake valve.

c. Air leaking through both the intake and exhaust valves indicates the engine is not set at TDC on its compression stroke.

d. Air leaking through the crankcase breather hole indicates the rings are not sealing properly in the bore.

13. If the cylinder leakdown is 10 percent or higher, further engine service is required.

14. Disconnect the test equipment and install all the previously removed parts. Readjust the drive chain if the chain was removed (Chapter Three).

CLUTCH

Basic clutch troubleshooting is listed in this section. Clutch service is covered in Chapter Six.

No Pressure at Clutch Lever

1. Incorrect clutch adjustment.
2. Broken clutch cable.
3. Damaged clutch lifter mechanism.

Clutch Lever Hard to Pull In

1. Dry or damaged clutch cable.
2. Kinked or stuck clutch cable.
3. Incorrect clutch cable routing.
4. Damaged clutch lifter mechanism.
5. Damaged clutch lifter thrust washer and needle bearing.

Rough Clutch Operation

Worn, grooved or damaged clutch hub and clutch housing slots.

Clutch Slip

If the engine speed increases without a corresponding increase in motorcycle speed, the clutch is probably slipping. The main causes of clutch slippage are:
1. No clutch lever free play.
2. Worn clutch plates.
3. Weak clutch springs.
4. Sticking or damaged clutch lifter.
5. Clutch plates contaminated by engine oil additive.

Clutch Drag

If the clutch does not disengage or if the motorcycle creeps with the transmission in gear and the clutch disengaged, the clutch is dragging. Some main causes of clutch drag are:
1. Excessive clutch lever free play.
2. Warped clutch plates.
3. Damaged clutch lifter assembly.
4. Loose clutch housing locknut.
5. High oil level.
6. Incorrect oil viscosity.
7. Engine oil additive being used.
8. Damaged clutch hub and clutch housing splines.

GEARSHIFT LINKAGE

The gearshift linkage assembly connects the shift pedal (external shift mechanism) to the shift drum (internal shift mechanism). Refer to Chapter Six and Chapter Seven to identify the shift mechanism components called out in this section.

Transmission Jumps Out of Gear

1. Damaged stopper arm.
2. Damaged stopper arm spring.
3. Loose stopper arm mounting bolt.
4. Loose guide plate mounting bolts.
5. Damaged shifter collar.
6. Worn or damaged shift drum cam.
7. Damaged shift shaft spring.

Difficult Shifting

1. Incorrect clutch operation or improper adjustment.
2. Incorrect oil viscosity.

3. Loose or damaged stopper arm assembly.
4. Bent shift fork shaft(s).
5. Bent or damaged shift fork(s).
6. Worn gear dogs or slots.
7. Damaged shift drum grooves.
8. Damaged shift shaft spindle.
9. Incorrect gearshift linkage installation.
10. Damaged shift lever assembly.

Shift Pedal Does Not Return

1. Bent shift shaft spindle.
2. Bent shift shaft engagement arm.
3. Damaged shift lever assembly.
4. Weak or damaged shift shaft arm return spring.
5. Shift shaft installed incorrectly (return spring not indexed around pin).

Excessive Transmission Noise

1. Damaged primary drive and driven gears or bearing.
2. Incorrect primary drive and drive gear installation.
3. Damaged transmission bearings or gears.

TRANSMISSION

Transmission symptoms are sometimes hard to distinguish from clutch symptoms. Basic transmission troubleshooting information is listed below. Refer to Chapter Seven for transmission service procedures. Before working on the transmission, make sure the clutch and gearshift linkage assembly are not causing the problem.

Difficult Shifting

1. Incorrect clutch operation.
2. Bent shift fork(s).
3. Damaged shift fork guide pin(s).
4. Bent shift fork shaft(s).
5. Damaged shift drum grooves.
6. Damaged gears.

Jumps Out of Gear

1. Loose or damaged shift drum cam mounting bolt.
2. Bent or damaged shift fork(s).
3. Bent shift fork shaft(s).
4. Damaged shift drum grooves.
5. Worn gear dogs or slots.

Incorrect Shift Lever Operation

1. Bent shift pedal or linkage.
2. Stripped shift pedal splines.
3. Damaged shift linkage.
4. Damaged shift shaft spindle.

Excessive Gear Noise

1. Worn or damaged transmission bearings.
2. Worn or damaged gears.
3. Excessive gear backlash.

ELECTRICAL TESTING

This section describes electrical troubleshooting and the use of test equipment. Never assume anything and do not overlook the obvious, such as a blown fuse or an electrical connector that has separated. Test the simplest and most obvious items first and try to perform tests at easily accessible points on the motorcycle. Make sure to troubleshoot problems systematically.

Refer to the color wiring diagrams at the end of the manual for component and connector identification. Use the wiring diagrams to determine how the circuit should work by tracing the current paths from the power source through the circuit components to ground. Also, check any circuits that share the same fuse, ground or switch. If the other circuits work properly and the shared wiring is good, the cause must be in the wiring used only by the suspect circuit. If all related circuits are faulty at the same time, the probable cause is a poor ground connection or blown fuse(s).

Preliminary Checks and Precautions

Before starting any electrical troubleshooting, perform the following:
1. Inspect the battery. Make sure it is fully-charged and that the battery leads are clean and securely attached to the battery terminals.
2. Electrical connectors are often the cause of electrical system problems. Inspect the connectors as follows:
    a. Disconnect each electrical connector in the suspect circuit and make sure there are no bent terminals in the electrical connector. A bent terminal will not connect to its mate, causing an open circuit.
    b. Make sure the terminals are pushed all the way into the connector. If not, carefully push them in with a narrow-bladed screwdriver.

    c. Check the wires where they attach to the terminals for damage.
    d. Make sure each terminal is clean and free of corrosion. Clean them, if necessary, and pack the connectors with dielectric grease.
    e. Push the connector halves together. Make sure the connectors are fully engaged and locked together.
    f. Never pull the wires when disconnecting a connector. Pull only on the connector housing.
3. Never use a self-powered test light on circuits that contain solid-state devices. The solid-state devices may be damaged.

Intermittent Problems

Problems that do not occur all the time can be difficult to isolate during testing, such as when a problem only occurs when the motorcycle is ridden over rough roads (vibration) or in wet conditions (water penetration). Note the following:
1. Vibration. This is a common problem with loose or damaged electrical connectors.
    a. Perform a continuity test as described in the appropriate service procedure or in *Continuity Test* (this section).
    b. Lightly pull or wiggle the connectors while repeating the test. Do the same when checking the wiring harness and individual components, especially where the wires enter a housing or connector.
    c. A change in meter readings indicates a poor connection. Find and repair the problem or replace the part. Check for wires with cracked or broken insulation.

NOTE
An analog ohmmeter is useful when making this type of test. Slight needle movements are visibly apparent, which indicate a loose connection.

2. Heat. This is a common problem with connectors or joints that have loose or poor connections. As these connections heat up, the connection or joint expands and separates, causing an open circuit. Other heat-related problems occur when a component starts to fail as it heats up.
    a. Troubleshoot the problem to isolate the circuit.

CAUTION
A heat gun will quickly raise the temperature of the component being tested. Do not apply heat directly to the part or use heat in excess of 60° C (140° F) on any electrical component.

b. To check a connector, perform a continuity test as described in the appropriate service procedure or in *Continuity Test* (this section). Then, repeat the test while heating the connector with a heat gun. If the meter reading was normal (continuity) when the connector was cold, and then fluctuated or read infinity when heat was applied, the connection is bad.

c. To check a component, allow the engine to cool. Then, start and run the engine. Note operational differences when the engine is cold and hot.

d. If the engine will not start, isolate and remove the suspect component. Test it at room temperature and again after heating it with a heat gun. A change in meter readings indicates a temperature problem.

3. Water. When the problem occurs when riding in wet conditions or in areas with high humidity, start and run the engine in a dry area. Then, with the engine running, spray water onto the suspected component/circuit. Water-related problems often stop after the component heats up and dries.

Test Light or Voltmeter

Use a test light to check for voltage in a circuit. Attach one lead to ground and the other lead to various points along the circuit. It does not make a difference which test lead is attached to ground. The bulb lights when voltage is present.

Use a voltmeter in the same manner as the test light to find out if voltage is present in any given circuit. The voltmeter, unlike the test light, also indicates how much voltage is present at each test point.

Voltage test

Unless otherwise specified, make all voltage tests with the electrical connectors still connected. Insert the test leads into the backside of the connector and make sure the test lead touches the electrical terminal within the connector housing. If the test lead only touches the wire insulation, it will cause a false reading.

Always check both sides of the connector because one side may be loose or corroded, thus preventing electrical flow through the connector. This type of test can be performed with a test light or a voltmeter.

1. Attach the voltmeter negative test lead to a confirmed ground location. If possible, use the battery ground connection. Make sure the ground is not insulated.

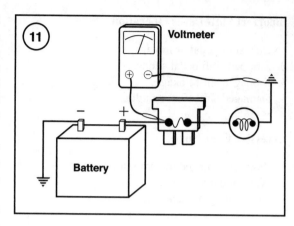

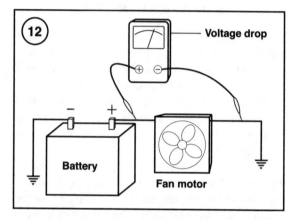

2. Attach the voltmeter positive test lead to the point to be tested (**Figure 11**).

3. Turn the ignition switch on. If using a test light, the test light will come on if voltage is present. If using a voltmeter, note the voltage reading. The reading should be within 1 volt of battery voltage. If the voltage is less there is a problem in the circuit.

Voltage drop test

The wires, cables, connectors and switches in the electrical circuit are designed to carry current with low resistance. This ensures current can flow through the circuit with a minimum loss of voltage. Voltage drop indicates where there is resistance in a circuit. A higher-than-normal amount of resistance in a circuit decreases the flow of current and causes the voltage to drop between the source and destination in the circuit.

Because resistance causes voltage to drop, a voltmeter is used to measure voltage drop when current is running through the circuit. If the circuit has no resistance, there is no voltage drop so the voltmeter indicates 0 volts. The greater the resistance in a circuit, the greater the voltage drop reading.

To perform a voltage drop:

1. Connect the positive meter test lead to the electrical source (where electricity is coming from).

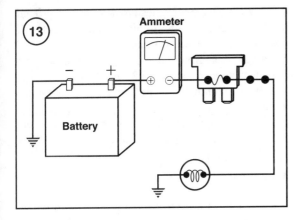

2. Connect the voltmeter negative test lead to the electrical load (where the electricity is going). Refer to **Figure 12**.

3. If necessary, activate the component(s) in the circuit.

4. Read the voltage drop (difference in voltage between the source and destination) on the voltmeter. Note the following:

   a. The voltmeter should indicate 0 volts. If there is a drop of 1 volt or more, there is a problem within the circuit. A voltage drop reading of 12 volts indicates a break in the circuit.

   b. A voltage drop of 1 or more volts indicates that a circuit has excessive resistance.

   c. For example, consider a starting problem where the battery is fully-charged but the starter turns over slowly. Voltage drop would be the difference in the voltage at the battery (source) and the voltage at the starter (destination) as the engine is being started (current is flowing through the battery cables). A corroded battery cable would cause a high voltage drop (high resistance) and slow engine cranking.

   d. Common sources of voltage drop are loose or contaminated connectors and poor ground connections.

Testing for a short with a voltmeter

A test light may also be used.

1. Remove the blown fuse from the fuse panel.

2. Connect the voltmeter across the fuse terminals in the fuse panel. Turn the ignition switch on and check for battery voltage.

3. With the voltmeter attached to the fuse terminals, wiggle the wiring harness relating to the suspect circuit at approximately 15.2 cm (6 in.) intervals. Start next to the fuse panel and work systematically away from the panel. Note the voltmeter reading while progressing along the harness.

4. If the voltmeter reading changes (test light blinks), there is a short-to-ground at that point in the harness.

Ammeter

Use an ammeter to measure the flow of current (amps) in a circuit (**Figure 13**). When connected in series in a circuit, the ammeter determines if current is flowing through the circuit and if that current flow is excessive because of a short in the circuit. Current flow is often referred to as current draw. Comparing actual current draw in the circuit or component to current draw specification (if specified by the manufacturer) provides useful diagnostic information.

Self-Powered Test Light

A self-powered test light can be constructed from a 12-volt light bulb, a pair of test leads and a 12-volt battery. When the test leads are touched together the light bulb should go on.

Use a self-powered test light as follows:

1. Touch the test leads together to make sure the light bulb goes on. If not, correct the problem.

2. Disconnect the motorcycle's battery or remove the fuse(s) that protects the circuit to be tested. Do not connect a self-powered test light to a circuit that has power applied to it.

3. Select two points within the circuit where there should be continuity.

4. Attach one lead of the test light to each point.

5. If there is continuity, the test light bulb will come on.

6. If there is no continuity, the test light bulb will not come on, indicating an open circuit.

Ohmmeter

> *CAUTION*
> *To prevent damage to the ohmmeter, never connect it to a circuit that has power applied to it. Always disconnect the battery negative lead before using an ohmmeter.*

Use an ohmmeter to measure the resistance (in ohms) to current flow in a circuit or component.

Ohmmeters may be analog-type (needle scale) or digital-type (LCD or LED readout). Both types of ohmmeters have a switch that allows the user to select different ranges of resistance for accurate readings. The analog ohmmeter also has a set-adjust control which is used to zero or calibrate the meter (digital ohmmeters do not require calibration). Refer to the ohmmeter's instructions to determine the correct scale setting.

Use an ohmmeter by connecting its test leads to the circuit or component to be tested. If an analog meter is used, it must be calibrated by touching the test leads together and turning the set-adjust knob until the meter needle reads zero. When the leads are uncrossed, the needle should move to the other end of the scale, indicating infinite resistance.

During a continuity test, a reading of infinite resistance indicates there is a break in the circuit or component. A reading of zero indicates continuity, that is, there is no measurable resistance in the circuit or component. A measured reading indicates the actual resistance to current flow that is present in that circuit. Even though resistance is present, the circuit has continuity.

Continuity test

Perform a continuity test to determine the integrity of a circuit, wire or component. A circuit has continuity if it forms a complete circuit; that is if there are no breaks in either the electrical wires or components within the circuit. A circuit with a break in it, on the other hand, has no continuity.

This type of test can be performed with a self-powered test light or an ohmmeter. An ohmmeter gives the best results.
1. Disconnect the negative battery cable (Chapter Ten or Chapter Eleven) or disconnect the test circuit/component from its power source.
2. Attach one test lead (test light or ohmmeter) to one end of the part of the circuit to be tested.
3. Attach the other test lead to the other end of the part or the circuit to be tested.
4. The self-powered test light comes on if there is continuity. An ohmmeter reads 0 or low resistance if there is continuity. A reading of infinite resistance indicates no continuity; the circuit is open.
5. If testing a component, note the resistance and compare this to the specification if available.

Testing for short with an ohmmeter

An analog ohmmeter or one with an audible continuity indicator works best for short testing.
1. Disconnect the negative battery cable (Chapter Ten or Chapter Eleven).
2. If necessary, remove the blown fuse from the fuse panel.
3. Connect one test lead of the ohmmeter to the load side (battery side) of the fuse terminal in the fuse panel.

4. Connect the other test lead to a confirmed ground location. Make sure the ground is not insulated. If possible, use the battery ground connection.
5. Wiggle the wiring harness relating to the suspect circuit at approximately 15.2 cm (6 in.) intervals. Watch the ohmmeter while progressing along the harness.
6. If the ohmmeter needle moves, or if it beeps, there is a short-to-ground at that point in the harness.

Jumper Wire

Use a jumper wire to bypass a potential problem and isolate it to a particular point in a circuit. If a faulty circuit works properly with a jumper wire installed, there is a break in the circuit between the two jumped points.

To troubleshoot with a jumper wire, first use the wire to determine if the problem is on the ground side or the load side of a device. Test the ground by connecting the wire between the device and a good ground. If the device comes on, the problem is the connection between the device and ground. If the device does not come on with the wire installed, the device's connection to ground is good, so the problem is between the device and the power source.

To isolate the problem, connect the wire between the battery and the device. If it comes on, the problem is between these two points. Next, connect the wire between the battery and the fuse side of the switch. If the device comes on, the switch is good. By successively moving the wire from one point to another, the problem can be isolated to a particular place in the circuit.

Note the following when using a jumper wire:
1. Make sure the wire gauge (thickness) is the same as that used in the circuit being tested. Smaller gauge wire rapidly overheats and could melt.
2. Make sure the jumper wire has insulated alligator clips. This prevents accidental grounding (sparks) or possible shock. Install an inline fuse/fuse holder in the jumper wire.
3. A jumper wire is a temporary test measure. Do not leave a jumper wire installed as a permanent solution. This creates a fire hazard.
4. Never use a jumper wire across any load (a component that is connected and turned on). This would cause a direct short and blow the fuse(s).

ELECTRIC STARTING SYSTEM

This section describes troubleshooting procedures for the electric starting system. A fully-charged battery, ohmmeter and jumper cables are required to perform many of these troubleshooting procedures.

Description

The electric starting system requires a fully-charged battery to provide the large amount of current required to operate the starter motor.

The starting circuit consists of the battery, starter motor, clutch lever switch, neutral switch, diode (CRF230L and CRF230M models), sidestand switch (CRF230L and CRF230M models), starter relay, ignition switch and engine stop switch. Refer to Chapter Ten or Chapter Eleven for the location of the starting system components.

The starter relay carries the heavy electrical current to the starter motor. Depressing the starter switch allows current to flow through the starter relay coil. The starter relay contacts close and allow current to flow from the battery through the starter relay to the starter motor.

When the ignition switch is turned on, and the engine stop switch is set to run on CRF230L and CRF230M models, the starter motor can be operated only if the transmission is in neutral or the clutch lever is gripped.

On CRF230L and CRF230M models, if the sidestand is down, the engine will stop if the transmission is shifted into gear.

Preliminary Troubleshooting

Before troubleshooting the starting circuit, verify that:
1. The battery is fully-charged.
2. Battery cables are the proper size and length. Replace cables that are undersize or damaged.
3. All electrical connections are clean and tight.
4. The wiring harness is in good condition, with no worn or frayed insulation or loose harness sockets.
5. The fuel system is filled with an adequate supply of fresh gasoline.

Starter Troubleshooting

> *CAUTION*
> *Do not operate an electric starter motor continuously for more than 5 seconds. Allow the motor to cool for at least 10 seconds between attempts to start the engine.*

When operating the starter switch, set the engine stop switch to run and turn the ignition switch on. Be sure the transmission is in neutral.

> *NOTE*
> *This procedure isolates a starter problem when attempting to start in neutral. If the starter operates in neutral but not when the transmission is in gear and the clutch lever is gripped, check the clutch lever switch circuit.*

If the starter does not operate, perform the following tests:
1. Refer to Chapter Ten or Chapter Eleven and check the main fuse. If the fuse is blown, replace it. If the main fuse is good, reinstall it and continue the procedure.
2. Test the battery as described in Chapter Three. Note the following:
    a. If the battery is fully-charged, continue the procedure.
    b. If necessary, clean and recharge the battery. If the battery is damaged, replace it.
3. Check for loose, corroded or damaged battery cables. Check at the battery, starter motor, starter relay and all cable-to-frame connections.
4. Turn the ignition switch on. Then, push the starter button and listen for a click sound at the starter relay switch. Note the following:
    a. If the relay clicked, continue the procedure.
    b. If the relay did not click, proceed to Step 6.
5. Test the battery as follows:
    a. Park the motorcycle on level ground. Make sure the transmission is in neutral.
    b. Disconnect the cable from the starter motor terminal (**Figure 14**).

> *WARNING*
> *Because a spark will be produced, perform this procedure away from gasoline or other volatile liquids. Make sure that there is no spilled gasoline on the motorcycle or gasoline fumes in the work area.*

    c. Momentarily connect a jumper cable (thick gauge wire) from the positive battery terminal to the starter motor terminal (**Figure 14**). If the starter motor is working properly, it will turn when making the jumper cable connection.

   d. If the starter motor did not turn, remove and service it (Chapter Ten or Chapter Eleven).

   e. If the starter motor turned, check for a loose or damaged starter motor cable. If the cable is okay, the starter relay is faulty. Replace the starter relay and retest.

6. Test the following items (Chapter Ten or Chapter Eleven):

   a. Neutral switch.

   b. Clutch lever switch.

   c. Sidestand switch (CRF230L and CRF230M models).

   d. Ignition switch.

   e. Diode (CRF230L and CRF230M models).

7. Perform the starter relay switch voltage test (Chapter Ten or Chapter Eleven). Note the following:

   a. If the voltmeter shows battery voltage, continue the procedure.

   b. If there was no voltage reading, check the ignition switch and starter switch (Chapter Ten or Chapter Eleven). If both switches are good, check continuity of the yellow/red wire between the starter switch and the starter relay switch.

8. Perform the starter relay switch continuity test (Chapter Ten or Chapter Eleven). Note the following:

   a. If the meter reading is correct, continue the procedure.

   b. If the meter reading is incorrect, check for an open circuit in the yellow/red and green/red wires. Check the wire ends for loose or damaged connectors.

9. If the starting system problem was not found after performing the steps of this procedure in order, recheck the wiring system for dirty or loose-fitting terminals or damaged wires. Clean and repair the wiring as required.

10. Make sure all connectors are free of corrosion and reconnected securely.

Starter Motor Turns Slowly

If the starter motor turns slowly and all engine components and systems are normal, perform the following:

1. Test the battery (Chapter Ten or Chapter Eleven).

2. Check for the following:

   a. Loose or corroded battery terminals.

   b. Loose or corroded battery ground cable.

   c. Loose starter motor cable.

3. Remove, disassemble and bench test the starter (Chapter Ten or Chapter Eleven).

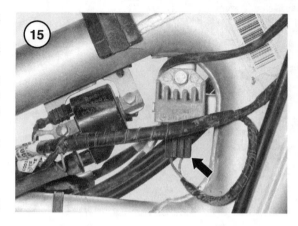

4. Check the starter for binding during operation. Disassemble the starter (Chapter Ten) and check the armature shaft for bending or damage. Also, check the starter clutch (Chapter Five).

Starter Motor Turns but the Engine Does Not

If the starter motor turns, but the engine does not, perform the following:

1. Check for a damaged starter clutch (Chapter Five).

2. Check for a damaged starter gear (Chapter Five).

CHARGING SYSTEM

The charging system consists of the battery, alternator and a voltage regulator/rectifier. A 20-amp main fuse protects the circuit.

A malfunction in the charging system generally causes the battery to remain undercharged.

Battery Discharging

1. Check all of the connections. Make sure they are securely tightened and free of corrosion.

2. Disconnect the negative battery cable (Chapter Ten or Chapter Eleven) from the battery.

CAUTION
Before connecting the ammeter into the circuit, set the meter to its highest amperage scale. This will prevent a large current flow from damaging the meter or blowing the meter's fuse, if so equipped.

3. Connect an ammeter between the battery ground cable and the negative battery terminal.

4. If the ammeter reading (current draw) exceeds 0.1 mA, continue the procedure. If the current draw is 0.1 mA or less, perform Step 6.

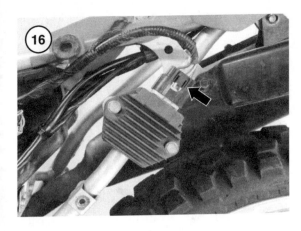

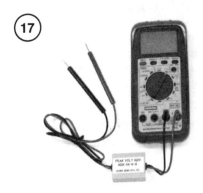

harness connector (Chapter Ten or Chapter Eleven). Note the following:

    a. If the test readings are correct, continue the procedure.

    b. If the test readings are incorrect, check for an open circuit in the wiring harness and for dirty or loose-fitting terminals. Clean and repair the terminals as required.

9. Perform the stator coil lead tests at the regulator/rectifier harness (Chapter Ten or Chapter Eleven). Note the following:

    a. If the test readings are incorrect, replace the alternator and retest.

    b. If the test readings are correct, replace the regulator/rectifier unit and retest.

Battery Overcharging

If the battery is overcharging, the regulator/rectifier unit is faulty. Replace the regulator/rectifier unit (Chapter Ten or Chapter Eleven).

IGNITION SYSTEM

Peak Voltage Tests and Equipment

WARNING
High voltage is present during ignition system operation. Do not touch ignition components, wires or test leads while cranking or running the engine.

Peak voltage tests check the voltage output of the ignition system components at normal cranking speed, thus making it possible to accurately test the voltage output under operating conditions.

The peak voltage specifications listed in **Table 1** are minimum values. If the measured voltage meets or exceeds the specification, the test results are satisfactory. In some cases, the voltage may greatly exceed the minimum specification.

A peak voltage tester is required. One of the following testers, or an equivalent, can be used to perform peak voltage tests described in this section. Refer to the tester manufacturer's instructions when using these tools.

1. Peak voltage adapter (Honda part No. 07HGJ-0020100). This tool (**Figure 17**) must be used in combination with a digital multimeter with a minimum impedance of 10M ohms/DC V. A meter with a lower impedance does not display accurate measurements.

2. IgnitionMATE (tecMATE part No. TS-91). Refer to **Figure 18**.

5. If the test results are incorrect, the ignition switch (CRF230L and CRF230M models) may be faulty or the wiring harness is shorted. On CRF230L and CRF230M models, test the ignition switch (Chapter Eleven).

6. Perform charging system testing (Chapter Ten or Chapter Eleven). Note the following:

    a. If the test readings are correct, continue the procedure.

    b. If the test readings are incorrect, go to Step 8.

7. Test the battery with a battery load tester and note the following:

NOTE
If a battery load tester is not accessible, remove the battery and take it to a dealership for testing.

    a. If the test readings are correct, check for an open circuit in the wiring harness and for dirty or loose-fitting terminals; clean and repair as required.

    b. If the test readings are incorrect, the battery is faulty or electrical components are overloading the charging system.

8. Perform the battery charging circuit lead and ground circuit lead tests at the regulator/rectifier

Preliminary Checks

Before testing the ignition system, check the following:

1. Make sure the battery is fully-charged and in good condition. A weak battery causes a slow engine cranking speed and low peak voltage readings.
2. Perform a spark test (Chapter Two). If a crisp, blue spark is noted, the ignition system is working correctly. Test each spark plug and note the following:

    a. If there is no spark at the spark plug, check for a disconnected or contaminated connector or a damaged ignition switch or engine stop switch. Test each switch as described in Chapter Ten or Chapter Eleven.

    b. Also check for a fouled or damaged spark plug, loose spark plug cap or water in the spark plug cap.

3. If the problem has not been found and the spark plugs, plug caps and all electrical system connectors are in good working order, the problem is probably due to a defective switch or ignition system component. Perform the peak voltage tests in this section to locate the damaged component.

Ignition Coil Signal Peak Voltage Test

This test requires a peak voltage tester (this section). Refer to **Figure 19** for ignition system testing procedures, and to **Table 1** for specifications.

1. Check the battery to make sure it is fully-charged and in good condition. A weak battery causes a slow engine cranking speed and inaccurate peak voltage tests results.
2. Remove the seat (Chapter Seventeen).
3. Remove the fuel tank (Chapter Eight or Chapter Nine).
4. Check engine compression (Chapter Three). If the compression is low in one or both cylinders, the test results will be inaccurate.
5. Check all of the ignition component electrical connectors and wiring harnesses. Check the electrical wires to and within the connector for any opens or poor connections. Make sure the connectors are clean and properly connected.
6. Disconnect the spark plug cap. Then, connect a new spark plug to the plug cap and ground the plug against the cylinder head (**Figure 20**). Do not remove the spark plug from the cylinder head. The spark plug must remain in the cylinder head to maintain engine compression.
7. If using the Honda peak voltage adapter, connect it to the multimeter as shown in **Figure 17**.

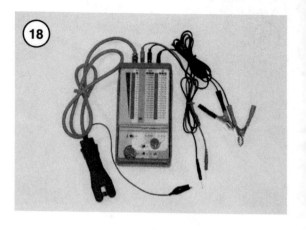

NOTE
If using the IgnitionMATE (Figure 18) tester, or a similar peak voltage tester, follow the equipment manufacturer's instructions for connecting the tester to the ignition coil.

NOTE
Do not disconnect the ignition coil primary connectors when performing this test.

8. Refer to Chapter Ten or Chapter Eleven to locate the ignition coil. Connect the peak voltage tester leads to the ignition coil terminals as follows:

    a. On CRF230F models, connect the negative test lead to the black/yellow wire terminal and the positive test lead to ground.

    b. On CRF230L and CRF230M models, connect the positive test lead to the black/yellow wire connector terminal and the negative test lead to ground.

9. Shift the transmission into neutral.
10. Turn the ignition switch on. On CRF230L and CRF230M models, set the engine stop switch to run.

WARNING
High voltage is present during ignition system operation. Do not touch spark plugs, ignition components, connectors or test leads while cranking the engine.

11. Press the starter button while reading the meter.
12. Turn the ignition switch off and note the following:

NOTE
All peak voltage specifications in the text and Table 1 are minimum voltages. As long as the measured voltage meets or exceeds the specification, consider the test results satisfactory. On some components, the voltage may greatly exceed the minimum specification.

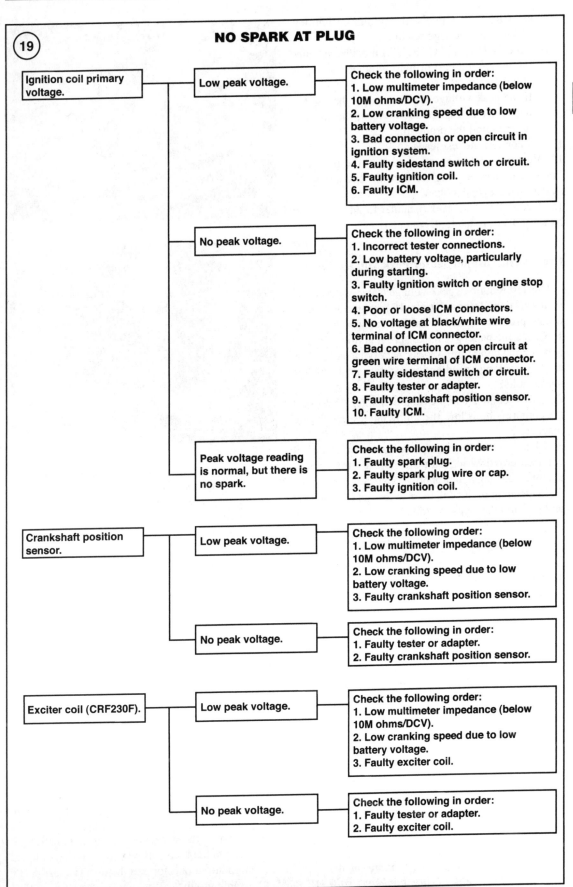

NO SPARK AT PLUG

19

Ignition coil primary voltage.	Low peak voltage.	Check the following in order: 1. Low multimeter impedance (below 10M ohms/DCV). 2. Low cranking speed due to low battery voltage. 3. Bad connection or open circuit in ignition system. 4. Faulty sidestand switch or circuit. 5. Faulty ignition coil. 6. Faulty ICM.
	No peak voltage.	Check the following in order: 1. Incorrect tester connections. 2. Low battery voltage, particularly during starting. 3. Faulty ignition switch or engine stop switch. 4. Poor or loose ICM connectors. 5. No voltage at black/white wire terminal of ICM connector. 6. Bad connection or open circuit at green wire terminal of ICM connector. 7. Faulty sidestand switch or circuit. 8. Faulty tester or adapter. 9. Faulty crankshaft position sensor. 10. Faulty ICM.
	Peak voltage reading is normal, but there is no spark.	Check the following in order: 1. Faulty spark plug. 2. Faulty spark plug wire or cap. 3. Faulty ignition coil.
Crankshaft position sensor.	Low peak voltage.	Check the following order: 1. Low multimeter impedance (below 10M ohms/DCV). 2. Low cranking speed due to low battery voltage. 3. Faulty crankshaft position sensor.
	No peak voltage.	Check the following in order: 1. Faulty tester or adapter. 2. Faulty crankshaft position sensor.
Exciter coil (CRF230F).	Low peak voltage.	Check the following order: 1. Low multimeter impedance (below 10M ohms/DCV). 2. Low cranking speed due to low battery voltage. 3. Faulty exciter coil.
	No peak voltage.	Check the following in order: 1. Faulty tester or adapter. 2. Faulty exciter coil.

a. On CRF230F models, the minimum ignition coil primary voltage reading is 70 volts.

b. On CRF230L and CRF230M models, the minimum ignition coil primary voltage reading is 100 volts.

c. If the peak voltage reading is less than specified, refer to **Figure 19**. Perform the steps in order to find the problem.

13. Disconnect the test leads.

14. Remove the test spark plug from the plug cap. Then, reconnect the plug cap onto the spark plug installed in the cylinder head.

15. Reinstall the fuel tank (Chapter Eight or Chapter Nine) and seat (Chapter Seventeen).

Crankshaft Position Sensor Peak Voltage Test

This test requires a peak voltage tester as described in this section. Refer to **Figure 19** for ignition system testing procedures, and to **Table 1** for specifications.

1. Check the battery to make sure it is fully-charged and in good condition. A weak battery causes a slow engine cranking speed and inaccurate peak voltage tests results.

2. Check engine compression (Chapter Three). If the compression is low, the following test results are inaccurate.

3. Check all of the ignition component electrical connectors and wiring harnesses. Make sure the connectors are clean and properly connected.

4. Depending on model, refer to the appropriate test and perform the steps in order.

CRF230F models

1. Remove the number plate as described in Chapter Seventeen.

2. Disconnect the connectors (**Figure 21**) from the ICM.

> *WARNING*
> *High voltage is present during ignition system operation. Do not touch spark plugs, ignition components, connectors or test leads while cranking the engine.*

> *NOTE*
> *If using the IgnitionMATE tester, or a similar peak voltage tester, follow the equipment manufacturer's instructions for connecting the tester to the ignition coil.*

> *NOTE*
> *All peak voltage specifications in the text and **Table 1** are minimum volt-*

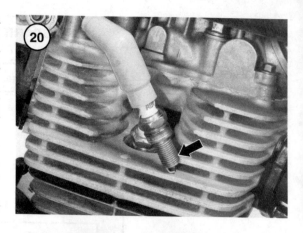

ages. If the measured voltage meets or exceeds the specification, consider the test results satisfactory. On some components, the voltage may greatly exceed the minimum specification.

3. Perform the following test:

a. Connect the peak voltage tester negative test lead to the wiring harness connector blue/yellow wire terminal and the positive test lead to frame ground.

b. Shift the transmission into neutral.

c. Turn the ignition switch on.

d. Press the starter button while reading the meter. The meter should indicate a minimum peak voltage reading of 0.7 volts DC.

e. Turn the ignition switch off and disconnect the test leads.

4. If the test indicates less than the specified voltage, perform the following test:

a. Remove the left side cover as described in Chapter Seventeen.

b. Disconnect the alternator connector (A, **Figure 22**).

c. Connect the peak voltage tester negative test lead to the blue/yellow wire terminal in the alternator connector and the positive test lead to frame ground.

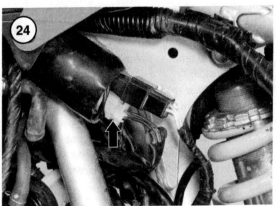

d. Shift the transmission into neutral.

e. Turn the ignition switch on.

f. Press the starter button while reading the meter. The meter should indicate a minimum peak voltage reading of 0.7 volts DC.

g. Turn the ignition switch off and disconnect the test leads.

5. If the voltage readings were incorrect, check the affected wires in the wiring harness between the ICM connector and the crankshaft position sensor for an open or short circuit. At the same time, check the connector for loose terminals or contamination.

6. Reinstall the left side cover and number plate (Chapter Seventeen).

CRF230L and CRF230M models

1. Remove the seat as described in Chapter Seventeen.

2. Disconnect the connector (**Figure 23**) from the ICM.

WARNING
High voltage is present during ignition system operation. Do not touch spark plugs, ignition components, connec-

tors or test leads while cranking the engine.

NOTE
If using the IgnitionMATE tester, or a similar peak voltage tester, follow the equipment manufacturer's instructions for connecting the tester to the ignition coil.

NOTE
All peak voltage specifications in the text and **Table 1** *are minimum voltages. If the measured voltage meets or exceeds the specification, consider the test results satisfactory. On some components, the voltage may greatly exceed the minimum specification.*

3. Perform the following test:

a. Connect the peak voltage tester positive test lead to the blue/yellow wire terminal and the negative test lead to the green wire terminal.

b. Shift the transmission into neutral.

c. Turn the ignition switch on and set the engine stop switch to run.

d. Press the starter button while reading the meter. The meter should indicate a minimum peak voltage reading of 0.7 volts DC.

e. Turn the ignition switch off and disconnect the test leads.

4. Perform the following test:

a. Remove the battery case (Chapter Eleven).

b. Disconnect the white crankshaft position sensor connector (**Figure 24**).

c. Connect the peak voltage tester positive test lead to the blue/yellow wire terminal and the negative test lead to the green wire connector terminal in the sensor end of the connector.

d. Shift the transmission into neutral.

e. Turn the ignition switch on and set the engine stop switch to run.

f. Press the starter button while reading the meter. The meter should indicate a minimum peak voltage reading of 0.7 volts DC.

g. Turn the ignition switch off and disconnect the test leads.

5. If the voltage readings were incorrect, check the affected wires in the wiring harness between the ICM connector and the crankshaft position sensor for an open or short circuit. At the same time, check the connector for loose terminals or contamination.

6. Install the the battery case (Chapter Eleven) and the seat (Chapter Seventeen).

Alternator Exciter Coil Peak Voltage Test (CRF230F Models)

This test requires a peak voltage tester as described in this section. Refer to **Figure 19** for ignition system testing procedures, and to **Table 1** for specifications.

1. Check the battery to make sure it is fully-charged and in good condition. A weak battery causes a slow engine cranking speed and inaccurate peak voltage tests results.

2. Check engine compression (Chapter Three). If the compression is low, the following test results are inaccurate.

3. Check all of the ignition component electrical connectors and wiring harnesses. Make sure the connectors are clean and properly connected.

4. Remove the number plate as described in Chapter Seventeen.

5. Disconnect the connectors (**Figure 21**) from the ICM.

> *WARNING*
> *High voltage is present during ignition system operation. Do not touch spark plugs, ignition components, connectors or test leads while cranking the engine.*

> *NOTE*
> *If using the IgnitionMATE tester, or a similar peak voltage tester, follow the equipment manufacturer's instructions for connecting the tester to the ignition coil.*

> *NOTE*
> *All peak voltage specifications in the text and **Table 1** are minimum voltages. If the measured voltage meets or exceeds the specification, consider the test results satisfactory. On some components, the voltage may greatly exceed the minimum specification.*

6. Perform the following test:

a. Connect the peak voltage tester positive test lead to the wiring harness connector black/red wire terminal and the negative test lead to frame ground.

b. Shift the transmission into neutral.

c. Turn the ignition switch on.

d. Press the starter button while reading the meter. The meter should indicate a minimum peak voltage reading of 100 volts DC.

e. Turn the ignition switch off and disconnect the test leads.

7. If the test indicates less than specified voltage, perform the following test:

a. Remove the left side cover as described in Chapter Seventeen.

b. Disconnect the exciter coil connector (B, **Figure 22**).

c. Connect the peak voltage tester positive test lead to the black/red wire terminal in the exciter coil connector and the negative test lead to frame ground.

d. Shift the transmission into neutral.

e. Turn the ignition switch on.

f. Press the starter button while reading the meter. The meter should indicate a minimum peak voltage reading of 100 volts DC.

g. Turn the ignition switch off and disconnect the test leads.

8. If the voltage reading was incorrect, check the affected wires in the wiring harness between the ICM connector and the exciter coil for an open or short circuit. At the same time, check the connector for loose terminals or contamination.

9. Install the left side cover and the number plate (Chapter Seventeen).

FRONT SUSPENSION AND STEERING

Steering is Sluggish

1. Tight steering adjustment.
2. Damaged steering head bearings.
3. Low tire pressure.
4. Damaged tire.

Motorcycle Steers to One Side

1. Bent axle.
2. Bent frame.
3. Worn or damaged wheel bearings.
4. Worn or damaged swing arm pivot bearings.
5. Damaged steering head bearings.
6. Bent swing arm.
7. Incorrectly-installed wheels.

8. Front and rear wheels are not aligned.
9. Front fork legs positioned unevenly in steering stem.
10. Damaged tire.

Front Suspension Noise

1. Loose mounting fasteners.
2. Damaged fork.
3. Low fork oil capacity.

Front Wheel Wobble/Vibration

1. Loose front wheel axle.
2. Loose or damaged wheel bearing(s).
3. Damaged wheel rim(s).
4. Damaged tire(s).
5. Loose or damaged spokes.

Front End Too Stiff

1. Decrease the fork oil capacity.
2. Change to a lighter weight fork oil.
3. Install softer fork springs.

Front End Oversteers

1. Install stiffer fork springs.
2. Increase fork oil capacity.

Front End Washes
Out or Understeers

1. Decrease fork oil capacity.
2. Install softer fork springs.

Front End Shakes or Jumps
Under Heavy Braking

1. Increase fork oil capacity.
2. Reduce the rear shock spring preload.

Front End is Unstable
at High Speed

1. Increase fork oil capacity.
2. Increase rear shock spring preload.

REAR SUSPENSION

Soft Suspension

1. Low tire pressure.
2. Weak shock spring.

3. Incorrect shock preload adjustment.
4. Damaged shock.

Stiff Suspension

1. High tire pressure.
2. Damaged suspension bearings.
3. Incorrect shock preload adjustment.
4. Damaged shock.

Wheel Rotates Hard

1. Tight drive chain.
2. Bad wheel bearings.
3. Bent axle.
4. Brake drags.

Rear Suspension Noise

1. Loose suspension components.
2. Worn or damaged suspension bearings.
3. Damaged shock.

BRAKE SYSTEM

Disc Brake

All models are equipped with a hydraulically-actuated front disc brake. CRF230L and CRF230M models are equipped with a rear disc brake. Inspect the brakes frequently and repair any problem immediately. When replacing or refilling the brake fluid, use only DOT 4 brake fluid from a closed container.

Refer to **Figure 25** for troubleshooting a disc brake problem.

Rear Drum Brake (CRF230F Models)

Model CRF230F is equipped with a mechanically-actuated rear drum brake. Inspect the brake frequently and repair any problem immediately.

If the rear drum brake is not working properly, check for one or more of the following conditions:
1. Incorrect rear brake adjustment.
2. Incorrect brake cam lever position.
3. Worn or damaged brake drum.
4. Worn or damaged brake linings.
5. Oil or grease on brake drum or bake lining surfaces.
6. Weak or damaged brake return springs.

2

(25) **BRAKE TROUBLESHOOTING**

Disc brake fluid leaks

Check:
- Loose or damaged line fittings
- Worn caliper piston seals
- Scored caliper piston or bore
- Loose banjo bolts
- Damaged oil line washers
- Leaking master clyinder diaphragm
- Leaking master cylinder secondary seal
- Cracked master cylinder housing
- Brake fluid level too high
- Loose or damaged master cylinder

Brake overheating

Check:
- Warped brake disc
- Incorrect brake fluid
- Caliper piston and/or brake pads hanging up
- Riding brakes during riding

Brake chatter

Check:
- Warped brake disc
- Incorrect caliper alignment
- Loose caliper mounting bolts
- Loose front axle nut and/or clamps
- Worn wheel bearings
- Damaged hub
- Restricted brake hydraulic line
- Contaminated brake pads

Brake locking

Check:
- Incorrect brake fluid
- Plugged passages in master cylinder
- Caliper piston and/or brake pads hanging up
- Warped brake disc

Insufficient brakes

Check:
- Air in brake lines
- Worn brake pads
- Low brake fluid
- Incorrect brake fluid
- Worn brake disc
- Worn caliper piston seals
- Glazed brake pads
- Leaking primary cup seal in master cylinder
- Contaminated brake pads and/or disc

Brake squeal

Check:
- Contaminated brake pads and/or disc
- Dust or dirt collected behind brake pads
- Loose parts

Table 1 IGNITION SYSTEM SPECIFICATIONS

Alternator exciter coil peak voltage (CRF230F models)	100 volts minimum
Ignition coil primary peak voltage	
CRF230F models	70 volts minimum
CRF230L and CRF230M models	100 volts minimum
Crankshaft position sensor peak voltage	0.7 volts minimum

2

CHAPTER THREE

LUBRICATION, MAINTENANCE AND TUNE-UP

This chapter describes lubrication, maintenance and tune-up procedures. Procedures that require more than minor disassembly or adjustment are covered in the appropriate subsequent chapter.

To maximize the service life of the motorcycle and gain the utmost in safety and performance, it is necessary to perform periodic inspections and maintenance. Minor problems found during routine service can be corrected before they develop into major ones. A neglected motorcycle will be unreliable and may be dangerous to ride.

Table 1 and **Table 2** list the recommended lubrication, maintenance and tune-up intervals. If the motorcycle is operated in extreme conditions, it may be appropriate to reduce the interval between some maintenance items.

Specifications are listed in **Tables 3-11** located at the end of this chapter.

PRE-RIDE INSPECTION

Perform the following inspections before the first ride of the day. If a component requires service, refer to the appropriate section or chapter.

1. Inspect all fuel lines and fittings for leaks.
2. Check fuel tank level.
3. Check engine oil level.

4. Check the throttle operation for proper operation in all steering positions. Open the throttle all the way and release it. The throttle should close quickly with no binding or roughness.
5. Check that the brake lever and brake pedal operate properly with no binding.
6. Check the brake fluid level in the front brake master cylinder reservoir. Add DOT 4 brake fluid if necessary.
7. On CRF230L and CRF230M models, check the brake fluid level in the rear brake master cylinder reservoir. Add DOT 4 brake fluid if necessary.
8. Check clutch operation.
9. Inspect the front and rear suspension. Make sure they have a good solid feel with no looseness. Turn the handlebar from side to side to check steering play. Service the steering assembly if excessive play is noted. Make sure the handlebar cables do not bind.
10. Check tire pressure.
11. Check wheel condition and spoke tightness.
12. Check drive chain condition and adjustment.
13. Check the exhaust system for looseness or damage.
14. Check fastener tightness, especially engine, steering and suspension mounting hardware.
15. Check the air filter drain tube for contamination.

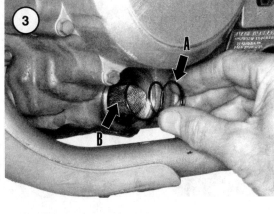

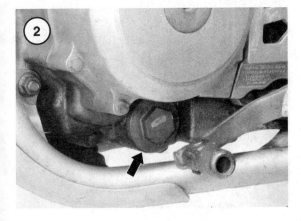

16. Start the engine, and then stop it with the engine stop switch. If the engine stop switch does not operate properly, test the switch.

FUEL TYPE

Refer to **Table 3** for fuel requirements. Using fuel with a lower octane number can cause pinging or spark knock, and lead to engine damage.

When choosing gasoline and filling the fuel tank, note the following:
1. When filling the tank, do not overfill it.
2. Because oxygenated fuels can damage plastic and paint, do not spill fuel onto the fuel tank during filling.
3. Do not use gasoline containing more than 10 percent ethanol by volume.
4. Do not use gasoline containing more than 15 percent MTBE (methyl tertiary butyl ether) by volume.

ENGINE OIL AND FILTER

Refer to *Shop Supplies* (Chapter One) for lubricant and fluid information.

Engine Oil Level Check

Check the engine oil level using the dipstick cap mounted on the right side of the engine.
1. Start the engine and allow it to warm up for 3 to 5 minutes. In colder weather, allow the engine to idle for at least 5 minutes.
2. Shut off engine.
3. Support the motorcycle so it is vertical and level. Allow the engine to rest in this position for 2 to 3 minutes before checking the oil level.
4. Unscrew and remove the dipstick cap (**Figure 1**) and wipe the dipstick clean.
5. Hold the motorcycle so it is not tipped to the side. Reinstall the dipstick cap onto the threads in the hole, but do not screw it in. Remove the dipstick and check the oil level.
6. The level should be between the two lines and not above the upper one.
7. If necessary, add the recommended engine oil (**Table 3**) through the dipstick hole to correct the level.
8. Replace the dipstick O-ring if damaged.
9. Install the dipstick cap (**Figure 1**) and tighten it securely.

Engine Oil Change

Change the engine oil at the intervals recommended in **Table 1** or **Table 2**. Use the appropriate grade and viscosity of oil as recommended in this section.

Always change the oil when the engine is warm. Contaminants will remain suspended in the oil and drain more completely and quicker.
1. Start the engine and allow it to warm up for several minutes. Shut off the engine.
2. Remove the dipstick (**Figure 1**).
3. Place a drain pan below the oil drain cap.
4. Remove the oil drain cap (**Figure 2**)
5. Remove the spring (A, **Figure 3**) and strainer (B) from the drain plug hole. Allow the oil to drain.

6. Examine the strainer for debris that may indicate engine damage. Clean the strainer in solvent and allow to dry.

7. Install a new O-ring onto the oil drain cap.

8. Install the strainer, spring and oil drain cap. Make sure the closed end of the strainer is out.

9. Tighten the oil drain cap to 15 N•m (11 ft.-lb.).

10. Unscrew and remove the dipstick cap (**Figure 1**).

11. Fill the engine with the correct quantity of the recommended engine oil. Refer to **Table 4** for engine oil capacity.

12. Screw in the dipstick cap securely.

13. Start the engine and run at idle speed.

14. Turn off the engine and check the oil drain cap for leaks.

15. Check the oil level and adjust if necessary.

Engine Oil Centrifugal Filter Cleaning

Clean the centrifugal oil filter at the interval listed in **Table 1** or **Table 2**.

1. Remove the right crankcase cover as described in Chapter Five.

2. Remove the rotor cover screws (A, **Figure 4**), and then remove the rotor (B).

3. Remove the gasket (A, **Figure 5**).

> *CAUTION*
> *Do not direct compressed air at the rotor. Debris may be blown into the crankshaft oil passage.*

4. Clean the cover (B, **Figure 5**) and rotor (C).

5. Install a new gasket (A, **Figure 5**).

6. Install the rotor cover. Tighten the rotor cover screws to 5 N•m (44 in.-lb.).

7. Install the right crankcase cover as described in Chapter Five.

AIR FILTER (CRF230F MODELS)

Service the air filter at the interval listed in **Table 1**.

Air Filter Element Removal/Cleaning/Installation

1. Remove the right side cover as described in Chapter Seventeen.

2. Remove the filter cover (**Figure 6**).

3. Unhook the element retaining rod (**Figure 7**).

4. Remove the filter element assembly from the air box.

5. Separate the air filter element (A, **Figure 8**) from the holder (B).

6. Clean the interior of the air box with a shop rag dampened with cleaning solvent. Remove any foreign matter that may have passed through a broken element.

7. Before cleaning the air filter element, check it for brittleness, separation or other damage. Replace the element if it is excessively worn or damaged.

8. If there is no visible damage, clean the air filter element as follows:

> *WARNING*
> *Do not clean the air filter element or holder with gasoline.*

a. Soak the air filter element in a container filled with solvent, kerosene or an air filter cleaning solution.

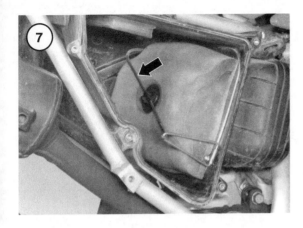

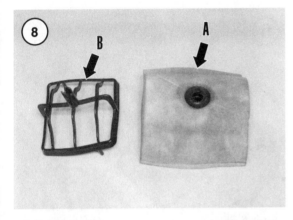

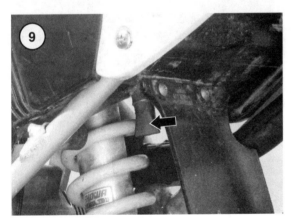

b. Gently squeeze the filter to dislodge and re-move the oil and dirt from the filter pores. Repeat this step a few times, while moving the filter around in the cleaner. Then, remove the air filter and set it aside to dry.

c. Fill a clean pan with warm soapy water.

CAUTION
Do not wring or twist the filter element when cleaning it. This could damage a filter pore or tear the filter element loose at a seam and allow unfiltered air to enter the engine.

d. Submerge the filter element into the cleaning solution and gently work the soap solution into the filter pores. Soak and squeeze the filter element gently to clean it.

e. Rinse the filter element under clear water while gently squeezing it.

f. Repeat this process until the filter element is clean.

9. After cleaning the filter element, inspect it carefully. Replace it if it is torn or damaged. Do not run the engine with a damaged air filter element as it allows dirt to enter the engine.

CAUTION
A filter that is damp when oiled will not trap fine dust. Make sure the filter element is dry before oiling it.

10. Allow the filter element to dry thoroughly.

11. Properly oiling an air filter element is a messy job. Wear a pair of disposable rubber gloves when performing this procedure. Oil the filter element as follows:

a. Place the air filter element into a one gallon-sized storage bag.

CAUTION
Do not use motor oils to lubricate foam air filters. Foam air filter oil is specifically formulated for easy and thorough application into the filter pores and provides a tacky viscous medium to trap airborne contaminants. Motor oils are too thin to remain suspended in the filter; the oil will be drawn into the engine and allow dirt to pass through the filter.

b. Pour foam air filter oil into the bag and onto the filter clement to soak it.

c. Gently squeeze and release the filter element, from the outside of the bag, to soak the filter oil into the filter element pores. Repeat until all of the pores are saturated.

d. Remove the filter element from the bag and check the pores for uneven oiling. Light or dark areas on the filter indicate this condition. If necessary, work more oil into the filter and repeat squeezing the filter until the oil is evenly distributed.

e. When the filter is oiled evenly, squeeze the filter a final time to remove excess oil.

f. Remove the air filter element from the bag.

12. Check the air box drain cap (**Figure 9**) for oil or debris. If necessary, remove and clean the cap. Allow any oil to drain from the air box.

13. Install the element onto the holder so the holder pins extend through the element holes (**Figure 10**).

14. Install the air filter element by reversing the removal steps.

AIR FILTER
(CRF230L AND CRF230M MODELS)

Service the air filter at the interval listed in **Table 2**.

Air Filter Element
Removal/Cleaning/Installation

1. Remove the seat as described in Chapter Seventeen.
2. Disengage the tabs (A, **Figure 11**) and remove the filter cover (B).
3. Push up the tab (A, **Figure 12**) to unlock the filter element (B).
4. Remove the filter element (**Figure 13**).

> *NOTE*
> *Due to the coating on the filter, washing or cleaning the filter element is not recommended.*

5. At the specified service intervals in **Table 2**, replace the air filter element. If the motorcycle has not yet reached the mileage interval for replacement, check the element for damage or dirt buildup. Replace the element if necessary.
6. Gently brush off debris from the filter element.

> *CAUTION*
> *Do not run the engine with a damaged element as it may allow dirt to enter the engine.*

7. Inspect the element. If it is torn or broken in any area, replace it.
8. Install the filter element by reversing the removal steps. Note the following:
  a. Install the filter element so the pads (**Figure 14**) are down. The pads fit into recesses in the bottom of the air box.
  b. Engage the tab (A, **Figure 12**) with the lip on the filter element (B) so it is locked in place.

CONTROL CABLE
INSPECTION AND LUBRICATION

This section describes lubrication procedures for the control cables. Clean and lubricate the throttle and clutch cables whenever cable operation becomes sluggish or stiffens. At the same time, check the cables for wear, fraying or other damage that could cause the cables to bind or break. The most positive method of cable lubrication involves using a cable

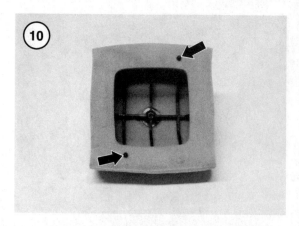

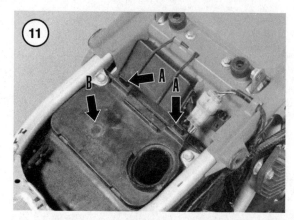

lubricator like the one shown in **Figure 15** and a can of cable lubricant.

> *CAUTION*
> *Do not use chain lubricant to flush and lubricate the control cables.*

1. Disconnect both clutch cable ends (Chapter Six).
2. Disconnect both throttle cable ends (Chapter Eight or Chapter Nine).
3. Attach a cable lubricator to one end of the cable, following the lubcricator manufacturer's instructions (**Figure 15**).

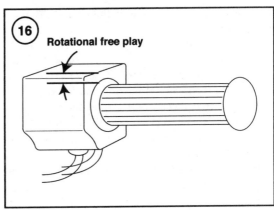

Rotational free play

3

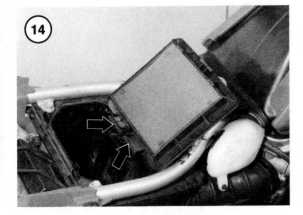

10. Lubricate the upper clutch cable end with grease.
11. Reconnect the cables as described in the appropriate chapter.
12. Adjust the cables as described in this chapter.

THROTTLE CABLE ADJUSTMENT

Cable wear and stretch affect the operation of the carburetor. Normal amounts of cable wear and stretch can be controlled by the free play adjustments described in this section. If the cables cannot be adjusted within their limits, the cables are excessively worn or damaged and require replacement.

Free play is the distance the throttle grip can be rotated, measured at the throttle grip flange (**Figure 16**), until resistance from the throttle shaft can be felt. Throttle cable free play is necessary to prevent variation in the idle speed when turning the handlebars. In time, the throttle cable free play increases as the cable stretches. This delays throttle response and affects low speed operation. On the other hand, if there is no throttle cable free play, an excessively high idle speed can result, possibly causing an accident.

1. Rotate the throttle grip from low idle position as if accelerating, with the handlebar pointed in different steering positions. In each position, the throttle must open and close smoothly and completely. If the throttle cables bind or move roughly, inspect the cables for kinks, bends or other damage. Replace damaged cables. If the cables move smoothly and are not damaged, continue with the procedure.

4. Tie a plastic bag around the opposite cable end to catch the lubricant.
5. Fit the nozzle of the cable lubricant into the hole in the lubricator.
6. Hold a rag over the lubricator. Then, press and hold the button on the lubricant can. Continue until lubricant drips from the opposite end.
7. Disconnect the cable lubricator. Then, pull the inner cable back and forth to help distribute the lubricant.
8. Allow time for excess lubricant to drain from the cable before reconnecting it.
9. Apply a light coat of grease to the upper throttle cable ends before reconnecting them.

2. Determine the throttle grip free play as shown in **Figure 16**. If the free play is more or less than 2-6 mm (3/32-1/4 in.), adjust the cables as described in this section.

NOTE
Throttle cable adjustment is made at either end of the pull cable. Make minor adjustments at the upper end of the pull cable. Make major adjustments at the lower end of the pull cable.

3. Slide the rubber cover (**Figure 17**) away from the throttle housing.

4. Loosen the pull cable locknut (A, **Figure 18**) and turn the cable adjuster (B) in or out to achieve the correct free play. Tighten the locknut securely.

5. Recheck the free play and note the following:

    a. If the free play is correct, reposition the rubber cover (**Figure 17**) over the throttle housing.

    b. If further adjustment is required, continue with the procedure.

6A. On CRF230F models, loosen the pull cable locknuts (A, **Figure 19**) and turn the adjuster (B) in or out to achieve the correct free play. Tighten the locknuts securely.

6B. On CRF230L and CRF230M models, proceed as follows:

    a. Remove the screws (A, **Figure 20**) securing the throttle pulley cover (B). Allow the cover to remain attached to the rubber cover.

    b. Loosen the pull cable locknut (A, **Figure 21**) and turn the adjuster (B) in or out to achieve the correct free play. Tighten the locknut securely.

    c. Install the throttle pulley cover.

    d. Install the long cover screw (A, **Figure 22**) in the rear hole of the cover. Place the rubber cover hole (B, **Figure 22**) onto the long screw end.

7. If the correct free play cannot be achieved, the throttle cables have stretched to the point where they need to be replaced. Replace both throttle cables (Chapter Eight or Chapter Nine).

8. Recheck the throttle cable free play.

9. Slide the rubber cover (**Figure 17**) over the throttle housing.

10. Make sure the throttle grip rotates freely from a fully-closed to fully-open position.

11. Start the engine and allow it to idle in neutral. Turn the handlebar from side to side. If the idle increases, the throttle cable is routed incorrectly or there is not enough throttle cable free play. Repair this condition before riding the motorcycle.

CLUTCH LEVER ADJUSTMENT

The clutch lever free play is continually changing due to the clutch cable wearing and stretching over time, as well as clutch plate wear. Maintain the clutch lever free play within the specification listed in this procedure. Insufficient free play causes clutch slippage and premature clutch plate wear. Excessive free play causes clutch drag and rough shift pedal operation.

NOTE
Clutch cable adjustment is possible at the clutch lever or at the inline cable adjuster. Make minor adjustments at

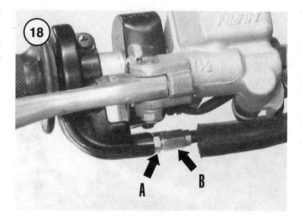

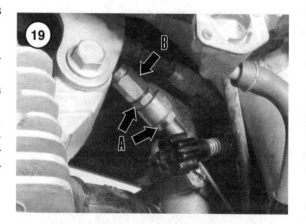

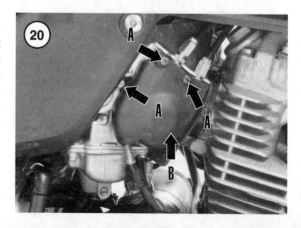

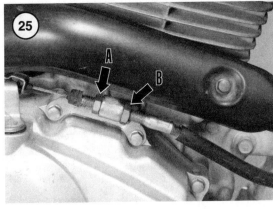

3

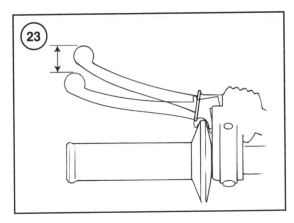

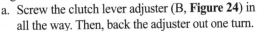

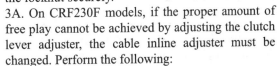

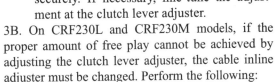

the clutch lever. Make major adjustments at the inline cable adjuster.

1. Determine the clutch lever free play at the end of the clutch lever as shown in **Figure 23**. If the free play is more or less than 10-20 mm (3/8-3/4 in.), adjust the cable as described in this section.

2. Slide the cover away from the adjuster. Loosen the locknut (A, **Figure 24**) and turn the cable end adjuster (B) either in or out as required to achieve the specified amount of free play (**Table 5**). Tighten the locknut securely.

3A. On CRF230F models, if the proper amount of free play cannot be achieved by adjusting the clutch lever adjuster, the cable inline adjuster must be changed. Perform the following:

  a. Screw the clutch lever adjuster (B, **Figure 24**) in all the way. Then, back the adjuster out one turn.

  b. Loosen the clutch cable left locknut (A, **Figure 25**). Then, turn the right adjuster nut (B, **Figure 25**) as required to obtain the free play specified (**Table 5**). Tighten the locknut securely. If necessary, fine-tune the adjustment at the clutch lever adjuster.

3B. On CRF230L and CRF230M models, if the proper amount of free play cannot be achieved by adjusting the clutch lever adjuster, the cable inline adjuster must be changed. Perform the following:

  a. Screw the clutch lever adjuster (B, **Figure 24**) in all the way. Then, back the adjuster out one turn.

  b. Loosen the clutch cable locknut (A, **Figure 26**). Then, turn the adjuster nut (B, **Figure 26**) as required to obtain the free play specified (**Table 5**). Tighten the locknut securely. If necessary, fine-tune the adjustment at the clutch lever adjuster.

4. If the correct free play cannot be obtained, either the cable has stretched to the point that it needs to be replaced or the clutch discs are worn. Refer to Chapter Six for clutch cable replacement and clutch service procedures.

5. Make sure the locknut(s) are all tightened securely.

6. Reinstall the clutch lever cover.

DISC BRAKES

This section describes routine service procedures for the front disc brake used on all models and the rear disc brakes used on CRF230L and CRF230M models. Refer to **Table 1** or **Table 2** for service intervals.

Disc Brake Pad Wear

Inspect the brake pads for grease or fork oil contamination, wear, scoring, or other damage. Inspect the thickness of the friction material on each pad. Each brake pad is equipped with wear grooves (**Figure 27**). If any one pad is worn to its wear grooves, replace both pads. Refer to Chapter Sixteen for brake pad service.

Front Brake Lever Adjustment (CRF230F Models)

Brake pad wear in the front brake caliper is automatically compensated as the pistons move outward in the caliper. However, the relationship of the brake lever position to the handlebar can be adjusted on these models.

1. Remove the dust cover from the adjuster.
2. To move the brake lever closer to or farther away from the handlebar, loosen the locknut (A, **Figure 28**) and turn the adjuster (B) in or out. Tighten the locknut (A, **Figure 28**) securely.
3. Check the front brake lever free play. There must be at least some free play so the tip of the lever adjuster does not push against the master cylinder piston (C, **Figure 28**) when the lever is released. Turn the adjuster (B, **Figure 28**) as needed to obtain lever free play.
4. Support the motorcycle with the front wheel off the ground. Rotate the front wheel and check for brake drag. Operate the front brake lever several

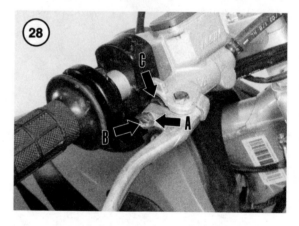

times to make sure it returns to the at-rest position after releasing it.
5. Tighten the locknut securely, making sure the adjuster does not move, and recheck the free play.
6. Move the brake lever away from the handlebar and lubricate the end of the adjuster and piston contact surfaces with silicone brake grease.
7. Install the dust cover.

Brake Fluid Level Inspection

The brake fluid level in the front or rear brake master cylinder reservoir must be kept above the minimum level line. If the fluid level is low in either reservoir, check for loose or damaged hoses or loose fittings. If there are no visible fluid leaks, check the brake pads for excessive wear. As the brake pads wear, the caliper pistons move farther out of the bores, thus causing the brake fluid level to drop in the reservoir. Also, check the master cylinder bore and the brake caliper piston areas for signs of leaking brake fluid. If there is a noticeable fluid leak, that component requires overhaul to replace the damaged part. Check the brake pads for wear as described in this section. Refer to Chapter Sixteen for brake service procedures.

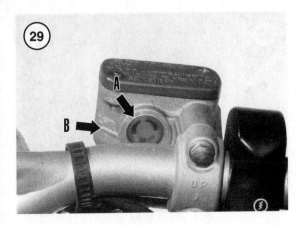

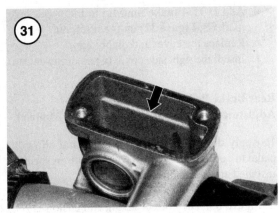

3

area immediately with soap and water, and then rinse thoroughly.

CAUTION
Do not remove the cover on the brake reservoir unless the reservoir is level.

CAUTION
When adding brake fluid to the reservoir, inspect the master cylinder reservoir diaphragm for tearing, cracks or other damage. A damaged diaphragm will allow moisture to enter the reservoir and contaminate the brake fluid.

3A. To check the front master cylinder reservoir level, perform the following:
   a. Turn the handlebar so the master cylinder reservoir is level.
   b. Observe the brake fluid level through the inspection window (A, **Figure 29**) on the master cylinder reservoir.
   c. The brake fluid level must be above the minimum level line (B, **Figure 29**).
   d. Remove the two screws and remove the cover (**Figure 30**) and diaphragm.
   e. Add DOT 4 brake fluid up to the upper level mark (**Figure 31**) inside the reservoir.
   f. Inspect the cover and diaphragm. Replace if damaged.
   g. Install the diaphragm and cover and tighten the screws securely.

3B. To check the rear master cylinder reservoir level (CRF230L and CRF230M models), perform the following:
   a. Remove the right side cover as described in Chapter Seventeen.
   b. Check that the brake fluid level is above the lower level mark (A, **Figure 32**) on the reservoir.
   c. Unscrew the top cap. Pull up and loosen the top cap and the diaphragm.

WARNING
If a reservoir is empty, or if the brake fluid level is so low that air is entering the brake system, bleed the brake system (Chapter Sixteen). Simply adding brake fluid to the reservoir does not restore the brake system to its full effectiveness.

1. Park the motorcycle on level ground.
2. Clean the master cylinder area before removing the cover to avoid contaminating the reservoir.

WARNING
Use a brake fluid that is marked DOT 4 and is specified for use with disc brakes. Others may vaporize and cause brake failure. Do not intermix different brands or types of brake fluid, as they may not be compatible. Do not intermix a silicone-based (DOT 5) brake fluid, as it can cause brake component damage, and possibly lead to brake system failure.

CAUTION
Be careful when handling brake fluid. Do not spill it on painted or plastic surfaces, as it will damage them. Wash the

d. Add DOT 4 brake fluid up to the upper level mark (B, **Figure 32**) on the reservoir.
e. Replace the cover and diaphragm.
f. Install the right side cover (Chapter Seventeen).

Rear Brake Pedal Height Adjustment (CRF230L and CRF230M Models)

1. Apply the rear brake a few times and allow the pedal to come to rest. Make sure the return spring is installed and in good condition.
2. Measure the pushrod height dimension as shown in **Figure 33**. The correct height dimension is 69.5 mm (2.74 in.).
3. If necessary, loosen the locknut (**Figure 33**) and turn the pushrod to adjust its height position.
4. Tighten the locknut to 17 N•m (13 ft.-lb.) and recheck the height dimension.

Rear Brake Light Switch Adjustment (CRF230L and CRF230M Models)

1. Turn the ignition switch on.
2. Depress the brake pedal and watch the brake light. The brake light should come on just before feeling pressure at the brake pedal. If necessary, adjust the rear brake light switch (this section).
3. To adjust the brake light switch:
   a. Hold the switch body (A, **Figure 34**) and turn the adjusting nut (B).
   b. To make the light come on earlier, turn the adjusting nut and move the switch body up.
   c. To delay the light coming on, move the switch body down.
4. Check that the brake light comes on when the pedal is depressed and goes off when the pedal is released. Readjust if necessary.
5. Turn the ignition switch off.

Brake Hose Replacement

Replace the brake hose when it becomes swollen or damaged. Refer to Chapter Sixteen for brake service procedures.

Brake Fluid Change

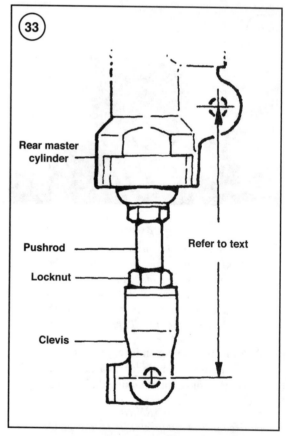

WARNING
Use brake fluid marked DOT 4 only. Others may vaporize and cause brake failure. Dispose of any unused fluid according to local regulations. Never reuse brake fluid. Contaminated brake fluid can cause brake failure.

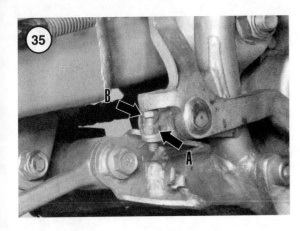

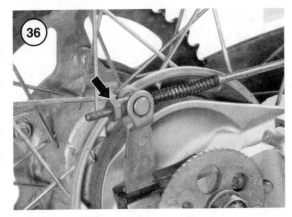

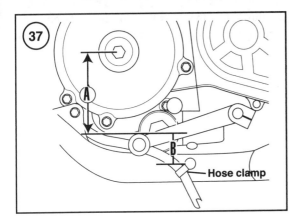

Hose clamp

REAR DRUM BRAKE (CRF230F MODELS)

Pedal Height and Free Play Adjustment

1. Apply the rear brake pedal a few times and allow the pedal to come to rest.
2. If necessary, loosen the locknut (A, **Figure 35**), and then turn the adjusting bolt (B) to adjust the pedal height.
3. Adjust the pedal height to the desired position. Tighten the locknut securely and recheck the height dimension.
4. Apply the rear brake and measure the distance from rest to applied positions, which is pedal freeplay. The rear brake pedal freeplay should be 20-30 mm (3/4-1 1/4 in.).
5. To change the freeplay distance, turn the adjuster nut (**Figure 36**) at the end of the brake rod. Turn the nut as needed to obtain the desired pedal freeplay.

GEARSHIFT LEVER HEIGHT

The gearshift lever height should be adjusted as follows:
1. Loosen and remove the gearshift lever pinch bolt, and then remove the gearshift lever.
2A. On CRF230F models, position the gearshift lever on the shaft so the top of the pedal is 79 mm (3 in.) from the center of the flywheel bolt cap (A, **Figure 37**).
2B. On CRF230L and CRF230M models, position the gearshift lever on the shaft so the top of the pedal is 40 mm (1.6 in.) above the hose clamp (B, **Figure 37**).
3A. On CRF230F models, tighten the gearshift lever pinch bolt to 12 N•m (106 in.-lb.).
3B. On CRF230L and CRF230M models, tighten the gearshift lever pinch bolt to 16 N•m (144 in.-lb.).

DRIVE CHAIN

Drive Chain Lubrication

Lubricate the drive chain at the intervals specified in **Table 1** and **Table 2**. During off-road use, lubricate the chain throughout the day as required. A properly maintained chain provides maximum service life and reliability.
1. Ride the motorcycle approximately 5 minutes to heat the chain.
2. Support the motorcycle so the rear wheel is off the ground.
3. Shift the transmission into neutral.
4A. Non-O-ring chain:
    a. Turn the rear wheel and lubricate the chain with an SAE 80 or 90-weight gear oil or a spray chain

Every time the master cylinder cover is removed, a small amount of dirt and moisture enters the brake system. The same thing happens if a leak occurs, or if any part of the hydraulic system is loosened or disconnected. Dirt can clog the system and cause unnecessary wear. Water in the brake fluid can vaporize at high brake system temperatures, impairing the hydraulic action and reducing stopping ability.

To maintain peak performance, change the brake fluid every year and when rebuilding the caliper or master cylinder. To change brake fluid, follow the brake bleeding procedure in Chapter Sixteen.

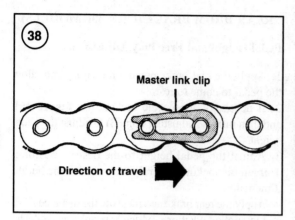

Master link clip

Direction of travel

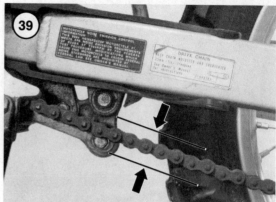

lubricant. Do not over-lubricate, as this causes dirt to collect on the chain and sprockets.

b. Wipe off all excess oil from the rear hub, wheel and tire.

4B. O-ring chain:

CAUTION
An O-ring chain is pre-lubricated during manufacturing. External oiling is only required to prevent chain rust and to keep the O-rings pliable. Do not use a tacky chain lubricant on O-ring chains. Dirt and other abrasive material that sticks to the lubricant also sticks against the O-rings and damages them. Clean the chain as described in this chapter.

a. Lubricate the chain with a lubricant specified by the chain manufacturer. If unavailable, lubricate the chain with an SAE 80 or 90-weight gear oil or a non-tacky chain lubricant specifically-formulated for O-ring chains.

b. Wipe off all excess oil from the rear hub, wheel and tire.

c. After lubricating the chain with gear oil, support the motorcycle with the rear wheel off the ground. Then, hold a cloth against the chain and rear sprocket and slowly turn the wheel to remove excess oil.

5. Check that the master link, if so equipped, is properly installed and secured (**Figure 38**).

Drive Chain Adjustment

The drive chain must have adequate free play to accommodate swing arm movement. A tight chain causes unnecessary wear to the driveline components while a loose chain may jump off the sprockets, possibly causing damage and injury.

1. Support the motorcycle so the rear wheel is off the ground.

2. Slowly turn the rear wheel and check the chain for binding and tight spots by moving the links up and down by hand. If a link or group of links does not move freely, remove and clean the chain. Check for swollen or damaged O-rings.

3. Support the motorcycle on the sidestand.

4. Check the amount of free play by measuring midway between the two sprockets at the lower chain run (**Figure 39**). Chains do not wear evenly. Rotate the rear wheel and check several sections of the chain to find the tightest length (least amount of play) and measure free play at this point. Refer to **Table 6** for the correct amount of free play. If the free play is out of specification, continue the procedure to adjust the chain.

CAUTION
Excessive free play may damage the frame.

CAUTION
When adjusting the drive chain, maintain rear wheel alignment. A misaligned rear wheel can cause poor handling and pulling to one side or the other, as well as causing increased chain and sprocket wear.

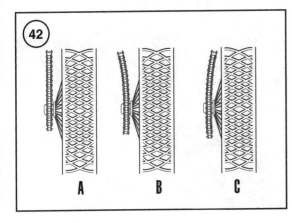

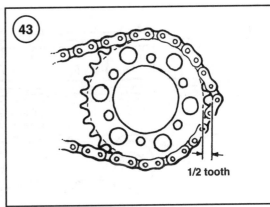

1/2 tooth

a. Recheck the free play at its tightest point. Make sure the free play is within specification.
b. Check the chain alignment as it runs through the chain guide.
c. Check rear brake operation.

Drive Chain Cleaning

1. If desired, remove the drive chain as described in Chapter Twelve.
2A. If the chain is installed, clean it as follows:
   a. Support the motorcycle so the rear wheel is off the ground.
   b. Increase chain slack as described in this section so the chain is as loose as possible.
   c. Liberally apply kerosene to the drive chain while turning the rear wheel.
2B. If the chain is removed, clean it as follows:
   a. Immerse the chain in a pan of kerosene.
   b. Flex the chain to loosen dirt and increase kerosene penetration.
3. Allow the kerosene to soak into the drive chain.

CAUTION
Brushes with coarse or wire bristles
may damage the O-rings.

4. Using a soft brush, clean dirt and debris from all exterior chain surfaces.
5. Check for binding or kinked links and damaged pins.
6. Clean the sprockets.
7. Rinse the chain with clean kerosene and allow to dry.
8. If removed, install the drive chain as described in Chapter Twelve.

5A. On CRF230F models, loosen the rear axle nut (A, **Figure 40**).
5B. On CRF230L and CRF230M models, loosen the rear axle nut (A, **Figure 41**).
6. Rotate the chain adjuster (B, **Figure 40** or **Figure 41**) on each side of the swing arm to adjust the chain. Turn the adjusters equally so the same chain adjuster plate index marks align with the index pin on each side of the swing arm. Remeasure chain free play at the original spot.
7. When the chain free play is correct, verify proper wheel alignment by sighting along the chain from the rear sprocket. The chain must leave the sprocket in a straight line (A, **Figure 42**). If it is turned to one side or the other (B and C, **Figure 42**), perform the following:
   a. Adjust wheel alignment by turning one adjuster or the other. Recheck chain free play.
   b. Confirm swing arm index mark accuracy, if necessary, by measuring from the center of the swing arm pivot shaft to the center of the rear axle.
8A. On CRF230F models, tighten the rear axle nut (A, **Figure 40**) to 108 N•m (80 ft.-lb.).
8B. On CRF230L and CRF230M models, tighten the rear axle nut (A, **Figure 41**) to 93 N•m (69 ft.-lb.).
9. Spin the wheel several times. Note the following:

Drive Chain and Sprocket Wear Inspection

A worn drive chain and sprockets are both unreliable and potentially dangerous. Inspect the chain and both sprockets for wear and replace if necessary. If there is

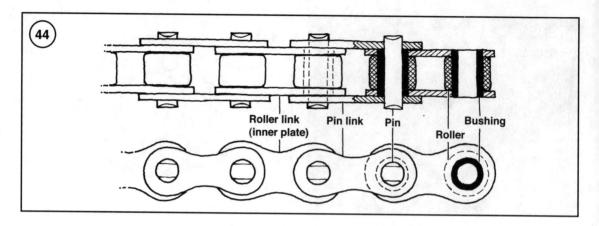

Roller link — Pin link — Pin — Bushing
(inner plate) — Roller

wear, replace both sprockets and the chain. Mixing old and new parts will prematurely wear the new parts.

1. Perform a quick inspection of the chain by pulling one link away from the rear sprocket. If more than half the height of the tooth is visible (**Figure 43**), the chain is probably worn out.

> *NOTE*
> *If both sprockets and chain were re-placed as a set, and the driven sprocket wore out quickly, inspect the condition of the sprocket teeth. If the worn area is halfway up on the sprocket teeth, the chain was adjusted too tightly. Sprocket wear contained to one side of the sprocket is normally caused by incorrect chain alignment. A bent or damaged chain guide will also cause the sprocket to wear on one side. Also, consider the condition of the swing arm bearings. Worn or damaged bearings will affect swing arm and chain alignment, even when the chain adjuster marks are correctly aligned.*

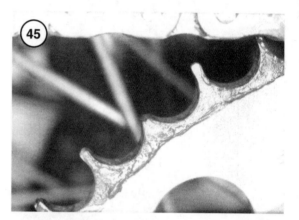

2. Inspect the inner plate chain faces (**Figure 44**). They should be polished evenly on both sides. If they show considerable uneven wear on one side, the sprockets are not aligned properly. Severe wear requires replacement of not only the drive chain, but also replacement of the drive and driven sprockets. Also check for a damaged chain guide and worn bushings and bearings in the swing arm and drive system.

3. Inspect the teeth on each sprocket. The teeth should be symmetrical and uniform. Look for hooked and broken teeth (**Figure 45**). Check the rear sprocket for cracks and damaged Allen bolt recesses.

Drive Chain Slider Inspection

Chain sliders protect the swing arm (A, **Figure 46**) and the frame tube (B) from frame damage.

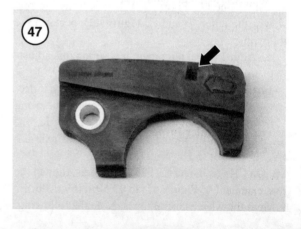

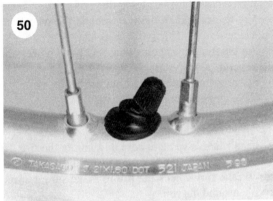

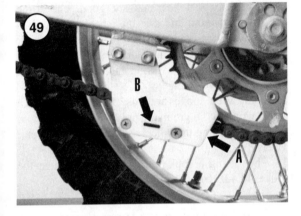

1. Remove the drive sprocket cover.

NOTE
On CRF230L and CRF230M models,
the wear limit groove on the swing arm
slider is adjacent to the frame down-
tube.

2. Inspect each chain slider for excessive wear or damage. Note the wear limit groove on the swing arm slider (C, **Figure 46**) and the frame slider (**Figure 47**). Replace the slider if it is worn to the bottom of the wear limit groove. Tighten the chain slider screw to the specification in **Table 11**.

3. For access to either chain slider, remove the swing arm (Chapter Fourteen or Chapter Fifteen).

4. If the slider is excessively worn, check for damage to the swing arm or frame tube.

5. If removed for access to the chain slider on CRF230L models, install the drive chain cover and tighten the stay screw to 6.0 N•m (53 in.-lb.).

Drive Chain Roller Inspection (CRF230F Models)

A drive chain roller (**Figure 48**) protects the frame from chain damage.

1. Measure the diameter of the chain roller.

2. Replace the chain roller if the diameter is less than 18 mm (0.7 in.).

Chain Guide Slider Inspection

1. Inspect the chain guide (A, **Figure 49**) for alignment, loose mounting bolts or damage.

2. Inspect the chain guide slider for wear and damage.

3. On CRF230F models, replace the chain guide slider when the chain is visible in the wear limit slot (B, **Figure 49**).

TIRES AND WHEELS

Tire Pressure

Periodically check the tire pressure to maintain good handling and to prevent unnecessary wear or damage. Refer to **Table 7** for standard tire pressures. Check the tire pressure when the tires are cold.

Tire Inspection

Inspect the tires weekly for damage. Check the sidewall for damage. Inspect the tire tread for tears or sharp objects embedded in the tire.

Tube Alignment

Check the valve stem alignment. **Figure 50** shows a valve stem that has slipped with the tire. If the tube is not repositioned, the valve stem will eventually pull away from the tube, causing a flat. To realign the tube and tire:

1. Wash the tire and rim.

2. Remove the valve stem core to deflate the tire.

3. Loosen the rim lock nuts, if so equipped.

4. With an assistant steadying the motorcycle, break the tire-to-rim seal all the way around the wheel on both sides.

5. Put the motorcycle on a stand with the wheel off the ground.

6. Spray soapy water along both tire beads.

7. Have an assistant apply the brake.

8. Grab the tire at two opposite places and turn it and the tube to straighten the valve stem.

9. Install the valve stem core and inflate the tire. If necessary, reapply the soap and water to help the tire seat on the rim. Check the tire to make sure it seats evenly around the rim.

> *WARNING*
> *Do not over-inflate the tire and tube. If the tire does not seat properly, remove the valve stem core and re-lubricate the tire with soap and water again.*

10. If so equipped, tighten the rim lock nut(s) to 13 N•m (115 in.-lb.).

11. Adjust the tire pressure (**Table 7**) and install the valve stem nut and cap.

Wheel Spoke Tension and Wheel Inspection

Inspect wheel runout and check spoke tension at regular intervals as described in this section:

> *CAUTION*
> *Most spokes loosen as a group rather than individually. Tighten loose spokes carefully. Over-tightened spokes put excessive pressure across the wheel. Never tighten spokes so tight that the spoke wrench rounds off the spoke nippies. If the spokes are stuck, apply penetrating oil into the top of each nipple and allow time for it to soak in and dissolve rust and corrosion on the mating threads.*

> *NOTE*
> *During break-in for a new or a respoked wheel, check the spoke tension at the end of each 15-minute interval for the first hour of riding. Most spoke seating takes place during initial use.*

1. Inspect the rims for cracks, warp or dents. Replace damaged rims.

2. Support the motorcycle with the front or rear wheel off the ground. Then, spin the wheel while watching the rim. If there is appreciable rim wobble or runout, note the following:

   a. Refer to *Wheel Bearing Inspection* (this chapter) to check the bearings.

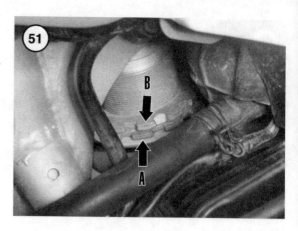

   b. If the wheel bearings are good, check the wheel runout and true the wheel as described in Chapter Twelve.

3. Tap each spoke in the same spot with a spoke wrench. Tight spokes will ring and loose spokes will make a dull, flat sound.

4. If only a few spokes are loose, tighten them with a spoke wrench. If a group of spokes are loose, tighten them while truing the wheel as described in Chapter Twelve.

5. When using a spoke torque wrench, tighten the spokes to 4.0 N•m (35 in.-lb.).

WHEEL BEARING INSPECTION

When inspecting the wheels at the intervals listed in **Table 1** or **Table 2**, check the condition of the seals and bearings. If the seals are reusable, wipe off their outer surface, and then pack the lip of each seal with grease. To replace the seals and wheel bearings, refer to the service procedures in Chapter Twelve.

Check the front and rear wheel bearings as follows:

1. Support the motorcycle with the wheel off the ground.

2. On the front wheel, push the caliper in to push the pistons into their bores. This will move the pads away from the disc.

3. Spin the wheel while checking for excessive wheel bearing noise or other damage. Stop the wheel.

4. Grab the wheel at two points and rock it. There should be no perceptible play at the wheel bearings. If any movement can be seen or felt, check the wheel bearings (Chapter Twelve) for excessive wear or damage.

5. Spin the wheel while applying the brake several times to reposition the pads against the disc.

> *WARNING*
> *Do not ride the motorcycle until the front and rear brakes operate correctly.*

FRONT FORK

Oil Change

There is no fork oil change interval specified. However, a one-year interval is a typical recommendation. Refer to Chapter Thirteen for fork service procedures.

STEERING

Steering Head Bearing Inspection

Inspect the steering head bearings at the intervals specified in **Table 1** or **Table 2**. Lubricate the bearings when necessary. Remove the steering stem to clean and lubricate the bearings. Refer to Chapter Thirteen for complete service procedures.

Steering Head Adjustment

The steering head assembly consists of upper and lower tapered roller bearings, the steering stem and the steering head. Because the motorcycle may be subjected to rough terrain and conditions, check the bearing play at the specified intervals (**Table 1**) or whenever it feels loose. A loose bearing adjustment hampers steering and causes premature bearing and race wear. In extreme conditions, a loose bearing adjustment can cause loss of control. Refer to *Steering Play Check and Adjustment* (Chapter Thirteen).

To check steering play:

1. Apply the front brake while compressing the fork. If the steering head pulls away from the frame, or looseness is felt, the steering is too loose.
2. Support the motorcycle with the front wheel off the ground. Turn the handlebar from side to side. Roughness or binding indicates a too tight steering adjustment or damaged bearings.

FRONT SUSPENSION

Inspection

1. With the front wheel touching the ground, apply the front brake and pump the fork up and down vigorously. Check fork movement, paying attention to any abnormal noises or oil leaks.
2. Check that the upper and lower fork bridge bolts are secure (Chapter Thirteen).

REAR SUSPENSION

Shock Spring Preload Adjustment

The spring preload adjustment can be performed with the shock mounted on the motorcycle. Adjust spring preload by changing the position of the adjuster (A, **Figure 51**, typical). Tightening the adjuster increases spring preload and loosening it decreases preload.

1. Support the motorcycle with the rear wheel off the ground.
2A. On CRF230F models, remove the left side cover (Chapter Seventeen).
2B. On CRF230L and CRF230M models, remove the battery case (Chapter Eleven).
3. Clean the threads on the shock body.
4. Loosen the spring locknut (B, **Figure 51**) with a spanner wrench. If the adjuster turns with the locknut, strike the locknut with a punch and hammer to break it free from the locknut.
5. Turn the adjuster to change the spring preload dimension.
6. Hold the adjuster and tighten the rear shock absorber spring locknut securely.
7A. On CRF230F models, install the left side cover (Chapter Seventeen).
7B. On CRF230L and CRF230M models, install the battery case (Chapter Eleven).

Shock Nitrogen Pressure

Refer all nitrogen pressure adjustment to a dealership or suspension specialist.

Rear Suspension Inspection

Inspect the rear suspension at the intervals in **Table 1** or **Table 2**.

1. With both wheels on the ground, check the shock absorber by bouncing on the seat several times.
2. Raise the rear of the motorcycle and securely support it so the rear wheel is off the ground.
3. With an assistant steadying the motorcycle, push hard on the rear wheel (sideways) to check for side play in the rear swing arm bearings.
4. Check the shock absorber for oil leaks, loose mounting fasteners or other damage.
5. Check for loose or missing suspension fasteners.
6. Make sure the rear axle nut is tight.

BATTERY

The original equipment battery is a sealed type. The electrolyte level cannot be adjusted in a sealed battery because there are no filler caps and the top is permanently attached.

Removal/Installation (CRF230F Models)

1. Turn the ignition switch off.
2. Remove the left side cover as described in Chapter Seventeen.
3. Remove the battery retaining strap (A, **Figure 52**).
4. Disconnect the negative (–) battery lead (B, **Figure 52**), and then the positive (+) lead (C) from the battery.
5. Slide the battery out of the battery box.
6. Reverse the removal steps for installation. Tighten all fasteners securely.

Removal/Installation (CRF230L and CRF230M Models)

1. Turn the ignition switch off.
2. Remove the left side cover as described in Chapter Seventeen.
3. Remove the battery retaining strap (A, **Figure 53**).
4. Disconnect the negative (–) battery lead (B, **Figure 53**), and then the positive (+) lead (C) from the battery.
5. Slide the battery out of the battery box.
6. Reverse the removal steps for installation. Tighten all fasteners securely.

Inspection

For a preliminary test, connect a digital voltmeter to the battery negative and positive terminals and measure battery voltage. A fully-charged battery will read 13.0 volts or more. If the voltmeter reads less, the battery is undercharged. If necessary, charge the battery as described in this section.

Charging

CAUTION
Always follow the charger manufacturer's instructions when using a battery charger. Never connect a battery charger to the battery with the leads still connected. Always disconnect the leads from the battery. During the charging procedure the charger may damage the voltage regulator/rectifier if the battery cables are connected.

1. Remove the battery as described in this section.

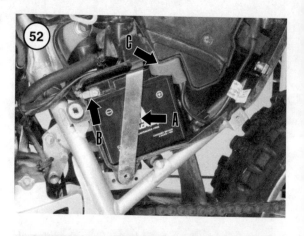

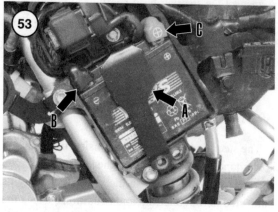

2. Connect the positive charger lead to the positive battery terminal and the negative charger lead to the negative battery terminal.

CAUTION
Do not exceed the recommended charging amperage rate or charging time on the battery charging time label attached to the battery.

3. Set the charger to 12 volts. If the output of the charger is variable, it is best to select a low setting. Use the following suggested charging amperage and length of charge time:
   a. Standard charge: 0.9 amps at 5 to 10 hours.
   b. Quick charge: 4.0 amps at 1 hour.
4. Turn on the charger.
5. After the battery has been charged for the specified amount of time, turn the charger off and disconnect the charger leads.
6. Connect a voltmeter between the battery negative and positive terminals and measure the battery voltage. A fully-charged battery should read 13.0-13.2 volts. If necessary, continue charging.
7. If the battery remains stable for 1 hour at the specified voltage, the battery is considered fully-charged.

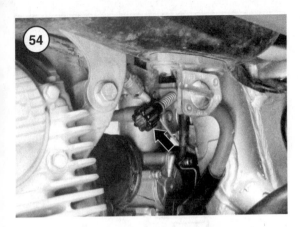

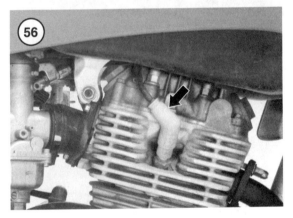

8. Clean the battery terminals and surrounding case. Coat the terminals with dielectric grease or silicone spray to prevent corrosion.

9. Reinstall the battery as described in this section.

New Battery Installation

Always replace the battery with another maintenance-free type. The charging system and battery box are designed for this type of battery.

When replacing the old battery with a new one, be sure to charge it completely before installing it in the

motorcycle. Failure to do so will permanently damage the battery.

> *NOTE*
> *Recycle the old battery. Most motorcycle dealers will accept batteries for recycling. Never place old batteries in household trash.*

CARBURETOR

Idle Speed Adjustment

1. Check the air filter for cleanliness. Clean or replace if necessary as described in this chapter.
2. Connect a tachometer to the engine following the gauge manufacturer's instructions.
3. Make sure the throttle cable free play is correct. Check and adjust as described in this chapter.
4. Start and allow the engine to reach operating temperature.
5A. On CRF230F models, adjust the idle speed using the idle speed screw (**Figure 54**) located near the fuel valve.
5B. On CRF230L and CRF230M models, adjust the idle speed using the idle speed screw (**Figure 55**) located near the throttle cable.
6. Adjust the idle speed to 1300-1500 rpm. Open and close the throttle a few times to make sure the idle speed returns to the specified rpm.
7. Turn off the engine and disconnect the tachometer.

Pilot Screw Adjustment

The pilot screw is pre-set at the factory and adjustment is not necessary unless the carburetor has been overhauled or it has been misadjusted. Refer to Chapter Eight or Chapter Nine.

FUEL SYSTEM

Fuel Filter and Shutoff Valve

The fuel filter is built into the shutoff valve and removes particles which might otherwise clog the carburetor. Refer to Chapter Eight or Chapter Nine for fuel valve service.

Fuel Line Inspection

Inspect the fuel line from the fuel shutoff valve to the carburetor. If it is cracked or starting to deteriorate, replace it. Make sure the hose clamps are in place and holding securely.

Emission Control System (CRF230L and CRF230M Models)

Periodically inspect the hoses and fittings of the emission control system. Make sure the hoses are correctly routed and attached. Refer to Chapter Nine.

At the interval listed in **Table 2**, replace the air supply filter as described in Chapter Nine.

SPARK PLUG

Spark Plug Removal

1. Grasp the spark plug lead (**Figure 56**) as near the plug as possible and pull it straight off the plug. If it is stuck to the plug, twist it slightly to break it loose.

> *CAUTION*
> *Whenever the spark plug is removed, dirt around it can fall into the plug hole. This can cause expensive engine damage.*

2. Blow away any dirt that has collected around the spark plug.

> *NOTE*
> *If the plug is difficult to remove, apply penetrating oil, like WD-40 or Liquid Wrench, around the base of the plug and let it soak about 10-20 minutes.*

3. Remove the spark plug using a spark plug socket.

4. Inspect the plug carefully. Look for a broken center porcelain, excessively-eroded electrodes and excessive carbon or oil fouling.

Spark Plug Gapping and Installation

Carefully adjust the electrode gap on a new spark plug to ensure a reliable, consistent spark. Use a spark plug gapping tool and a wire feeler gauge.

1. If using the stock spark plug cap, remove the small terminal from the end of the plug (A, **Figure 57**).

2. Insert a wire feeler gauge between the center and side electrode of the plug (**Figure 58**). The correct gap is listed in **Table 8**. If the gap is correct, a slight drag will be felt while pulling the wire through. If there is no drag, or the gauge will not pass through, bend the side electrode with a gapping tool (**Figure 59**) to set the proper gap.

3. Apply an antiseize compound to the plug threads before installing the spark plug. Do not use engine oil on the plug threads.

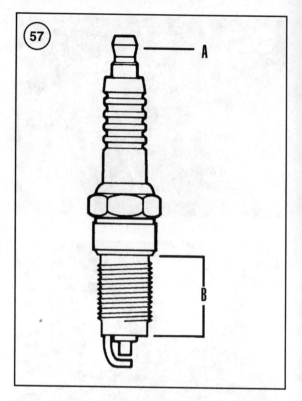

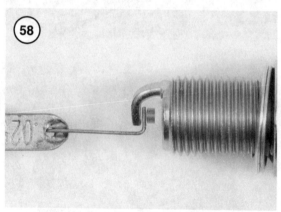

> *NOTE*
> *Antiseize compound can be purchased at most automotive parts stores.*

4. Screw the spark plug in by hand until it seats. Very little effort should be required. If force is necessary, the plug may be cross-threaded. Unscrew it and try again.

> *CAUTION*
> *Do not overtighten. This may crush the gasket and cause a compression leak or damage the cylinder head threads.*

5A. When installing a used spark plug without a torque wrench, tighten the spark plug an additional 1/8 turn after it seats.

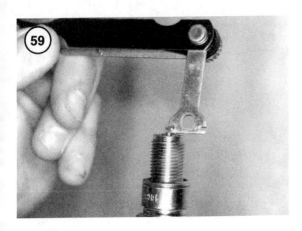

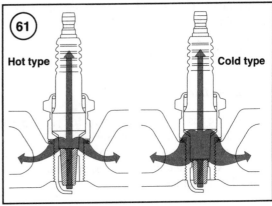

d. Tighten the spark plug until it seats, and then tighten it an additional 1/8 turn.

Inspection

Reading a spark plug that has been in use can provide information about spark plug operation, air/fuel mixture composition and engine operating conditions (oil consumption due to wear for example). Before checking the spark plug, operate the motorcycle under a medium load for approximately 10 km (6 miles). Avoid prolonged idling before shutting off the engine. Remove the spark plug as described in this section. Examine the plug and compare it to the typical plugs and conditions shown in **Figure 60**.

When reading a plug to evaluate carburetor jetting, start with a new plug and operate the motorcycle at the load that corresponds to the jetting information desired. For example, if the main jet is in question, operate the motorcycle at full throttle, shut off the engine and coast to a stop.

Heat range

Spark plugs are available in various heat ranges that are either hotter or colder than the original plugs (**Figure 61**). Select plugs of the heat range designed for the anticipated loads and operating conditions. Use of the incorrect heat range can cause the plug to foul or overheat and cause piston damage.

In general, use a hot plug for low speeds and low temperatures. Use a cold plug for high speeds, high engine loads and high temperatures. The plug should operate hot enough to burn off unwanted deposits, but not so hot that it burns itself or causes preignition. A spark plug of the correct heat range shows a light tan color on the insulator after the plug has been in service.

The reach, or length, of a plug is also important (B, **Figure 57**). A plug that is too short causes excessive carbon buildup, hard starting and plug fouling.

Normal

Gap-bridged

Carbon-fouled

Overheated

Oil-fouled

Sustained preignition

5B. When installing a used spark plug with a torque wrench, after seating it tighten the spark plug to 18 N•m (13 ft.-lb.).

6. When installing a new spark plug, tighten the spark plug twice to prevent it from loosening. Note the following:

    a. Denso spark plug: Tighten the spark plug 1/2 turn after it seats.

    b. NGK spark plug: Tighten the spark plug 3/4 turn after it seats.

    c. Loosen the spark plug.

A plug that is too long causes overheating or may contact the top of the piston. Both conditions cause engine damage.

Table 8 lists the standard heat range spark plug.

Normal condition

If the plug has a light tan- or gray-colored deposit and no abnormal gap wear or erosion, good engine, carburetion and ignition condition are indicated. The plug in use is of the proper heat range and may be serviced and returned to use.

Carbon-fouled

Soft, dry, sooty deposits covering the entire firing end of the plug are evidence of incomplete combustion. Even though the firing end of the plug is dry, the plug's insulation decreases. An electrical path is formed that lowers the voltage from the ignition system. Engine misfiring is a sign of carbon fouling. Carbon fouling can be caused by one or more of the following:
1. Too rich fuel mixture.
2. Spark plug heat range too cold.
3. Clogged air filter.
4. Retarded ignition timing.
5. Ignition component failure.
6. Low engine compression.
7. Prolonged idling.

Oil-fouled

The tip of an oil-fouled plug has a black insulator tip, a damp oily film over the firing end and a carbon layer over the entire nose. The electrodes are not worn. Common causes for this condition are:
1. Incorrect carburetor jetting.
2. Low idle speed or prolonged idling.
3. Ignition component failure.
4. Spark plug heat range too cold.
5. Engine still being broken in.

An oil-fouled spark plug may be cleaned in an emergency, but it is better to replace it. It is important to correct the cause of fouling before the engine is returned to service.

Gap bridging

Plugs with this condition exhibit gaps shorted out by combustion deposits between the electrodes. If this condition is encountered, check for an improper oil type or excessive carbon in the combustion chamber. Be sure to locate and correct the cause of this condition.

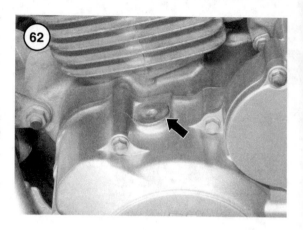

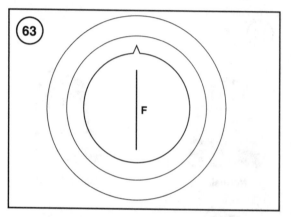

Overheating

Badly-worn electrodes and premature gap wear, along with a gray or white blistered porcelain insulator surface are signs of overheating. The most common cause for this condition is using a spark plug of the wrong heat range (too hot). If a hotter spark plug has not been installed, but the plug is overheated, consider the following causes:
1. Lean fuel mixture.
2. Ignition timing too advanced.
3. Engine lubrication system malfunction.
4. Engine vacuum leak.

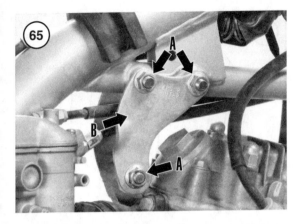

3

5. Improper spark plug installation (too tight).
6. No spark plug gasket.

Worn out

Corrosive gases formed by combustion and high voltage sparks have eroded the electrodes. Spark plugs in this condition require more voltage to fire under hard acceleration. Replace with a new spark plug.

Preignition

If the electrodes are melted, preignition is almost certainly the cause. Check for carburetor mounting or intake manifold leaks and over-advanced ignition timing. It is also possible that a plug of the wrong heat range (too hot) is being used. Find the cause of the preignition before returning the engine to service.

IGNITION TIMING

All models are equipped with an electronic ignition system. Ignition timing is factory set and is not adjustable. Check the ignition timing to make sure all components within the ignition system are working correctly. If the ignition timing is incorrect, trou-

bleshoot the ignition system as described in Chapter Two. Incorrect ignition timing can cause a drastic loss of engine performance and efficiency. It may also cause overheating.

Before starting this procedure, check all electrical connections related to the ignition system. Make sure all connections are tight and free from corrosion and that all ground connections are clean and tight.
1. Start the engine and let it warm approximately 2-3 minutes. Shut off the engine.
2. Park the motorcycle on level ground.
3. Remove the timing hole cap (**Figure 62**) and O-ring.
4. Connect a portable tachometer following the gauge manufacturer's instructions.
5. Connect a timing light following the tool manufacturer's instructions.
6. Restart the engine and let it run at 1300-1500 rpm. Adjust the idle speed if necessary (this chapter).
7. Aim the timing light at the timing hole and pull the trigger. The F mark on the flywheel should align with the index mark on the left crankcase cover as shown in **Figure 63**.
8. If the ignition timing is incorrect, troubleshoot the ignition system as described in Chapter Two.
9. Turn off the ignition switch and disconnect the timing light and portable tachometer.
10. Install the timing hole cap and O-ring. Tighten the timing hole cap to the specification listed in **Table 1**.

VALVE CLEARANCE ADJUSTMENT (CRF230F MODELS)

Perform the valve clearance measurements and adjustments with the engine cool, at room temperature (below 35° C [95° F]). The correct valve clearance is listed in **Table 10**. The exhaust valve is located at the front of the engine and the intake valve is located at the rear of the engine.
1. Remove the fuel tank as described in Chapter Eight.
2. Remove the rubber caps (**Figure 64**).
3. Remove the retaining bolts (A, **Figure 65**), and then remove the mounting plates (B).
4. Remove the two inspection caps (A and B, **Figure 66**) on the left crankcase cover.
5. Unscrew each valve adjuster cover (**Figure 67**) at the front and rear of the engine.
6. Remove the spark plug. This will make it easier to rotate the crankshaft.
7. Insert a wrench through the crankshaft cap hole (A, **Figure 66**) and rotate the crankshaft using the flywheel bolt. Rotate the crankshaft counterclockwise until the engine is at top dead center (TDC) on the compression stroke. Look through the timing cap hole (B, **Figure 66**), and verify that the flywheel T

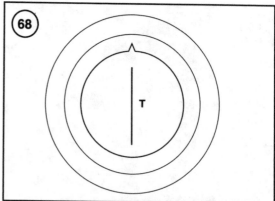

mark aligns with the index mark on the crankcase (**Figure 68**).

NOTE
A cylinder at TDC on its compression stroke will have free play in both of its rocker arms, indicating that the intake valve and exhaust valve are closed.

8. With the flywheel mark aligned on the T, if both rocker arms are not loose, rotate the crankshaft an additional 360° until both rockers have free play.

9. Check the clearance of both valves.

10. Insert a flat feeler gauge between the adjusting screw (A, **Figure 69**) and the valve stem. When the clearance is correct, there will be a slight drag on the feeler gauge when it is inserted and withdrawn.

11. To adjust the clearance, perform the following:

 a. Loosen the valve adjuster locknut (B, **Figure 69**).

 b. Screw the adjuster (A, **Figure 69**) in or out so there is a slight resistance felt on the feeler gauge.

 c. Apply clean engine oil to the locknut threads and the locknut contact surfaces.

 d. Hold the adjuster to prevent it from turning any farther and tighten the valve adjuster locknut to 14 N•m (10 ft.-lb.).

 e. Recheck the clearance to make sure the adjuster did not turn after the correct clearance was achieved; readjust if necessary.

12. Inspect the rubber gaskets on each valve adjuster cover. Replace if damaged or hardened. Install the covers and tighten to 15 N•m (11 ft.-lb.).

13. Install the spark plug (this chapter).

14. Install the mounting plates (B, **Figure 65**). Note that each plate is identified for its correct position upon reinstallation.

15. Install the mounting plate bolts (A, **Figure 65**). Tighten the 8-mm bolts to 34 N•m (25 ft.-lb.). Tighten the 10-mm bolt to 59 N•m (44 ft.-lb.).

16. Install the rubber caps (**Figure 64**) onto the bolts.

17. Install the two inspection caps (A and B, **Figure 66**) into the left crankcase cover and tighten securely.

18. Install the fuel tank as described in Chapter Eight.

VALVE CLEARANCE ADJUSTMENT (CRF230L AND CRF230M MODELS)

Perform the valve clearance measurements and adjustments with the engine cool, at room temperature (below 35° C [95° F]). The correct valve clearance is listed in **Table 10**. The exhaust valve is located at the front of the engine and the intake valve is located at the rear of the engine.

1. Remove the fuel tank as described in Chapter Nine.

2. Remove the EVAP canister as described in Chapter Nine.

3. Remove the ignition coil as described in Chapter Eleven.

4. Disconnect the electrical connectors from the horn.

5. Move aside the wiring harness near the cylinder head cover.

6. Detach the rubber cover (A, **Figure 70**) from the retaining hook (B).

7. Remove the upper engine mount bolts (**Figure 71**) and plates.

8. Remove the two inspection caps (A and B, **Figure 66**) on the left crankcase cover.

9. Unscrew each valve adjuster cover (**Figure 67**).

10. Remove the spark plug. This will make it easier to rotate the crankshaft.

11. Insert a wrench through the crankshaft cap hole (A, **Figure 66**) and rotate the crankshaft using the flywheel bolt. Rotate the crankshaft counterclockwise until the engine is at top dead center (TDC) on the compression stroke. Look through the timing cap hole (B) and verify that the flywheel T mark aligns with the index mark on the crankcase (**Figure 68**).

NOTE
A cylinder at TDC on its compression stroke will have free play in both of its rocker arms, indicating that the intake valve and exhaust valve are closed.

12. With the flywheel mark aligned on the T, if both rocker arms are not loose, rotate the crankshaft an additional 360° until both rockers have free play.

13. Check the clearance of both valves.

14. Insert a flat feeler gauge between the adjusting screw (A, **Figure 69**) and the valve stem (**Figure 69**). When the clearance is correct, there will be a slight drag on the feeler gauge when it is inserted and withdrawn.

15. To adjust the clearance, perform the following:

  a. Loosen the adjuster locknut (B, **Figure 69**).

  b. Screw the adjuster (A, **Figure 69**) in or out so there is a slight resistance felt on the feeler gauge.

  c. Hold the adjuster to prevent it from turning any farther and tighten the valve adjuster locknut to 14 N•m (10 ft.-lb.).

  d. Recheck the clearance to make sure the adjuster did not turn after the correct clearance was achieved; readjust if necessary.

16. Inspect the rubber gaskets on each valve adjuster cover. Replace if damaged or hardened. Install the covers and tighten to 15 N•m (11 ft.-lb.).

17. Install the spark plug (this chapter).

18. Install the upper engine mount plate and bolts (**Figure 71**). Tighten the bolts to 34 N•m (25 ft.-lb.).

19. Attach the rubber cover (A, **Figure 70**) to the retaining hook (B).

20. Return the wiring harness to its original position.

21. Connect the electrical connectors to the horn.

22. Install the ignition coil as described in Chapter Eleven.

23. Install the EVAP canister as described in Chapter Nine.

24. Install the fuel tank as described in Chapter Nine.

EXHAUST SYSTEM

Refer to Chapter Four for exhaust system service and repair procedures.

Inspection

1. Inspect the exhaust pipe for cracks or dents that could alter performance. Refer all repairs to a qualified dealership or welding shop.

2. Check all the exhaust pipe fasteners and mounting points for loose or damaged parts.

Spark Arrestor Cleaning

Remove and clean the spark arrestor at the intervals specified in **Table 1** or **Table 2**.

> *WARNING*
> *Perform the cleaning procedure when the exhaust system is cold. Work in a well-ventilated area. Wear safety eyewear and clothing.*

1. Remove the bolts (**Figure 72**) securing the spark arrestor to the rear of the muffler. Remove the spark arrestor (A, **Figure 73**) and gasket.
2. Using a soft brush, remove the carbon deposits from the spark arrestor screen (B, **Figure 73**).
3. Inspect the spark arrestor screen. If it is torn, deteriorated or otherwise damaged, replace the spark arrestor.
4. Reverse the removal steps to install the spark arrestor. Note the following:
   a. On CRF230F models, install the spark arrestor using a new gasket. Install the spark arrestor bolts and tighten to 14 N•m (10 ft.-lb.).
   b. On CRF230L and CRF230M models, inspect the gasket and replace it if damaged or deteriorated. Apply molybdeum-disulfide grease to the spark arrestor bolt threads. Then, install the spark arrestor, gasket and bolts. Tighten the bolts to 6.35 N•m (56 in.-lb.).

CRANKCASE BREATHER

Crankcase gases are routed through a breather hose from a fitting on the rear of the crankcase into the air box. A drain hose at the bottom of the air box allows removal of residue.

1. On CRF230F models, remove the cap (**Figure 74**) and drain any residue from the drain hose at the intervals specified in **Table 1**.
2. On CRF230L and CRF230M models, remove the plug (**Figure 75**) and drain any residue from the drain hose at the intervals specified in **Table 2**.
3. Clean the air box and make sure all hoses and clamps are in good condition and tight to prevent the entrance of water or debris into the engine.

ENGINE COMPRESSION TEST

A cranking compression test is one of the quickest ways to check the internal condition of the engine (piston rings, piston, head gasket, valves and cylinder). It is a good idea to check compression at each tune-up, record it and compare it with the reading obtained at the next tune-up.

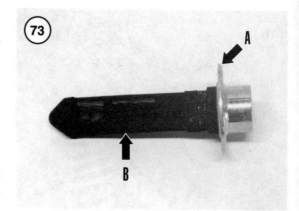

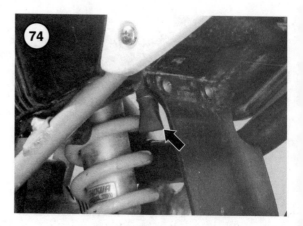

Use a screw-in type compression gauge with a flexible adapter. Before using the gauge, check that the rubber gasket on the end of the adapter is not cracked or damaged; this gasket seals the cylinder to ensure accurate compression readings.

1. Make sure the battery is fully charged to ensure proper engine cranking speed.
2. Run the engine until it reaches normal operating temperature, and then turn it off.
3. Remove the spark plug as described in this chapter.
4. Lubricate the threads of the compression gauge adapter with a small amount of antiseize compound and carefully thread the gauge into the spark plug hole. Tighten the hose by hand to form a good seal.

> *CAUTION*
> *When the spark plug lead is disconnected, the electronic ignition will produce the highest voltage possible. This can damage the ignition control module. To protect the ignition system, install a grounding tool (Chapter One) in the spark plug cap. Do not crank the engine more than necessary.*

5. Open the throttle completely and operate the starter to turn the engine over while reading the compression gauge until there is no further rise in pres-

sure. The compression reading should increase on each stroke. Record the reading.

6. Refer to **Table 10** for the compression specification. If the compression reading is low, continue the procedure. If the compression reading is high, go to Step 8.

NOTE
An engine with low compression cannot be tuned to maximum performance.

7. A low compression reading can be caused by the following:
  a. Incorrect valve adjustment.
  b. Worn piston rings, piston or cylinder bore.
  c. Leaking valve seat.
  d. Damaged cylinder head gasket.
8. A high compression reading can be caused by excessive carbon deposits on the piston crown or combustion chamber.
9. To isolate the problem to a valve or ring problem, perform a wet compression test. Pour about a teaspoon of engine oil into the spark plug hole. Repeat the compression test and record the reading. If the compression increases significantly, the valves are good but the piston rings are defective. If compression does not increase, the valves require servicing.
10. Reverse the steps to complete installation. Reinstall the spark plug (this chapter).

TUNE-UP

Performing the maintenance jobs listed in **Table 1** or **Table 2** at the specified intervals should result in a motorcycle that operates optimally under normal riding conditions. However, a motorcycle that is operated in severe conditions, or raced, may require a tune-up to restore lost performance.

The frequency of tune-ups depends on motorcycle use. Creating a record that contains the type of operation and when tune-ups occur will help establish the frequency for future tune-ups.

Which tasks are included in the tune-up should be determined by the operating conditions. For instance, air filter service is dictated by the amount of airborne debris. A tune-up may differ between motorcycles due to different operating conditions.

As a guideline, the following items may be included in a tune-up:
1. Air filter.
2. Engine oil and filter.
3. Idle speed.
4. Spark plug.
5. Battery.
6. Engine compression test.
7. Brake system.
8. Clutch system.
9. Fuel system.
10. Tires.
11. Suspension components.
12. Steering.
13. Drive chain.
14. Fasteners.

Table 1 MAINTENANCE SCHEDULE (CRF230F MODELS)

Initial maintenance: 150 km (100 miles) or 1 month, whichever comes first	Inspect valve clearance
	Replace engine oil
	Check engine idle speed
	Inspect brake system
	Inspect clutch system
	Check for loose or missing fasteners
	Inspect wheels and tires
	Inspect front steering for looseness
	Lubricate and adjust the drive chain

(continued)

Table 1 MAINTENANCE SCHEDULE (CRF230F MODELS) (continued)

Every 100 operating hours or 1600 km (1000 miles)	Clean spark arrestor
Every 3 months or 500 km (300 miles)	Lubricate and adjust the drive chain*
Every 6 months or 1000 km (600 miles)	Clean and inspect air filter element* Check air box drain. Inspect spark plug; regap if necessary Check and adjust valve clearance Change engine oil Check and adjust engine idle speed Inspect drive chain slider Inspect brake system, including brake pads/shoes, for operation and wear Inspect and, if necessary, adjust clutch system Inspect wheel and tires
Every 12 months or 2000 km (1200 miles)	Inspect fuel line, fuel tank vent and fuel tank valve screen Check and adjust throttle operation and free play Clean oil strainer screen and centrifugal filter Lubricate side stand pivot point Check all suspension components Inspect front steering for looseness Inspect all fasteners for tightness and damage

*Service more frequently if operated in a wet or dusty environment.

Table 2 MAINTENANCE SCHEDULE (CRF230L AND CRF230M MODELS)

Initial maintenance after 1000 km (600 miles)	Inspect valve clearance Replace engine oil Check engine idle speed Inspect brake fluid level Inspect brake system Inspect clutch system Check for loose or missing fasteners Check steering for free play
Every 800 km (500 miles)	Lubricate and adjust drive chain*
Every 3000 km (2000 miles)	Change engine oil
Every 6400 km (4000 miles)	Inspect spark plug, regap if necessary Check and adjust valve clearance Check and adjust carburetor idle speed Check and adjust clutch free play Clean and inspect fuel filter screen Adjust front brake lever and rear brake pedal Inspect brake pads for wear Inspect drive chain sliders Inspect wheels and tires* Clean spark arrestor Clean and drain crankcase breather
Every 12800 km (8000 miles)	Clean engine oil strainer and centrifugal filter Replace spark plug Inspect fuel lines for chafed, cracked or swollen ends Inspect throttle operation Inspect choke operation Check all nuts, bolts and other fasteners for tightness* Check steering for free play Check all suspension components Inspect entire brake system Check and adjust headlight aim Lubricate rear suspension linkage

(continued)

Table 2 MAINTENANCE SCHEDULE (CRF230L AND CRF230M MODELS) (continued)

Every 12800 km (8000 miles) (continued)	Lubricate swing arm bearings Inspect crankcase and emission hoses for cracks or loose hose clamps—drain out all residue
Every 19200 km (12000 miles)	Replace air filter* Replace emission system air supply filter
Every 19200 km (12000 miles) or two years, whichever occurs first	Replace brake fluid

*Service more frequently when operated in severe conditions.

Table 3 RECOMMENDED LUBRICANTS AND FUEL

Air filter	Foam air filter oil
Brake fluid	DOT 4
Engine oil	
Grade	API SG or higher/JASO MA*
Viscosity	SAE10W-30*
Fork oil	Pro Honda Suspension Fluid SS-8
Fuel	
CRF230F models	Octane rating of 91 or higher
CRF230L and CRF230M models	Octane rating of 86 or higher
Steering and suspension lubricant	Multipurpose grease

*Refer to text for additional information.

Table 4 ENGINE OIL CAPACITY

	Liters	Quarts
Oil change only	1.0	1.1
After engine disassembly	1.2	1.3

Table 5 CLUTCH, BRAKE AND THROTTLE ADJUSTMENTS

Clutch lever free play	10-20 mm (3/8-3/4 in.)
Rear brake master cylinder pushrod height (CRF230L and CRF230M models)	69.5 mm (2.74 in.)
Rear brake pedal free play (CRF230F models)	20-30 mm (3/4-1 3/16 in.)
Throttle grip free play	2-6 mm (3/32-1/4 in.)

Table 6 DRIVE CHAIN SPECIFICATIONS

Drive chain	
CRF230F models	DID 520V6 (110 links) RK520MOZ2 (110 links)
CRF230L models	DID 520VC5 (100 links) RK520MOZ9 (100 links)
CRF230M models	DID 520V (100 links) RK520MOZ9 (100 links)
Drive chain slack	
CRF230F models	20-30 mm (3/4-1 3/16 in.)
CRF230L and CRF230M models	25-35 mm (1.0-1 3/8 in.)
Drive chain roller diameter (CRF230F models)	18 mm (0.7 in.) min.

Table 7 TIRE INFLATION PRESSURE

	kPa (psi)
CRF230F models	
Front and rear tires	100 (15)
CRF230L models	
Front	125 (18)
Rear	150 (22)
CRF230M models	
Front and rear tires	200 (29)

Table 8 SPARK PLUG SPECIFICATIONS

Spark plug gap	0.8-0.9 mm (0.03-0.04 in.)
Spark plug type	
Standard	NGK DPR8EA-9 or Denso X24EPR-U9
Cold weather operation*	NGK DP7EA-9 or Denso X22EP-U9

*Below 5° C (41° F).

Table 9 IDLE SPEED SPECIFICATION

Engine idle speed	1300-1500 rpm

Table 10 ENGINE COMPRESSION AND VALVE CLEARANCE SPECIFICATIONS

Engine compression	1294 kPa (187 psi) @ 450 rpm
Valve clearance	
CRF230L and CRF230M models	
Intake and exhaust	0.08-0.12 mm (0.003-0.005 in.)
CRF230F models	
Intake and exhaust	0.10 mm (0.004 in.)

Table 11 MAINTENANCE TORQUE SPECIFICATIONS

	N•m	in.-lb.	ft.-lb.
Clutch lever pivot bolt			
2004-on CRF230F models	1	9	–
Clutch lever pivot nut			
2004-on CRF230F models	6	53	–
Crankshaft hole cap	8	71	–
Drive chain cover stay screw	6.0	53	–
Drive chain slider screw			
CRF230F models	4	35	–
CRF230L and CRF230M models	4.2	37	–
Engine mounting plate bolts			
8-mm	34	–	25
10-mm	59	–	44
Gearshift lever pinch bolt			
CRF230F models	12	106	–
CRF230L and CRF230M models	16	144	–
Oil centrifugal filter rotor cover screws	5	44	–
Oil drain cap	15	132	–
Rear axle nut			
CRF230F models	108	–	80
CRF230L and CRF230M models	93	–	69
Rear brake pedal locknut	17.2	156	–
Spark arrestor bolts			
CRF230F models	14	120	–
CRF230L and CRF230M models*	6.35	56	–
Spark plug			
New		Refer to text	
Used	18	156	–
Timing hole cap			
CRF230F models	6	53	–
CRF230L and CRF230M models	10	89	–
Valve adjuster cover	15	132	–
Valve adjuster locknut	14	120	–
Wheel rim locknut	13	115	–
Wheel spokes	4	35	–

* Apply molybdenum-disulfide grease to bolt threads.

ENGINE TOP END

4

ENGINE TOP END

This chapter provides service and overhaul procedures for the exhaust system and engine top end components. **Tables 1-3** at the end of this chapter provide engine top end specifications.

EXHAUST SYSTEM (CRF230F MODELS)

Muffler Removal/Installation

1. Remove the right side cover (Chapter Seventeen).
2. Loosen the muffler clamp bolt (A, **Figure 1**).
3. Remove the lower muffler mounting bolt (B, **Figure 1**).
4. Support the muffler. Remove the upper muffler bolt (**Figure 2**), and then remove the muffler.
5. Inspect the muffler mounting cushion and sleeve. Replace if necessary.
6. Inspect the muffler gasket (**Figure 3**) on the exhaust pipe. Replace if necessary.
7. Reverse the removal steps for installation. Note the following:
   a. Tighten the muffler clamp bolt (A, **Figure 1**) to 20 N•m (15 ft.-lb.).
   b. Tighten the muffler mounting bolts to 26 N•m (19 ft.-lb.).

Exhaust Pipe Removal/Installation

1. Loosen the muffler clamp bolt (A, **Figure 1**).
2. Remove the exhaust pipe retaining nuts (**Figure 4**).
3. Remove the exhaust pipe.
4. Remove the exhaust pipe gasket (A, **Figure 5**).
5. Inspect the muffler gasket (**Figure 3**) on the exhaust pipe. Replace if necessary.
6. Inspect the exhaust pipe retaining studs (B, **Figure 5**). If necessary, tighten them. The exposed stud length should be 25 mm (1.0 in.).
7. Reverse the removal steps for installation. Note the following:
   a. Install a new exhaust pipe gasket (A, **Figure 5**).
   b. Tighten the exhaust pipe retaining nuts to 20 N•m (15 ft.-lb.).
   c. Tighten the muffler clamp bolt to 20 N•m (15 ft.-lb.).

EXHAUST SYSTEM (CRF230L AND CRF230M MODELS)

Muffler Removal/Installation

1. Loosen the muffler clamp bolt (A, **Figure 6**).
2. Remove the lower muffler mounting bolt (B, **Figure 6**).

3. Support the muffler. Remove the upper muffler mounting bolt (**Figure 7**), and then remove the muffler.

4. Inspect the muffler mounting cushion and sleeve. Replace if necessary.

5. Inspect the muffler gasket (**Figure 3**) on the exhaust pipe. Replace if necessary.

6. Reverse the removal steps for installation. Note the following:

    a. On 2008 models, install the upper muffler mounting bolt (**Figure 7**) and collar from the right side. Install the nut from the opposite side.

    b. On 2009 models, install the upper muffler mounting bolt and collar from the left side. Install the nut from the opposite side.

    c. Tighten the muffler clamp bolt to 20 N•m (15 ft.-lb.).

    d. Tighten the muffler mounting bolts to 26.5 N•m (19 ft.-lb.).

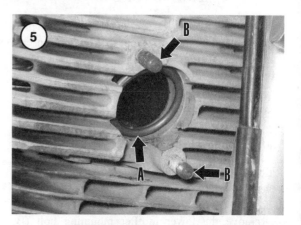

Exhaust Pipe Removal/Installation

1. Loosen the muffler clamp bolt (A, **Figure 6**).

2. Remove the nuts (**Figure 8**) securing the exhaust pipe flanges to the cylinder head. Remove the two individual exhaust pipe flanges from the exhaust pipe.

3. Remove the exhaust pipe.

4. Remove the exhaust pipe gasket (A, **Figure 5**).

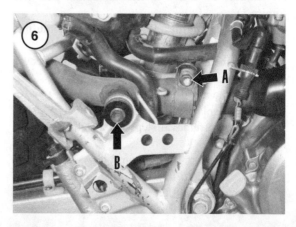

4

5. Inspect the muffler gasket (**Figure 3**) on the exhaust pipe. Replace if necessary.

6. Inspect the exhaust pipe retaining studs (B, **Figure 5**). If necessary, tighten them. The exposed stud length should be 20 mm (0.8 in.).

7. Reverse the removal steps for installation. Note the following:

    a. Install a new exhaust pipe gasket (A, **Figure 5**).

    b. Install the exhaust pipe retaining flanges so they interlock as shown in **Figure 9**.

    c. Tighten the exhaust pipe retaining nuts to 10 N•m (89 in.-lb.).

    d. Tighten the muffler clamp bolt to 20 N•m (15 ft.-lb.).

CYLINDER HEAD COVER AND CAMSHAFT

The cylinder head cover contains the rocker arm assemblies. The camshaft is held in place between the cylinder head cover and the cylinder head. The camshaft is driven by a chain attached to the crankshaft sprocket.

Removal

> *CAUTION*
> *Remove the cylinder head cover when the engine is at room temperature to prevent damage.*

1. Remove the engine as described in Chapter Five.

2. Remove the starter (Chapter Ten or Chapter Eleven).

3. Remove the two inspection caps (A and B, **Figure 10**) on the left crankcase cover.

4. Unscrew each valve adjustment cover (**Figure 11**).

5. Remove the spark plug (Chapter Three). This will make it easier to rotate the crankshaft.

6. Insert a wrench through the crankshaft cap hole (A, **Figure 10**) and rotate the crankshaft using the flywheel bolt. Rotate the crankshaft counterclockwise until the

engine is at top dead center (TDC) on the compression stroke. Look through the timing cap hole (B, **Figure 10**) and verify that the flywheel T mark aligns with the index mark on the crankcase (**Figure 12**).

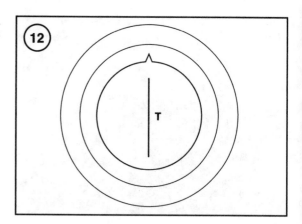

> *NOTE*
> *A cylinder at TDC on its compression stroke will have free play in both of its rocker arms, indicating that the intake valve and exhaust valve are closed.*

7. With the flywheel mark aligned on the T, if both rocker arms are not loose, rotate the crankshaft an additional 360° until both rockers have free play.
8. Remove the cam chain tensioner as described in this chapter.
9. Remove the cover retaining bolts (A, **Figure 13**), and then remove the cam sprocket cover (B).

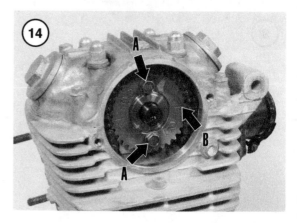

> *CAUTION*
> *Do not drop the camshaft bolts into the engine.*

> *NOTE*
> *If necessary, prevent camshaft rotation when loosening the sprocket bolts by holding the flywheel bolt.*

10. Remove the cam sprocket mounting bolts (A, **Figure 14**).

> *NOTE*
> *Hold the chain during sprocket removal so it cannot fall into the engine.*

11. Separate the cam chain from the cam sprocket (B, **Figure 14**) and remove the sprocket.
12. Tie a piece of wire to the cam chain and secure the loose end to the exterior of the engine. This will prevent the cam chain from falling into the crankcase.
13. Using a crossing pattern, remove the cylinder head cover retaining bolts (A, **Figure 15**).
14. Using a crossing pattern, remove the cap nuts and washers (B, **Figure 15**).
15. Remove the cylinder head cover. Do not lose the locating dowels.
16. Remove the dowels (A, **Figure 16**).
17. Remove the camshaft (B, **Figure 16**).
18. Remove the oil passage plug (A, **Figure 17**).

> *CAUTION*
> *If the crankshaft must be rotated when the camshaft is removed, pull up on the camshaft chain and keep it taut while rotating the crankshaft. Make certain that the chain is positioned correctly on the crankshaft sprocket. If this is not done, the chain may become kinked*

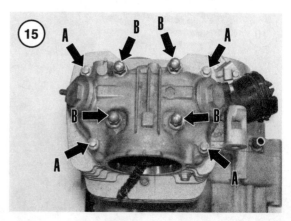

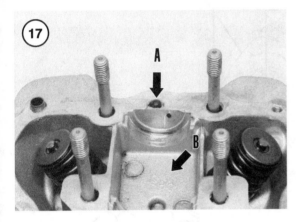

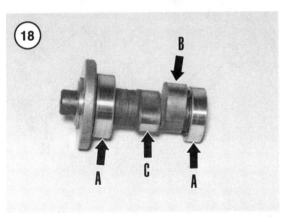

by hand. If any roughness or play can be felt in a bearing, replace the camshaft.

2. Check the camshaft lobes for wear. The lobes must be smooth with no scoring, galling or roughness.

3. Measure both the intake (B, **Figure 18**) and exhaust (C) lobes of the camshaft. Compare to the camshaft specifications listed in **Table 2**.

4. Inspect the camshaft sprocket for wear and replace if necessary.

Cylinder Head Cover
Disassembly/Inspection/Assembly

The rocker arm assemblies are identical. To avoid intermixing parts, inspect one rocker arm assembly (**Figure 19**) at a time. Individual parts develop a specific wear pattern. Label parts as they are removed and keep them together as a set.

1. Unscrew the valve adjuster covers.

2. Remove the set plate retaining screw (A, **Figure 20**), and then remove the set plate (B).

3. Thread a 6-mm bolt (A, **Figure 21**) into the end of the rocker arm shaft (B).

4. Using the bolt, pull out the rocker arm shaft (**Figure 21**) while also removing the rocker arm.

5. Remove the remaining rocker arm shaft and rocker arm.

6. Wash all parts in cleaning solvent and dry thoroughly.

7. Inspect the rocker arm components as follows:

   a. Inspect the rocker arm contact pad (A, **Figure 22**). If the pad is scratched or unevenly worn, inspect the cam lobe for scoring, chipping or flat spots. Replace the rocker arm if defective.

   b. Inspect the valve adjuster contact pad (B, **Figure 22**) and locknut (C) for thread damage or wear. Replace if necessary.

   c. Measure the inside diameter of the rocker arm bore (**Figure 23**) and compare with the specifications in **Table 2**. Replace if worn to the service limit or greater.

   d. Inspect the rocker arm shafts (**Figure 24**) for signs of wear or scoring. Measure the outside diameter and compare with the specifications in **Table 2**. Replace if worn to the service limit or less.

8. Lubricate the rocker arm shaft and rocker arm bores with molybdenum oil (a 1:1 mixture of engine oil and molybdenum grease).

9. Reverse the disassembly steps to complete assembly. Note the following:

   a. Insert each rocker shaft so the flat portion (**Figure 25**) is toward the center of the cover.

   b. Tighten the set plate retaining screw (A, **Figure 20**) securely.

and may damage both the chain and the sprocket on the crankshaft.

Camshaft Inspection

NOTE
The cam is dark in color due to the manufacturing heat treating process. It is not due to lack of oil pressure or excessive engine heat.

1. Check the camshaft bearings (A, **Figure 18**) for roughness, pitting, galling and play by rotating them

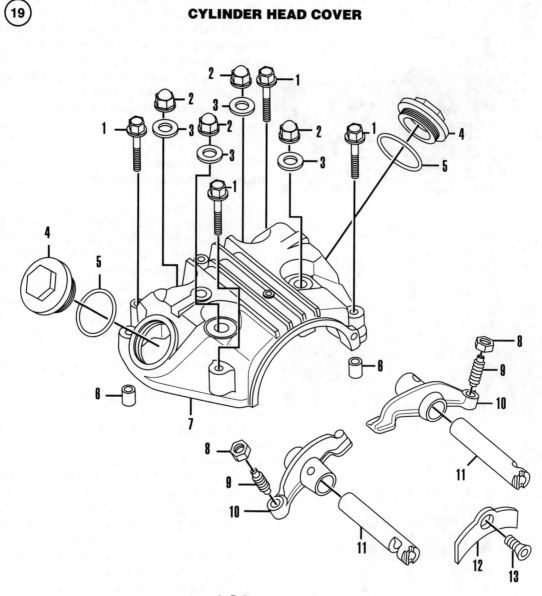

⑲ **CYLINDER HEAD COVER**

1. Bolt
2. Nut
3. Washer
4. Cover
5. O-ring
6. Dowel
7. Cylinder head cover
8. Nut
9. Adjuster
10. Rocker arm
11. Rocker shaft
12. Set plate
13. Screw

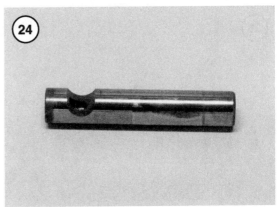

4

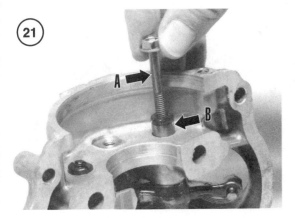

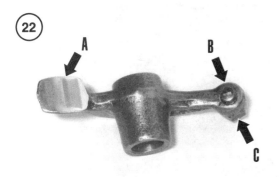

Installation

CAUTION
When rotating the crankshaft, keep the camshaft chain taut and engaged with the timing sprocket on the crankshaft.

1. The engine must be at top dead center (TDC) for correct valve timing. Hold the camshaft chain out and taut while rotating the crankshaft to avoid damage to the chain and/or the crankcase.

2. Pull up on the chain, making sure it is properly engaged on the crankshaft sprocket. Rotate the engine until the T timing mark on the flywheel aligns with the fixed notch on the crankcase (**Figure 12**).

3. Install the oil passage plug (A, **Figure 17**).

4. Install the dowel pins (A, **Figure 16**).

5. Lubricate both camshaft lobes with molybdenum disulfide grease. Apply clean engine oil to the camshaft bearings.

6. Install the camshaft (B, **Figure 16**) so both cam lobes point down.

7. Fill the oil pocket in the cylinder head (B, **Figure 17**) with engine oil.

8. Make sure all mating surfaces are clean and dry.

CAUTION
Do not allow sealant into the oil pas-
sage (Figure 26) during application.

9. Apply a nonhardening, liquid gasket sealant such as Hondabond 4, or its equivalent, to the mating surfaces on the cylinder head.

NOTE
Hold the rocker arms in place so they
don't snag the valves or camshaft dur-
ing cylinder head cover installation.

10. Install the cylinder head cover onto the cylinder head.

11. Lubricate the threads of the cap nuts and new washers.

12. Install the washers, cap nuts and flange bolts.

13. Following a crossing pattern, tighten the cap nuts and flange bolts evenly in several steps as follows.

    a. Tighten the cap nuts to the specifications listed in **Table 3**.

    b. Tighten the flange bolts to 12 N•m (106 in.-lb.).

14. Verify that the crankshaft is at TDC.

15. Make sure the cam chain is meshed properly with the drive sprocket on the crankshaft.

16. Install the camshaft sprocket through the camshaft chain and into position on the camshaft. The timing marks (A, **Figure 27**) must be visible and aligned with the cylinder head cover/cylinder head mating surfaces (B).

17. Lubricate the cam sprocket retaining bolts with engine oil, and then install the bolts. Tighten the bolts to 12 N•m (106 in.-lb.). Check that the alignment marks (A, **Figure 27**) are still aligned with the top surface of the cylinder head (B) and that the flywheel T mark is still aligned (**Figure 12**) with the fixed notch on the crankcase.

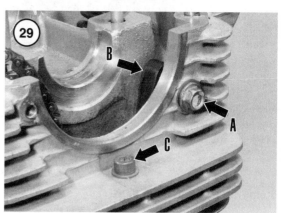

CAUTION
Very expensive damage could result from
improper camshaft and camshaft chain
alignment. Be sure alignment is correct.

18. If alignment is incorrect, reposition the camshaft chain on the sprocket and recheck the alignment.

19. Install a new gasket onto the cam sprocket cover.

20. Install a new O-ring into the sprocket cover groove. Lubricate the O-ring with engine oil.

21. Install the sprocket cover so the oil pocket (**Figure 28**) is down. Tighten the bolts securely.

4

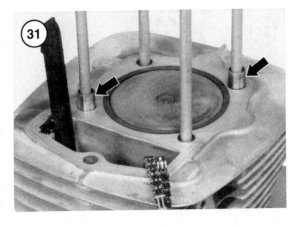

22. Install the spark plug (Chapter Three).
23. Install the valve adjustment covers (**Figure 11**).
24. Install the two inspection caps (A and B, **Figure 10**) on the left crankcase cover.
25. Install the starter (Chapter Ten or Chapter Eleven).
26. Install the engine as described in Chapter Five.

CYLINDER HEAD

Removal/Installation

CAUTION
To prevent any warping or other damage, remove the cylinder head only when the engine is at room temperature.

1. Remove the cylinder head cover and camshaft (this chapter).
2. Remove the rear cam chain guide retaining bolt (A, **Figure 29**).
3. Remove the rear cam chain guide (B, **Figure 29**).
4. Remove the cylinder head Allen bolt (C, **Figure 29**).

CAUTION
The cooling fins are fragile and easily damaged.

5. Loosen the cylinder head by tapping around the perimeter with a rubber-faced or other soft mallet.
6. Lift the cylinder head straight up and off the cylinder. Guide the camshaft chain through the opening in the cylinder head and resecure the wire to the exterior of the engine. This will prevent the drive chain from falling down into the crankcase.
7. Remove the cylinder head gasket and discard it. Do not lose the locating dowels.
8. Place a clean shop cloth into the camshaft chain opening in the cylinder to prevent the entry of foreign matter.
9. If necessary, remove the intake tube (**Figure 30**).
10. Install the cylinder head by reversing the removal steps. Note the following:
    a. Clean the mating surface of the cylinder and cylinder head of any old gasket material.
    b. If removed, install the locating dowels (**Figure 31**) around the studs in the cylinder.
    c. Make sure the bottom end of the front camshaft chain guide (A, **Figure 32**) properly fits into the chain guide holder cast into the crankcase. The camshaft chain guide pin must fit into the notch (B, **Figure 32**) in the cylinder.
    d. Route the cam chain through the cylinder head during installation.
    e. Install the cylinder head Allen bolt and finger-tighten it after the cylinder head is installed. After the cylinder head cover is installed, tighten the cylinder head Allen bolt (C, **Figure 29**) to 10 N•m (89 in.-lb.).
    f. Tighten the rear cam chain guide retaining bolt (A, **Figure 29**) to 10 N•m (89 in.-lb.).
    g. On CRF230F models, if the intake tube was removed, install a new gasket and O-ring onto the intake tube. Then, install the intake tube and bolts. Tighten the bolts securely.
    h. On CRF230L and CRF230M models, if the intake tube was removed, install a new O-ring onto the intake tube. Then, install the intake tube and bolts. Tighten the bolts securely.

Cylinder Head Inspection

1. Remove all gasket residue from the cylinder head gasket surfaces. Do not scratch the gasket surface.

> *CAUTION*
> *Do not clean the combustion chamber after removing the valves. The valve seat surfaces may be damaged, which may cause poor valve seating.*

2. Without removing the valves, remove all carbon deposits from the combustion chamber. Use a fine wire brush dipped in solvent or make a scraper from hardwood. Do not damage the head, valves or spark plug threads.

> *NOTE*
> *When using a tap to clean spark plug threads, coat the tap with cutting fluid or kerosene.*

> *NOTE*
> *Aluminum spark plug hole threads can be damaged by galling, cross-threading and overtightening. To prevent galling, apply an anti-seize compound on the plug threads before installation and do not overtighten.*

3. Examine the spark plug threads in the cylinder head for damage. If damage is minor or if the threads are dirty or clogged with carbon, use a spark plug thread tap to clean the threads following the manufacturer's instructions. If thread damage is excessive, restore the threads with a steel thread insert.

4. After cleaning the combustion chamber, valve ports and spark plug thread hole, clean the entire head in solvent.

> *NOTE*
> *If the cylinder head was bead-blasted, clean the head first with solvent, and then with hot, soapy water. Residual grit that seats in small crevices and other areas can be hard to dislodge. Also, chase each exposed thread with a tap to remove grit trapped between the threads. Residual grit left in the engine will cause premature piston, ring and bearing wear.*

5. Examine the piston crown. The crown must not be worn or damaged. If the crown appears pecked or spongy-looking, also check the spark plug, valves and combustion chamber for aluminum deposits. If these deposits are found, the cylinder is suffering from excessive heat caused by a lean fuel mixture or preignition.

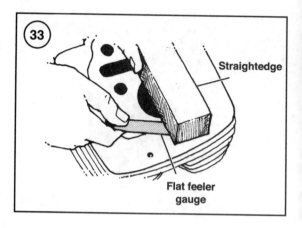

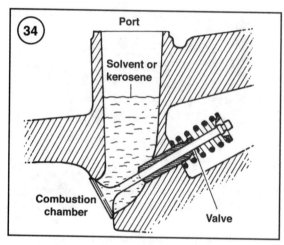

6. Inspect the carburetor intake tube for cracks or other damage that would allow unfiltered air to enter the engine.

7. Check the exhaust pipe studs for damage. If necessary, replace the studs (Chapter One).

8. Inspect the combustion chamber and exhaust port for cracks.

9. Place a straightedge across the gasket surface (**Figure 33**). Measure warp by inserting a feeler gauge between the straightedge and cylinder head at several locations. Measure warp between each set of bolt holes. **Table 2** specifies the maximum allowable warp. Warping or nicks in the cylinder head surface could cause an air leak and overheating. If the cylinder is warped, resurface or replace the cylinder head. Consult with a dealership or a machine shop for this type of work.

10. Service the valves as described in this chapter.

VALVES AND VALVE COMPONENTS

A complete valve job, consisting of reconditioning the valve seats and replacing the valve guides, requires specialized tools and experience. This section describes service procedures on checking the valve

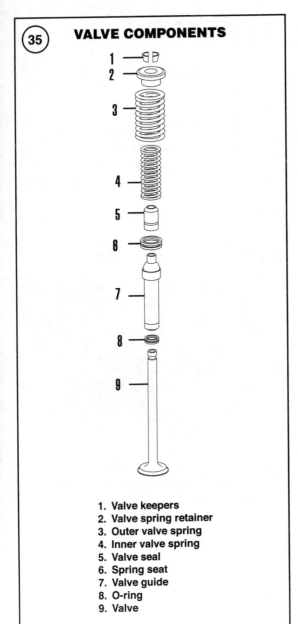

VALVE COMPONENTS

1. Valve keepers
2. Valve spring retainer
3. Outer valve spring
4. Inner valve spring
5. Valve seal
6. Spring seat
7. Valve guide
8. O-ring
9. Valve

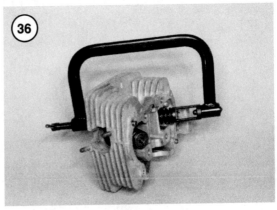

components for wear and how to determine what type of service is required. Refer all valve machining to a qualified machine shop.

A valve spring compressor designed for motorcycle applications is required to remove and install the valves.

Solvent Test

For proper engine operation, the valves must seal tightly against their seats. Any condition that prevents the valves from sealing properly can cause valve burning and reduced engine performance. Before removing the valves from the cyl-

inder head, perform the following to check valve sealing.

1. Remove the cylinder head (this chapter).
2. Support the cylinder so that the exhaust port faces up (**Figure 34**) and pour solvent or kerosene into the port. Then, check the combustion chamber for fluid leaking past each exhaust valve seat.
3. Repeat the solvent test for the intake port and the intake valves and seats.
4. If there is fluid leaking around a valve seat, the valve is not sealing properly on its seat. The following conditions can cause poor valve sealing:
   a. A bent valve stem.
   b. A worn or damaged valve seat (in cylinder head).
   c. A worn or damaged valve face.
   d. A crack in the combustion chamber.

Valve Removal

Refer to **Figure 35** when performing this procedure.
1. Remove the cylinder head (this chapter).

WARNING
Wear safety glasses or goggles when compressing the valve springs.

NOTE
Do not compress the springs any more than necessary to remove the keepers.

2. Compress the valve springs using a valve compressor tool (**Figure 36**). Remove the valve keepers and release the spring compression. Remove the valve compressor tool.
3. Remove the valve spring retainer (A, **Figure 37**) and valve springs (B).
4. Before removing the valve, remove any burrs from the valve stem (**Figure 38**). Otherwise the valve guide will be damaged during removal.
5. Remove the valve from the cylinder head.

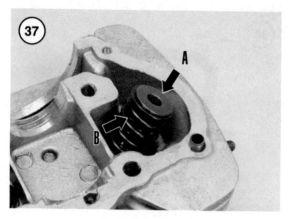

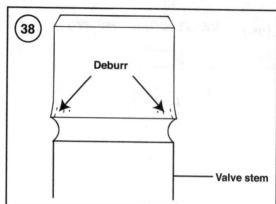

6. Remove the spring seats (A, **Figure 39**). There is a spring seat for the inner spring and the outer spring.

7. Pull the valve stem seal (B, **Figure 39**) off the valve guide and discard it.

> *CAUTION*
> *Keep all parts of each valve assembly together. Do not mix components.*

8. Repeat the procedure to remove the remaining valve.

Inspection

When measuring the valve components (**Figure 35**) in this section, compare the actual measurements to the specifications listed in **Table 2**. Replace parts that are out of specification or show damage as described in this section.

Refer to the troubleshooting chart in **Figure 40** when inspecting and troubleshooting the valves in this section.

1. Clean the valves in solvent. Do not gouge or damage the valve seating surface.

2. Inspect the contact surface (**Figure 41**) of each valve for burning. Minor roughness and pitting can be removed by lapping the valve (this section). Excessive unevenness in the contact surface is an indication that the valve is not serviceable.

3. Inspect the valve stems for wear and roughness. Measure the valve stem outside diameter for wear (**Figure 42**).

4. Remove all carbon and varnish from the valve guides with a stiff spiral wire brush before measuring wear.

> *NOTE*
> *If the required measuring tools are not available, go to Step 7.*

5. Measure each valve guide at its top, center and bottom inside diameter with a small hole gauge.

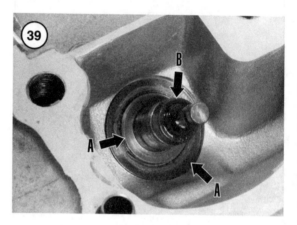

Then, measure the small hole gauge with a micrometer to determine the valve guide inside diameter.

6. Subtract the valve stem outside diameter measurement from the valve guide inside diameter measurement. The difference is the valve stem-to-guide clearance. Replace any guide or valve that is not within tolerance. Refer valve guide replacement to a dealership.

7. If a small hole gauge is not available, insert each valve in its guide. Hold the valve just slightly off its seat and rock it sideways (**Figure 43**). If the valve rocks more than slightly, the guide is probably worn. However, as a final check, take the cylinder head to a dealership and have the valve guides measured.

8. Check the inner and outer valve springs as follows:

    a. Check each valve spring for visible damage.

    b. Use a square and check each spring for distortion or tilt (**Figure 44**).

    c. Measure the valve spring free length with a caliper (**Figure 45**).

    d. Replace worn or damaged springs as a set.

9. Check the valve spring seats and valve keepers for cracks or other damage.

10. Inspect the valve seats (**Figure 46**) for burning, pitting, cracks, excessive wear or other damage. If worn or burned, they may be reconditioned as de-

VALVE TROUBLESHOOTING

| Valve deposits |

Check:
- Worn valve guide
- Carbon buildup from incorrect tuning
- Carbon buildup from incorrect carburetor adjustment
- Dirty or gummed fuel
- Dirty engine oil

| Valve sticking |

Check:
- Worn valve guide
- Bent valve stem
- Deposits collected on valve stem
- Valve burning or overheating

| Valve burning |

Check:
- Valve sticking
- Cylinder head warped
- Valve seat distorted
- Incorrect valve clearance
- Incorrect valve spring
- Valve spring worn
- Valve seat worn
- Carbon buildup in engine
- Engine ignition and/or carburetor adjustment incorrect

| Valve seat/face wear |

Check:
- Valve burning
- Incorrect valve clearance
- Abrasive material on valve face and seat

| Valve damage |

Check:
- Valve burning
- Incorrectly installed or serviced valve guides
- Incorrect valve clearance
- Incorrect valve, spring seat and retainer assembly
- Detonation caused by incorrect ignition and/or carburetor adjustment

4

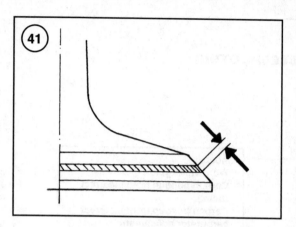

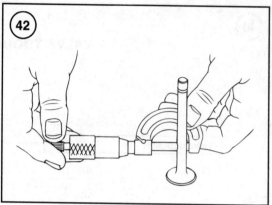

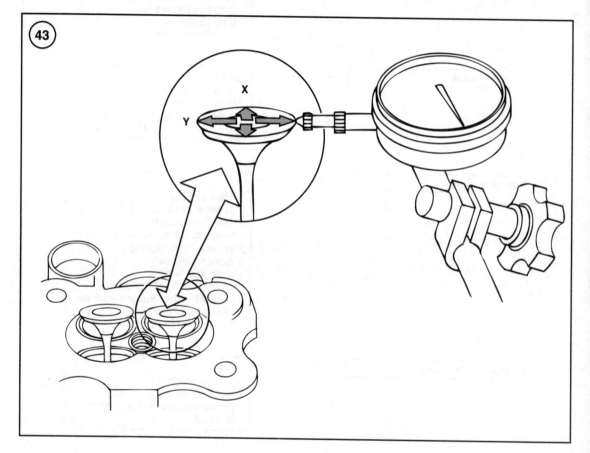

scribed in this chapter. Seats and valves in near-perfect condition can be reconditioned by lapping with fine carborundum paste. Check as follows:

a. Clean the valve seat and valve mating areas with contact cleaner.

b. Coat the valve seat with machinist's dye.

c. Install the valve into its guide and rotate it against its seat with a valve lapping tool. Refer to *Valve Lapping* (this section).

d. Lift the valve out of the guide and measure the seat width (**Figure 47**) with a caliper.

e. The seat width for intake and exhaust valves should measure within the specifications listed

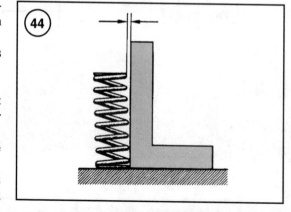

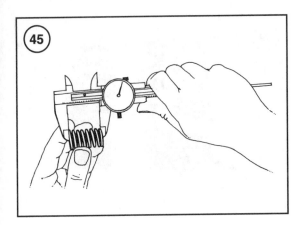

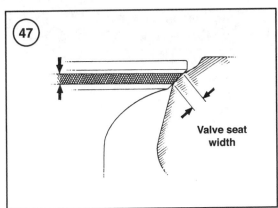

Valve seat
width

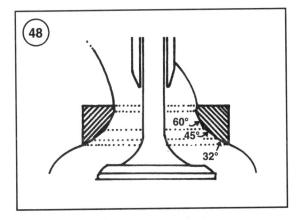

60°
45°
32°

in **Table 2** all the way around the seat. If the seat width exceeds the service limit, have a dealership machine the seats.

   f. Remove all machinist's blue dye from the seats and valves.

Valve Guide Replacement

Refer valve guide replacement to a machine shop. A valve guide reamer (Honda part No. 07984-098000D) may be used.

Valve Seat Reconditioning

The valve seats are an integral part of the cylinder head and cannot be replaced separately. Minor valve seat wear and damage can be repaired by regrinding. Refer this service to a dealership. If the necessary tools and expertise are available, refer to **Figure 48** for the valve seat grinding angles required. Refer to **Table 2** for valve seat width dimensions.

Valve Lapping

Valve lapping is a simple operation used to restore the valve seal without machining—if the amount of wear or distortion is not excessive.

This procedure should only be performed after determining that the valve seat width and outside diameter are within specification (this section).

1. Smear a light coating of fine-grade valve lapping compound on the valve face seating surface.

2. Insert the valve into the head.

3. Wet the suction cup of the lapping stick and stick it onto the head of the valve. Lap the valve to the seat by spinning the lapping stick in both directions. Every 5 to 10 seconds, rotate the valve in the valve seat. Continue this action until the mating surfaces on the valve and seat are smooth and equal in size.

4. Closely examine the valve seat in the cylinder head. It should be smooth and even with a smooth, polished seating ring.

5. Thoroughly clean the valves and cylinder head in solvent. Then, wash with hot soapy water to remove all lapping compound. Any compound left on the valves or the cylinder head will contaminate the engine oil and cause excessive wear and damage. After drying the cylinder head, lubricate the valve guides with engine oil to prevent rust.

6. After installing the valves into the cylinder, perform a solvent test to check the valve seat seal. If fluid leaks past the seat, remove the valve assembly and repeat the lapping procedure until there are no leaks. When there are no leaks, remove all valve sets and reclean the cylinder head assembly.

Valve Installation

1. Clean and dry all parts. If the valve seats were reground or lapped, or the valve guides replaced, thoroughly clean the valves and cylinder head in solvent. Then, wash with hot soapy water to remove all lapping and grinding compound. Any abrasive residue left on the valves or in the cylinder head will contaminate the engine oil and cause excessive wear and damage. After drying the cylinder head, lubricate the valve guides with engine oil to prevent rust.

2. Install the new valve seal (B, **Figure 39**) onto the valve guide and seat it into place.

3. Install the spring seats (A, **Figure 39**).

4. Coat the valve stem with molybdenum-disulfide paste, and then install the valve into the correct guide.

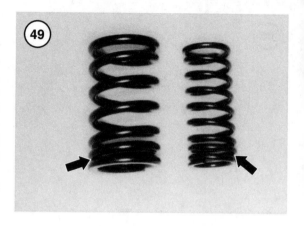

> *NOTE*
> *Install each valve spring so the end with coils closest together (**Figure 49**) is toward the cylinder head.*

5. Install the inner and outer valve springs.

6. Install the valve spring retainer.

> *WARNING*
> *Wear safety glasses or goggles when compressing the valve springs.*

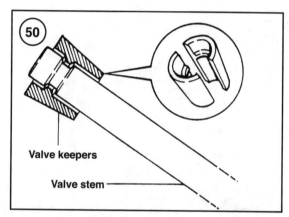

Valve keepers

Valve stem

7. Install the valve spring compressor (**Figure 36**). Push down on the valve spring retainer and compress the springs. Then, install the valve keepers (**Figure 50**). Release tension from the compressor and check that the keepers seat evenly around the end of the valve. Tap the end of the valve stem with a soft-faced hammer to ensure that the keepers are properly seated.

8. Repeat the installation procedure for the remaining valve.

9. After installing the cylinder head cover onto the engine, adjust the valve clearance (Chapter Three).

CAM CHAIN TENSIONER

Removal/Installation

> *CAUTION*
> *The cam chain tensioner is a non-return type. The internal push rod will not return to its original position once it has moved out, even the slightest amount. After the tensioner mounting bolts are loosened, the tensioner assembly must be **completely removed** and the pushrod reset. If the mounting bolts are loosened, do not simply retighten the mounting bolts. The pushrod has already moved out to an*

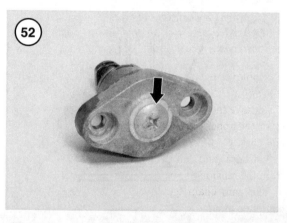

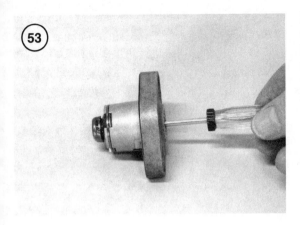

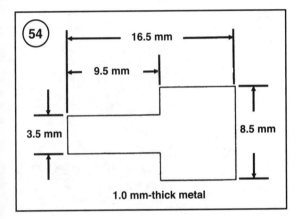

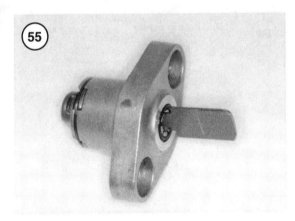

Inspect the housing and rod for damage. Replace the tensioner assembly if necessary.

5. Remove all gasket residue from the cam chain tensioner and cylinder mounting surfaces.

6A. Reset the tensioner on CRF230F models using the following procedure:

    a. Insert a small, flat-bladed screwdriver and turn the inner adjuster *clockwise* until the rod is fully retracted and locked (**Figure 53**).

    b. If the rod does not fully retract and lock, replace the tensioner.

> *NOTE*
> *Before installing the cam chain tensioner on CRF230L and CRF230M models, the tensioner must be locked in the retracted position using a stopper plate. A stopper plate may be fabricated from a piece of thin metal using the dimensions shown in **Figure 54**.*

6B. Reset the tensioner on CRF230L and CRF230M models using the following procedure:

    a. Use a narrow, flat-bladed screwdriver and turn the inner adjuster *clockwise* to retract the rod (**Figure 53**).

    b. Hold the rod in the retracted position.

    c. Remove the screwdriver and insert the stopper plate (**Figure 55**) into the grooves of the rod and housing to keep the spring tension locked.

7. Install a new gasket onto the tensioner.

8. Install the cam chain tensioner and the tensioner mounting bolts. Tighten the mounting bolts to 12 N•m (106 in.-lb.).

9A. On CRF230F models, turn the inner adjuster slightly counterclockwise to release the plunger.

> *NOTE*
> *The tensioner should "click" after removing the stopper plate, which indicates the rod has extended. If not, remove the tensioner and check tensioner operation.*

9B. On CRF230L and CRF230M models, remove the stopper plate from the tensioner body to allow the rod to extend.

10. Install a new, lubricated O-ring (**Figure 56**) into the center of the tensioner body.

11. Install the seal bolt on the tensioner and tighten it to 4 N•m (35 in.-lb.).

CYLINDER

Removal

1. Remove the cylinder head cover and cylinder head (this chapter).

extended position, and it will exert excessive pressure on the chain leading to costly engine damage.

1. Remove the starter (Chapter Ten or Chapter Eleven).

2. Remove the bolts (A, **Figure 51**) securing the cam chain tensioner (B). Remove the cam chain tensioner and gasket.

3. Unscrew and remove the seal bolt (**Figure 52**) from the tensioner.

4. The cam chain tensioner is available only as a complete assembly. Do not attempt to disassemble it.

2. Remove the front cam chain guide (A, **Figure 32**).

CAUTION
The cooling fins are fragile and easily
damaged.

3. Loosen the cylinder by tapping around the perimeter with a rubber or plastic mallet.

4. Pull the cylinder straight up and off the piston. Pass the camshaft chain wire through the opening in the cylinder. Resecure the wire to the exterior of the crankcase.

5. Install a piston holding fixture (A, **Figure 57**) under the piston. This can be a commercial tool or a homemade device as shown in **Figure 58**.

6. If necessary, remove the piston (this chapter).

7. Remove and discard the cylinder base gasket (B, **Figure 57**).

8. If necessary, remove the two dowel pins (C, **Figure 57**).

9. Cover the crankcase opening to prevent objects from falling into the crankcase.

Inspection

The cylinder is plated and oversize pistons are not available. Major damage requires cylinder replacement. If the cylinder is only slightly damaged, refer to a dealership for possible repair recommendations.

Refer to **Table 2** when measuring the cylinder block in this section.

1. Remove all gasket residue from the top and bottom cylinder block gasket surfaces.

2. Wash the cylinder block (**Figure 59**) in solvent. Dry with compressed air.

3. Check the dowel pin holes for cracks or other damage.

4. Check the cylinder block for warping with a feeler gauge and straightedge as shown in **Figure 60**. Measure at several places on the cylinder block and compare results to **Table 2**. If out of specification, refer service to a dealership.

5. Measure the cylinder bore using a bore gauge or inside micrometer (**Figure 61**) at the points shown in **Figure 62**. Measure at three different depths along two separate axes—aligned with the piston pin, and at 90° to the pin. Use the maximum bore dimension to determine cylinder wear. Average the other measurements to determine taper and out-of-round. If any dimension is out of specification (**Table 2**), install a new cylinder, piston and ring assembly.

6. If the cylinder is not worn past the service limit, check the bore for scratches or gouges. If damaged, install a new cylinder.

7. If the cylinder is glazed, use a suitable deglazing tool to recondition the cylinder.

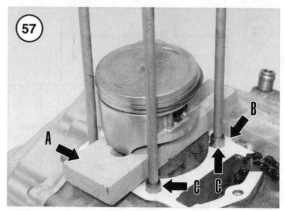

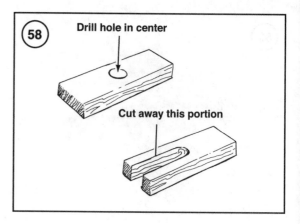

Drill hole in center

Cut away this portion

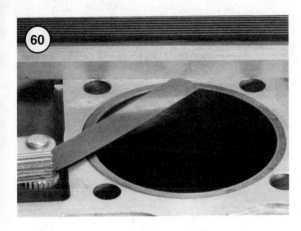

60

CAUTION
A combination of soap and hot water is the only solution that will completely clean cylinder walls. Solvent and kerosene cannot wash fine grit out of cylinder crevices. Any grit remaining in the cylinder will cause premature engine wear.

8. After servicing the cylinder, wash the bore in hot soapy water. This is the only way to clean the cylinder wall of the fine grit material left from the bore or honing job. After washing the cylinder wall, run a clean white cloth through it. The cylinder must be free of all grit and other residue. If the rag is dirty, rewash the cylinder wall again and recheck with the white cloth. Repeat until the cloth comes out clean. When the cylinder is clean, lubricate it with engine oil to prevent the cylinder liner from rusting.

9. Make sure the oil passage (**Figure 63**) adjoining the cylinder stud is clean and unobstructed.

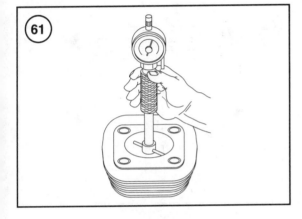

61

Installation

1. Remove any covering(s) from the crankcase opening(s).

2. Check that the top surface of the crankcase and the bottom surface of the cylinder are clean before installing a new base gasket.

3. Apply a small amount of liquid sealant to the mating surfaces of the crankcase halves in the area where the cylinder base gasket fits. This will help prevent an oil leak.

4. Install the dowel pins (C, **Figure 57**) into the holes in the crankcase.

5. Install a new cylinder base gasket (B, **Figure 57**). Make sure all holes align.

6. Install a piston holding fixture under the piston.

7. Make sure the end gaps of the piston rings are positioned correctly as described in this chapter. Lightly oil the piston rings and the inside of the cylinder bore with engine oil.

8. Carefully feed the camshaft chain and wire up through the opening in the cylinder and resecure the wire to the engine.

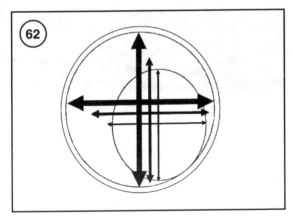

62

NOTE
It is easier to install the cylinder over the piston by compressing the rings first with a ring compressor. As the cylinder is installed over the piston, the rings pass into the cylinder compressed. Then, the rings expand out once they are free of the ring compressor. A hose clamp works well for this. Before using a ring compressor or hose clamp, lubricate its ring contact side with en-

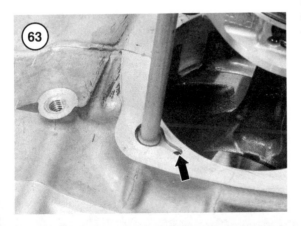

63

gine oil. When using a ring compressor or hose clamp, do not overtighten. The tool should be able to slide freely as the cylinder pushes against it.

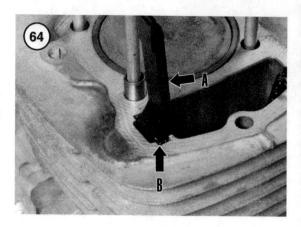

9. While compressing the piston rings, slide the cylinder down over the piston. If used, remove the ring compressor.

10. Remove the piston holding fixture and slide the cylinder down into place on the crankcase.

11. Make sure the cylinder is completely seated on the crankcase.

12. Install the front cam chain guide (A, **Figure 64**). Make sure the bottom end properly fits into the guide holder cast into the crankcase. The camshaft chain guide pin must fit into the notch (B, **Figure 64**) in the cylinder.

13. Install the cylinder head, camshaft and cylinder head cover (this chapter).

14. Follow the *Engine Break-in* procedure (Chapter Five) if the cylinder, piston or piston rings were replaced.

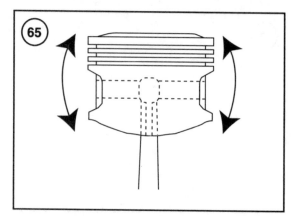

PISTON, PISTON PIN AND PISTON RINGS

Piston Removal

1. Remove the cylinder (this chapter).

2. Cover openings in the crankcase below the piston to prevent the piston pin circlips from falling into the crankcase.

3. Before removing the piston, hold the rod and rock the piston (**Figure 65**). Any rocking motion (do not confuse with the normal sliding motion) indicates wear on the piston pin, rod bore, pin bore, or a combination of all three.

WARNING
Wear safety glasses or goggles when removing the piston pin circlips.

NOTE
Discard the piston circlips. Install new circlips during reassembly.

4. Remove the circlips from the piston pin bore grooves (**Figure 66**).

5. Push out the piston pin (**Figure 67**) by hand. If the pin is tight, use a homemade tool (**Figure 68**) to remove it. Do not drive the piston pin out as the force may damage the piston pin, connecting rod or piston.

6. Lift the piston off the connecting rod.

7. Inspect the piston (this chapter).

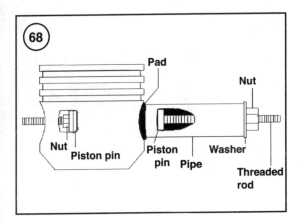

Piston Inspection

1. Remove the piston rings (this section).
2. Clean the carbon from the piston crown (**Figure 69**) with a soft scraper. Large carbon accumulations reduce piston cooling and result in detonation and piston damage.
3. After cleaning, examine the piston crown. The crown must show no signs of wear or damage. If the crown appears pecked or spongy-looking, also check the spark plug, valves and combustion chamber for aluminum deposits. If these deposits are found, the engine is overheating.
4. Examine each ring groove (**Figure 70**) for burrs, dented edges or other damage. Pay particular attention to the top compression ring groove as it usually wears more than the others. Because the oil rings are bathed in oil, their rings and grooves wear less than compression rings and their grooves. If there is evidence of oil ring groove wear or if the oil ring is tight and difficult to remove, the piston skirt may have collapsed due to excessive heat. Replace the piston.
5. Check the piston oil control holes for carbon or oil sludge buildup. Clean the holes with wire.

> *CAUTION*
> *Do not clean the piston skirt using a wire brush.*

> *NOTE*
> *If the piston skirt is worn or scuffed unevenly from side-to-side, the connecting rod may be bent or twisted.*

6. Inspect the piston skirt (**Figure 71**) for cracks or other damage. If the piston shows signs of partial seizure (bits of aluminum on the piston skirt), replace the piston.
7. Check the piston circlip grooves for wear, cracks or other damage. If a circlip groove is worn, replace the piston.
8. Measure piston-to-cylinder clearance as described in *Piston Clearance* (this section). Compare the results with the specification in **Table 2**.

Piston Pin Inspection

Refer to **Table 2** when measuring the piston pin components in this section. Replace parts that are out of specification or show damage.
1. Clean and dry the piston pin.
2. Inspect the piston pin for chrome flaking, cracks or signs of heat damage.
3. Lubricate the piston pin and install it in the piston. Slowly rotate the piston pin and check for excessive play as shown in **Figure 72**. Determine piston pin clearance by performing the following steps:

a. Measure the piston pin bore diameter (**Figure 73**) in the piston.

b. If within specification, record the dimension and continue with the procedure.

4. Measure the piston pin outside diameter (**Figure 74**). If within specification, record the dimension and continue with the procedure.

5. Subtract the piston pin bore diameter measurement from the piston pin outside diameter measurement to determine the piston-to-piston pin clearance (**Table 2**). Replace the piston and/or piston pin if the clearance is excessive.

Connecting Rod Small End Inspection

1. Inspect the connecting rod small end (**Figure 75**) for cracks or signs of heat damage.

2. Measure the connecting rod bore diameter (**Figure 75**) with a telescoping gauge. Measure the telescoping gauge with a micrometer (**Figure 76**, typical) and compare the measurement with the dimension in **Table 2**. If the bore wear is excessive, replace the crankshaft assembly. The connecting rod cannot be replaced separately.

Piston Clearance

1. Make sure the piston and cylinder walls are clean and dry.

2. Measure the cylinder bore (this chapter). Record the bore diameter measurement.

3. Measure the piston diameter with a micrometer at a right angle to the piston pin bore (**Figure 77**). Measure 10 mm (0.4 in.) from the bottom edge of the piston skirt. Record the piston diameter measurement.

4. Subtract the piston diameter from the largest bore diameter; the difference is piston-to-cylinder clearance. If clearance exceeds the service limit in **Table 2**, refer to Cylinder: Inspection in this chapter for service options.

Piston Installation

1. Install the piston rings onto the piston (this section).

2. Coat the connecting rod bore, piston pin and piston with engine oil.

3. Slide the piston pin into the piston until its end is flush with the piston pin boss (**Figure 78**).

4. Place the piston onto the connecting rod so the IN mark (**Figure 79**) on the piston crown faces toward the intake side of the engine.

5. Align the piston pin with the hole in the connecting rod. Push the piston pin (**Figure 67**) through the connecting rod and into the other side of the piston and center it in the piston.

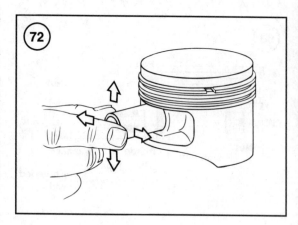

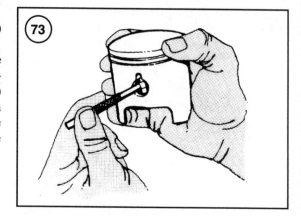

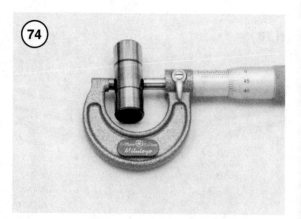

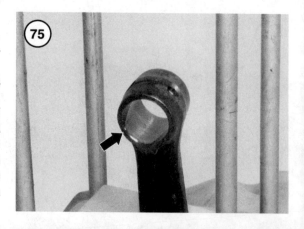

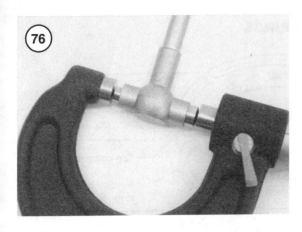

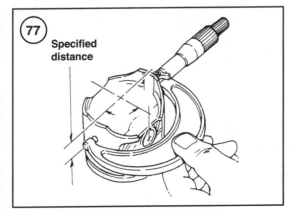

Specified distance

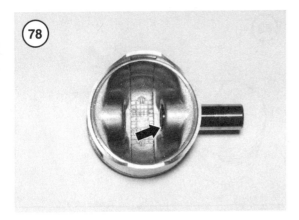

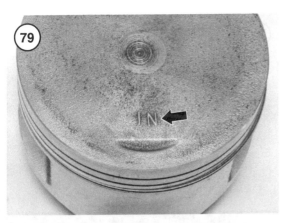

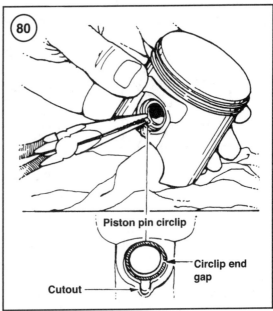

Piston pin circlip

Circlip end gap

Cutout

6. Cover the crankcase openings.

WARNING
Wear safety glasses or goggles when installing the piston pin circlips.

7. Install new piston pin circlips (**Figure 66**) in both ends of the piston pin bore. Make sure the circlips seat in the piston clip grooves completely. Turn the circlips so that their end gaps do not align with the cutout in the piston (**Figure 80**).
8. Remove any covering from the crankcase opening.
9. Install the cylinder (this chapter).

Piston Ring Inspection and Removal

The piston is equipped with a three-ring type piston and ring assembly (**Figure 81**). The top and second rings are compression rings. The lower ring is an oil control ring assembly (consisting of two ring rails and an expander spacer).

WARNING
The edges of all piston rings are very sharp. Be careful when handling them to avoid cut fingers.

1. Measure the side clearance of each compression ring in its groove with a flat feeler gauge (**Figure 82**) and compare with the specifications in **Table 2**. If the clearance is greater than specified, replace the rings. If the clearance is still excessive with the new rings, replace the piston.

NOTE
Store the rings in order of removal.

PISTON RINGS

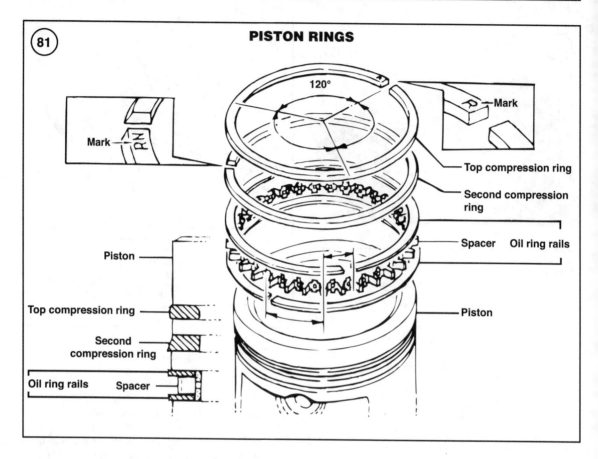

2. Remove the compression rings with a ring expander tool (**Figure 83**) or spread the ring ends by hand using thumbs (**Figure 84**) and lift the rings out of their grooves and up over the piston.

3. Remove the oil ring assembly (**Figure 85**) by first removing the upper (A, **Figure 86**), and then the lower (B) ring rails. Then, remove the expander spacer (C, **Figure 86**).

> *CAUTION*
> *Do not remove aluminum material from the ring grooves as this will increase ring side clearance.*

> *NOTE*
> *When cleaning the piston ring grooves, use the same type of ring that operates in the groove. Using a ring that is dissimilar to the groove will damage the groove.*

4. Using a broken piston ring, remove carbon and oil residue from the piston ring grooves (**Figure 87**).

5. Inspect the ring grooves for burrs, nicks or broken or cracked lands. Replace the piston if necessary.

> *NOTE*
> *When measuring the oil control ring end gap, measure the upper and lower*

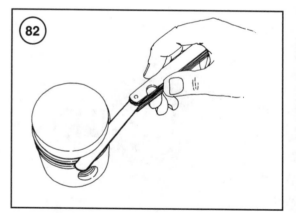

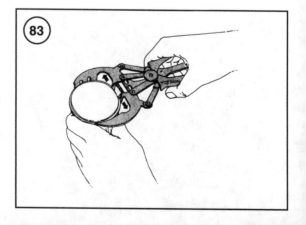

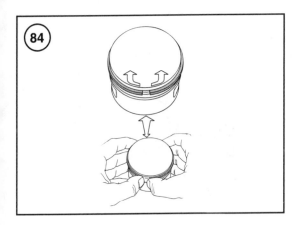

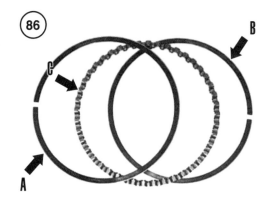

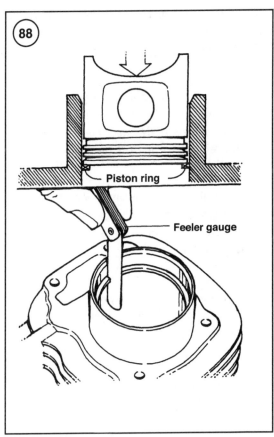

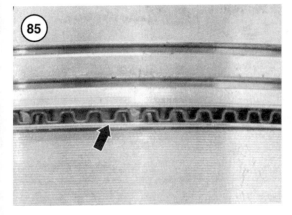

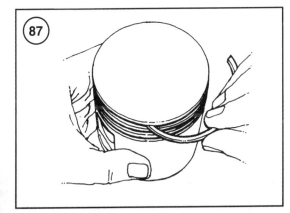

ring rail end gaps only. Do not measure the expander spacer (C, Figure 86).

6. Check the end gap of each ring. To check, insert the ring into the bottom of the cylinder bore and square it with the cylinder wall by tapping it with the piston (**Figure 88**). Measure the end gap with a feeler gauge (**Figure 88**). Compare the end gap dimension with **Table 2**. Replace the rings if the gap is too large. If the gap on the new ring is smaller than specified, hold a fine-cut file in a vise. File the ends of the ring to enlarge the gap.

7. Roll each ring around its piston groove (**Figure 89**) to check for binding. Repair minor binding with a fine-cut file.

Piston Ring Installation

1. Hone or deglaze the cylinder before installing new piston rings. This machining process will help the new rings seat in the cylinder. If necessary, refer this job to a dealership or motorcycle repair shop. After honing, measure the end gap of each ring and compare to the dimensions in **Table 2**.

2. If the cylinder was honed, clean the cylinder as described in this chapter.

3. Clean the piston and rings in solvent. Dry with compressed air.

4. Install the piston rings as follows:

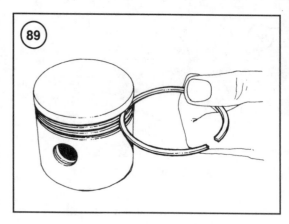

NOTE
*Use a ring expander tool (**Figure 83**) or spread the ring ends by hand with thumbs (**Figure 84**), and then slip the rings over the top of the piston to install them.*

a. Install the oil ring assembly into the bottom ring groove. Install the expander spacer first, and then install the bottom and top ring rails (**Figure 85**).

NOTE
*The top and second compression rings are different. Refer to **Figure 81** to identify the rings.*

b. Install the compression rings with the marks facing up (**Figure 81**).

c. Install the second compression ring.

d. Install the top compression ring.

5. Check that the piston rings rotate freely. Position the end gaps around the piston as shown in Figure 81.

Table 1 ENGINE SPECIFICATIONS

Engine	4-stroke, overhead camshaft engine
Displacement	223 cc (13.6 cu.-in.)
Bore	65.5 mm (2.58 in.)
Stroke	66.2 mm (2.61 in.)
Compression ratio	9.0:1
Cooling system	Air-cooled
Valve timing*	
CRF230F models	
Intake valve opens	10° BTDC
Intake valve closes	40° ABDC
Exhaust valve opens	35° BBDC
Exhaust valve closes	10° ATDC
CRF230L and CRF230M models	
Intake valve opens	5° BTDC
Intake valve closes	30° ABDC
Exhaust valve opens	35° BBDC
Exhaust valve closes	5° ATDC
*Specified at 1 mm (0.039 in.) lift.	

Table 2 ENGINE TOP END SERVICE SPECIFICATIONS

	New mm (in.)	Service limit mm (in.)
Camshaft lobe height		
CRF230F models		
Intake	31.610-31.690 (1.2445-1.2476)	31.30 (1.232)
Exhaust	31.452-31.532 (1.2383-1.2414)	31.20 (1.228)
CRF230L and CRF230M models		
Intake	31.372-31.612 (1.2531-1.2445)	31.3 (1.23)
Exhaust	31.212-31.452 (1.2288-1.2382)	31.0 (1.22)
Connecting rod small end inside diameter	15.010-15.028 (0.5909-0.5917)	15.06 (0.593)
Connecting rod-to-piston pin clearance	0.010-0.034 (0.0004-0.0013)	0.10 (0.004)
Cylinder bore diameter (standard bore)	65.500-65.510 (2.5787-2.5791)	65.60 (2.583)
Cylinder head warp limit	– –	0.10 (0.004)
Cylinder out-of-round limit	– –	0.10 (0.004)
Cylinder taper limit	–	0.10 (0.004)
Cylinder warp limit	–	0.10 (0.004)
Exhaust pipe retaining stud height		
CRF230F models	–	25 (1.0)
CRF230L and CRF230M models	–	20 (0.8)
Piston diameter (standard piston)	65.470-65.490 (2.5776-2.5783)	65.40 (2.575)
Piston diameter measuring point	Refer to text	–
Piston-to-cylinder clearance	0.010-0.040 (0.0004-0.0016)	0.20 (0.008)
Piston pin bore diameter	15.002-15.008 (0.5906-0.5909)	15.04 (0.592)
Piston pin outside diameter	14.994-15.000 (0.5903-0.5906)	14.96 (0.589)
Piston-to-piston pin clearance	0.002-0.014 (0.00008-0.0006)	0.02 (0.0008)
Piston ring end gap		
Top compression ring	0.20-0.35 (0.008-0.014)	0.5 (0.02)
Second compression ring	0.35-0.50 (0.014-0.020)	0.65 (0.026)
Oil ring (side rails)	0.20-0.70 (0.008-0.028)	0.9 (0.04)
Piston ring side clearance		
Top compression ring		
CRF230F models	0.025-0.060 (0.0010-0.0024)	0.09 (0.004)
CRF230L and CRF230M models	0.010-0.045 (0.0004-0.0018)	0.09 (0.004)
Second compression ring	0.015-0.050 (0.0006-0.0020)	0.08 (0.003)
Rocker arm bore inside diameter	12.000-12.018 (0.4724-0.4732)	12.05 (0.474)
Rocker arm shaft outside diameter	11.966-11.984 (0.4711-0.4718)	11.93 (0.470)
Rocker arm-to-shaft clearance	0.016-0.052 (0.0006-0.0020)	0.08 (0.003)

(continued)

Table 2 ENGINE SERVICE SPECIFICATIONS (continued)

	New mm (in.)	Service limit mm (in.)
Valve clearance	See Chapter 3	–
Valve guide inside diameter	5.475-5.485 (0.2156-0.2159)	5.50 (0.217)
Valve seat width	1.1-1.3 (0.04-0.05)	1.5 (0.06)
Exhaust	5.430-5.445 (0.2146-0.2152)	5.40 (0.213)
Valve stem-to-guide clearance		
Intake	0.010-0.035 (0.0004-0.0014)	0.08 (0.003)
Exhaust	0.030-0.055 (0.0012-0.0022)	0.10 (0.004)
Valve spring free length		
Inner	39.2 (1.54)	38.0 (1.50)
Outer	44.9 (1.77)	43.5 (1.71)
Valve stem diameter		
Intake	5.450-5.465 (0.2589-0.2594)	5.42 (0.213)

Table 3 ENGINE TOP END TORQUE SPECIFICATIONS

	N•m	in.-lb.	ft.-lb.
Cam chain tensioner			
Mounting bolts	12	106	–
Seal bolt	4	35	–
Cam sprocket retaining bolts	12	106	–
Crankshaft hole cap	8	71	–
Cylinder head Allen bolt	10	89	–
Cylinder head cover			
Cap nuts			
CRF230F models	26	–	19
CRF230L and CRF230M models	27	–	20
Flange bolts	12	106	–
Exhaust (CRF230F models)			
Muffler clamp bolt	20	–	15
Muffler mounting bolts	26	–	19
Pipe retaining nuts	20	–	15
Exhaust (CRF230L and CRF230M models)			
Muffler clamp bolt	20	–	15
Muffler mounting bolts	26.5	–	20
Pipe retaining nuts	10	89	–
Rear cam chain guide retaining bolt	10	89	–
Timing hole cap			
CRF230F models	6	53	–
CRF230L and CRF230M models	10	89	–

CHAPTER FIVE

ENGINE LOWER END

This chapter describes service procedures for the engine lower end. Engine removal and installation procedures are also included.

Specifications are located in **Tables 1-3** at the end of this chapter.

SERVICING ENGINE IN FRAME

The following components can be serviced while the engine is installed in the frame:

1. Clutch (Chapter Six).
2. External shift mechanism (Chapter Six).
3. Starter clutch and flywheel (this chapter).
4. Starter (Chapter Ten or Chapter Eleven).
5. Carburetor assembly (Chapter Eight or Chapter Nine).
6. Oil pump (this chapter).
7. Alternator (Chapter Ten or Chapter Eleven).

ENGINE REMOVAL/INSTALLATION (CRF230F MODELS)

1. Support the motorcycle securely.
2. Drain the engine oil (Chapter Three).
3. Remove the skid plate (Chapter Seventeen).
4. Remove both side covers and the seat (Chapter Seventeen).
5. Disconnect the negative battery cable from the battery (Chapter Ten).
6. Remove the footpegs (Chapter Seventeen). Remove the shift pedal.
7. Remove the exhaust system (Chapter Four).
8. Remove the carburetor (Chapter Eight).
9. Disconnect the spark plug lead and secure it out of the way.
10. Detach the drive sprocket and chain from the engine (Chapter Twelve).
11. Detach the rear brake return spring (**Figure 1**).
12. Remove the rear brake adjuster (**Figure 2**). Allow the rear brake pedal to drop down.
13. Remove the two bolts (A, **Figure 3**) that secure the clutch cable holder (B) to the crankcase cover. Disconnect the clutch cable from the clutch release lever (C, **Figure 3**).
14. Slide back the rubber boot (A, **Figure 4**) on the starter battery cable connector.
15. Disconnect the starter battery cable from the starter terminal (B, **Figure 4**).
16. Remove the bolt (C, **Figure 4**) securing the ground wire terminal to the starter.
17. Detach the breather hose (D, **Figure 4**) from the engine.
18. Detach the clips (**Figure 5**) that secure the alternator and exciter wires.
19. Disconnect the alternator connector (A, **Figure 6**) and the exciter wire connector (B).
20. Verify that all engine wiring has been disconnected from the frame.
21. Place tape or other material on the frame to protect it and the engine.

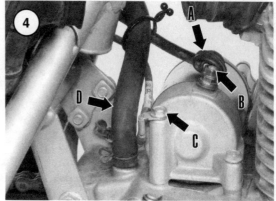

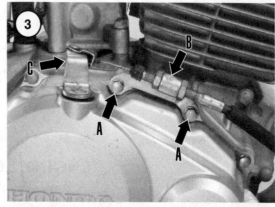

CAUTION
Continually adjust jack pressure during engine removal and installation to prevent damage to the mounting bolt threads and hardware.

22. Place a suitable size jack, with a piece of wood to protect the crankcase, under the engine. Apply a small amount of jack pressure up against the engine.

23. Remove the rubber caps (**Figure 7**) on the upper engine hanger bolts.

24. Remove the upper engine mounting bolt (A, **Figure 8**).

25. Remove the hanger bolts and nuts, and then remove the hanger plates (B, **Figure 8**).

26. Remove the front, upper engine mounting bolt (A, **Figure 9**).

27. Remove the bolts securing the front hanger plates (B, **Figure 9**), and then remove the hanger plates.

28. Remove the front, lower engine mounting bolt (A, **Figure 10**). Note the spacer (B, **Figure 10**) on the right side of the engine.

29. Remove the rear, upper engine mounting bolt (A, **Figure 11**).

30. Remove the bolts securing the rear hanger plate (B, **Figure 11**) and remove the hanger plate.

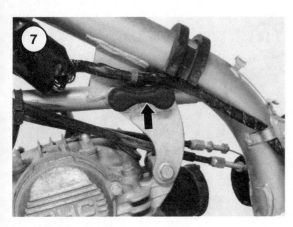

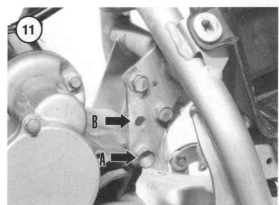

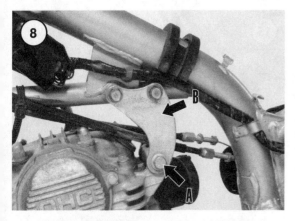

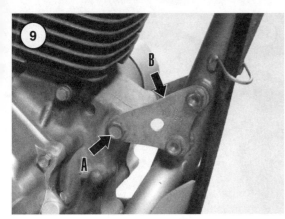

31. Remove the rear, lower engine mounting bolt (**Figure 12**).

32. Remove the engine from the left side of the frame. Take it to a workbench for further disassembly, if required.

33. Install by reversing the removal steps. Note the following:

    a. Install all engine mounting hardware loosely before starting the final tightening of the bolts.

    b. Be sure to install the spacer (B, **Figure 10**) on the right side of the engine when installing the lower front engine mounting bolt.

    c. The front hanger plates (B, **Figure 9**) are marked R and L to indicate installation on right or left side of frame.

    d. Note that each upper hanger plate is identified for its correct position upon reinstallation.

    e. Tighten the 8-mm engine mounting bolts and nuts to 34 N•m (25 ft.-lb.). Tighten the 10-mm engine mounting bolts and nuts to 59 N•m (43 ft.-lb.).

    f. Fill the engine with the recommended type and quantity of oil (Chapter Three).

    g. Adjust the clutch and shift pedal (Chapter Three).

    h. Adjust the rear brake (Chapter Three).

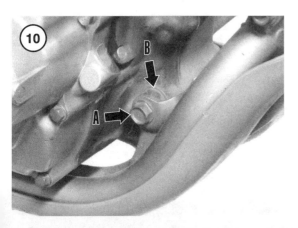

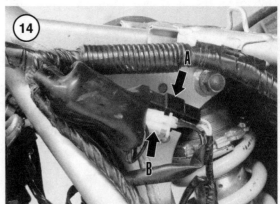

ENGINE REMOVAL/INSTALLATION
(CRF230L AND CRF230M MODELS)

1. Support the motorcycle securely.
2. Drain the engine oil (Chapter Three).
3. Remove both side covers and the seat (Chapter Seventeen).
4. Remove the fuel tank (Chapter Nine).
5. Remove the battery case (Chapter Eleven).
6. Remove the exhaust system (Chapter Four).
7. Remove the carburetor (Chapter Nine).
8. Remove the purge control valve (PCV) and canister (Chapter Nine).
9. Disconnect the spark plug lead and tie it up out of the way.
10. Detach the drive sprocket and chain from the engine (Chapter Twelve).
11. Detach the wires from the retaining clips (**Figure 13**).
12. Disconnect the black alternator connector (A, **Figure 14**) and white crankshaft position sensor connector (B).
13. Slide back the rubber boot (A, **Figure 15**) on the starter battery cable connector.
14. Disconnect the starter battery cable from the starter terminal (B, **Figure 15**).
15. Remove the bolt (C, **Figure 15**) securing the ground wire terminal to the starter.
16. Detach the breather hose (D, **Figure 15**) from the engine.
17. Remove the retaining bolts, and then detach the air supply tube (**Figure 16**) from the engine.
18. Rotate the clutch cable adjuster (A, **Figure 17**) to increase cable slack. Detach the cable from the holder, and then disconnect the clutch cable from the clutch release lever (B, **Figure 17**).
19. Remove the rubber cover (**Figure 18**) by disengaging the cover from the upper hook.
20. Verify that all engine wiring has been disconnected from the frame.
21. Place tape or other material on the frame to protect it and the engine.

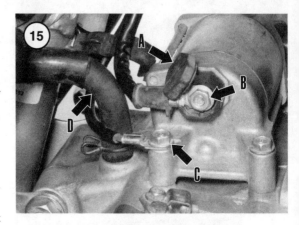

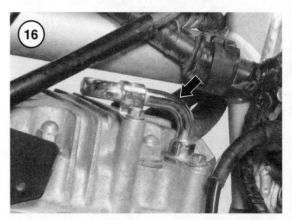

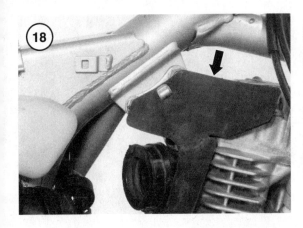

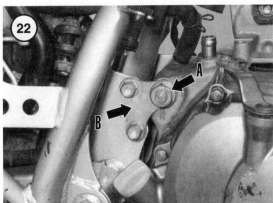

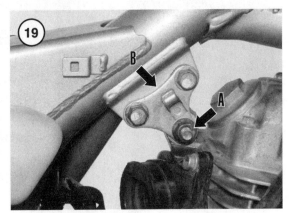

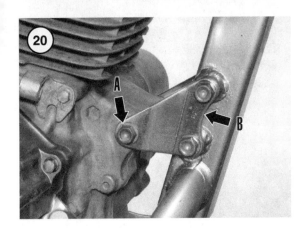

CAUTION
Continually adjust jack pressure during engine removal and installation to prevent damage to the mounting bolt threads and hardware.

22. Place a suitable size jack, with a piece of wood to protect the crankcase, under the engine. Apply a small amount of jack pressure up against the engine.

23. Remove the upper engine mounting bolt (A, **Figure 19**).

24. Remove the upper engine hanger bolts and nuts, and then remove the hanger plates (B, **Figure 19**).

25. Remove the front, upper engine mounting bolt (A, **Figure 20**).

26. Remove the front hanger bolts and nuts, and then remove the hanger plates (B, **Figure 20**).

27. Remove the front, lower engine mounting bolt (A, **Figure 21**). Note the spacer (B, **Figure 21**) on the right side of the engine.

28. Remove the rear, upper engine mounting bolt (A, **Figure 22**).

29. Remove the bolts securing the rear hanger plate (B, **Figure 22**), and then remove the hanger plate.

30. Remove the rear, lower mounting bolt (**Figure 23**).

31. Remove the engine from the right side of the frame. Take it to a workbench for further disassembly, if required.

32. Install by reversing the removal steps. Note the following:

    a. Install all engine mounting hardware loosely before starting the final tightening of the bolts.

    b. Be sure to install the spacer (B, **Figure 21**) on the right side of the engine when installing the front, lower mounting bolt.

    c. Tighten the 8-mm mounting bolts and nuts to 34 N•m (25 ft.-lb.). Tighten the 10-mm mounting bolts and nuts to 64 N•m (47 ft.-lb.).

    d. Fill the engine with the recommended type and quantity of oil (Chapter Three).

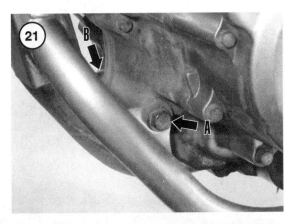

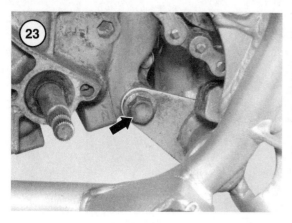

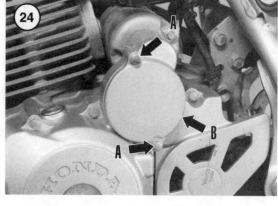

e. Adjust the clutch (Chapter Three).

STARTER GEAR

Removal/Inspection/Installation

1. Remove the bolts (A, **Figure 24**) securing the starter gear cover and remove the cover (B).
2. Remove the shaft (A, **Figure 25**) and gear (B).
3. Inspect the gear and shaft for abnormal wear or tooth damage. Replace if necessary.
4. Installation is the reverse of the removal steps. Note the following:
    a. Lubricate the shaft and gear with engine oil.
    b. Install a new O-ring onto the cover. Lubricate the O-ring.
    c. Tighten the cover bolts securely.

LEFT CRANKCASE COVER
(CRF230F MODELS)

Removal/Installation

1. Remove the drive sprocket cover (Chapter Twelve).
2. Remove the left side cover (Chapter Seventeen).
3. Move back the rubber boot, and then disconnect the exciter coil (A, **Figure 26**) and alternator (B) connectors.
4. Remove the starter gear (this chapter).
5. Disconnect the wire end (**Figure 27**) from the neutral switch.
6. Following a crossing pattern, loosen and remove the bolts securing the left crankcase cover (**Figure 28**).
7. Remove the cover. Do not lose the locating dowels (**Figure 29**).
8. Remove the left crankcase cover gasket.
9. Reverse the removal steps for installation. Note the following:

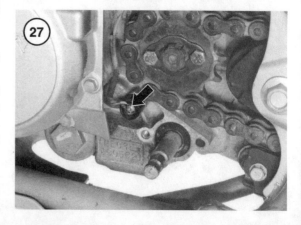

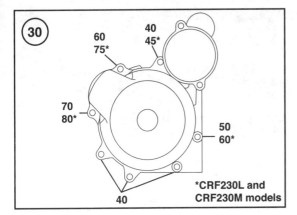

40
40*
45*
60
75*
70
80*
50
60*

*CRF230L and CRF230M models

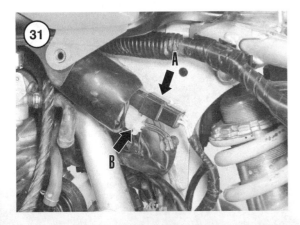

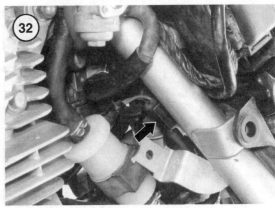

a. Install a new O-ring onto the end of the starter. Lubricate the O-ring.
b. Make sure the locating dowels (**Figure 29**) are in place.
c. Install a new gasket.
d. Note the bolt lengths in **Figure 30** and install the cover bolts.
e. Following a crossing pattern, tighten the cover bolts securely.

LEFT CRANKCASE COVER (CRF230L AND CRF230M MODELS)

Removal/Installation

1. Remove the drive sprocket cover (Chapter Twelve).
2. Remove the battery case (Chapter Eleven).
3. Disconnect the alternator connector (A, **Figure 31**) and crankshaft position (CKP) sensor connector (B).
4. Remove the alternator wires from the wire clamps.
5. Remove the starter gear (this chapter).
6. Disconnect the wire connector (**Figure 32**) from the neutral switch.
7. Remove the bolts securing the charcoal canister bracket (A, **Figure 33**). Move the canister (B, **Figure 33**) and bracket (A) out of the way.
8. Following a crossing pattern, remove the bolts securing the left crankcase cover (**Figure 34**).
9. Remove the cover. Do not lose the locating dowels (**Figure 35**).
10. Remove the gasket.
11. Reverse the removal steps for installation. Note the following:
    a. Install a new O-ring onto the end of the starter. Lubricate the O-ring.
    b. Make sure the locating dowels (**Figure 35**) are in place.
    c. Install a new gasket.

d. Note the bolt lengths in **Figure 30** and install the bolts.

e. Following a crossing pattern, tighten the cover bolts securely.

FLYWHEEL AND STARTER CLUTCH

Tool

A flywheel puller (Honda part No. 07733-0020001 or 07933-2160000), or its equivalent, is required to remove the flywheel from the crankshaft.

Flywheel Removal

1. Remove the left crankcase cover (this chapter).

2. Remove the starter idler gear shaft (A, **Figure 36**) and gear (B).

3. Hold the flywheel using a strap wrench (**Figure 37**).

4. Remove the bolt (**Figure 38**) and washer securing the flywheel.

> *CAUTION*
> *Do not try to remove the flywheel without a puller; doing so will damage the engine and/or flywheel. If a puller is not available, have a dealership remove the flywheel.*

> *NOTE*
> *Apply grease to the puller threads and the tip of the puller stem.*

5. Screw in the flywheel puller (**Figure 39**) until it stops.

> *CAUTION*
> *If the flywheel is difficult to remove, strike the puller with a hammer a few times. The shock may break it loose. Do*

5

not force the puller as the threads may strip out of the flywheel. Take the motorcycle to a dealership and have the flywheel removed.

6. Turn the flywheel puller with a wrench until the flywheel separates from the crankshaft.

7. Remove the flywheel (**Figure 40**) and remove the puller from the flywheel.

NOTE
*When removing the flywheel the starter driven gear (**Figure 41**) may remain on the crankshaft.*

8. If still in place, remove the starter driven gear (**Figure 41**).

9. Remove the collar (A, **Figure 42**).

10. If necessary, remove the Woodruff key (B, **Figure 42**) from the crankshaft keyway.

Starter Clutch Removal/Inspection/Installation

1. Check the one-way clutch operation as follows:
   a. Place the flywheel and starter clutch on the workbench with the driven gear facing up (**Figure 43**).
   b. Hold the flywheel. Try to turn the driven gear clockwise, and then counterclockwise. The driven gear should only turn counterclockwise as shown in **Figure 43**.
   c. If the driven gear turns clockwise, the one-way clutch is damaged and must be replaced (this section).

2. Remove the driven gear (**Figure 43**) from the one-way clutch assembly.

3. Inspect the driven gear (A, **Figure 44**) for the following conditions:
   a. Worn or damaged gear teeth.
   b. Worn or damaged bearing shoulder.
   c. Measure the outside diameter of the starter driver boss (B, **Figure 44**) and refer to **Table 2**.

4. Inspect the one-way clutch (**Figure 45** for CRF230F models or **Figure 46** for CRF230L and CRF230M models) for the following conditions:

   a. Severely worn or damaged one-way clutch rollers.

   b. Loose one-way clutch bolts.

5. To replace the one-way clutch, perform the following:

   a. Secure the flywheel with a strap or band wrench.

   b. Using an impact driver, remove the one-way clutch mounting bolts (**Figure 47**). Torx bolts are used on CRF230F models, while Allen-head bolts are used on CRF230L and CRF230M models.

   c. Separate the clutch outer race (A, **Figure 48**) and the one-way clutch (B).

   d. Install the one-way clutch into the outer race so the flange on the one-way clutch fits into the recess in the outer race as shown in **Figure 49**.

   e. Apply a medium-strength threadlock to the threads of each mounting bolt.

   f. Install the one-way clutch mounting bolts finger-tight. Then, tighten the bolts to 16 N•m (12 ft.-lb.).

6. Inspect the collar for excessive wear or damage. Replace if necessary.

Flywheel Inspection

> *WARNING*
> *Replace a cracked or chipped flywheel. A damaged flywheel can fly apart at high rpm, throwing metal fragments into the engine. Do not attempt to repair a damaged flywheel.*

> *CAUTION*
> *Carefully inspect the inside of the flywheel for small bolts, washers or other metal debris that may have been picked up by the magnets. Any metal attached to the magnets can damage the alternator stator assembly.*

1. Clean and dry the flywheel.

2. Check the flywheel for cracks or breaks.

3. Check the tapered bore in the flywheel and the crankshaft taper for damage.

4. Replace damaged parts as required.

Flywheel Installation

1. Apply engine oil to the one-way clutch rollers and the driven gear shoulder.

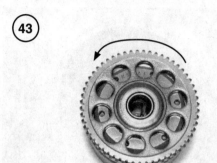

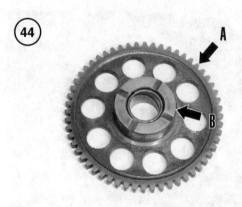

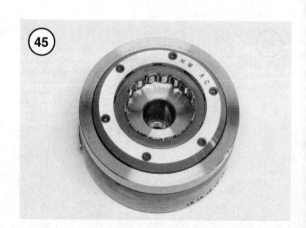

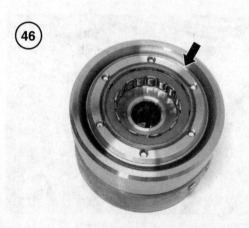

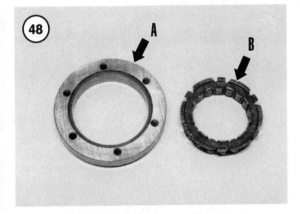

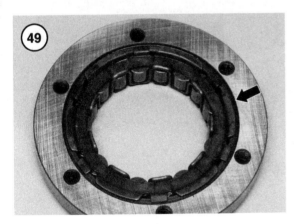

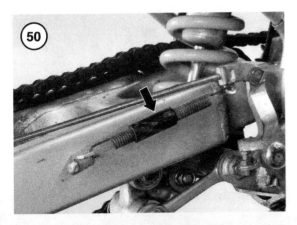

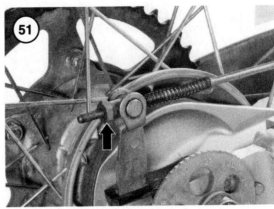

2. To install the driven gear:
  a. Place the flywheel on the workbench so that the one-way clutch faces up.
  b. Rotate the driven gear counterclockwise and slide it into the one-way clutch (**Figure 43**).
3. Apply engine oil onto the collar and install the collar (A, **Figure 42**) onto the crankshaft.
4. If removed, install the Woodruff key (B, **Figure 42**) into the crankshaft keyway.
5. Align the keyway in the flywheel with the Woodruff key in the crankshaft and install the flywheel.
6. Lubricate the flywheel bolt and flange surface with engine oil. Install the flywheel bolt (**Figure 38**) and washer.
7. Tighten the flywheel bolt to 74 N•m (55 ft.-lb.).
8. Install the starter idler shaft (A, **Figure 36**) and gear (B).
9. Install the left crankcase cover (this chapter).

RIGHT CRANKCASE COVER (CRF230F MODELS)

Removal/Installation

1. Drain the engine oil (Chapter Three).
2. Detach the brake return spring (**Figure 50**).
3. Remove the rear brake adjuster (**Figure 51**). Allow the rear brake pedal to drop down.
4. Remove the two bolts that secure the clutch cable holder (A, **Figure 52**) to the crankcase cover. Disconnect the clutch cable from the clutch release lever (B, **Figure 52**).
5. Following a crossing pattern, remove the bolts securing the right crankcase cover (**Figure 53**). Remove the right crankcase cover and gasket. Do not lose the locating dowels (**Figure 54**).
6. Reverse the removal steps to install the right crankcase cover. Note the following:
  a. Make sure the locating dowels (**Figure 54**) are in place.

b. Install a new gasket.

c. Install the 50-mm long bolt (B, **Figure 53**) at the front of the cover.

d. Install the two 43-mm long bolts (A, **Figure 53**) securing the clutch cable holder and cover.

e. Following a crossing pattern, tighten the bolts securely.

f. Refill the engine with the correct type and quantity of engine oil (Chapter Three).

g. Check clutch operation. If necessary, adjust the clutch (Chapter Three).

h. Adjust brake pedal freeplay (Chapter Three).

RIGHT CRANKCASE COVER (CRF230L AND CRF230M MODELS)

Removal/Installation

1. Drain the engine oil (Chapter Three).

2. Rotate the clutch cable adjuster (A, **Figure 55**) to increase cable slack. Detach the cable from the holder, and then disconnect the clutch cable from the clutch release lever (B, **Figure 55**).

3. Remove the rear brake pedal (Chapter Sixteen).

4. Following a crossing pattern, remove the bolts securing the right crankcase cover (A, **Figure 56**).

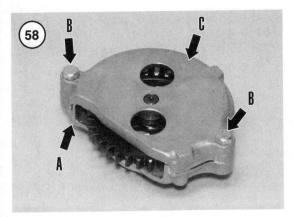

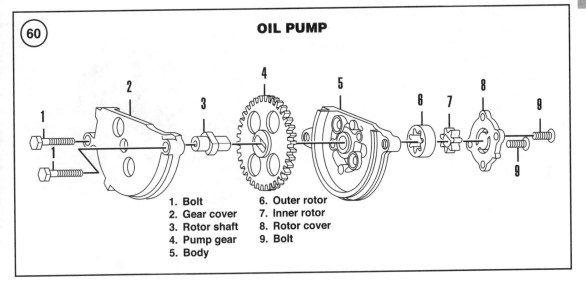

OIL PUMP

1. Bolt
2. Gear cover
3. Rotor shaft
4. Pump gear
5. Body
6. Outer rotor
7. Inner rotor
8. Rotor cover
9. Bolt

Remove the right crankcase cover and gasket. Do not lose the locating dowels (**Figure 54**).

5. Reverse the removal steps to install the right crankcase cover. Note the following:

  a. Make sure the locating dowels (**Figure 54**) are in place.

  b. Install a new gasket.

  c. Install the 50-mm long bolt (B, **Figure 56**) at the front of the cover.

  d. Following a crossing pattern, tighten the cover bolts securely.

  e. Refill the engine with the correct type and quantity of engine oil (Chapter Three).

  f. Adjust the clutch (Chapter Three).

OIL PUMP

Removal/Installation

1. Remove the right crankcase (this chapter).

2. Rotate the clutch housing or flywheel bolt so the oil pump retaining screws (A, **Figure 57**) appear in the holes of the gear cover (B).

CAUTION
The oil pump retaining screws may be very tight. Use an impact driver to loosen the screws. If necessary, apply heat to the screws using a heat gun.

3. Remove the oil pump retaining screws (**Figure 57**) and the oil pump (A, **Figure 58**).

4. Reverse the removal steps for installation. Note the following:

  a. Install new O-rings (**Figure 59**).

  b. Lubricate the O-rings prior to pump installation.

  c. Tighten the oil pump retaining screws (A, **Figure 57**) securely.

Disassembly

Refer to **Figure 60**.

1. Remove the rotor cover screws (A, **Figure 61**).

2. Remove the cover (B, **Figure 61**).

NOTE
If the rotors are not marked, mark them so they can be installed in their original positions.

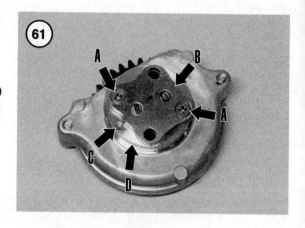

3. Remove the inner (A, **Figure 62**) and outer (B) rotors.
4. Remove the gear cover bolts (B, **Figure 58**).
5. Remove the gear cover (C, **Figure 58**).
6. Remove the rotor shaft (A, **Figure 63**).
7. Remove the pump gear (B, **Figure 63**).

Cleaning and Inspection

An excessively-worn or damaged oil pump will not maintain oil pressure and should be repaired or replaced before it causes engine damage. Inspect the oil pump carefully when troubleshooting a lubrication or oil pressure problem.

Refer to **Table 2** when measuring the oil pump components in this section. Replace parts that are out of specification or show damage as described in this section.

1. Clean and dry all parts. Place the parts on a clean, lint-free cloth.
2. Check the pump shaft for scoring, cracks or signs of heat discoloration.
3. Check the oil pump body for:
   a. Warped or cracked mating surfaces.
   b. Rotor bore damage.
4. Check the oil pump rotors for:
   a. Cracked or damaged outer surface.
   b. Worn or scored inner mating surfaces.
5. If the rotor cover, body and both rotors are in good condition, check the rotor operating clearances (this procedure).
6. Install the inner and outer rotors and pump shaft into the pump body (**Figure 62**).
7. Using a flat feeler gauge, measure the clearance between the outer rotor and the oil pump body (**Figure 64**). Then, refer to the outer rotor-to-body clearance specification in **Table 2**. If out of specification, replace the outer rotor and remeasure. If still out of specification, replace the oil pump assembly.

8. Using a flat feeler gauge, measure the clearance between the inner rotor tip and the outer rotor (**Figure 65**). Then, refer to the tip clearance specification in **Table 2**. If out of specification, replace the inner and outer rotors.
9. Using a flat feeler gauge and straightedge, measure the clearance between the body surface and rotors (**Figure 66**). Then, refer to the end clearance specification in **Table 2**. If out of specification, replace the oil pump assembly.

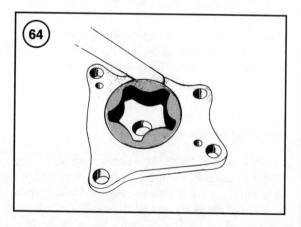

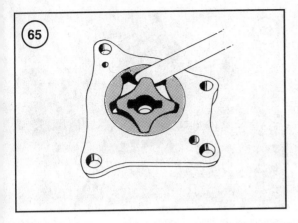

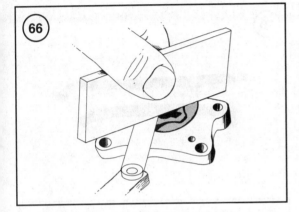

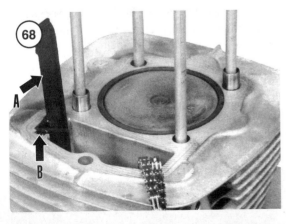

Reassembly

1. If necessary, clean the parts again (this section). Lubricate the rotors and body rotor bore with engine oil when installing them in the following steps.
2. Install the pump gear (B, **Figure 63**) and rotor shaft (A) into the pump body.
3. Install the gear cover (C, **Figure 58**).
4. Install the gear cover bolts (B, **Figure 58**) and tighten the bolts to 10 N•m (89 in.-lb.).
5. Install the outer and inner rotors (**Figure 62**). If installing the original rotors, install them with their original side facing up as identified during disassembly.
6. Install the cover (B, **Figure 61**) so the point on the cover (C) aligns with the dimple on the body (D).
7. Install the rotor cover screws (A, **Figure 61**) and tighten the screws to 3 N•m (27 in.-lb.).
8. Rotate the pump shaft. If there is any roughness or binding, disassemble the oil pump and check it for damage.
9. Store the oil pump in a plastic bag until installation.

PRIMARY DRIVE GEAR

Removal/Installation

1. Remove the clutch (Chapter Six).
2. Remove the primary drive gear (**Figure 67**).
3. On CRF230F models, remove the Woodruff key if necessary.
4. Reverse the removal steps for installation. Note the following:
   a. On CRF230F models, install the gear so the smooth diameter is out (**Figure 67**).
   b. On CRF230F models, install the Woodruff key, if it was removed.

CAMSHAFT CHAIN AND GUIDES

Removal/Installation

1. Remove the cylinder head (Chapter Four). The rear cam chain guide is removed during that procedure.
2. Remove the front cam chain guide (A, **Figure 68**).
3. Remove the flywheel, starter clutch and collar (this chapter).
4. Remove the bolt (A, **Figure 69**) and cam chain retainer (B).
5. Remove the cam chain (C, **Figure 69**) from the crankshaft sprocket.
6. Inspect the camshaft chain for wear and damage. If chain replacement is necessary, also inspect the drive sprocket and the camshaft sprocket.

7. Inspect the chain guides (**Figure 70**). Replace if excessively worn or damaged.

8. Install by reversing the removal steps. Note the following:

    a. Make sure the bottom end of the front chain guide is seated in its socket in the crankcase casting.

    b. Make sure the front chain guide boss is seated in the notch (B, **Figure 68**) in the cylinder.

    c. Tighten the cam chain retainer bolt (A, **Figure 69**) securely.

CRANKCASE

Disassembly of the crankcase requires engine removal from the frame. If transmission service is the only repair necessary, the crankcase may be disassembled and assembled without removing the crankshaft. The crankcase is made in two halves that can be replaced separately.

Reference in the text to the right and left side of the engine refers to the engine as it sits in the frame, not as it sits on a workbench.

Disassembly

1. Remove all of the following exterior engine assemblies:

    a. Starter (Chapter Ten or Chapter Eleven).

    b. Cylinder and piston (Chapter Four).

    c. Camshaft chain (this chapter).

    d. Clutch assembly (Chapter Six).

    e. Flywheel and starter clutch (this chapter).

    f. External shift mechanism (Chapter Six).

    g. Oil pump (this chapter).

    h. Primary drive gear (this chapter) and primary drive gear key (CRF230F models only).

2. Remove the engine (this chapter).

3. Remove the bolt from the right crankcase side (A, **Figure 71**). On CRF230L and CRF230M models, the bolt also secures the clutch cable holder (B, **Figure 71**).

4. Following a crossing pattern, remove the bolts (**Figure 72**) from the left crankcase side.

5. Set the crankcase down on the left side. Set the engine on wood blocks or fabricate a holding fixture (**Figure 73**) of wood.

> *CAUTION*
> *Do not pry between the crankcase mating surfaces when separating the crankcase halves. Doing so may cause an oil leak.*

6. Hold onto the right crankcase half and tap on the right end of the crankshaft and transmission shafts with

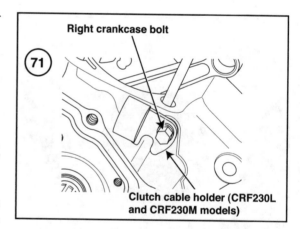

Right crankcase bolt

Clutch cable holder (CRF230L and CRF230M models)

a plastic or soft-faced mallet until the crankshaft and crankcase separate. Remove the right crankcase half.

7. If the crankcase and crankshaft will not separate after tapping on them with a mallet, check to make sure that all bolts are removed. If crankcase remains intact, it may be necessary to use a puller to remove the right crankcase half. If the proper tools are not available, take the crankcase assembly to a dealer and have it separated. Do not risk expensive crankcase damage with improper tools or techniques.

8. Remove the crankcase gasket. Do not lose the locating dowels if they came out of the case. Dowel removal is not necessary if they are secure.

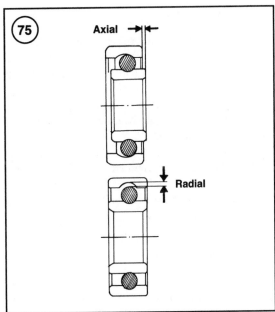

5

CAUTION
When drying the bearings with compressed air, do not allow the air jet to spin the bearing or the inner bearing races. The bearings are not lubricated and damage may result.

3. Clean both crankcase halves and all crankcase bearings with solvent. Thoroughly dry with compressed air.
4. Flush all crankcase oil passages with compressed air.
5. Lightly oil all of the crankcase bearings with engine oil before checking the bearings.
6. Check the bearings for roughness, pitting, galling and play by rotating them slowly by hand. Replace any bearing that turns roughly or has excessive play (**Figure 75**).
7. Replace any worn or damaged crankcase bearings (this section).
8. Carefully inspect the crankcase for cracks and fractures, especially in the lower areas where it is vulnerable to rock damage.
9. Check the areas around the stiffening ribs, around bearing bosses and threaded holes for damage. Refer crankcase repair to a shop specializing in the repair of precision aluminum castings.
10. Check the threaded holes in both crankcase halves for thread damage, dirt or oil buildup. If necessary, clean or repair the threads with the correct size metric tap. Coat the tap threads with kerosene or tap cutting fluid before use.
11. Install the countershaft and shift shaft oil seals (**Figure 74**) with the flat side facing out. Pack the lips of the new oil seals with grease.

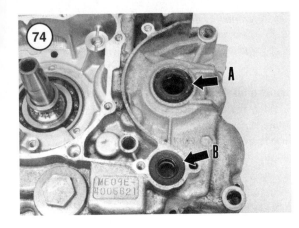

9. For further disassembly, refer to the appropriate section or chapter. Note that the transmission may be serviced without removing the crankshaft.

Inspection

1. Remove all gasket residue from the crankcase mating surfaces.
2. Pry out the countershaft oil seal (A, **Figure 74**) and shift shaft oil seal (B) from the left crankcase half using a wide-bladed screwdriver or seal puller. Protect the crankcase surface to prevent damage.

Bearing Replacement

The crankcase contains bearings for the crankshaft and transmission. Refer to the general bearing replacement procedures (Chapter One) and note the following:

1. Before removing the bearings, note and record the direction in which the bearings size codes face for proper reinstallation.

2. A retainer (A, **Figure 76**) holds the transmission mainshaft bearing in the right crankcase half. During bearing installation, apply threadlock to the retainer bolt threads. Tighten the retainer bolt (B, **Figure 76**) to 23 N•m (17 ft.-lb.).

Stud Replacement

The crankcase studs are different lengths. When replacing the studs, measure their length before removal and note their original location.

Assembly

1. Apply assembly oil to the inner race of all bearings in both crankcase halves and to the crankshaft main bearings.

> *NOTE*
> *Set the crankcase half assembly on wood blocks or the wood holding fixture (**Figure 73**).*

2. Install the transmission assemblies, shift shafts and shift drum in the left crankcase half (Chapter Seven). Lubricate all transmission components with engine oil.

> *NOTE*
> *Make sure the crankcase mating surfaces are clean and free of all old sealant material.*

3. Install the locating dowels if they were removed.
4. Apply a thin film of sealant to both case halves at the areas shown in **Figure 77**.
5. Install a new crankcase gasket.
6. Set the right crankcase half onto the left crankcase half. Push it down squarely into place until it reaches the crankshaft bearing. There is usually about 1/2 inch gap between the halves.

> *CAUTION*
> *The crankcase halves should fit together without force. Do not attempt to pull the case halves together with the crankcase bolts. Separate the crankcase halves and investigate the cause of the inter-*

ference. If the transmission shafts were disassembled, recheck to make sure that a gear is not installed backwards.

7. Lightly tap the case halves together with a rubber mallet until they mate.
8. After the crankcase halves are completely mated, rotate the crankshaft and transmission shafts to make sure there is no binding. If any is present, disassemble the crankcase and correct the problem.

> *NOTE*
> *The left crankcase half bolts are all the same length. The single long bolt is installed in the right crankcase half.*

9. Install and finger-tighten the left crankcase half bolts (**Figure 72**).
10. Following a crossing pattern, tighten the bolts in two stages to 9 N•m (80 in.-lb.).
11A. On CRF230F models, install the bolt (**Figure 71**) into the right crankcase half and tighten to 9 N•m (80 in.-lb.).
11B. On CRF230L and CRF230M models, install the clutch cable holder and bolt (**Figure 71**) . Tighten the bolt to 9 N•m (80 in.-lb.).
12. After the crankcase halves are completely assembled, again rotate the crankshaft and transmis-

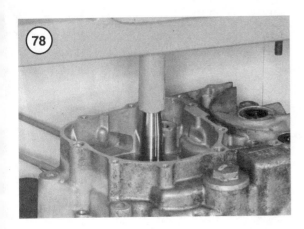

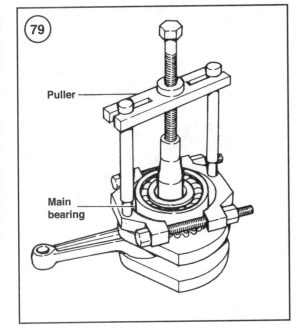

Puller

Main bearing

CAUTION
When supporting the crankcase half in the press, confirm that there is adequate room to press the crankshaft out without the connecting rod hitting against the press bed. If this happens, a bent connecting rod may result. Check the setup carefully before applying pressure to the crankshaft.

CAUTION
Catch the crankshaft once the crankshaft is free of the crankcase half. Otherwise, the crankshaft can fall to the floor, causing severe damage.

2. Center the crankshaft under the press ram (**Figure 78**) and press the crankshaft out of the crankcase.
3. Remove the crankshaft from the crankcase half.
4. Remove the left crankshaft bearing (this section).

Left Crankshaft Bearing Replacement

1A. If the left crankshaft bearing came out with the crankshaft, use a suitable puller to separate the bearing from the crankshaft (**Figure 79**).
1B. If the left crankshaft bearing remains in the crankcase half, drive the bearing from the case half.
2. Discard the bearing.
3. Install a new bearing into the crankcase half (Chapter One). Drive the bearing in until it bottoms in the crankcase.

Inspection

Handle the crankshaft carefully when performing the cleaning and inspection procedures in this section. Contact a dealership for crankshaft parts availability. If crankshaft overhaul is necessary, contact a dealership or repair shop.
1. Clean the crankshaft thoroughly with solvent.
2. Check the crankshaft journals for scratches, heat discoloration or other defects.
3. Check the flywheel taper, threads and keyway for damage.
4. Check the connecting rod big end for signs of damage, as well as bearing or thrust washer damage.
5. Check the connecting rod small end for signs of excessive heat (blue coloration) or other damage.
6. Measure the connecting rod small end inside diameter (**Figure 80**) and compare with the dimension in **Table 2**.
7. Slide the connecting rod big end to one side and check the side clearance with a flat feeler gauge

sion shafts to make sure there is no binding. If any binding is present, disassemble the crankcase and correct the problem.
13. If the new crankcase gasket protrudes above the cylinder seating surface, carefully trim off all excess gasket material. If it is not trimmed the cylinder base gasket will not seal properly.
14. Install all exterior engine assemblies as described in this chapter and other related chapters.

CRANKSHAFT (CRF230F MODELS)

Removal

NOTE
The left crankshaft bearing must be replaced whenever the crankshaft is removed.

1. Support the left crankcase half in a press.

(**Figure 81**) and compare with the dimension in **Table 2**.

8. Place the crankshaft on a set of V-blocks and measure runout with a dial indicator at the points listed in **Figure 82**. If the runout exceeds the service limit in **Table 2**, take the crankshaft to a dealership for service or replacement.

9. Place the crankshaft on a set of V-blocks and measure the connecting rod big end radial clearance with a dial indicator. Measure in the two directions shown in **Figure 83** and compare with the dimension in **Table 2**.

Installation Tools

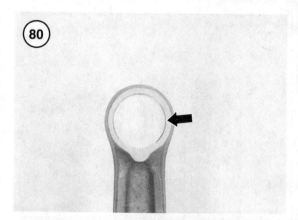

> *CAUTION*
> *Do not attempt to drive the crankshaft into the left main bearing. Doing so will affect crankshaft alignment.*

Use the following special tools, or their equivalents, to install the crankshaft into the left crankcase half.

1. Threaded adapter (Honda part No. 070MF-KPS0100 or 07VMF-HM8010A).
2. Shaft puller/nut (Honda part No. 07931-ME4010B and 07931-HB3020A or 07965-VM00200).
3. Assembly collar (Honda part No. 07965-VM00100).

Installation

1. Lubricate the crankshaft main bearing with oil.
2. Insert the crankshaft into the main bearing.
3. Install the threaded adapter into the end of the crankshaft.
4. Install the crankshaft puller assembly (**Figure 84**) onto the end of the crankshaft and thread it onto the adapter. Center the tool assembly on the main bearing inner race.

> *CAUTION*
> *When installing the crankshaft, position the connecting rod at the top dead center position. Otherwise, the connecting rod may contact the side of the crankcase, causing expensive connecting rod and crankcase damage.*

5. Hold the threaded adapter and turn the shaft puller (**Figure 84**) to pull the crankshaft into the main bearing. When installing the crankshaft, frequently check that it is going straight into the bearing and not binding to one side.

6. Continue to turn the shaft puller until the crankshaft bottoms against the main bearing. Remove the

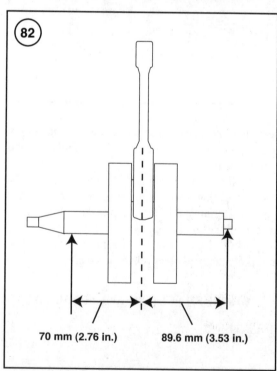

70 mm (2.76 in.)   89.6 mm (3.53 in.)

crankshaft installation tools and turn the crankshaft. The crankshaft must turn with no binding or roughness.

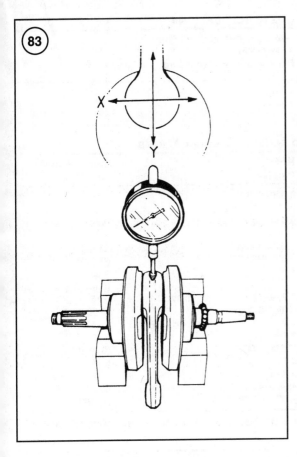

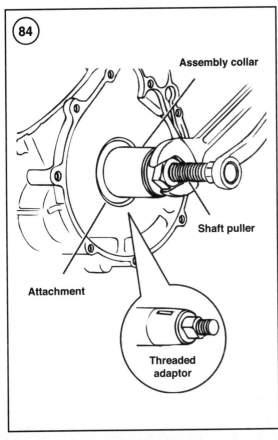

Assembly collar

Shaft puller

Attachment

Threaded
adaptor

CRANKSHAFT
(CRF230L AND CRF230M MODELS)

Removal/Installation

1. Remove the crankshaft assembly from the left crankcase half. The crankshaft bearing should free itself from the crankcase without the use of tools. If force is used, the bearing will be damaged, which will require crankshaft replacement.
2. Inspect the crankshaft assembly (this section).
3. Prior to installation, lubricate the crankshaft and main bearing.
4. Insert the crankshaft into the crankcase.
5. After the crankshaft is seated, check that it moves freely. The crankshaft must turn with no binding or roughness.

Inspection

NOTE
Measure crankshaft runout with the left main bearing installed on the crank-shaft.

Except for the right crankshaft main bearing, the crankshaft, connecting rod, crankpin, rod bearing, left crankshaft main bearing and cam chain sprocket are replaced as an assembly.

For inspection procedures, refer to *Crankshaft (CRF230F models) Inspection* (this chapter). Refer to **Table 2** for specifications.

Left Crankshaft Bearing Replacement

Do not attempt to remove the left crankshaft bearing from the crankshaft. The left crankshaft bearing is not available separately, but only as a part of the crankshaft assembly.

ENGINE BREAK-IN

If new piston rings were installed or major repair work was performed, break in the engine as if new. The performance and service life of the engine depends greatly on a careful and sensible break-in.

On CRF230F models, avoid full throttle starts and rapid acceleration for the first day of operation or 25 km (15 miles).

On CRF230L and CRF230M models, avoid full throttle starts and rapid acceleration for the first 500 km (300 miles) of operation.

Table 1 GENERAL ENGINE SPECIFICATIONS

Crankshaft type	Two main journals, unit type
Engine weight (approximate)	31 kg (68 lb.)
Lubrication system	Dry sump, forced pressure

Table 2 ENGINE LOWER END SERVICE SPECIFICATIONS

	New mm (in.)	Service limit mm (in.)
Connecting rod big end radial clearance	0.000-0.008 (0.0000-0.0003)	0.05 (0.002)
Connecting rod big end side clearance	0.05-0.30 (0.002-0.012)	0.80 (0.032)
Connecting rod small end inside diameter	15.010-15.028 (0.5909-0.5917)	15.06 (0.593)
Crankshaft runout*	– –	0.03 (0.001)
End clearance	0.03-0.12 (0.001-0.005)	0.15 (0.006)
Oil pump		
Outer rotor-to-body clearance	0.15-0.21 (0.006-0.008)	0.35 (0.014)
Tip clearance	0.15 (0.006)	0.20 (0.008)
Starter driven gear boss outside diameter	45.660-45.673 (1.7976-1.7981)	45.56 (1.794)

*Measure crankshaft runout at points identified in **Figure 82**. Measure distance from connecting rod center-line.

Table 3 ENGINE LOWER END TORQUE SPECIFICATIONS

	N•m	in.-lb.	ft.-lb.
Crankcase bolts	9	80	–
Engine mounting fasteners			
8-mm	34	–	25
10-mm			
CRF230F	59	–	44
CRF230L, CRF230M	64	–	47
Flywheel bolt	74	–	55
Footpeg mounting bolt (CRF230F models)	12	106	–
Gearshift pedal pinch bolt			
CRF230F models	12	106	–
CRF230L and CR230F models	16	144	–
Oil pump			
Gear cover bolts	10	89	–
Rotor cover screws	3	27	–
Starter one way clutch mounting bolts	16	144	–
Transmission mainshaft bearing retainer bolt	23	–	17

CLUTCH AND EXTERNAL SHIFT MECHANISM

6

This chapter provides service procedures for the clutch, clutch release mechanism and external shift mechanism. Specifications are listed in **Table 1** and **Table 2** located at the end of this chapter.

The clutch is a wet (operates in the engine oil), multi-plate design. The clutch assembly is located on the right side of the engine. The clutch hub is mounted on the splines of the transmission mainshaft. The clutch housing is driven by the primary drive gear on the crankshaft.

CLUTCH

The clutch can be removed with the engine mounted in the frame. Refer to **Figure 1**.

Special Tools

Before removing the oil filter rotor nut (A, **Figure 2**) or clutch nut (**Figure 3**), note the following:
1. The clutch nut (**Figure 3**) is staked to a notch in the mainshaft. Purchase a new nut for reassembly.
2. Use a wrench (Honda part No. 07716-0020100, or equivalent) (**Figure 4**), to turn the oil filter rotor nut or clutch nut.
3. When loosening and tightening the clutch nut, some means of holding the clutch will be required. Suggested methods for holding the clutch include the following:

a. A clutch center holder tool (Honda part No. 07JMB-MN50300 or Honda part No. 07HGB-001010B), or its equivalent, (**Figure 5**) is designed to hold the clutch when loosening and tightening the clutch nut.
b. Use an air impact wrench and air compressor. This tool setup can be used to loosen the clutch nut. However, when tightening the nut during clutch assembly, a separate tool setup (**Figure 6**) will be required to hold the clutch so that the clutch nut can be tightened with a torque wrench.
c. Use a gear holder (Honda part No. 07724-001A100), or its equivalent (**Figure 6**), to prevent clutch gear and primary gear rotation. A copper penny placed between the teeth of the clutch gear and primary gear may also be used.

Removal/Disassembly

1. Remove the right crankcase cover (Chapter Five).
2. Remove the centrifugal oil filter rotor cover (Chapter Three).
3. Remove the oil pump (Chapter Five).
4A. Install the gear holder (Honda part No. 07724-001A100), or its equivalent, (**Figure 7**) to prevent clutch gear and primary gear rotation.

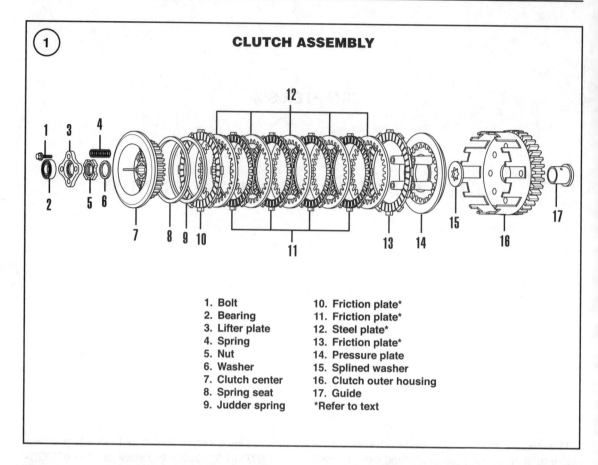

CLUTCH ASSEMBLY

1. Bolt
2. Bearing
3. Lifter plate
4. Spring
5. Nut
6. Washer
7. Clutch center
8. Spring seat
9. Judder spring
10. Friction plate*
11. Friction plate*
12. Steel plate*
13. Friction plate*
14. Pressure plate
15. Splined washer
16. Clutch outer housing
17. Guide
*Refer to text

4B. Install a copper penny (**Figure 8**) between the clutch gear teeth and primary gear teeth to prevent gear rotation.

5. Use a wrench (Honda part No. 07716-0020100), or its equivalent, to loosen the oil filter rotor nut (**Figure 2**).

6. Remove the nut (**Figure 2**), washer (A, **Figure 9**) and oil filter rotor (B).

7A. Following a crossing pattern, loosen the lifter plate bolts (A, **Figure 10**) 1/4 turn at a time. Remove the bolts (A **Figure 10**), lifter plate (B) and clutch springs if the clutch plates require service.

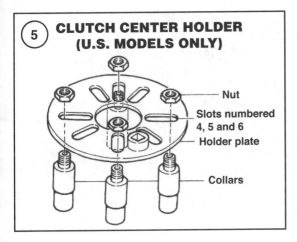

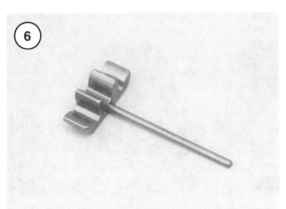

7B. If clutch plate service is not required, keep the clutch assembled with a clutch spring, flat washer and clutch bolt as shown in A, **Figure 11**.

> *CAUTION*
> *Be sure to unstake the clutch locknut where it contacts the mainshaft (B, **Figure 11**). This will prevent the nut from damaging the mainshaft threads as the nut is being removed.*

8. Using a die grinder or other metal removal tool, unstake the clutch locknut from the groove in the

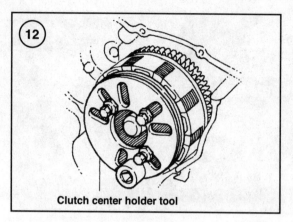

Clutch center holder tool

mainshaft (B, **Figure 11**). Cover the parts so that metal particles do not enter the clutch or engine.

NOTE
*The clutch center tool (**Figure 12**, typical) is shown in use to lock the clutch center.*

9. Lock the clutch center using one of the methods listed in this section. Loosen and remove the clutch locknut and washer.

10. Remove the clutch center, clutch plates and pressure plate assembly (**Figure 13**).

11. Remove the splined washer (A, **Figure 14**) and clutch housing (B).

12. Remove the clutch guide (**Figure 15**).

Inspection

Refer to **Table 1** when measuring the clutch components (**Figure 1**) in this section. Replace parts that are out of specification or damaged.

1. Clean all parts in solvent and dry with compressed air.

2. Measure the free length of each clutch spring (**Figure 16**) with a caliper. Replace the springs as a set if any spring is too short.

3. Measure the thickness of each friction plate at several places around the plate (**Figure 17**). Replace

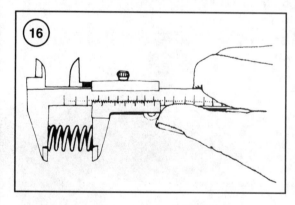

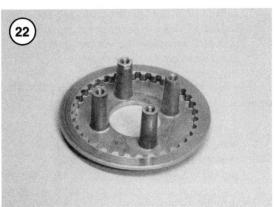

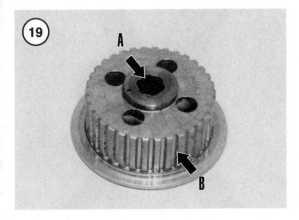

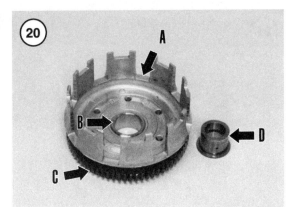

all friction plates as a set if any one plate is too thin or damaged. Do not replace only one or two plates.

4. Place each clutch steel plate on a surface plate or a thick piece of glass and measure warp with a feeler gauge (**Figure 18**). Replace the steel plate if it is out of specification.

5. Examine the clutch center splines (A, **Figure 19**) and plate grooves (B) for cracks or excessive wear.

6. Examine the clutch housing slots (A, **Figure 20**) for grooves, steps, cracks or other damage. The slots must be smooth for proper clutch operation. Repair light damage with a fine-cut file or oilstone. Replace the clutch housing if the damage is not repairable.

7. Examine the clutch housing bore (B, **Figure 20**) for excessive wear or damage. Measure the inside diameter and compare with **Table 1**.

8. Examine the clutch housing gear (C, **Figure 20**) for damaged gear teeth.

9. Examine the clutch guide (D, **Figure 20**) inside and outside surfaces for cracks, deep scoring or other damage. If there is no visible damage, measure the clutch guide inside and outside diameters. Replace if either dimension is out of specification (**Table 1**).

10. Measure the mainshaft outside diameter (**Figure 21**) where the clutch guide rides. Replace the mainshaft if out of specification (**Table 1**).

11. Examine the pressure plate (**Figure 22**) for stripped threads, cracked spring towers or other damage.

12. Check the lifter bearing (A, **Figure 23**) by turning the inner race. The bearing should turn smoothly with no signs of roughness or damage. Examine the lifter plate (B, **Figure 23**) for damage.

Assembly/Installation

Refer to **Figure 1** when assembling and installing the clutch assembly.

CAUTION
Never assemble the clutch without lubricating the clutch plates with oil, especially if the clutch was cleaned in

solvent or if new plates are being installed. Otherwise, the plates may grab and lock up when the engine is first started and cause clutch damage.

1. Lubricate the mainshaft and all clutch parts with engine oil.

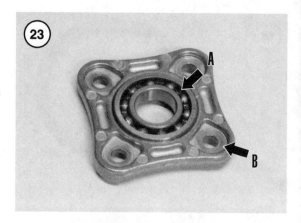

NOTE
If the clutch plates were not separated from the clutch center and clutch housing, go to Step 4.

2. Identify the friction plates.
   a. There is one plate (**Figure 24**) with a larger inner diameter than the remaining friction plates. The plate is located against the clutch center flange (A, **Figure 25**).
   b. The four middle friction plates (B, **Figure 25**) have 45 friction pads on each side.
   c. The friction plate next to the pressure plate (C, **Figure 25**) has 48 friction pads on each side.

3. Assemble the clutch plates, clutch center, and pressure plate as follows:
   a. Place the clutch center (**Figure 26**) on the workbench.
   b. Lubricate the friction and steel clutch plates with engine oil.
   c. Install the spring seat (A, **Figure 27**) and judder spring (B) onto the clutch center. The cupped side of the judder spring must face up or outward.

NOTE
The next friction plate installed must fit around the judder spring and spring seat.

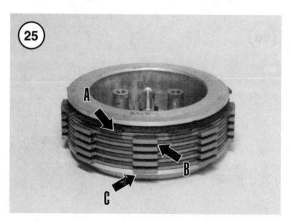

   d. Install the large inner diameter friction plate (**Figure 24**), and then install a steel clutch plate. Alternately install the remaining clutch plates. Last, install the friction plate with 48 friction pads. Refer to **Figure 28**.
   e. Install the pressure plate (**Figure 29**) and seat it against the outer friction plate. Check that the friction plate tabs engage with the clutch center splines and that the clutch center sits flush against the friction plate as shown in **Figure 30**.

NOTE
*Installing the spring, washer and bolt (A, **Figure 11**) will align the clutch plates with the clutch center. Aligning the clutch plates now will make it easier to install the clutch plate assembly later in this procedure.*

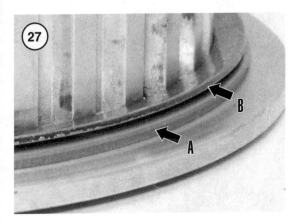

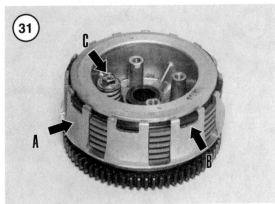

f. Align the friction plates with the clutch housing, and then install the clutch plate assembly into the clutch housing (A, **Figure 31**). Align the tabs on the outer friction plate so they are located in the shallow slots (B, **Figure 31**).

g. After properly inserting the plates, install one clutch spring, a flat washer and clutch spring bolt as shown in C, **Figure 31**. Tighten the bolt to hold the clutch plate assembly together. Then, remove the clutch plate assembly from the clutch housing.

h. Check again that all of the friction plates are properly aligned and that the pressure plate seats flush against the outer friction plate (**Figure 30**).

i. Set the clutch plate assembly aside until installation.

4. If removed, install the primary drive gear (Chapter Five).

NOTE
The clutch guide on CRF230L and CRF230M models does not have a flange and may be installed in either direction.

5. Slide the clutch guide (**Figure 15**), flanged end toward engine, onto the mainshaft.

6. Install the clutch housing (B, **Figure 14**) onto the mainshaft and seat it onto the clutch guide.

7. Install the splined washer (A, **Figure 14**) onto the mainshaft and seat it against the clutch housing.

8. Mesh the clutch center with the mainshaft splines and slide the clutch center into the clutch housing (**Figure 32**). Remove the temporary bolt, washer and spring holding the clutch pack assembly.

NOTE
A flat washer is used on CRF230F models and may be installed in either direction. A concave washer is used on CRF230L and CRF230M models.

*Install the washer so the side marked OUTSIDE (**Figure 33**) is visible.*

9. Install the washer (**Figure 33**) onto the mainshaft and seat it against the clutch center.

10. Lock the clutch center to the clutch housing, using one of the special tools described in this section. Note the following:

   a. If using a gear or penny to lock the clutch housing gear to the primary drive gear, install two or more clutch springs, flat washers and bolts (A, **Figure 11**) to prevent the clutch center from slipping when tightening the clutch nut (B).

   b. Install the gear holder or a penny to lock the clutch housing gear to the primary drive gear.

   c. If using the clutch center holder tool (**Figure 12**, typical), remove the clutch bolt (A, **Figure 11**), washer and clutch spring set that were installed during assembly.

11. Lubricate the threads and inner side of the clutch nut with engine oil.

12. Install the clutch locknut so the flanged side (**Figure 34**) faces out. Tighten the clutch locknut to 93 N•m (69 ft.-lb.).

13. Remove the clutch holding tools.

14. Using a punch, stake the locknut shoulder into the mainshaft notch. Refer to **Figure 34**.

15. Remove the clutch spring bolts and flat washers if not already removed.

16. Install the clutch springs (**Figure 35**).

17. Install the lifter plate and bearing (A, **Figure 36**).

18. Install the four clutch spring bolts (B, **Figure 36**). Following a crossing pattern, tighten the clutch spring bolts in several steps to 12 N•m (106 in.-lb.).

19. Install the oil filter rotor (A, **Figure 37**) and washer (B).

20. Lubricate the threads and inner face of the rotor nut with engine oil.

21. Install the rotor nut (**Figure 38**) so the chamfered side faces in.

22. Use one of the following procedures to prevent clutch gear and primary gear rotation:

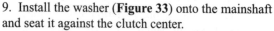

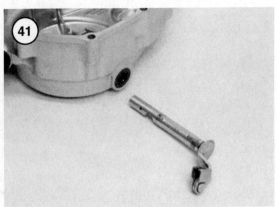

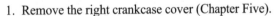

a. Install a gear holder(Honda part No. 07724-001A100), or an equivalent (**Figure 6**).

b. Install a copper penny between the clutch gear teeth and primary gear teeth.

23. Tighten the rotor nut to 83 N•m (61 ft.-lb.).

24. Install the oil pump (Chapter Five).

25. Install the oil filter cover (Chapter Three).

26. Install the right crankcase cover (Chapter Five).

CLUTCH RELEASE MECHANISM

Removal/Installation

1. Remove the right crankcase cover (Chapter Five).

2. Remove the clutch lifter piece (**Figure 39**).

3. Measure and record the standout height of the return spring pin (**Figure 40**). The pin will be returned to this height during assembly.

4. Drive the return spring pin in until it is flush with the lifter arm shaft surface.

5. Remove the lifter arm (**Figure 41**) and the return spring.

6. Replace the lifter arm shaft seal (**Figure 42**) if leaking or otherwise damaged.

7. Inspect the bearings (**Figure 43**) in the cover. Replace if worn or damaged.

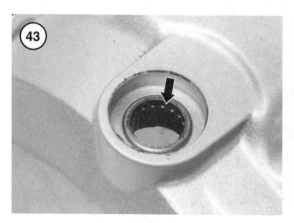

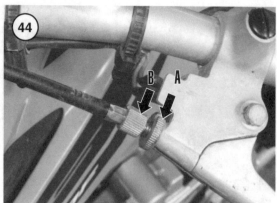

8. Replace the lifter arm if excessively worn or damaged.

9. Lubricate the bearings and the seal lips with grease.

10. Install the lifter arm and spring.

11. Drive the return spring pin into the lifter arm hole so it protrudes to the standout height measured during removal (**Figure 40**).

12. Hook the return spring onto the return spring pin.

13. Align the cutout in the lifter arm shaft with the lifter piece hole in the crankcase cover. Then, install the lifter piece (**Figure 39**) into the hole.

CLUTCH CABLE

Replacement

1. Move the rubber boot away from the clutch lever assembly.

2. Increase cable slack by loosening the adjuster nut (A, **Figure 44**), and then screwing in the cable adjuster (B).

3A. On CRF230F models, loosen both cable nuts on the lower end of the clutch cable (**Figure 45**).

3B. On CRF230L and CRF230M models, loosen both cable nuts (**Figure 46**) on the lower end of the clutch cable.

4. Detach the lower end of the clutch cable from the clutch actuating lever and cable holder.

5. Detach the clutch cable from the clutch lever.

6. Remove the clutch cable, while noting the routing.

7. Reverse the removal steps to install the clutch cable. Adjust the clutch lever free play (Chapter Three).

EXTERNAL GEARSHIFT LINKAGE

Removal

The external gearshift linkage is located behind the right crankcase cover and is partially covered by the clutch (**Figure 47**). Visual inspection of the

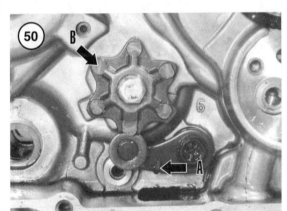

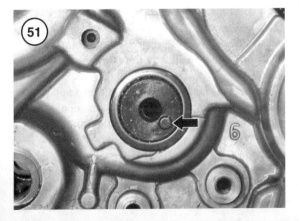

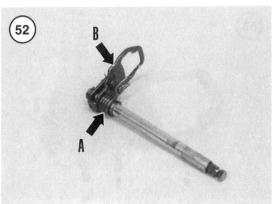

shift shaft assembly is possible without removing the clutch. To completely remove the external gearshift linkage, perform the following:

1. Remove the right crankcase cover (this chapter).
2. Remove the clutch (this chapter).
3. Put the transmission in neutral. This can be verified by the position of the lever on the shift cam. The roller should rest in the neutral detent on the shift cam (**Figure 48**).
4. Remove the shift lever from the left side of the engine. Mark the location of the shift lever on the splines so the lever can be reinstalled in the same position.
5. Pull the shift shaft assembly from the engine (**Figure 49**).
6. Remove the stopper arm (A, **Figure 50**), return spring and washer.
7. Remove the shift cam (B, **Figure 50**).
8. Remove the pin from the end of the shift drum (**Figure 51**).
9. Inspect the parts (this section).

Inspection

Inspect the components of the gearshift linkage and replace any parts that are worn, damaged or fatigued. Perform the following:

1. Clean the parts in solvent.
2. Inspect the shift shaft assembly (**Figure 52**).
   a. Inspect the return spring (A, **Figure 52**) for fatigue or damage.
   b. Inspect the pawl tips for wear.
   c. Inspect the gearshift plate (B, **Figure 52**) for wear, damage or deformation. Make sure the gearshift plate moves freely.
   d. Check the shaft for wear and straightness. Inspect the condition of the splines on the shaft and in the shift lever.
3. If necessary, remove the gearshift plate from the shift shaft as follows:
   a. Remove the cotter pin (A, **Figure 53**).

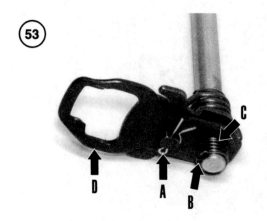

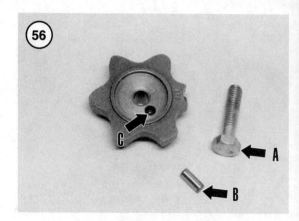

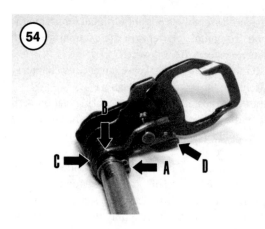

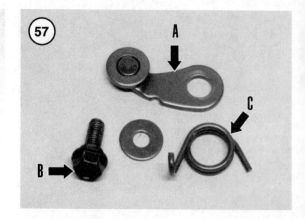

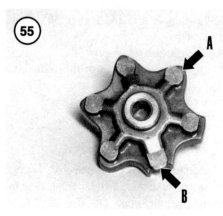

b. Remove the snap ring (B, **Figure 53**) and spring (C).

c. Remove the gearshift plate (D, **Figure 53**).

d. Reverse the disassembly steps to assembly the shift shaft.

4. If necessary, remove the return spring from the shift shaft assembly as follows:

a. Remove the snap ring (A, **Figure 54**).

b. Remove the washer (B, **Figure 54**) and return spring (C).

c. Install the return spring so the spring ends surround the pin on the gearshift plate (D, **Figure 54**)

5. Inspect the shift cam. The ramps (A, **Figure 55**) must be smooth and free from burrs or wear. The neutral detent (B, **Figure 55**) should not be worn away and should allow the lever roller to rest in the detent.

6. Inspect the shift cam bolt (A, **Figure 56**), pin (B) and pin bore (C). The pin and bore should not be worn. Inspect the fit of the pin in the shift drum. The pin should fit with minimal perceptible play.

7. Inspect the lever (A, **Figure 57**), bolt (B) and spring (C). The lever roller should be round, turn freely and have no play in its pivot. The shoulder on the bolt should fit into the lever with minimal percep-

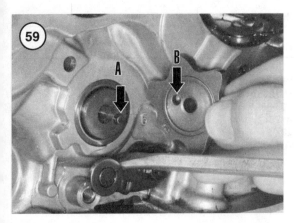

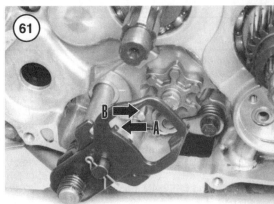

c. Make sure the bolt shoulder is seated into the stopper arm before tightening.

d. Tighten the stopper arm bolt to 12 N•m (106 in.-lb.).

2. Install the pin (A, **Figure 59**) in the end of the shift drum.

3. Depress the stopper arm so it is out of the way. Install the shift cam, engaging the pin hole (B, **Figure 59**) in the shift cam with the pin (A).

4. Install the bolt and tighten securely.

5. Make sure the thrust washer (**Figure 60**) is installed on the shift shaft. Then, insert the shift shaft assembly through the engine. Position the return spring ends (A, **Figure 61**) around the post (B).

tible play. If either part is loose, replace both parts. Inspect the ends of the spring for wear.

6. Install the shift lever onto the left side of the engine. If necessary, get assistance to hold the shaft in place on the right side while the lever is installed.

7. Check the shifting action of the linkage.

Installation

1. Install the stopper arm assembly (**Figure 58**).

a. Install the washer (A, **Figure 58**) between the spring and crankcase.

b. Make sure the spring ends (B, **Figure 58**) are located as shown.

a. Turn the transmission shaft to aid in shifting.

b. The lever roller should lock into each dent on the shift cam as the transmission is shifted. In neutral, the lever roller should rest in the neutral detent (**Figure 48**).

8. Install the clutch (this chapter).

9. Install the right crankcase cover (Chapter Five).

Table 1 CLUTCH SERVICE SPECIFICATIONS

	New mm (in.)	Service limit mm (in.)
Clutch friction plate thickness		
CRF230F models		
Plate A	3.62-3.70 (0.143-0.146)	3.3 (0.13)
Plates B and C	2.90-3.00 (0.114-0.118)	2.6 (0.10)
CRF230L and CRF230M models		
Plate A	2.92-3.08 (0.115-0.121)	2.6 (0.10)
Plates B and C	2.62-2.78 (0.103-0.109)	2.3 (0.09)
	(continued)	

Table 1 CLUTCH SERVICE SPECIFICATIONS (CONTINUED)

	New mm (in.)	Service limit mm (in.)
Clutch guide		
Outside diameter	27.959-27.980	27.93
	(1.1007-1.1016)	(1.100)
Inside diameter	19.983-19.996	20.02
	(0.7867-0.7872)	(0.788)
Clutch housing bore inside diameter	28.000-28.021	28.05
	(1.1024-1.1032)	(1.104)
Clutch spring free length		
CRF230F models	39.2	36.1
	(1.54)	(1.42)
CRF230L and CRF230M models	37.1	35.1
	(1.46)	(1.38)
Clutch steel plate warp limit		
CRF230F models	–	0.20
		(0.008)
CRF230L and CRF230M models	–	0.30
		(0.012)
Mainshaft outside diameter at outer guide	19.959-19.980	19.92
	(0.7858-0.7866)	(0.784)

Table 2 CLUTCH TORQUE SPECIFICATIONS

	N·m	in.-lb.	ft.-lb.
Clutch lever pivot bolt			
2004-on CRF230F models	1	9	–
Clutch lever pivot nut			
2004-on CRF230F models	6	53	–
Clutch locknut	93	–	69
Clutch spring bolts	12	106	–
Oil filter rotor locknut	83	–	61
Stopper arm bolt	12	106	–

CHAPTER SEVEN

TRANSMISSION
AND INTERNAL SHIFT MECHANISM

This chapter provides service procedures for the transmission and internal shift mechanism. The external shift mechanism is covered in Chapter Six. Transmission and internal shift mechanism service requires crankcase disassembly as described in Chapter Five.

Transmission and internal shift mechanism specifications are listed in **Table 1** and **Table 2** at the end of this chapter.

SERVICE NOTES

Careful inspection of the parts is required, as is keeping the parts correctly oriented so they can be reinstalled in the correct direction on the shafts. The gears, washers and snap rings must be installed in the same direction as they were before disassembly. If necessary, slide the parts onto a long dowel or screwdriver as the parts are removed, or make an identification mark on each part to indicate position and orientation.

Always install new snap rings. The snap rings fatigue and distort when they are removed. Although they appear to be in good condition, do not reuse them. To install a new snap ring without distorting it, hold the closed side of the snap ring with a pair of pliers while the open side is spread with snap ring pliers (**Figure 1**). While holding the spread ring with both tools, slide it over the shaft and into position (**Figure 2**). This technique is particularly useful when removing a notched-type snap ring (**Figure 1**). During removal, this type of snap ring tends to bind and grip the shaft.

Usually, snap rings have one rounded edge, while the other side has a sharp edge (**Figure 3**). The inner sharp edge prevents the snap ring from lifting out of the shaft groove when lateral pressure is applied to the snap ring. Always look at the inner and outer edges of the snap ring. Some snap rings are manufactured with the inner and outer sharp edge on opposite sides. If a snap ring has no identifiable sharp edge, the snap ring can be installed in either direction. In all cases, new snap rings must be installed at assembly, and when applicable, must be installed in the same direction as the removed snap rings.

When installed on a splined shaft, the snap ring gap should be positioned over a groove in the shaft (**Figure 4**).

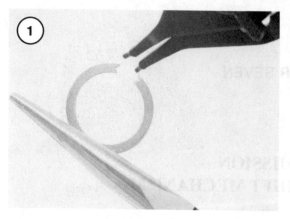

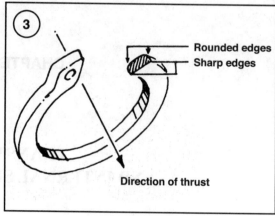

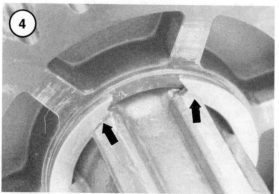

Rounded edges

Sharp edges

Direction of thrust

TRANSMISSION

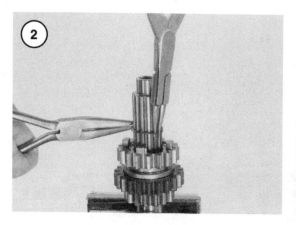

Removal/Installation

1. Split the crankcase (Chapter Five).
2. Remove the shift fork shaft (A, **Figure 5**).
3. Remove the shift drum (B, **Figure 5**).
4. Remove the shift forks (**Figure 6**).
5. Remove both transmission shaft assemblies (**Figure 7**) together as a unit.

> *NOTE*
> *During assembly, lubricate all moving contact surfaces with clean engine oil.*

6. To install the transmission shaft assemblies, mesh them both together in their proper relationship to each other (**Figure 8**).
7. Make sure the thrust washers (**Figure 9**) are installed on the shafts. If necessary, apply a small amount of grease to hold the washers in place.
8. Insert the transmission shaft assemblies (**Figure 7**) into the left crankcase half together as a unit.
9. Make sure the thrust washer (**Figure 10**) is installed on the countershaft.
10. Identify the shift forks according to position. Each shift fork has a letter L, C or R (**Figure 11**) cast onto it to indicate left, center or right, respectively.

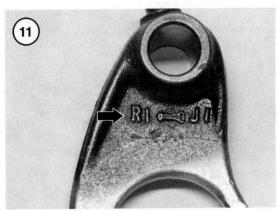

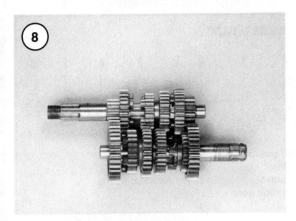

7

11. Install the left shift fork (A, **Figure 12**), center shift fork (B) and right shift fork (C) into the gear slots. The identifying letter on the left shift fork must be up (toward right end of transmission shafts). Install the center and right shift forks so the identifying letter is down (toward the left crankcase half).

NOTE
*It may be necessary to move the sliding gears up the transmission shafts so the shift fork pins (D, **Figure 12**) will fit into the shift drum slots.*

12. Install the shift drum (**Figure 13**). Insert the end pins of the shift forks into the corresponding slots in the shift drum.

13. Install the shift fork shaft (**Figure 14**) through all three shift forks. Push the shaft in until it bottoms in the crankcase hole.

14. Turn both transmission shafts. Make sure there is no binding.

15. Tilt the left crankcase half and transmission assemblies up to about a 45° angle from horizontal. This will relieve some of the weight of the gears against each other so the gears will shift properly.

16. Turn the transmission shafts and shift through all gears using the shift drum. Make sure all gears prop-

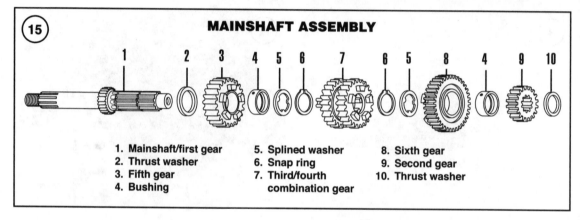

MAINSHAFT ASSEMBLY

1. Mainshaft/first gear
2. Thrust washer
3. Fifth gear
4. Bushing
5. Splined washer
6. Snap ring
7. Third/fourth combination gear
8. Sixth gear
9. Second gear
10. Thrust washer

erly engage. This is the last opportunity to determine if something is installed incorrectly.

17. Reassemble the crankcase (Chapter Five).

Mainshaft Disassembly/Assembly

Refer to **Figure 15**.

1. Remove the thrust washer (A, **Figure 16**).
2. Remove second gear (B, **Figure 16**).
3. Remove sixth gear (**Figure 17**).
4. Slide off the bushing (A, **Figure 18**).
5. Remove the splined washer (B, **Figure 18**) and snap ring (**Figure 19**).
6. Slide off third/fourth combination gear (**Figure 20**).
7. Remove the snap ring (A, **Figure 21**) and splined washer (B).
8. Slide off fifth gear (**Figure 22**).
9. Remove the bushing (A, **Figure 23**) and thrust washer (B).
10. Inspect the mainshaft assembly (this section).
11. Assemble by reversing the disassembly steps. Note the following:

    a. Refer to **Figure 24** for correct gear orientation.

    b. Make sure each gear properly engages the adjoining gear, where applicable.

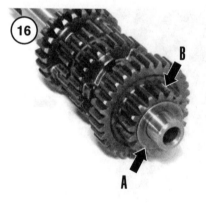

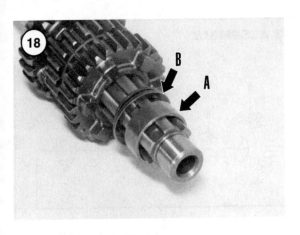

7

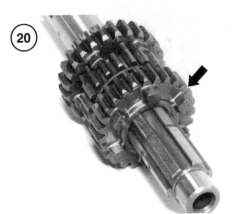

Countershaft
Disassembly/Assembly

Refer to **Figure 25**.

1. At the inner end of the countershaft, remove the thrust washer (A, **Figure 26**) and first gear (B).

2. Remove the bushing (A, **Figure 27**) and thrust washer (B).

3. Remove fifth gear (C, **Figure 27**).

4. At the drive sprocket end of the shaft, remove the thrust washer (A, **Figure 28**) and second gear (B).

5. Remove the bushing (A, **Figure 29**) and thrust washer (B).

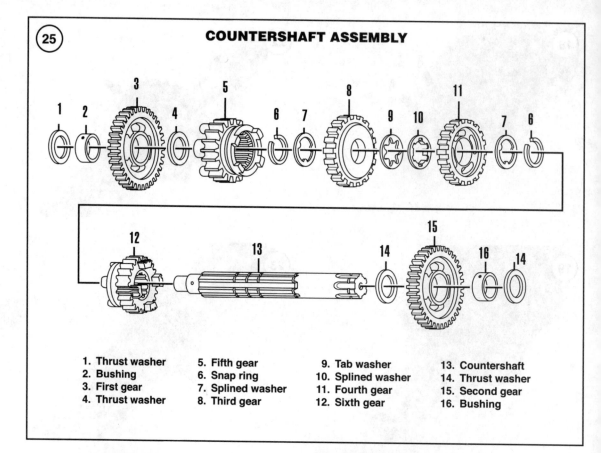

COUNTERSHAFT ASSEMBLY

1. Thrust washer
2. Bushing
3. First gear
4. Thrust washer
5. Fifth gear
6. Snap ring
7. Splined washer
8. Third gear
9. Tab washer
10. Splined washer
11. Fourth gear
12. Sixth gear
13. Countershaft
14. Thrust washer
15. Second gear
16. Bushing

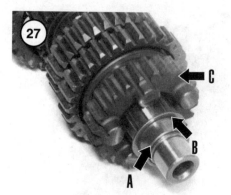

6. At the opposite end of the shaft, remove the snap ring (A, **Figure 30**) and splined washer (B).

7. Remove the third gear (C, **Figure 30**)

8. Remove the tab washer (A, **Figure 31**) and splined washer (B).

9. Remove fourth gear (C, **Figure 31**).

10. Remove the splined washer (A, **Figure 32**) and snap ring (B) .

11. Remove fifth gear (C, **Figure 32**).

12. Inspect the countershaft assembly (this section).

13. Assemble by reversing the disassembly steps. Note the following:

a. Install the splined washer (B, **Figure 31**) and seat it against third gear (C). Rotate the washer so its splines align with the countershaft splines.

b. Position the tab washer so the tabs point inward (**Figure 33**). Push the tab washer (A, **Figure 31**) in so the tabs fit into the splined washer (B).

c. Refer to **Figure 34** for correct placement of the gears.

d. Make sure each gear engages properly to the adjoining gear, where applicable.

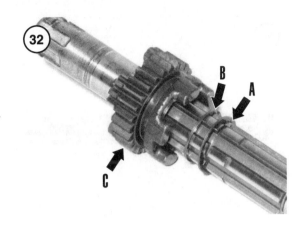

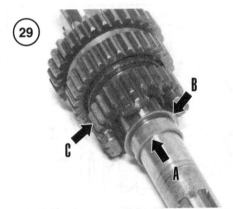

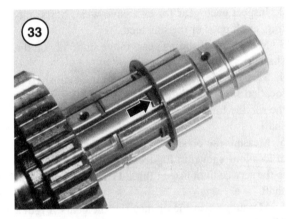

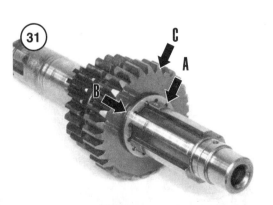

Inspection

1. Clean all parts in solvent and dry thoroughly.

NOTE
Replace defective gears. It is a good idea to replace the mating gear on the opposite shaft even though it may not show as much wear or damage.

NOTE
The first gear is part of the mainshaft. Replace the shaft if the gear is defective.

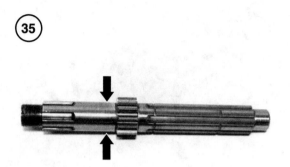

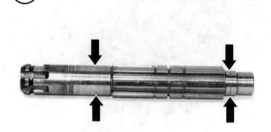

2. Inspect each gear for excessive wear, burrs, pitting, or chipped or missing teeth.

3. Make sure all sliding gears move smoothly on the shaft.

4. Measure the outside diameter of the mainshaft at location shown in **Figure 35**. If the shaft is worn to the service limit listed (**Table 1**) or less, replace the shaft.

5. Measure the outside diameter of the countershaft at locations shown in **Figure 36**. If the shaft is worn to the service limit listed (**Table 1**) or less, replace the shaft.

6. Measure the inside diameter of the gears (**Figure 37**). If the gear is worn to, or beyond the service limit (**Table 1**), replace the gear.

7. Measure the inside and outside diameters of the bushings (**Figure 38**). Replace a bushing if it is worn to or beyond the service limit dimension listed (**Table 1**).

8. Inspect the engagement dogs and slots on the gears (**Figure 39**) for rounded or damaged edges. In particular inspect the sides that carry the engine load. Any wear on the dogs or slots should be uniform. If the dogs are not worn evenly, the dogs may fail. Check the engagement of the dogs by placing the gears at their appropriate positions on the shaft, then twist the gears together. Check for positive engagement in both directions. Rounded dogs will cause the transmission to jump out of gear. If damage is evident, also check the condition of the shift forks.

9. Replace worn or damaged washers.

10. Discard the snap rings and replace them during assembly.

INTERNAL SHIFT MECHANISM

The internal shift mechanism is removed and installed during the transmission removal and installation procedures described in this chapter.

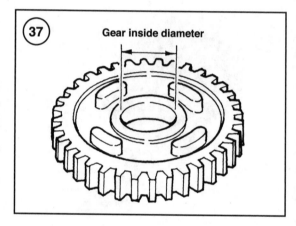

Gear inside diameter

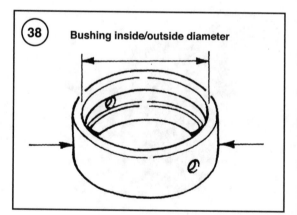

Bushing inside/outside diameter

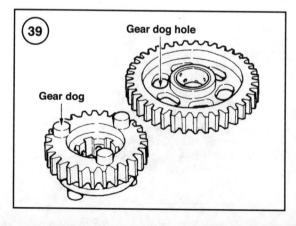

Gear dog hole

Gear dog

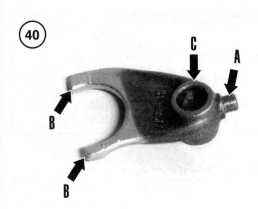

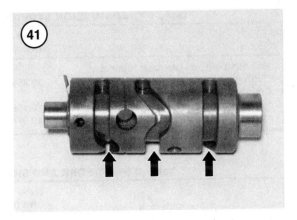

Inspection

1. Inspect each shift fork for signs of wear or cracking. Check for bending and make sure each fork slides smoothly on the shaft; replace any worn or damaged forks.
2. Check the follower pin (A, **Figure 40**) on each shift fork for wear or damage; replace if necessary.
3. Check the grooves in the shift drum (**Figure 41**) for wear or roughness. If any of the groove profiles have excessive wear or damage, replace the thrift drum.
4. Measure the thickness (B, **Figure 40**) of the shift fork fingers. Replace forks that are worn to the service limit (**Table 2**) or less.

5. Check for any arc-shaped wear or burned marks on the shift forks. This indicates that the shift fork has come in contact with the gear. The fork fingers have become excessively worn and the fork must be replaced.
6. Roll the shift fork shaft on a flat surface such as a piece of plate glass. Replace a bent shaft.
7. Measure the outside diameter of the shift fork shaft. Replace the shaft if worn to the service limit listed (**Table 2**) or less.
8. Measure the inside diameter (C, **Figure 40**) of each shift fork shaft bore. Replace forks that are worn to the service limit (**Table 2**) or greater.
9. Apply a light coat of oil to the shift fork shafts and the inside bores of the shift forks before installation.

Table 1 TRANSMISSION SERVICE SPECIFICATIONS

	New mm (in.)	Service limit mm (in.)
Transmission gears–inside diameter		
Mainshaft		
Fifth and sixth gear	23.020-23.041 (0.9063-0.9071)	23.08 (0.909)
Countershaft		
First gear	19.520-19.541 (0.7685-0.7693)	19.57 (0.770)
Second gear	23.020-23.041 (0.9063-0.9071)	23.08 (0.909)
Third and fourth gear	22.020-22.041 (0.8669-0.8678)	22.08 (0.869)
Bushings		
Mainshaft		
Fifth and sixth gear inside diameter		
CRF230F	20.000-20.021 (0.7874-0.7882)	20.05 (0.789)
CRF230L and CRF230M	20.020-20.041 (0.7882-0.7890)	20.07 (0.790)
Fifth and sixth gear outside diameter	22.979-23.000 (0.9047-0.9055)	22.93 (0.903)
Countershaft		
First gear inside diameter	16.516-16.534 (0.6502-0.6509)	16.60 (0.654)
First gear outside diameter	19.479-19.500 (0.7669-0.7677)	19.43 (0.765)
Second gear inside diameter		
CRF230F	20.000-20.021 (0.7874-0.7882)	20.05 (0.789)
CRF230L and CRF230M	20.020-20.041 (0.7882-0.7890)	20.07 (0.790)
Second gear outside diameter	22.979-23.000 (0.9047-0.9055)	22.93 (0.903)
(continued)		

Table 1 TRANSMISSION SERVICE SPECIFICATIONS (CONTINUED)

	New mm (in.)	Service limit mm (in.)
Mainshaft outside diameter location:		
Fifth gear bushing	19.959-19.980 (0.7858-0.7866)	19.90 (0.783)
Countershaft outside diameter location:		
First gear bushing	16.466-16.484 (0.6483-0.6490)	16.41 (0.646)
Second gear bushing	19.974-19.987 (0.7864-0.7869)	19.94 (0.785)

Table 2 SHIFT FORK AND SHAFT SERVICE SPECIFICATIONS

	New mm (in.)	Service limit mm (in.)
Shift fork shaft bore inside diameter	12.000-12.021 (0.4724-0.4733)	12.05 (0.474)
Shift fork finger thickness	4.93-5.00 (0.194-0.197)	4.50 (0.177)
Shift fork shaft outside diameter	11.976-11.994 (0.4715-0.4722)	11.96 (0.471)

FUEL SYSTEM (CRF230F MODELS)

This chapter covers the fuel system. Air filter service is covered in Chapter Three. Refer to *Safety* in Chapter One when working on the fuel system and related components.

Specifications are located in **Tables 1-3** at the end of this chapter.

CARBURETOR

Removal/Installation

1. Remove the fuel tank (this chapter).
2. Place a container under the carburetor drain hose. Loosen the drain screw (A, **Figure 1**) to drain the fuel from the float bowl.
3. Loosen the clamp screws (B, **Figure 1**) on both the front intake tube and rear rubber boot.
4. Release the drain tube and air vent hose from the clamps on the frame.
5. Carefully pull the carburetor free of the intake tube and the rear rubber boot. Remove the carburetor from the right side.
6. Loosen the locknuts (A, **Figure 2**) on each throttle cable. Detach each throttle cable (B and C, **Figure 2**) from the mounting bracket. Then, detach the cables from the carburetor pulley. Disconnect both throttle cables from the carburetor pulley (D, **Figure 2**).
7. Install by reversing the removal steps. Note the following during installation:
   a. Install the carburetor so the boss on the carburetor aligns with the notch (**Figure 3**) in the rubber intake tube.

b. Make sure the pull cable (B, **Figure 2**) is installed in the bottom receptacle on the carburetor pulley and the return cable (C) is installed in the top receptacle.
   c. Make sure the screws on the clamping bands are tightened securely to avoid a vacuum leak and possible engine damage.
   d. Route the drain tube and air vent hose along their original path and secure with frame clamps.
   e. Make sure the fuel drain screw (A, **Figure 1**) is tightened securely.
   f. Adjust the throttle cables (Chapter Three).

Disassembly/Assembly

Refer to **Figure 4**.
1. Remove the fuel (A, **Figure 5**), vent (B) and overflow (C) tubes.
2. Remove the screws (**Figure 6**) securing the top cover and remove the cover and gasket.
3. Remove the link arm retaining screw (A, **Figure 7**).
4. Remove the throttle shaft and pulley assembly (**Figure 8**). Don't lose the internal washer (B, **Figure 7**).
5. Remove the throttle valve and link arm (**Figure 9**).
6. Remove the screws (**Figure 10**) and separate the throttle valve from the link arm.
7. If necessary, remove the jet needle (A, **Figure 11**) from the throttle valve. Record the position of the clip (B, **Figure 11**) if removal is necessary.

8. Remove the choke lever (A, **Figure 12**) and bracket (B).

9. Remove the screws (A, **Figure 13**) securing the air cutoff valve cover and remove the cover (B).

10. Remove the spring (A, **Figure 14**) and diaphragm (B).

11. Remove the small O-ring (C, **Figure 14**).

12. Remove the screws (A, **Figure 15**) securing the float bowl (B) and remove the float bowl.

13. Unscrew the main jet cover (C, **Figure 15**) from the float bowl.

14. Remove the plastic baffle (A, **Figure 16**).

15. Carefully screw in the pilot screw (B, **Figure 16**) until it lightly seats. Count and record the number of turns so it can be installed in the same position.

16. Unscrew and remove the pilot screw assembly (**Figure 17**). Remove the O-ring if it remained in the pilot screw hole.

17. Remove the float pivot pin (**Figure 18**).

18. Remove the float and fuel inlet valve (**Figure 19**).

19. Remove the main jet (A, **Figure 20**), needle jet holder (**Figure 21**) and needle jet (**Figure 22**).

20. Turn the carburetor over and gently tap the side of the body. Catch the needle jet as it falls out. If the needle jet does not fall out, use a plastic or fiber tool and gently push the needle jet out. Do not use metal tools for this purpose.

21. Remove the slow jet (B, **Figure 20**).

22. Remove the idle speed screw assembly (C, **Figure 13**).

23. Remove the O-ring gasket from the float bowl.

> *NOTE*
> *Further disassembly is not necessary. The throttle and choke plates and shafts are available only as part of the carburetor body.*

24. Clean and inspect all parts (this chapter).

25. Assembly is the reverse of the disassembly steps. Note the following:

   a. Install the needle jet (**Figure 22**) so the chamfered end faces up toward the needle jet holder.

   b. If removed, install the needle jet clip in its original position (**Table 1**).

   c. Install the plastic main jet baffle (A, **Figure 16**) so the wide notch (C) fits around the bosses (D).

   d. Make sure the end of the jet needle (A, **Figure 23**) enters the spring (B) on the link arm.

   e. Check the float height and adjust, if necessary (this chapter).

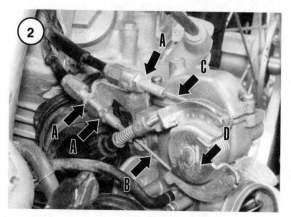

Cleaning/Inspection

> *CAUTION*
> *Do not clean the carburetor body or O-rings in carburetor cleaner or other solution that damages rubber parts.*

1. Clean and dry the carburetor parts.

2. Clean the overflow tube (**Figure 24**) in the float bowl.

3. Inspect the end of the fuel inlet valve (**Figure 25**) for wear or damage. Also, check the inside of the valve seat in the carburetor body. If either part is

CARBURETOR

④

1. Screw	18. Body	32. Spring
2. Top cover	19. Spring	33. Pilot screw
3. Gasket	20. Throttle pulley	34. Needle jet
4. Screw	and shaft	35. Needle jet holder
5. Washer	21. Choke lever	36. Main jet
6. Link arm	22. Bracket	37. Slow jet
7. Washer	23. Screw	38. Baffle
8. Link	24. Diaphragm	39. Fuel inlet valve
9. Spring	25. Spring	40. Float
10. Screw	26. O-ring	41. Float pin
11. Pivot	27. Air cut-off	42. Gasket
12. Spring	cover	43. Float bowl
13. Clip	28. Screw	44. Drain screw
14. Jet needle	29. Idle speed	45. O-ring
15. Throttle valve	screw	46. O-ring
16. Bracket	30. O-ring	47. Main jet cover
17. Screw	31. Washer	48. Screw

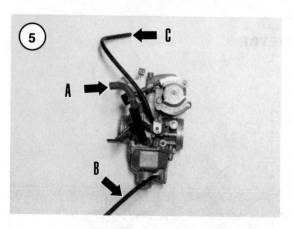

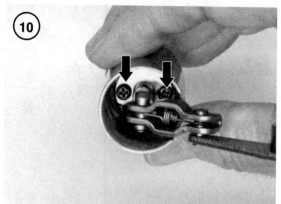

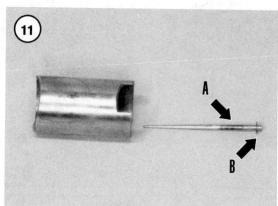

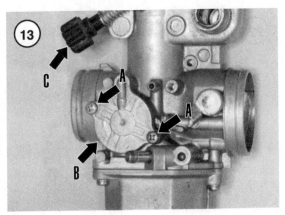

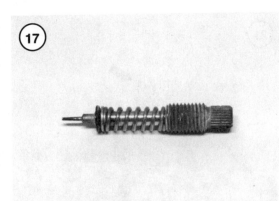

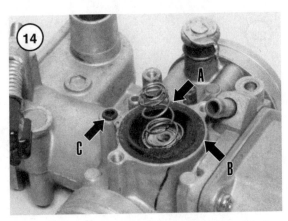

8

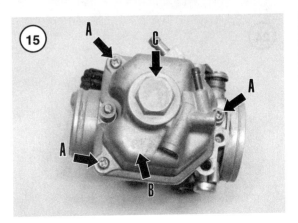

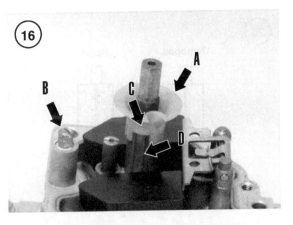

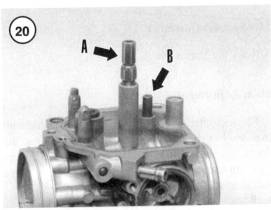

damaged, replace the valve and carburetor body as a set. A damaged valve or a particle of dirt or grit in the valve seat assembly will cause the carburetor to flood and overflow fuel.

4. Inspect all O-ring seals. O-ring seals tend to become hardened with prolonged use and heat.

5. Inspect the pilot screw (**Figure 26**) and spring for damage. Replace the screw if damaged.

6. Inspect the float for deterioration or damage. Check the float by submerging it in a container of water. If water enters the float, replace it.

7. Move the throttle pulley from stop-to-stop and check for free movement. If it does not move freely, replace the carburetor body.

8. Make sure all openings in the carburetor body are clear. Clean with compressed air.

9. Inspect the air cutoff diaphragm (B, **Figure 14**) for cracks, deterioration or other damage. Replace diaphragm if damaged.

> *CAUTION*
> *Do not use wire or drill bits to clean the jets. Minor gouges in the jet can alter the air/fuel mixture.*

10. Make sure all jet openings are clear. Replace any jet that cannot be cleaned.

CARBURETOR ADJUSTMENTS

Idle Speed Adjustment

Refer to Chapter Three.

Float Adjustment

The fuel inlet valve and float maintain a constant fuel level in the carburetor float bowl. Because the float level affects the fuel mixture throughout the engine's operating range, this level must be maintained within specification.

1. Remove the carburetor (this chapter).

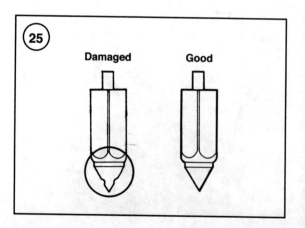

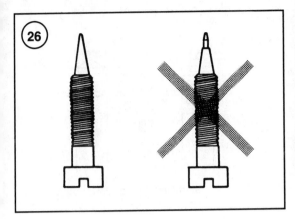

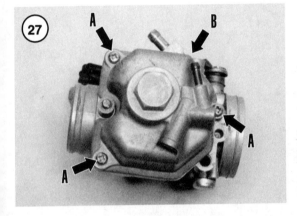

Float level gauge

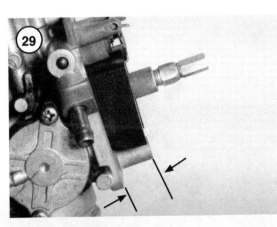

2. Remove the screws (A, **Figure 27**) securing the float bowl (B) and remove the float bowl.

3. Hold the carburetor assembly with the carburetor inclined 15-45° from vertical so that the float arm is just touching the float needle, and not pushing it down. Use a float gauge (**Figure 28**), caliper or small ruler and measure the distance (**Figure 29**) from the carburetor body to the bottom surface of the float. The correct float height is listed in **Table 1**.

4. Adjust by carefully bending the tang on the float arm. If the float level is too high, the result will be a rich air/fuel mixture. If it is too low, the mixture will be too lean.

5. Reassemble and install the carburetor (this chapter).

Pilot Screw Adjustment

NOTE
Pilot screw adjustment is not necessary unless the carburetor has been over-hauled or it has been misadjusted.

The air filter element must be clean before starting this procedure or the results will be inaccurate. Refer to Chapter Three.

1. If so equipped, remove the tamper-proof plug for access to the pilot screw.

2. For the preliminary adjustment, carefully turn the pilot screw (**Figure 30**) in until it seats lightly, and then back it out the number of turns listed in **Table 1**.

3. Start the engine and let it reach normal operating temperature. Approximately 10 minutes of stop and go riding is sufficient. Shut off the engine.

4. Connect a portable tachometer capable of reading 50 rpm increments following the gauge manufacturer's instructions.

5. Start the engine, and then turn the idle speed screw (**Figure 31**) to obtain the idle speed listed in **Table 1**.

6. Turn the pilot screw (**Figure 30**) as needed to obtain the highest idle speed.

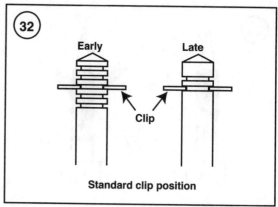

Standard clip position

7. Reset the idle speed. Open and close the throttle a couple of times while checking for variation in idle speed. Readjust if necessary.

8. While running the engine, turn the pilot screw in slowly until the engine speed drops 50 rpm. Turn the pilot screw out 1/4 turn. Turn the idle speed screw (**Figure 31**) to obtain the idle speed listed in **Table 1.**

9. Stop the engine and disconnect the portable tachometer.

10. Apply Three Bond 7737, or an equivalent high-strength instant adhesive, to a new tamper-proof plug and install the plug over the pilot screw.

Needle Jet Adjustment

Early models are equipped with a jet needle that has five clip grooves. Later models are equipped with a jet needle that has two clip grooves. Refer to **Figure 32**.

1. Remove the carburetor assembly (this chapter).

2. Remove the screws (A, **Figure 33**) securing the top cover (B). Then, remove the cover and gasket.

3. Remove the link arm retaining screw (A, **Figure 34**).

4. Remove the throttle shaft and pulley assembly (**Figure 35**). Don't lose the internal washer (B, **Figure 34**).

5. Remove the throttle valve and link arm (**Figure 36**).

6. Remove the screws (**Figure 37**) and separate the throttle valve from the link arm.

7. Remove the jet needle (**Figure 38**) and note the original position of the needle clip (**Figure 39**). The standard clip position setting is listed in **Table 1**.

8. Raising the needle (lowering the clip) will enrich the mixture during mid-throttle openings, while lowering the needle (raising the clip) will lean the mixture. Refer to **Figure 40**.

9. Reassemble and install the carburetor by reversing the disassembly and removal steps. Make sure the end of the jet needle (A, **Figure 41**) enters the spring (B) on the link arm.

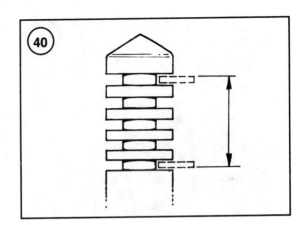

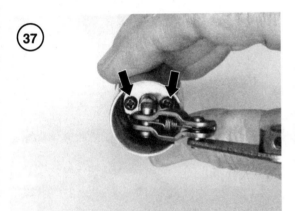

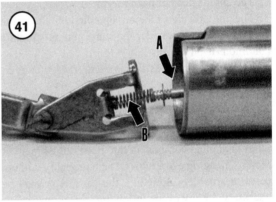

8

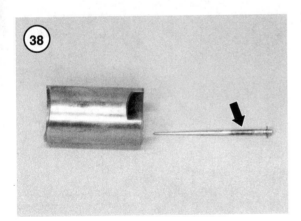

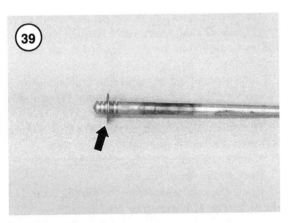

High-Altitude Adjustment

> *CAUTION*
> *If the carburetor is adjusted for higher elevations, change it back to the standard settings when the motorcycle is returned to elevations lower than 1000 m. (5000 ft). Engine overheating and piston seizure will occur if the engine runs lean.*

High-altitude and temperature adjustments consist of three different changes to the carburetor: main jet size change, a different location of the clip on the jet needle and a different pilot screw setting. Refer to **Table 1** for high-altitude specifications.

Never change a jet by more than one size at a time without test riding the motorcycle and inspecting the spark plug (Chapter Three).

Carburetor Rejetting

Do not try to solve a poor running engine problem by rejetting the carburetor if all of the following conditions hold true.

1. The engine maintained a good tune in the past with the standard jetting.

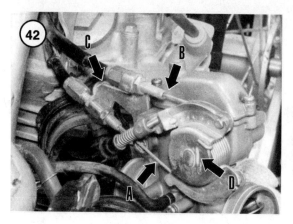

2. The engine has not been modified.

3. The motorcycle is being operated in the same geographical region under the same general climatic conditions as in the past.

4. The motorcycle was and is being ridden at average highway speeds.

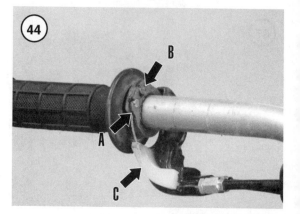

If those conditions all hold true, chances are that the problem is due to a malfunction in the carburetor or in another component that needs adjustment or repair. Changing carburetor jet size probably will not solve the problem. Rejetting the carburetor may be necessary for any of the following conditions:

1. Installation of a non-standard type of air filter element.

2. Installation of a non-standard exhaust system.

3. Modification of the top end components in the engine (pistons, cams, valves, compression ratio, etc.).

4. Operation at considerably higher or lower altitudes or in a considerably hotter or colder climate than in the past.

5. Operation at considerably higher speeds than before and changing to colder spark plugs does not solve the problem.

6. Previously changed carburetor jetting.

7. Inconsistent engine tune.

If it is necessary to rejet the carburetor due to installation of aftermarket parts, check with the manufacturer or a dealer for jetting recommendations.

When rejetting a carburetor, change the jets one size at a time, unless specific recommendations are available. After rejetting, test ride the motorcycle and inspect the spark plug as described in Chapter Three.

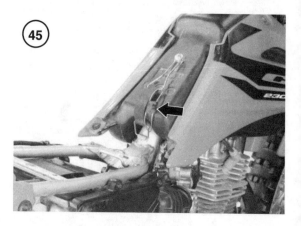

THROTTLE CABLE REPLACEMENT

1. Remove the carburetor (this chapter) sufficiently for access to the throttle cables on the carburetor (**Figure 42**).

2. On the carburetor loosen the nuts on the pull cable (A, **Figure 42**) and return cable (B). Disengage the cables from the bracket (C, **Figure 42**) and throttle pulley (D).

3. Slide the boot off the handlebar throttle housing.

4. Remove the throttle housing bolts (**Figure 43**) and separate the housing.

5. Disconnect the throttle cables (A and B, **Figure 44**) from the throttle grip pulley.

6. Note the routing of the throttle cables.

7. Remove the throttle cables.

8. Route the new cables from the throttle control to the carburetor following their original path.

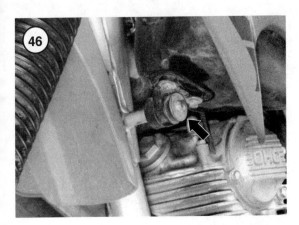

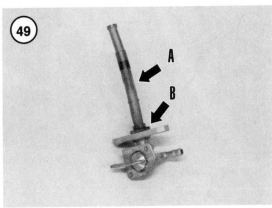

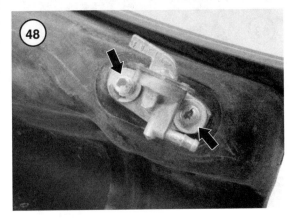

12. Mate both housing covers together so the cable guide fits inside the housing. Install the mounting bolts finger-tight.

13. Slide the boot over the throttle housing.

14. Align the clamp mating surface on the throttle housing with the punch mark on the handlebar. Tighten the upper throttle housing bolt, and then tighten the lower bolt. Tighten the bolts securely.

15. Operate the throttle grip and make sure it turns smoothly. Turn the handlebar and check the throttle operation in both lock positions.

16. Adjust the throttle cables (Chapter Three).

17. Reinstall the carburetor (this chapter).

FUEL TANK

Removal/Installation

1. Remove the seat (Chapter Seventeen).

2. Disconnect the negative battery lead (Chapter Ten).

3. Turn the fuel valve off.

4. Detach the fuel line to the carburetor.

5. Unhook the rubber strap (**Figure 45**) securing the rear of the tank.

6. Remove the bolt, washer and collar (**Figure 46**) on each side of the fuel tank.

7. Pull the fuel filler cap vent tube from the steering stem nut hole.

8. Lift up and pull the tank to the rear and remove the fuel tank.

> *WARNING*
> *If the protective bands or rubber covers are worn through or not installed, the bolt heads or nuts may wear a hole through the fuel tank.*

9. Attach the throttle cables to the carburetor throttle pulley (D, **Figure 42**) and bracket (C) as shown. Note that the pull cable (A, **Figure 42**) is equipped with two nuts.

10. Lubricate the ends of the cable with lithium grease. Then, insert the ends into the handlebar throttle control.

11. Reconnect the pull (A, **Figure 44**) and return (B) throttle cables. Route the pull cable (A, **Figure 44**) into the groove in the cable guide (C) and position the cable guide into the outer throttle housing.

9. Inspect the rubber protective covers (**Figure 47**) on the nuts of the engine upper hanger plate. Replace as a set if any are damaged or starting to deteriorate.

10. Install by reversing the removal steps. Note the following:

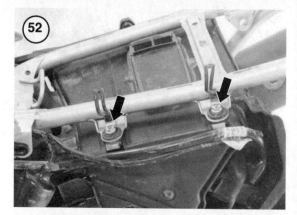

   a. Tighten the fuel tank mounting bolts (**Figure 46**) securely.

   b. Route the fuel filler cap vent tube through the steering stem nut hole.

   c. Make sure the rubber protective covers (**Figure 47**) are in place on the nuts of the upper engine hanger plate.

FUEL VALVE

Removal/Installation

1. Remove the fuel tank (this chapter).
2. Drain the fuel tank.
3. Remove the bolts (**Figure 48**) securing the fuel valve to the bottom of the fuel tank, and then remove the fuel valve.
4. Clean the strainer screen (A, **Figure 49**) in solvent. The strainer screen is not available separately.
5. Install a new fuel valve O-ring (B, **Figure 49**).
6. Install the fuel valve by reversing the removal steps. Note the following:

   a. Tighten the fuel valve mounting screws to 9 N•m (80 in.-lb.).

   b. After turning on the fuel valve, check the fuel valve and hose for leaks.

AIR BOX

Removal/Installation

1. Remove the seat (Chapter Seventeen).
2. Remove both side covers (Chapter Seventeen).
3. Remove the rear fender (Chapter Seventeen).
4. Remove the mud guard from the air box.
5. Remove the rear mounting bolt (**Figure 50**).
6. Detach the breather hose (A, **Figure 51**).
7. Detach the wiring connector boot from the battery box (B, **Figure 51**).

8. Unbolt the wiring clamps (C, **Figure 51**).

9. Remove the bolts (**Figure 52**) securing the air box to the frame.

10. Loosen the clamp band screw (**Figure 53**) on the carburetor for the air box inlet tube.

11. Remove the air box from the right side of the frame.

12. Install by reversing the removal steps. Note the following:

    a. Tighten the mudguard mounting screws to 1 N•m (9 in.-lb.).

    b. Tighten all remaining fasteners securely.

CRANKCASE BREATHER SYSTEM

Crankcase gases are routed through a breather hose (**Figure 54**) from a fitting on the rear of the crankcase into the air box. A drain hose at the bottom of the air box allows removal of residue.

Make sure all hoses and clamps are in good condition and tight to prevent the entrance of water or debris into the engine.

Table 1 CARBURETOR SPECIFICATIONS

Type	Piston valve
Throttle bore size	28 mm (1.1 in.)
Identification number	
2003-2005 models	PD9CA
2006-2007 models	
USA	PD9CD
Canada	PD9CA
2008-on models	PD9CF
Float level	12.5 mm (0.49 in.)
Main jet	
Sea level	102
High altitude	98
Slow jet	42
Jet needle clip position	
2003-2005 models	3rd groove[1]
2006-on models	Bottom groove[2]
Idle speed	1300-1500 rpm
Pilot screw adjustment[3]	1-5/8 turns out

1. High altitude: 2nd groove from top of jet needle.
2. High altitude: Upper groove on jet needle.
3. Initial adjustment only. Refer text for procedure and final pilot air screw adjustment (turns out).

Table 2 FUEL TANK SPECIFICATIONS

	Liters	Gallons
Fuel tank capacity	7.0	1.85
Reserve capacity	1.3	0.34

Table 3 FUEL SYSTEM TORQUE SPECIFICATIONS

	N•m	in.-lb.	ft.-lb.
Fuel valve mounting bolts	9	80	–
Mudguard mounting screws	1	9	–

CHAPTER NINE

FUEL AND EMISSION CONTROL SYSTEMS
(CRF230L AND CRF230M MODELS)

This chapter covers the fuel and emission control systems. Air filter service is covered in Chapter Three. Refer to *Safety* in Chapter One when working on the fuel system and related components.

Specification are located in **Tables 1-3** at the end of this chapter.

CARBURETOR

Removal/Installation

1. Remove the fuel tank (this chapter).

NOTE
If necessary, move the purge control valve out of the way for access to the carburetor heater connector.

2. Disconnect the carburetor heater connector (**Figure 1**).
3. Place a container under the carburetor drain hose. Loosen the drain screw (**Figure 2**) to drain the fuel from the float bowl.
4. Remove the screws securing the throttle pulley cover (**Figure 3**). Disengage the pulley cover from the rubber cover and remove the pulley cover.
5. Loosen the locknuts (A, **Figure 4**) on each throttle cable. Detach each throttle cable (B and C, **Figure 4**) from the mounting bracket. Disconnect the throttle cables from the carburetor pulley (D, **Figure 4**).
6. Disconnect the evaporative emission control hose (A, **Figure 5**) from the carburetor.

7. Disconnect the hose (B, **Figure 5**) from the air cutoff valve.
8. Disconnect the evaporative emission control hose (**Figure 6**) from the carburetor.
9. Separate the carburetor vent hose (**Figure 7**) from the retaining guide.
10. Release the drain tube from the guide on the frame.
11. Loosen the screw (A, **Figure 8**) on the air box tube clamping band.
12. Loosen the screw (B, **Figure 8**) on the intake tube clamping band.

CAUTION
Do not damage the air box tube when separating it from the carburetor.

CAUTION
Support the carburetor after separating it from the tubes since the choke cable is still attached.

13. Separate the carburetor from the air box tube. Pull the carburetor assembly toward the rear and free the assembly from the intake tube on the cylinder head.
14. Slide back the boot. Then, unscrew the choke valve nut (A, **Figure 9**). Remove the carburetor.
15. Install by reversing the removal steps. Note the following:

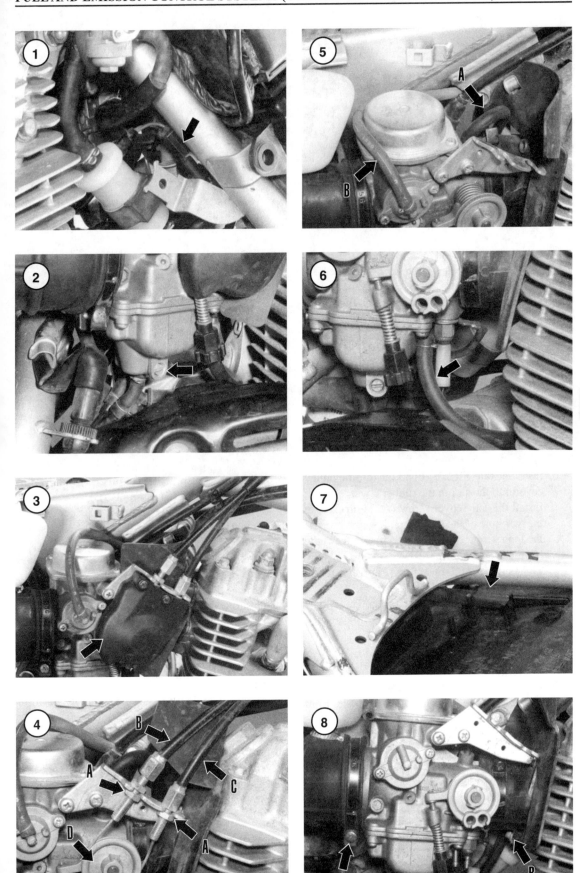

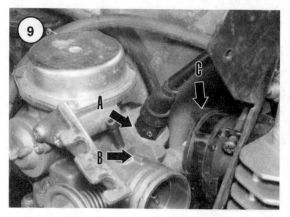

a. Install the choke valve and tighten the choke valve nut to 2.5 N•m (22 in.-lb.). Slide the boot back into place.

b. Install the carburetor so the boss on the carburetor (B, **Figure 9**) aligns with the notch (C) in the rubber intake tube.

c. When installing the throttle cables, be sure to install the pull cable (B, **Figure 4**) to the rear holder on the carburetor pulley and the return cable (C) to the front holder.

d. Make sure the screws (A and B, **Figure 8**) on the clamping bands are tightened securely to avoid a vacuum leak and possible engine damage.

e. Insert the tab (**Figure 10**) on the throttle pulley cover into the slot in the rubber cover.

f. Install the long cover screw (A, **Figure 11**) in the rear hole of the throttle pulley cover. Insert the long screw end into the rubber cover hole (B, **Figure 11**).

g. Tighten the fuel drain screw (**Figure 2**) to 1.5 N•m (13 in.-lb.).

h. Adjust the throttle cables (Chapter Three).

Disassembly/Assembly

Refer to **Figure 12**.

1. Note the location of the fuel hose, vent hose and drain hose in **Figure 13**. Then, detach the hoses from the carburetor.

2. Disconnect the heater wire connector (A, **Figure 14**).

3. Unscrew and remove the carburetor heater (B, **Figure 14**), ground wire end (C) and washer.

4. Remove the screws (A, **Figure 15**) securing the top cover and remove the cover (B).

5. Remove the spring (**Figure 16**) and the diaphragm (**Figure 17**).

6. Remove the air cut-off valve as follows:

a. Remove the screws (A, **Figure 18**) securing the air cut-off valve cover and remove the cover (B).

b. Remove the spring (A, **Figure 19**) and the diaphragm and piston assembly (B).

7. Remove the screws (A, **Figure 20**) securing the float bowl (B) and remove the float bowl and gasket.

8. Remove the main jet baffle (**Figure 21**).

9. Push the float pin (A, **Figure 22**) toward the fuel inlet side of the carburetor and remove the pin.

10. Remove the float (B, **Figure 22**) and the fuel valve.

11. Unscrew the main jet (A, **Figure 23**).

12. Unscrew the needle jet holder (B, **Figure 23**).

13. Turn the carburetor over and remove the needle jet (**Figure 24**).

14. Loosen the slow jet (**Figure 25**), and then remove it.

15. To disassemble the jet needle assembly, perform the following:

a. Using an 8-mm socket or flat-jawed needle-nose pliers, turn the needle holder (**Figure 26**) 90° counterclockwise and remove the holder (**Figure 27**) and small spring.

b. Remove the jet needle (**Figure 28**).

NOTE
Do not remove the pilot screw unless it is damaged or requires replacement.

16. Unscrew and remove the pilot screw (**Figure 29**), spring, washer and O-ring.

CARBURETOR

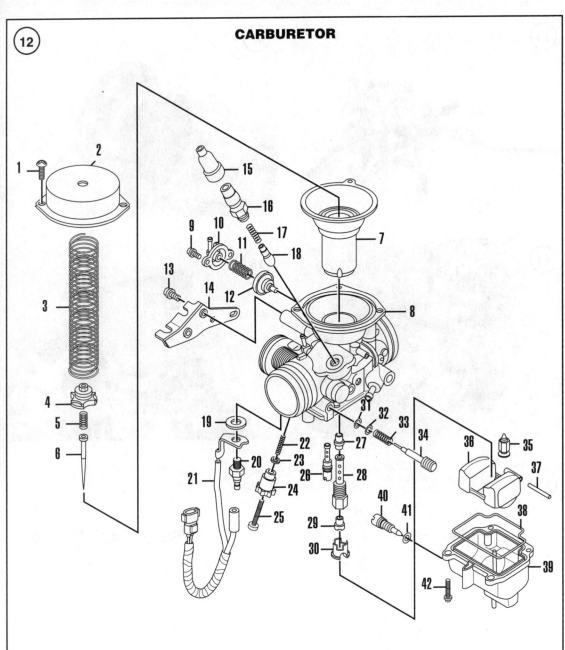

1. Screw	14. Cable bracket	28. Needle jet holder
2. Top cover	15. Boot	29. Main jet
3. Spring	16. Choke valve nut	30. Baffle
4. Jet needle holder	17. Spring	31. O-ring
5. Spring	18. Choke valve	32. Washer
6. Jet needle	19. Washer	33. Spring
7. Vacuum piston/ diaphragm	20. Carburetor heater	34. Pilot screw
8. Body	21. Ground/carburetor heater wires	35. Fuel inlet valve
9. Screw	22. Spring	36. Float
10. Air cut-off valve cover	23. Washer	37. Float pin
11. Spring	24. Idle speed knob	38. Gasket
12. Diaphragm	25. Bolt	39. Float bowl
13. Screw	26. Slow jet	40. Drain screw
	27. Needle jet	41. O-ring
		42. Screw

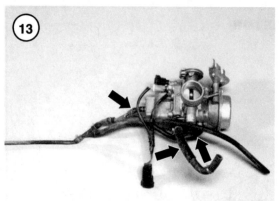

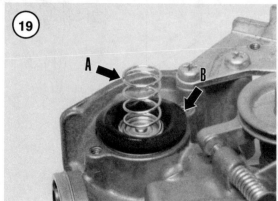

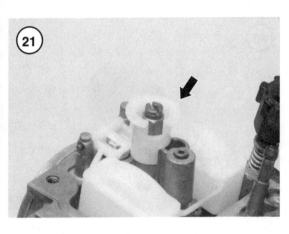

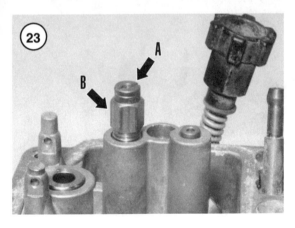

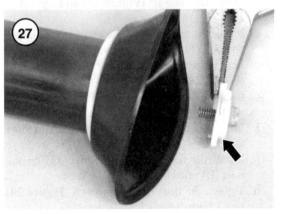

9

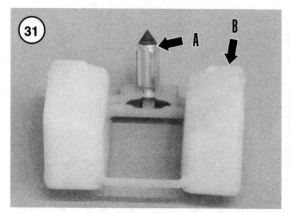

NOTE
Further disassembly is neither neces-
sary nor recommended. Do not remove
the throttle shaft and throttle valve as-
semblies. If these parts are damaged,
replace the carburetor.

17. Clean and inspect all parts (this section).

18. Assemble the carburetor by reversing the disassembly steps. Note the following:

   a. If removed, install the jet needle and needle
   holder. Using an 8-mm socket or flat-jaw needle-nose pliers, press the needle holder in and
   turn 90° clockwise to secure it in place.

   b. Install the slow jet (**Figure 25**) and tighten to
   1.8 N•m (16 in.-lb.).

   c. Install the needle jet so the end with the larger
   opening (**Figure 30**) enters first.

   d. Make sure the needle jet is completely seated
   (**Figure 24**).

   e. Install the needle jet holder (B, **Figure 23**) and
   tighten to 2.5 N•m (22 in.-lb.).

   f. Install the main jet (A, **Figure 23**) and tighten
   to 2.1 N•m (19 in.-lb.).

   g. Install the fuel valve (A, **Figure 31**) on the
   float (B) prior to installing the float.

   h. Tighten the float bowl screws (A, **Figure 20**)
   to 2.1 N•m (19 in.-lb.).

   i. Install the air cut-off valve cover (B, **Figure 18**),
   and tighten the screws (A) to 2.1 N•m (19 in.-lb.).

   j. When installing the diaphragm, position the
   tab (A, **Figure 32**) on the diaphragm into the
   recess in the carburetor body.

   k. Install the top cover so the ear (B, **Figure 32**)
   on the cover aligns with the tab (A) on the
   diaphragm. Install the top cover screws and
   tighten to 2.1 N•m (19 in.-lb.).

   l. After the top cover has been installed, move
   the piston valve up. The piston valve should
   slide back down immediately with no binding. If it binds or if the movement is sluggish,
   the diaphragm may have seated incorrectly or

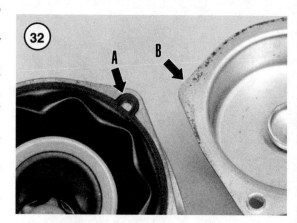

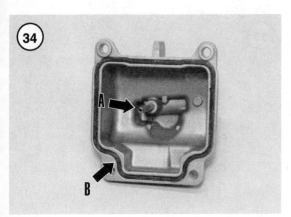

may be folded over. The diaphragm rubber is very soft and may fold over during top cover installation.

m. Check the float lever (this chapter).

n. Install the heater (A, **Figure 33**), ground wire end (B) and washer (C). Tighten the heater body to 4.9 N•m (43 in.-lb.).

o. If removed, reinstall and adjust the pilot screw (this chapter).

p. After the carburetor has been installed, adjust the idle speed (Chapter Three) and choke (this chapter).

Cleaning and Inspection

CAUTION
Do not clean the carburetor body or O-rings in carburetor cleaner or other solution that damages rubber parts.

1. Clean and dry the carburetor parts.

CAUTION
Do not use wire or drill bits to clean the jets. Minor gouges in the jet can alter the air/fuel mixture.

2. Remove the drain screw from the float bowl.

3. Make sure the float bowl overflow tube (A, **Figure 34**) is clear. Blow tube out with compressed air if necessary.

4. Inspect the float bowl O-ring gasket (B, **Figure 34**) for damage, hardening or deterioration; replace if necessary.

5. Inspect the diaphragm, slide and needle (**Figure 35**) for wear, damage or deterioration; replace if necessary.

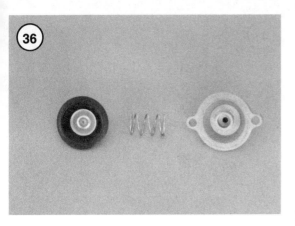

6. Inspect the air cut-off valve assembly (**Figure 36**) for wear, damage or deterioration. Replace any defective part.

7. Inspect the end of the fuel valve (**Figure 37**) for wear or damage. Also, check the inside of the valve seat (**Figure 38**). If either part is damaged, replace as a set.

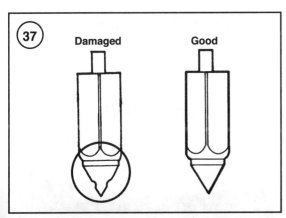

Damaged   Good

8. Inspect the needle jet, the jet holder and spring (**Figure 39**) for wear, damage or deterioration. Replace any defective part.

9. Make sure the holes in the needle jet and slow jet (**Figure 40**) are clear. Clean out using compressed air, if plugged.

10. Inspect the float (**Figure 41**) for deterioration or damage. If a float leak is suspected, place it in a container of non-caustic solution and push it down. If the float sinks or if bubbles appear (indicating a leak), replace the float.

11. Make sure the throttle valve screws (**Figure 42**) are tight. Tighten if necessary.

12. Move the throttle pulley back and forth from stop-to-stop and check for free movement. If it does not move freely or if it sticks in any position, replace the carburetor body.

13. Make sure all openings in the carburetor body are clear. Clean out using compressed air if they are plugged.

14. If necessary, test the carburetor heater (this chapter).

CARBURETOR ADJUSTMENTS

Idle Speed Adjustment

Refer to Chapter Three.

Float Level

The fuel valve and float maintain a constant fuel level in the carburetor float bowl. Because the float level affects the fuel mixture throughout the engine's operating range, this level must be maintained within factory specifications.

1. Remove the carburetor (this chapter).

2. Remove the float bowl mounting screws and float bowl (**Figure 43**). Do not remove the O-ring from the float bowl groove.

3. Hold the carburetor so the fuel valve just touches the float arm without pushing it down. Measure the distance from the carburetor body gasket surface to the float (**Figure 44**) using a float level gauge, ruler or caliper.

4. The float is non-adjustable. If the float level is incorrect, check the float pin and fuel valve for damage. If these parts are in good condition, replace the float and remeasure the float level.

5. Install the float bowl, O-ring gasket and mounting screws. Tighten the float bowl screws to 2.1 N•m (19 in.-lb.).

6. Install the carburetor (this chapter).

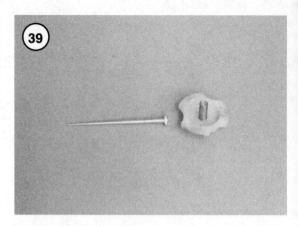

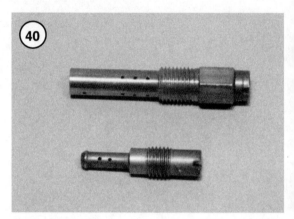

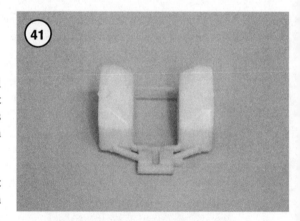

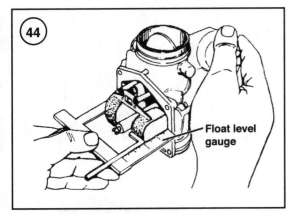

Float level gauge

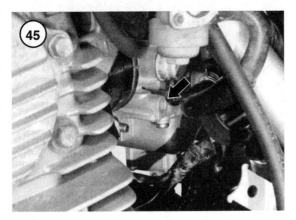

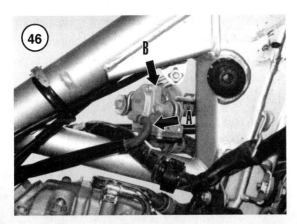

Pilot Screw Adjustment

The air filter element must be clean before starting this procedure or the results will be inaccurate. Refer to Chapter Three.

Pilot screw adjustment is not necessary unless the carburetor has been overhauled or it has been mis-adjusted.

NOTE
Figure 45 *shows the purge control valve and hoses moved out of the way for clarity.*

1. For a preliminary adjustment, carefully turn the pilot screw (**Figure 45**) in until it seats lightly. Then, back the pilot screw out the correct number of turns (**Table 1**.)
2. Start the engine and let it reach normal operating temperature. Approximately 5-10 minutes of stop-and-go riding is usually sufficient. Shut off the engine.
3. Remove the fuel tank (this chapter).
4. Disconnect the vacuum hose (A, **Figure 46**) from the PAIR valve (B). Plug the end of the hose.
5. Reinstall the fuel tank (this chapter).
6. Connect a portable tachometer capable of reading 50 rpm increments following the gauge manufacturer's instructions.
7. Start the engine and turn the idle speed screw (**Figure 47**) to obtain the correct idle speed (**Table 1**).
8. Turn the pilot screw in or out to obtain the highest engine idle speed.
9. Reset the idle speed. Open and close the throttle several times; check for variation in idle speed. Readjust if necessary.
10. Turn the pilot screw in gradually until the engine speed drops by 50 rpm and note this setting.
11. Turn the pilot screw out 3/8 turn from the position noted when the idle speed dropped by 50 rpm.
12. Disconnect the portable tachometer.
13. Remove the fuel tank (this chapter).

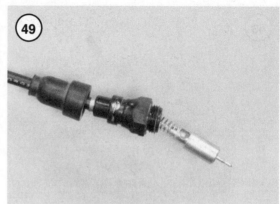

14. Reconnect the vacuum hose (A, **Figure 46**) to the PAIR valve (B).

15. Reinstall the fuel tank (this chapter).

16. After this adjustment is complete, test ride the motorcycle. Throttle response should be rapid and without any hesitation.

Choke Cable Adjustment

Make sure the choke (starter enrichment valve) operates smoothly with no binding before starting adjustment. If the cable binds, lubricate it (Chapter Three). If the cable still does not operate smoothly, replace it (this chapter).

1. Remove the carburetor (this chapter) for access to the choke valve nut (**Figure 48**).

2. Unscrew the choke valve nut. Then, remove the choke valve and spring assembly (**Figure 49**) from the carburetor.

3. Push the choke lever all the way to the fully-on position.

4. Using a caliper, measure the distance between the end of the threads of the choke valve nut and the choke valve (**Figure 50**). The correct distance is 27.5-30.5 mm (1.08-1.20 in.). Replace the choke cable if distance is incorrect.

5. Install the valve and spring. Then, install and tighten the choke valve nut to 2.5 N•m (22 in.-lb.).

6. Install the carburetor (this chapter).

High-Altitude Adjustment

CAUTION
If the carburetor is adjusted for higher elevations, change it back to the standard settings when the motorcycle is returned to lower elevations (near sea level). Engine overheating and piston seizure will occur if the engine runs lean.

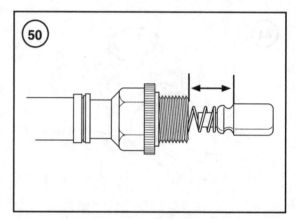

Honda does not provide carburetor specifications for operation at high altitude. Contact a dealership for recommended carburetor changes that apply to the riding area environment.

Carburetor Rejetting

Refer to Chapter Eight for recommendation on rejetting the carburetor. Note that the jet needle position is not adjustable on the CRF230L or CRF230M models.

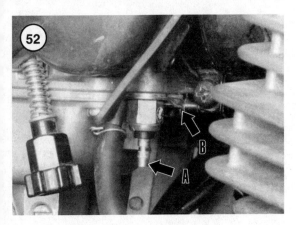

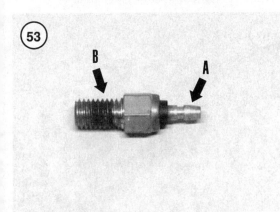

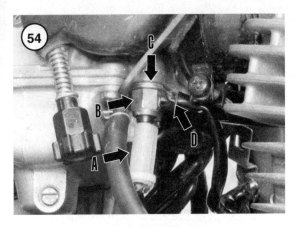

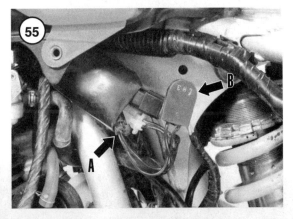

CARBURETOR HEATER AND AIR TEMPERATURE SWITCH

The carburetor is equipped with a heater element that improves cold-weather running. An air temperature switch regulates heater operation.

Carburetor Heater Test

The carburetor heater may be tested while it is installed on the carburetor or while it is removed from the carburetor.

1A. If testing will be done with the heater installed on the motorcycle, disconnect the heater connector (**Figure 51**). Use an ohmmeter and measure the resistance between the heater terminal (A, **Figure 52**) and the ground wire end (B).

1B. If testing will be done while the heater is removed, use an ohmmeter and measure the resistance between the heater terminal (A, **Figure 53**) and the heater body (B).

2. Replace the heater if the resistance is out of specification (**Table 1**).

3. If the heater tests good, check the air temperature switch. Also, test for the presence of 12 volts in the circuit with the ignition switch on.

Carburetor Heater Removal/Installation

1. Disconnect the heater connecter (A, **Figure 54**) from the heater terminal.

2. Unscrew and remove the heater (B, **Figure 54**). Do not lose the washer (C, **Figure 54**).

3. Reverse the removal steps for installation. Note the following:

    a. Install the ground wire end (D, **Figure 54**) and washer (C) as shown.

    b. Tighten the heater to 4.9 N•m (43 in.-lb.).

Air Temperature Switch Test and Replacement

1. Remove the battery case (Chapter Eleven).

2. Disconnect the air temperature switch connector (A, **Figure 55**) and remove the switch (B).

3. Connect an ohmmeter to the switch terminals.

4. Use a suitable temperature reading tool and check the temperature of the switch.

5. Heat or cool the switch to check switch operation.

6. The ohmmeter should indicate continuity or no continuity at the specified temperatures.

7. Replace the air temperature switch if the test results are not within specifications (**Table 1**).

8. Reverse removal steps to install the switch.

9

THROTTLE CABLE REPLACEMENT

1. Remove the fuel tank as described in this chapter.

2. Slide the boot off the handlebar throttle housing.

3. Remove the throttle housing bolts (**Figure 56**) and separate the housing.

4. Disconnect the throttle cables (A and B, **Figure 57**) from the throttle grip pulley.

5. Remove the screws securing the throttle pulley cover (**Figure 58**). Disengage the tab on the pulley cover from the slot in the rubber cover, and then remove the pulley cover.

6. Loosen the locknuts (A, **Figure 59**) on each throttle cable. Detach each throttle cable (B and C, **Figure 59**) from the mounting bracket. Disconnect the throttle cables from the carburetor pulley (D, **Figure 59**).

7. Note the routing of the throttle cables.

8. Remove the throttle cables.

9. Route the new cables from the throttle control to the carburetor along the original path noted during removal.

10. Install the throttle cables on the carburetor. Connect the pull cable (B, **Figure 59**) to the rear holder on the carburetor pulley and the return cable (C) to the front holder.

11. Insert the tab (**Figure 60**) on the throttle pulley cover into the slot in the rubber cover.

12. Install the long cover screw (A, **Figure 61**) in the rear hole of the throttle pulley cover. Insert the long screw end into the rubber cover hole (B, **Figure 61**).

13. Lubricate the ends of the throttle cables with lithium grease. Then, insert the cable ends into the handlebar throttle control.

14. Reconnect the pull (A, **Figure 57**) and return (B) throttle cables. Route the pull cable (A, **Figure 57**) into the groove in the cable guide (C) and position the cable guide into the outer throttle housing.

15. Mate both throttle housing covers together so the cable guide fits inside the housing. Install the mounting bolts finger-tight.

16. Slide the boot over the throttle housing.

17. Align the clamp mating surface on the throttle housing with the punch mark on the handlebar. Tighten the upper, and then the lower throttle housing bolt. Tighten the bolts securely.

> *WARNING*
> *Do not ride the motorcycle until the throttle cables are installed and adjusted properly and the throttle opens and returns smoothly.*

18. Operate the throttle grip and make sure it turns smoothly. Turn the handlebar and check the throttle operation in both lock positions.

19. Adjust the throttle cables (Chapter Three).

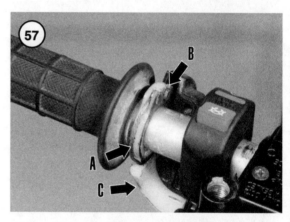

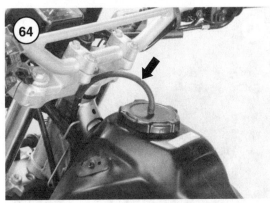

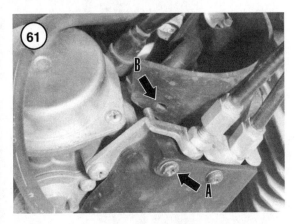

20. Install the fuel tank (this chapter).

CHOKE CABLE REPLACEMENT

The choke cable operates the starter enrichment valve on the carburetor.

1. Remove the fuel tank (this chapter).

2. Note the choke cable routing path from the handlebar to the carburetor.

3. Remove the carburetor (this chapter) for access to the choke valve nut (**Figure 48**).

4. Remove the choke valve and spring from the end of the choke cable (**Figure 49**) to prevent loss.

5. Disconnect the choke cable from the handlebar lever (**Figure 62**).

6. Detach the cable from any cable guides and remove the choke cable.

7. Reverse the removal steps to install the choke cable. Note the following:

   a. Tighten the choke valve nut to 2.5 N•m (22 in.-lb.).

   b. Adjust the choke cable (this chapter).

   d. Check the choke operation.

FUEL TANK

Removal/Installation

1. Remove the seat (Chapter Seventeen).

2. Remove the fuel tank shrouds (Chapter Seventeen).

3. Disconnect the negative battery lead (Chapter Eleven).

4. Turn the fuel valve off.

5. Disconnect the fuel hose (**Figure 63**) from the fuel valve.

6. Disconnect the hose (**Figure 64**) from the fuel cap.

7. Remove the bolt (**Figure 65**) and washer securing the rear of the fuel tank.

8. Lift up and pull the tank to the rear. Then, remove the fuel tank.

9. Install by reversing the removal steps. Note the following:

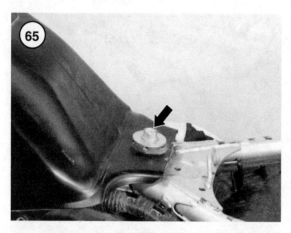

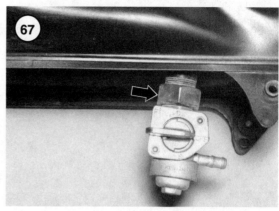

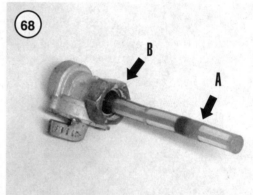

a. Inspect the front rubber support cushions (**Figure 66**). Replace the cushions if damaged or starting to deteriorate.

b. Turn the fuel valve on and check for fuel leaks.

FUEL VALVE

Removal/Installation

1. Remove the fuel tank (this chapter).
2. Drain the fuel tank of all gas.
3. Loosen the fuel valve nut (**Figure 67**) and remove the fuel valve.
4. Clean the strainer screen (A, **Figure 68**) in solvent. If damaged, replace the strainer screen.
5. Install a new fuel valve O-ring (B, **Figure 68**).
6. Install the fuel valve by reversing the removal steps. Note the following:

   a. Tighten the fuel valve nut (**Figure 67**) securely.
   b. After turning on the fuel valve, check the fuel valve and hose for leaks.

CRANKCASE BREATHER SYSTEM

The crankcase breather system captures blow-by gases from the crankcase and recirculates them

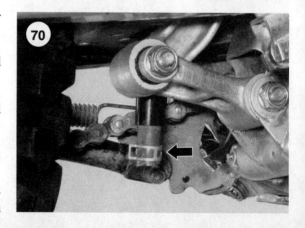

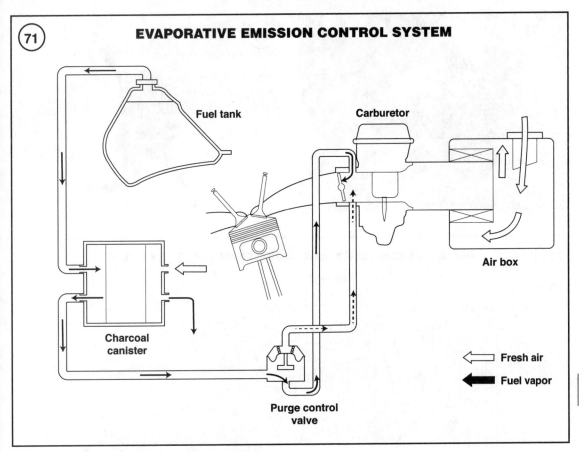

EVAPORATIVE EMISSION CONTROL SYSTEM

Fuel tank

Carburetor

Air box

Charcoal
canister

⇐ Fresh air

◀ Fuel vapor

Purge control
valve

into the air/fuel mixture to be burned. The crankcase breather hose (**Figure 69**) routes the blow-by gases from the crankcase to the air box.

Inspection/Cleaning

Make sure all hose clamps are tight. Check all hoses for deterioration and replace as necessary.

Remove the cap on the end of the air box drain tube (**Figure 70**) and drain out all residue. Perform this cleaning procedure more frequently if a considerable amount of riding is done at full throttle

or in the rain. Make sure the drain hose plug is secure.

EVAPORATIVE EMISSION CONTROL SYSTEM

Fuel vapor from the fuel tank is routed into a charcoal canister located on the left side of the frame. This vapor is stored when the engine is not running. When the engine is running, these vapors are drawn through a purge control valve and into the carburetor. Refer to **Figure 71** for system flow.

Make sure all hose clamps are tight. Check all hoses for deterioration and replace as necessary.

When removing the hoses from any component in the system, mark the hose and the fitting with a piece of masking tape and identify where the hose goes.

Purge Control Valve and Charcoal Canister Removal/Installation

1. Disconnect the hoses routed to the charcoal canister (A, **Figure 72**).
2. Remove the bolts securing the charcoal canister bracket (B, **Figure 72**). These bolts also retain the

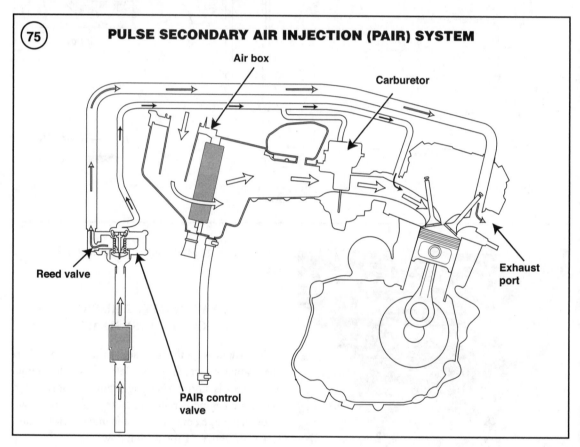

left crankcase cover. If necessary, separate the canister from the bracket.

3. Disconnect the hoses (A, **Figure 73**) connected to the purge control valve (B).

4. Dismount the purge control (B, **Figure 73**) valve from the rubber holder.

5. Install by reversing the removal steps. Note the following:

   a. Make sure the hoses are connected to the correct fitting on the charcoal canister and the vacuum control valves and that they are routed correctly through the frame.

   b. Make sure the hoses are not kinked, twisted or in contact with any sharp surfaces.

Purge Control Valve (PCV) Testing

If the engine is difficult to restart when hot, test the purge control valve as follows.

A hand-operated vacuum pump and pressure pump are required.

1. Remove the purge control valve (this section).

2. Connect a vacuum pump to the PCV output port hose fitting (A, **Figure 74**) that goes to the upper fitting on the carburetor.

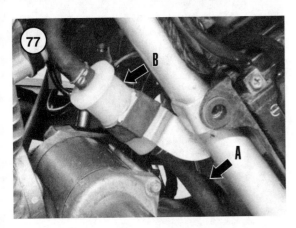

3. Apply 250 mm (9.8 in.) Hg of vacuum and watch the pump gauge. The vacuum should not bleed down. If the valve loses vacuum, replace the PCV.

4. Disconnect the vacuum pump.

5. Connect a vacuum pump to the PCV vacuum port hose fitting (B, **Figure 74**) that goes to the lower carburetor fitting.

6. Apply 250 mm (9.8 in.) Hg of vacuum and watch the pump gauge. The vacuum should not bleed down. If the valve loses vacuum, replace the PCV.

7. With the vacuum pump still connected to the PCV vacuum port hose fitting (B, **Figure 74**), connect a *pressure* pump on the PCV input port hose fitting (C, **Figure 74**) that goes to the EVAP canister.

CAUTION
Do not use compressed air, or the PCV will be damaged internally. Use only a hand-operated pump.

8. Apply 250 mm (9.8 in.) Hg of vacuum to the PCV vacuum port hose fitting (B, **Figure 74**). While the vacuum is applied, apply air pressure with the pressure pump. Air should blow out of the PCV output port hose fitting (A, **Figure 74**).

9. If air does not blow out the PCV output port (A, **Figure 74**) as described, replace the PCV.

10. If the PCV tests good, reinstall it (this section).

PULSE SECONDARY AIR INJECTION SYSTEM

The pulse secondary air injection (PAIR) system consists of an air injection control valve incorporating reed valves and air and vacuum hoses (**Figure 75**). This system does not pressurize air, but uses the momentary pressure differentials generated by the exhaust gas pulses to introduce fresh air into the exhaust ports. Make sure all air and vacuum hoses are correctly routed and attached. Inspect the hoses and replace any if necessary.

Testing

The PAIR system can be tested with the system installed.

1. Run the engine until it reaches normal operating temperature, and then shut off the engine.

2. Remove the fuel tank (this chapter).

3. Disconnect the vacuum hose (A, **Figure 76**) from the PAIR control valve (B). Plug the end of the vacuum hose.

4. Connect a hand-operated vacuum pump to the vacuum fitting on the PAIR control valve.

5. Run the engine. Verify that air is drawn into the end of the lower air supply hose (A, **Figure 77**). If not, check for a clogged or blocked air supply filter (B, **Figure 77**) or hose.

6. While the engine is running, operate the vacuum pump and apply 360 mm Hg (14.2 in. Hg) to the PAIR control valve vacuum fitting. Air flow should stop in the air supply hose (A, **Figure 77**).

7. If air continues to flow into the air supply hose with specified vacuum applied, replace the PAIR control valve.

8. If specified vacuum cannot be maintained, check for a damaged hose or leaking connection. If the hose is good, replace the PAIR control valve.

9. Reconnect the vacuum hose (A, **Figure 76**) to the PAIR control valve (B).

10. Install the fuel tank (this chapter).

Air Supply Filter Removal/Installation

A filter cleans air entering the air supply hose.

1. Remove the left side cover (Chapter Seventeen).

2. Remove the bolt securing the purge control valve bracket (**Figure 78**) and move the valve assembly out of the way.

3. Detach the hoses from the air supply filter (B, **Figure 77**) and remove it.

4. Reverse the removal steps for installation. Install the filter so the arrow on the filter body points up

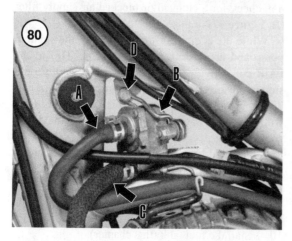

toward the PAIR control valve (mounted above the engine).

Control Valve Removal/Installation

1. Remove the fuel tank (this chapter).

2. Remove the bolts (A, **Figure 79**) securing the air injection pipe (B). Remove the pipe from the cylinder head cover.

3. Detach the vacuum hose (A, **Figure 76**) from the PAIR control valve (B).

4. Detach the air supply hose (A, **Figure 80**) from the PAIR control valve (B).

5. Detach the air injection hose (C, **Figure 80**) from the PAIR control valve.

6. Remove the retaining bolt (D, **Figure 80**), and then remove the PAIR control valve.

7. Reverse the removal steps for installation. Note the following:

    a. Install a new O-ring (**Figure 81**) onto the air injection pipe.

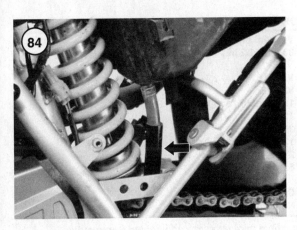

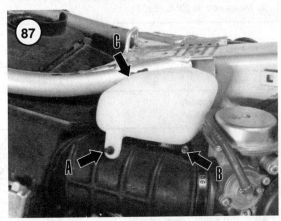

b. Tighten the PAIR control valve retaining bolt (D, **Figure 80**) and the air injection pipe bolts (A, **Figure 79**) securely.

AIR BOX

Removal/Installation

1. Remove the air filter (Chapter Three).
2. Remove the rear fender (Chapter Seventeen).
3. Remove the battery case (Chapter Eleven).

CAUTION
Keep the brake reservoir level to prevent fluid leaks.

4. Remove the rear brake reservoir mounting bolt (**Figure 82**). Support the reservoir in an upright position.

5. Detach the crankcase breather hose (A, **Figure 83**) from the air box.
6. Loosen the air box tube clamp screw (B, **Figure 83**).
7. Detach the drain hose (**Figure 84**) from the air box.
8. Remove the air box mounting bolts (**Figure 85**).
9. Separate the carburetor vent hose from the guide (**Figure 86**).
10. Detach the resonator chamber tab from the pin (A, **Figure 87**) on the air box tube.
11. Loosen the clamp screw (B, **Figure 87**), and then remove the resonator chamber (C).
12. Remove the air box from the left side of the frame.
13. Reverse the removal steps for installation. Tighten the air box mounting bolts (**Figure 85**) to 2.45 N•m (22 in.-lb.).

TABLES 1-3 ARE ON THE FOLLOWING PAGE.

Table 1 CARBURETOR SPECIFICATIONS

Type	Vacuum piston
Throttle bore size	30 mm (1.2 in.)
Identification number	
USA	VE3AH
Canada	VE3AG
Float level	18.5 mm (0.73 in.)
Main jet	118
Slow jet	35
Idle speed	1300-1500 rpm
Pilot screw adjustment (turns out)[1]	2 1/4
Carburetor heater resistance[2]	8.3-13.4 ohms
Air temperature switch	
Below 13°C (56° F)	Continuity (switch on)
13° C (56° F) and above	No continuity (switch off)

1. Initial adjustment only. Refer to text for procedure and final pilot air screw adjustment (turns out).
2. Measured at 20° C (68° F).

Table 2 FUEL TANK SPECIFICATIONS

	Liters	Gallons
Fuel tank capacity	8.7	2.3
Reserve capacity	2.7	0.7

Table 3 FUEL SYSTEM TORQUE SPECIFICATIONS

	N.m	in.-lb.	ft.-lb.
Air box mounting bolts	2.45	22	–
Air cutoff valve cover screw	2.1	19	–
Carburetor drain screw	1.5	13	–
Carburetor heater	4.9	43	–
Choke valve nut	2.5	22	–
Float bowl screw	2.1	19	–
Main jet	2.1	19	–
Needle jet holder	2.5	22	–
Slow jet	1.8	16	–
Throttle cable stay screw	3.4	30	–
Top cover screw	2.1	19	–

CHAPTER TEN

ELECTRICAL SYSTEM (CRF230F MODELS)

This chapter contains service and test procedures for the electrical and ignition system components. Procedures covering the battery and spark plug are located in Chapter Three.

Refer to **Table 1** and **Table 2** at the end of this chapter. Wiring diagrams are located at the end of this manual.

ELECTRICAL COMPONENT REPLACEMENT

Most parts suppliers will not accept returned electrical components. If the exact cause of any electrical system malfunction has not been determined, do not attempt to remedy the problem with guesswork and unnecessary parts replacement. If possible, have the suspect component or system tested by a professional technician before purchasing electrical components.

Consider any test results carefully before replacing a component that tests only slightly out of specification, especially for resistance. A number of variables can affect test results dramatically. These include: the internal tester circuitry, ambient temperature and motorcycle operating conditions. All instructions and specifications have been checked for accuracy; however, successful test results depend to a great degree upon individual accuracy.

CONTINUITY TESTING GUIDELINES

Circuits, switches, light bulbs and fuses can be checked for continuity (a completed circuit) using an ohmmeter connected to the appropriate color-coded wires in the circuit. Tests can be made at the connector or at the part. Use the following procedure as a guide to performing general continuity tests.

CAUTION
When performing continuity checks, do not turn on the ignition switch. Damage to parts and test equipment could occur. Also, verify that power from the battery is not routed directly into the test circuit, regardless of ignition switch position.

1. Refer to the wiring diagram at the back of this manual and find the part to be checked.
2. Identify the wire colors leading to the part and determine which pairs of wires should be checked. For any check, the circuit should begin at the connector, pass through the part, and then return to the connector.
3. Determine when continuity should exist.
   a. Typically, whenever a switch or button is turned on, it closes the circuit, and the meter should indicate continuity.

b. When the switch or button is turned off, it opens the circuit, and the meter should not indicate continuity.

4. Trace the wires from the part to the nearest connector. Separate the connector.

5. Connect an ohmmeter to the connector half that leads to the part being checked. If the test is being made at the terminals on the part, remove all other wires connected to the terminals so they do not influence the meter reading.

6. Operate the switch/button and check for continuity.

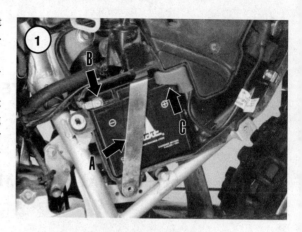

ELECTRICAL CONNECTORS

The position of the connectors may have been changed during previous repairs. Always confirm the wire colors to and from the connector and follow the wiring harness to the various components when performing tests.

> *CAUTION*
> *Although connectors may appear rugged, the internal pins are easily damaged and dislodged, which may cause a malfunction. Exercise care when handling or testing the connectors.*

Under normal operating conditions the connectors are weather-tight. If continuous operation in adverse operating condition is expected, the connectors may be packed with dielectric grease to prevent the intrusion of water or other contaminants. Do not use a substitute that may interfere with current flow. Dielectric grease is specifically formulated to seal the connector and not increase current resistance.

The ground connections are often overlooked when troubleshooting electrical problems. Make sure they are corrosion-free and tight. Apply dielectric grease to the terminals before reconnecting them.

BATTERY

Negative Battery Terminal

Some service procedures require disconnection of the battery cable from the negative battery terminal.

1. Turn the ignition switch off.
2. Remove the left side cover (Chapter Seventeen).
3. Remove the battery holder (A, **Figure 1**).
4. Remove the bolt and disconnect the cable from the negative battery terminal (B, **Figure 1**).
5. Move the cable out of the way and secure it so it cannot accidentally touch the negative battery terminal.

6. Reconnect the cable to the negative battery terminal and tighten the bolt securely.
7. Install the battery holder (A, **Figure 1**). Tighten the holder bolts securely.
8. Install the left side cover (Chapter Seventeen).

Battery Service

Refer to Chapter Three for battery replacement, inspection and charging procedures.

CHARGING SYSTEM

The charging system consists of the battery, alternator and a voltage regulator/rectifier. Alternating current generated by the alternator is rectified to direct current. The voltage regulator maintains the correct voltage to the battery regardless of variations in engine speed and load. A 7.5 amp main fuse protects the circuit.

Testing

1. Remove the left side cover (Chapter Seventeen).
2. Start the engine and let it reach normal operating temperature. Turn off the engine.

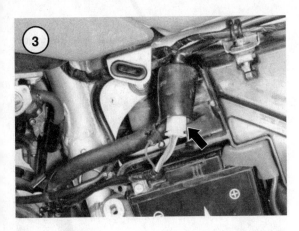

3. Leave the battery wires connected to the battery and connect a DC voltmeter to both battery terminals (B and C, **Figure 1**). The no-load voltage should be greater than 13 volts. If the no-load voltage is less than 13 volts, the battery requires service (Chapter Three).

CAUTION
Do not short either of the voltmeter test probes during this test.

4. Start the engine and let it idle.
5. Gradually increase engine speed to 5000 rpm. At 5000 rpm, the voltmeter should read between 15.5 volts and the measured no-load voltage.
6. If the charging voltage is not within specifications, first check the alternator-to-battery wire harness for loose or damaged connectors. If the wire harness connectors are good, check the alternator stator and voltage regulator/rectifier (this chapter).
7. Disconnect the voltmeter.
8. Install the left side cover (Chapter Seventeen).

ALTERNATOR

The alternator consists of the flywheel, which contains the rotor magnets, and stator coil assembly. Flywheel removal and installation procedures are covered in Chapter Five.

Flywheel Testing

The flywheel is permanently magnetized and cannot be tested except by replacing it with a known good unit. The rotor can lose magnetism over time or from a sharp blow. Replace the flywheel if defective or damaged.

Stator

The stator coil (A, **Figure 2**) is mounted inside the left crankcase cover. The exciter coil that triggers the crankshaft position sensor is contained in the stator coil assembly.

The stator coil can be tested with the left crankcase cover mounted on the engine.

The stator coil is also referred to as the charge coil.

Testing

1. Remove the left side cover (Chapter Seventeen).
2. Disconnect the alternator connector (**Figure 3**).
3. Use an ohmmeter and measure resistance between the white wire at the stator end of the connector and ground.
4A. If the resistance is as specified (**Table 1**), the stator coil is good.
4B. If the resistance is not correct, the coil is damaged. Replace the stator assembly.

NOTE
Before replacing the stator assembly, check the electrical wires to and within the electrical connector for any breaks or poor connections.

5. Reconnect the alternator connector.
6. Reinstall the left side cover (Chapter Seventeen).

Removal/installation

NOTE
The stator coil, exciter coil and crankshaft position sensor are wired together and must be serviced as an assembly.

1. Remove the flywheel and starter clutch (Chapter Five).
2. Remove the bolt and wire clamp (B, **Figure 2**) securing the wires to the cover.
3. Remove the bolts (C, **Figure 2**) securing the alternator stator to the left crankcase cover.
4. Remove the bolts (D, **Figure 2**) securing the crankshaft position sensor.
5. Carefully pull the rubber grommet and electrical wire harness from the left crankcase cover.
6. Install by reversing the removal steps. Note the following:
   a. Be sure to install the wire clamp (B, **Figure 2**).
   b. Tighten the wire clamp bolt securely.
   c. Apply oil to the stator mounting bolt threads and contact surfaces, and then install the bolts.
   d. Apply medium-strength threadlock to the crankshaft position (CKP) sensor mounting bolt threads, and then install the bolts.
   e. Tighten the stator mounting bolts (C, **Figure 2**) securely.

10

f. Tighten the crankshaft position (CKP) sensor mounting bolts (D, **Figure 2**) to 5 N•m (44 in.-lb.).

VOLTAGE REGULATOR/RECTIFIER

Regulator/Rectifier Wiring Harness Test

1. Remove the fuel tank (Chapter Eight).
2. Disconnect the voltage regulator/rectifier connector (A, **Figure 4**).

> *NOTE*
> *Perform all tests at the wiring harness connector, not at the regulator/rectifier.*

> *NOTE*
> *When checking for faulty wiring, also check for dirty or loose connector terminals.*

3. Check the battery circuit lead as follows:
   a. Connect a voltmeter between the red wire connector terminal and a good engine ground.
   b. With the ignition switch off, the voltmeter should read battery voltage.
   c. If the measured voltage is less than battery voltage, check the wire for damage.
   d. Disconnect the voltmeter leads.
4. Check the ground wire as follows:
   a. Connect an ohmmeter between the green wire connector terminal and a good engine ground.
   b. The ohmmeter must read continuity.
   c. If there is no continuity (zero or low resistance), check the green wire for damage.
5. Check the stator coil lead (white wire) as described in *Alternator* (this chapter).
6. If the above tests do not indicate a fault, the regulator/rectifier still may be defective. Substitute a known good unit, or have the regulator/rectifier tested by a dealership.

Regulator/Rectifier Removal/Installation

1. Remove the fuel tank (Chapter Eight).
2. Disconnect the voltage regulator/rectifier connector (A, **Figure 4**).
3. Remove the bolt (B, **Figure 4**) securing the voltage regulator/rectifier, and then remove the voltage regulator/rectifier (C).
4. Install by reversing the removal steps. Make sure all electrical connections are tight and free of corrosion.

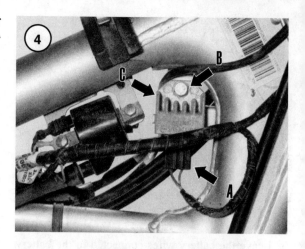

IGNITION SYSTEM

All models are equipped with an electronic ignition system.

Servicing Precautions

Take certain measures to protect the ignition system when working on it.
1. Never disconnect any of the electrical connections while the engine is running.
2. Apply dielectric grease to all electrical connectors before reconnecting them. This will help seal out moisture.
3. The electrical connectors must be free of corrosion and properly connected.
4. The ignition control module (ICM) is held in a rubber mount. If removed, be sure to reinstall it into the rubber mount.

Troubleshooting

Refer to Chapter Two for electrical system troubleshooting and component tests.

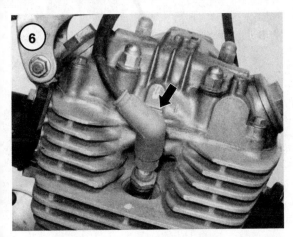

IGNITION
CONTROL MODULE (ICM)

Removal/Installation

1. Remove the number plate (Chapter Seventeen).
2. Disconnect the negative battery lead (this chapter).
3. Disconnect the electrical connectors (A, **Figure 5**) from the ICM.
4. Remove the ICM (B, **Figure 5**) from the rubber mount.
5. Reverse the removal steps for installation.

CRANKSHAFT
POSITION (CKP) SENSOR

Removal/Installation

The stator coil, exciter coil and crankshaft position sensor (D, **Figure 2**) are wired together and must be serviced as an assembly. Refer to *Stator Removal/Installation* (this chapter) for crankshaft position (CKP) sensor replacement.

IGNITION COIL

Removal/Installation

1. Remove the fuel tank (Chapter Eight).
2. Disconnect the high voltage lead from the spark plug (**Figure 6**).
3. Disconnect the primary electrical wire (A, **Figure 7**) from the coil.
4. Disconnect the ground wire (B, **Figure 7**) from the coil.
5. Remove the bolts (C, **Figure 7**) securing the ignition coil (D) to the frame.
6. Remove the ignition coil.
7. Install by reversing the removal steps. Note the following:
   a. Make sure all electrical connections are free of corrosion and tight.
   b. Tighten the mounting bolts (C, **Figure 7**) securely.

Testing

Refer to Chapter Two for ignition coil testing procedures.

STARTING SYSTEM

> *CAUTION*
> *Operate the starter for no more than 5 seconds at a time. Do not operate it for approximately 10 seconds between starting periods.*

The starting system consists of the starter, starter gears, starter relay and starter switch.

When the starter switch is pressed, it engages the starter relay that completes the circuit allowing electricity to flow from the battery to the starter. The neutral switch and clutch switch complete the starter relay circuit when closed.

The starter gears are covered in Chapter Five.

Troubleshooting

Refer to Chapter Two.

ELECTRIC STARTER (2003-2007 MODELS)

Removal/Installation

1. Disconnect the negative battery lead (this chapter).
2. Remove the exhaust pipe (Chapter Four).
3. Slide back the rubber boot (A, **Figure 8**) on the starter electrical cable.
4. Disconnect the starter electrical cable from the starter terminal (B, **Figure 8**).

5. Remove the bolts (A, **Figure 9**) securing the starter and ground wire to the crankcase.

> *NOTE*
> *Due to the tight fit of the O-ring on the starter nose, the starter may be difficult to pull out of the mounting hole.*

6. Remove the starter (B, **Figure 9**) from the top of the crankcase.
7. Install by reversing the removal steps. Note the following:
   a. Lubricate the starter O-ring (**Figure 10**) with grease.
   b. Clean any rust or corrosion from the starter electrical cable eyelet.
   c. Install the ground cable under the rear starter mounting bolt.
   d. Tighten the starter mounting bolts securely.

Disassembly

Refer to **Figure 11** while performing this procedure.
1. Find the alignment marks (**Figure 12**) on the case and both end covers. If necessary, scribe new marks.
2. Remove the two case throughbolts (A, **Figure 13**), set plates (B), and O-rings (C).
3. Remove the front cover (**Figure 14**)
4. Remove the lockwasher (**Figure 15**) from the front cover.

> *NOTE*
> *Write down the thickness and alignment of each shim and washer removed during disassembly. The number of shims used in each starter varies.*

5. Remove the front shims (**Figure 16**) from the armature shaft.
6. Remove the case (**Figure 17**) and rear cover (**Figure 18**).
7. Remove the rear shim set (**Figure 19**).

> *CAUTION*
> *Do not immerse the wire windings in the case or the armature coil in solvent as the insulation may be damaged. Wipe the windings with a cloth lightly moistened with solvent.*

8. Clean all grease, dirt and carbon from the armature, case and end covers.

Inspection

1. Pull the brush plate (A, **Figure 20**) out of the end cover.
2. Pull the spring away from each brush, and then pull the brushes (B, **Figure 20**) out of their guides.
3. Measure the length of each brush (**Figure 21**). If the brush length is less than the service limit (**Table 1**), replace both brushes as a set. When replacing the brushes, note the following:
   a. Soldering is not necessary when replacing the starter brushes.
   b. Replace the terminal bolt and brush as an assembly. Remove the terminal bolt (C, **Figure 20**) and brush, and then replace them. Be sure to install the washer set in the proper order (**Figure 11**).

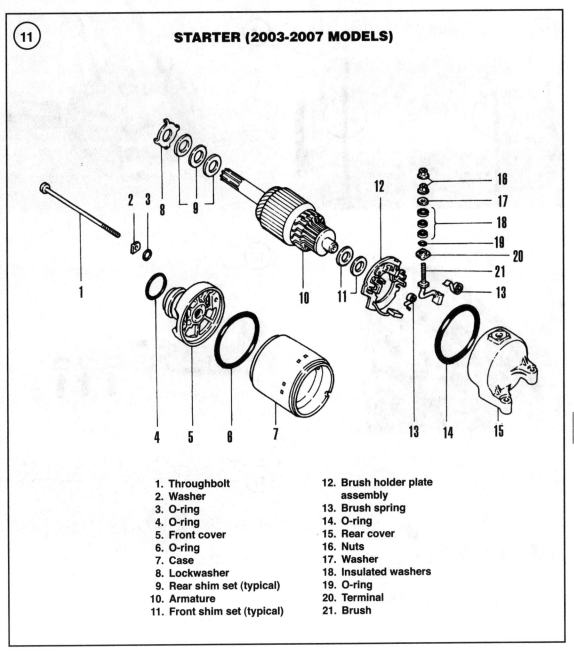

STARTER (2003-2007 MODELS)

1. Throughbolt
2. Washer
3. O-ring
4. O-ring
5. Front cover
6. O-ring
7. Case
8. Lockwasher
9. Rear shim set (typical)
10. Armature
11. Front shim set (typical)
12. Brush holder plate assembly
13. Brush spring
14. O-ring
15. Rear cover
16. Nuts
17. Washer
18. Insulated washers
19. O-ring
20. Terminal
21. Brush

10

c. The brush plate (A, **Figure 20**) and brushes are replaced as a set. Remove the brush and brush plate, and then replace them.

4. Inspect the brush springs, and replace them if weak or damaged. To replace the brush springs, perform the following:

a. Make a drawing that shows the location of the brush springs on the brush holder. Also, indicate the direction in which each spring coil turns.

b. Remove and replace both brush springs as a set.

5. Inspect the commutator (**Figure 22**). The mica must be below the surface of the copper bars. On a worn commutator the mica and copper bars may be worn to the same level (**Figure 23**). If necessary,

have the commutator serviced by a dealership or electrical repair shop.

6. Inspect the commutator copper bars for discoloration. A discolored pair of bars indicates grounded armature coils.

7. Inspect the armature shaft (**Figure 24**) for excessive wear, scoring or other damage.

8. Use an ohmmeter and perform the following:

a. Check for continuity between the commutator bars (**Figure 25**). There should be continuity (low resistance) between pairs of bars.

b. Check for continuity between the commutator bars and the shaft (**Figure 26**). There should be no continuity (infinite resistance).

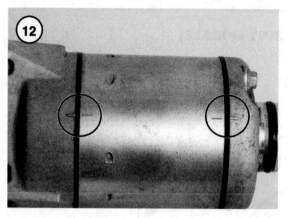

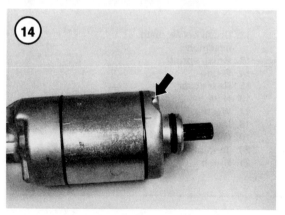

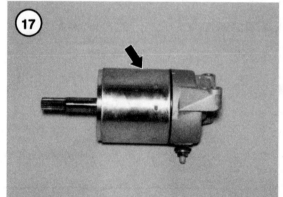

   c. If the armature fails either of these tests, re-
      place the starter assembly.

9. Use an ohmmeter and perform the following:

   a. Check for continuity between the starter cable
      terminal and the rear cover (**Figure 27**). There
      should be no continuity.

   b. Check for continuity between the starter cable
      terminal and the brush black wire terminal
      (**Figure 28**). There should be continuity.

   c. If the unit fails either of these tests, replace the
      starter assembly.

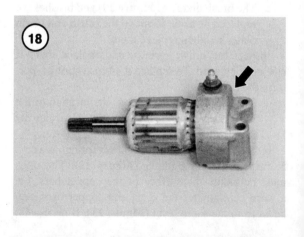

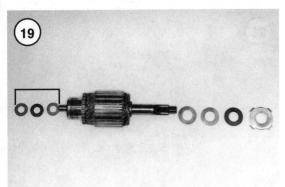

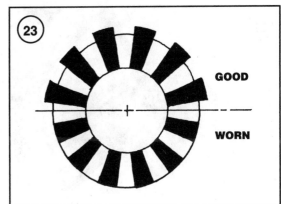

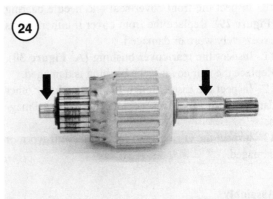

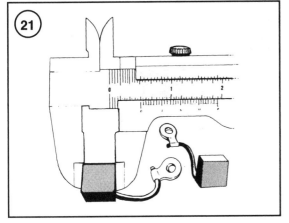

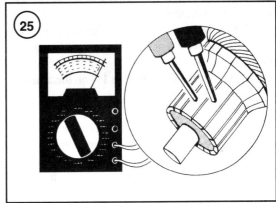

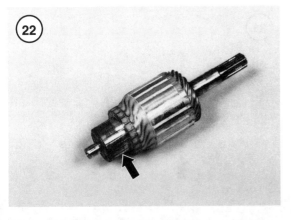

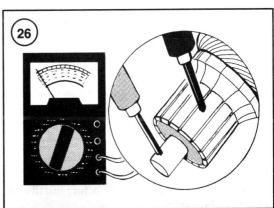

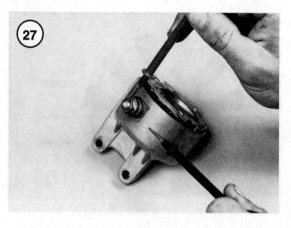

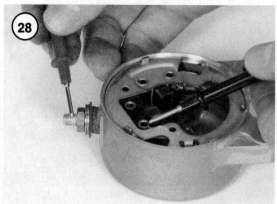

10. Inspect the front cover seal and needle bearing (**Figure 29**). Replace the front cover if either part is excessively worn or damaged.

11. Inspect the rear cover bushing (A, **Figure 30**). Replace the rear cover if the bushing is damaged.

12. Inspect the case (**Figure 17**) for cracks or other damage. Inspect for loose, chipped or damaged magnets.

13. Inspect the O-rings and replace them if worn or damaged.

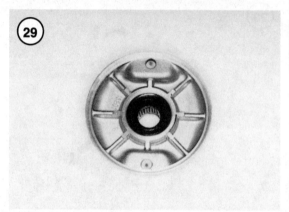

Assembly

1. If removed, install the brushes into their holders and secure the brushes with the springs.

2. Align the brush plate arm (A, **Figure 20**) with the notch (B, (**Figure 30**) in the rear cover and install the brush plate.

3. Install the rear shims (**Figure 19**) on the armature shaft next to the commutator.

4. Insert the armature coil assembly into the rear cover (**Figure 18**). Turn the armature during installation so the brushes engage the commutator properly. Make sure the armature is not turned upside down or the shims could slide off the end of the shaft. Do not damage the brushes.

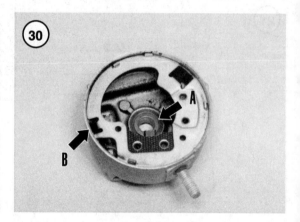

5. Install the two O-rings (**Figure 31**) onto the case. Then, slide the case (**Figure 17**) over the armature. Align the marks (**Figure 32**) on the case and end cover.

6. Install the front shims (**Figure 16**) onto the armature shaft.

7. Install the lockwasher (**Figure 15**) onto the front cover so that the lockwasher tabs (**Figure 33**) engage the cover slots.

8. Install the front cover (A, **Figure 34**) onto the armature shaft. Align the marks on the front cover and the case (B, **Figure 34**).

9. Lubricate the O-rings with oil before installation of the case throughbolts.

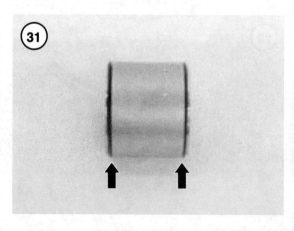

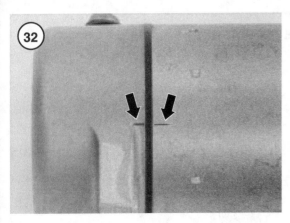

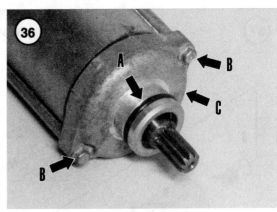

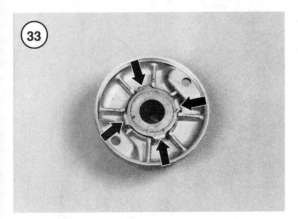

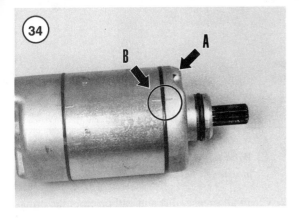

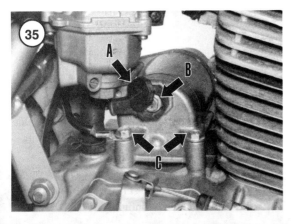

10

NOTE
If one or both throughbolts will not pass through the starter, the end covers and/or brush plate are installed incorrectly.

10. Install the throughbolts (A, **Figure 13**), set plates (B) and O-rings (C). Tighten the throughbolts securely.

ELECTRIC STARTER (2008-ON MODELS)

Removal/Installation

1. Disconnect the negative battery lead (this chapter).
2. Remove the exhaust pipe (Chapter Four).
3. Slide back the rubber boot (A, **Figure 35**) on the electrical cable.
4. Disconnect the starter electrical cable from the starter terminal (B, **Figure 35**).
5. Remove the bolts (C, **Figure 35**) securing the starter and ground wire to the crankcase.

NOTE
Due to the tight fit of the O-ring on the starter nose, the starter may be difficult to pull out of the mounting hole.

6. Remove the starter from the top of the crankcase.
7. Install by reversing the removal steps. Note the following:
   a. Lubricate the starter O-ring (A, **Figure 36**) with grease.
   b. Clean any rust or corrosion from the starter electrical cable eyelet.
   c. Install the ground cable under the rear starter mounting bolt.
   d. Tighten the starter mounting bolts securely.

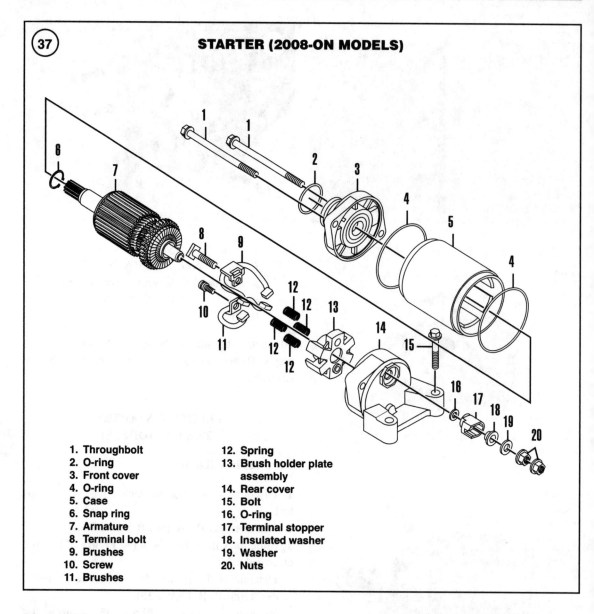

STARTER (2008-ON MODELS)

1. Throughbolt
2. O-ring
3. Front cover
4. O-ring
5. Case
6. Snap ring
7. Armature
8. Terminal bolt
9. Brushes
10. Screw
11. Brushes
12. Spring
13. Brush holder plate assembly
14. Rear cover
15. Bolt
16. O-ring
17. Terminal stopper
18. Insulated washer
19. Washer
20. Nuts

Disassembly

Refer to **Figure 37** while performing this procedure.

1. Find the alignment marks (**Figure 38**) on the case and front end cover. If necessary, highlight the existing marks or scribe new marks.

2. Remove the two throughbolts (B, **Figure 36**).

3. Remove the front cover (C, **Figure 36**).

4. Remove the rear cover (**Figure 39**).

5. Separate the armature (A, **Figure 40**) from the case (B).

6. Remove the O-rings (C, **Figure 40**) on the case.

CAUTION
Do not immerse the armature in solvent as the insulation may be damaged.

Wipe the windings with a cloth lightly moistened with solvent.

7. Clean all grease, dirt and carbon from the armature, case and end covers.

Inspection

1. Note the location of the positive brushes (A, **Figure 41**) and negative brushes (B).

2. Use an ohmmeter and perform the following:
   a. Check for continuity between the starter cable terminal (C, **Figure 41**) and the positive brushes (A); there should be continuity.
   b. Check for continuity between the positive brushes (A, **Figure 41**) and the rear cover; there should be no continuity.

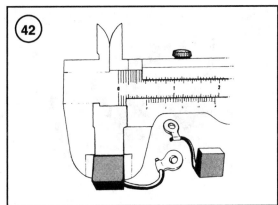

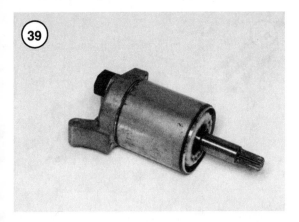

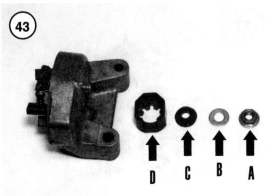

10

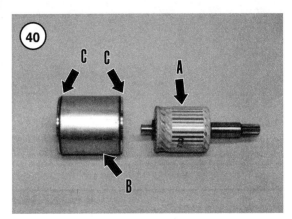

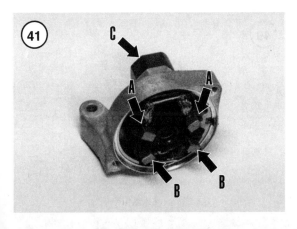

c. Check for continuity between the positive brushes (A, **Figure 41**) and the negative brushes (B); there should be no continuity.

d. Check for continuity between the starter cable terminal and the rear cover; there should be no continuity.

3. Measure the length of each brush with a caliper (**Figure 42**). If the length is less than the service limit (**Table 1**), replace the brushes.

4. To replace the positive brush set, perform the following:

a. Remove the nut (A, **Figure 43**), washer (B), insulating washer (C) and terminal stopper (D).

b. Remove the terminal bolt (A, **Figure 44**) and brush set (B).

c. Remove the springs (A, **Figure 45**) from the brush holder (B).

d. Reverse the brush removal steps for installation. Make sure the O-ring (C, **Figure 44**) is installed on the terminal bolt (A). Install the insulating washer (C, **Figure 43**) so the small ID is toward the terminal stopper.

5. To replace the negative brush set, remove the screw (C, **Figure 45**) and washer, brush set (D) and springs.

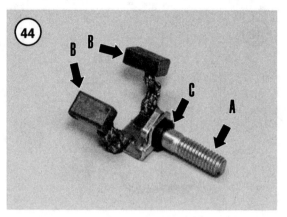

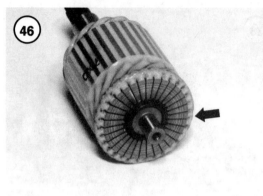

6. Inspect the commutator (**Figure 46**). The mica in a good commutator is below the surface of the copper bars. On a worn commutator the mica and copper bars may be worn to the same level. Clean any foreign material from between the commutator bars. If necessary, have the commutator serviced by a dealer or electrical repair shop.

7. Inspect the commutator copper bars for discoloration. If a pair of bars are discolored, the armature coils are grounded.

8. Use an ohmmeter and perform the following:

   a. Check for continuity between the commutator bars (**Figure 47**); there should be continuity (indicated resistance) between pairs of bars.
   b. Check for continuity between the commutator bars and the shaft (**Figure 48**); there should be no continuity (infinite resistance).
   c. If the unit fails either of these tests, replace the starter. The armature cannot be replaced individually.

9. Inspect the oil seal (**Figure 49**) and bearing in the front cover for wear or damage. If either is damaged, replace the starter.

10. Inspect the bushing (**Figure 50**) in the rear cover for wear or damage. If it is damaged, replace the starter.

11. Inspect the case assembly for wear or damage. Make sure the field magnets are bonded securely in

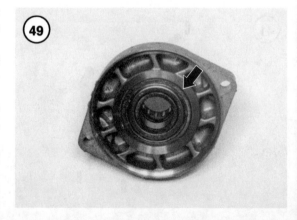

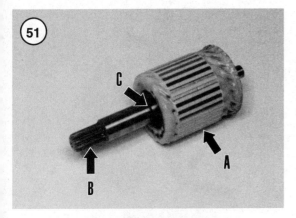

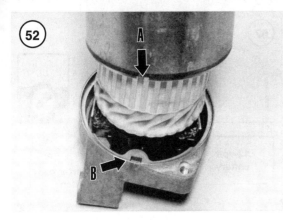

place. If there is damage, or if any field magnets are loose, replace the case.

12. Inspect the armature (A, **Figure 51**) for damage or wear. Inspect the gear splines (B, **Figure 51**) on the armature shaft for wear or damage. The snap ring (C, **Figure 51**) should be securely seated in the groove on the armature shaft. If the armature is damaged, replace the starter.

Assembly

1. Install the two O-rings (C, **Figure 40**) onto the case.
2. Carefully insert the armature into the rear cover.
3. Install the case. Position the case so the notch (A, **Figure 52**) in the case engages the tab (B) in the rim of the rear cover.

> *NOTE*
> *If the correct alignment marks are unknown, position the front cover so the bolt holes align with the rear cover bolt holes.*

4. Install the front cover onto the case. Align the marks (**Figure 53**) on the case and front cover.
5. Install the throughbolts and tighten securely.
6. Replace the front cover O-ring seal (A, **Figure 36**) if deteriorated or damaged.

STARTER RELAY SWITCH

Removal/Installation

1. Remove the left side cover (Chapter Seventeen).
2. Disconnect the negative battery cable (this chapter).
3. Open the cable clamps (A, **Figure 54**). Remove the starter cable and wiring harness from the clamps.
4. Remove the starter relay switch (B, **Figure 54**) from the frame bracket.

10

5. Detach the connector (**Figure 55**) from the switch.

6. Slide the rubber boots (A, **Figure 56**) off the two large cable leads (B).

7. Disconnect the two large cable leads (B, **Figure 56**) from the starter relay switch.

8. Install by reversing the removal steps. Transfer the 7.5 amp main fuse (and spare) to the new starter relay switch.

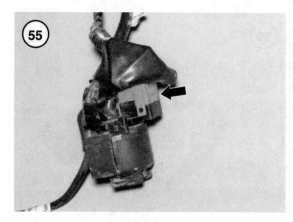

Testing

Troubleshoot the starting circuit (Chapter Two). If the problem has been isolated to the starter relay switch, perform the following test:

1. Remove the left side cover (Chapter Seventeen).

2. Shift the transmission into neutral.

3. Turn the ignition switch on and press the starter button. The starter relay switch should click when the starter button is pressed. If a click is not heard, continue with the test procedure.

4. Test the starter relay switch ground circuit as follows:

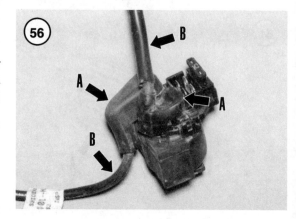

> *NOTE*
> *It is not necessary to disconnect the cables (B, **Figure 56**) when removing the switch.*

  a. Remove the starter relay switch (this section) for access to the connector (**Figure 55**).

  b. Disconnect the starter relay switch electrical connector.

  c. Connect an ohmmeter to the light green/red starter relay wire terminal in the connector and a good engine ground.

  d. Shift the transmission into neutral and release the clutch lever.

  e. The ohmmeter must read continuity.

  f. Place the transmission in gear and pull in the clutch lever fully.

  g. The ohmmeter must read continuity.

  h. Disconnect the ohmmeter leads.

5. Check for voltage at the starter relay switch as follows:

  a. If removed, reinstall the starter relay (this section) and reconnect the negative battery cable (this chapter).

  b. Shift the transmission into neutral.

  c. Connect the positive lead of a voltmeter to the starter relay switch yellow/red wire and the negative voltmeter lead to a good engine ground.

  d. Turn the ignition switch on and press the starter button while reading the voltmeter.

  e. The voltmeter must indicate battery voltage. If not, check the circuit.

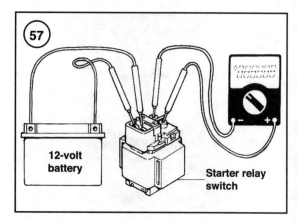

12-volt battery

Starter relay switch

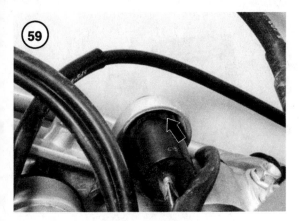

f. Turn the ignition switch off and remove the voltmeter leads.

6. Check the starter relay switch operation as follows:

a. Remove the starter relay switch (this section).

b. Connect an ohmmeter to the two blade terminals nearest the fuse on the starter relay switch. The ohmmeter should show no continuity.

c. Connect a fully-charged 12-volt battery to the starter relay switch. Connect the positive battery terminal to the yellow/red wire terminal and the negative battery terminal to the green/red wire terminal (**Figure 57**). The ohmmeter should now read continuity.

d. Disconnect the battery and ohmmeter leads.

7. Replace the starter relay switch if it fails any part of this test.

SWITCHES

Ignition Switch

Removal/installation

1. Remove the number plate (Chapter Seventeen).
2. Remove the fuel tank (Chapter Eight).
3. Disconnect the ignition switch connectors (**Figure 58**).
4. Push in the latches (**Figure 59**) on both sides of the switch to disengage the switch body from the upper fork bridge. Remove the switch.
5. Install by reversing the removal steps. Position the switch so the tab (A, **Figure 60**) on the switch body engages the groove (B) in the fork bridge.

Engine Stop Switch

Removal/installation

1. Remove the switch mounting screw (A, **Figure 61**).
2. Remove the engine stop switch (B, **Figure 61**).
3. Install by reversing the removal steps. Note the following:

a. Place the ground wire terminal (C, **Figure 61**) under the screw and washer.

b. Align the clamp gap with the punch mark (D, **Figure 61**) on the handlebar.

c. Make sure all connectors are secure.

d. Tighten the switch mounting screw securely.

Starter Switch

Removal/installation

1. Remove the fuel tank (Chapter Eight).

2. Disconnect the white starter switch connector (**Figure 62**).

3. Remove the retaining bolts, and then remove the starter switch (**Figure 63**).

4. Install by reversing the removal steps. Note the following:

   a. Insert the housing locating pin into the hole in the handlebar.

   b. Tighten the front screw first, and then tighten the rear screw. Tighten both screws securely.

Neutral Switch
Test/Replacement

The neutral switch is mounted in the lower left side of the crankcase, next to the gearshift shaft assembly.

1. Shift the transmission into neutral.

2. Remove the drive sprocket cover (Chapter Twelve).

3. Remove the insulator (**Figure 64**).

4. Disconnect the neutral switch wire (A, **Figure 65**) from the neutral switch. Push in the spring-loaded washer to release the wire.

5. Connect one ohmmeter lead to the neutral switch terminal and the other lead to a good engine ground.

6. Read the ohmmeter scale with the transmission in neutral, and then read it again with the transmission in gear. Note the following:

   a. The ohmmeter must read continuity with the transmission in neutral.

   b. The ohmmeter must read infinity with the transmission in gear.

   c. If either reading is incorrect, check the wiring harness for damaged, dirty or loose-fitting terminals. If the wiring harness is good, replace the neutral switch.

7. Loosen and remove the neutral switch (B, **Figure 65**).

8. Install a new O-ring (**Figure 66**) onto the neutral switch.

9. Lubricate the O-ring and install the neutral switch. Push in the switch until bottomed.

10. Reconnect the wire to the switch.

11. Install the insulator (**Figure 64**).

12. Install the drive sprocket cover (Chapter Twelve).

Clutch Lever Switch

Testing

1. Disconnect the connectors (A, **Figure 67**) from the switch.

2. Connect an ohmmeter to the switch terminals.

3. Pull in the lever. There should be continuity.

4. If there is no continuity, replace the switch.

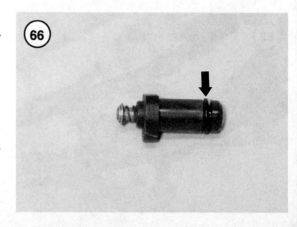

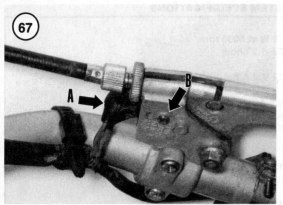

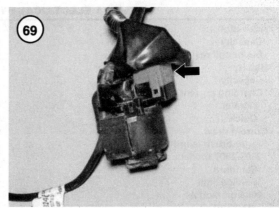

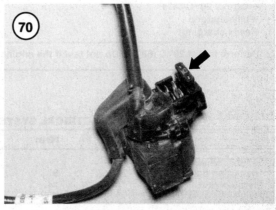

10

Removal/installation

1. Disconnect the connectors (A, **Figure 67**) from the switch.

2. Remove the switch mounting screw (B, **Figure 67**), and then remove the switch.

3. Install the switch, and then tighten the mounting screw securely.

4. Connect the connectors to the switch.

5. Check operation.

MAIN FUSE

A 7.5 amp fuse that protects the electrical system is located on the starter relay.

Replacement

1. Remove the left side cover (Chapter Seventeen).

2. Disconnect the negative battery cable (this chapter).

3. Open the cable clamps (A, **Figure 68**). Remove the starter cable and wiring harness from the clamps.

4. Remove the starter relay switch (B, **Figure 68**) from the frame bracket.

5. Detach the connector (**Figure 69**) from the switch.

6. Remove the fuse (**Figure 70**) and inspect it.

7. Reverse the removal steps to install the fuse and starter relay.

WIRING DIAGRAMS

The wiring diagrams are located at the end of this manual.

NOTE
Scan the QR code or search for "Clymer Manuals YouTube Tech Tips" to see an overview on electrical troubleshooting with a wiring diagram.

TABLES 1-2 ARE ON THE FOLLOWING PAGE.

Table 1 ELECTRICAL SYSTEM SPECIFICATIONS

Alternator	
Capacity	60 W at 5000 rpm
Stator coil resistance*	0.5-1.2 ohms
Battery	
Capacity	12 V, 4 A.h.
Charging current	
Normal	0.5 A/5-10 hour
Quick	5.0 A/0.5 hour
Current draw	0.1 mA max.
Starter brush length	
2003-2007 models	
Standard	12.5 mm (0.49 in.)
Service limit	9.0 mm (0.35 in.)
2008-on models	
Standard	12.0 mm (0.47 in.)
Service limit	6.5 mm (0.26 in.).\
Voltage @ 20° C/68° F	
Fully-charged	13.0-13.2V
Needs charging	Below 12.3V

*Perform test at 20° C (68° F). Do not test if the engine or component is hot.

Table 2 ELECTRICAL SYSTEM TORQUE SPECIFICATIONS

	N•m	in.-lb.	ft.-lb.
Crankshaft position (CKP) sensor			
mounting bolt	5	44	–
Flywheel bolt	74	–	54

CHAPTER ELEVEN

ELECTRICAL SYSTEM
(CRF230L AND CRF230M MODELS)

This chapter contains service and test procedures for the electrical and ignition system components. Procedures covering the battery and spark plug are located in Chapter Three.

Refer to **Tables 1-5** at the end of this chapter. Wiring diagrams are located at the end of this manual.

ELECTRICAL COMPONENT REPLACEMENT

Most parts suppliers will not accept returned electrical components. If the exact cause of any electrical system malfunction has not been determined, do not attempt to remedy the problem with guesswork and unnecessary parts replacement. If possible, have the suspect component or system tested by a professional technician before purchasing electrical components.

Consider any test results carefully before replacing a component that tests only slightly out of specification, especially for resistance. A number of variables can affect test results dramatically. These include: the internal tester circuitry, ambient temperature and motorcycle operating conditions. All instructions and specifications have been checked for accuracy; however, successful test results depend to a great degree upon individual accuracy.

CONTINUITY TESTING GUIDELINES

Circuits, switches, light bulbs and fuses can be checked for continuity (a completed circuit) using an ohmmeter connected to the appropriate color-coded wires in the circuit. Tests can be made at the connector or at the part. Use this procedure as a guide to performing general continuity tests.

CAUTION
When performing continuity checks, do not turn on the ignition switch. Damage to parts and test equipment could occur. Also, verify that power from the battery is not routed directly into the test circuit, regardless of ignition switch position.

1. Refer to the wiring diagram at the back of this manual and find the part to be checked.
2. Identify the wire colors leading to the part and determine which pairs of wires should be checked. For any check, the circuit should begin at the connector, pass through the part, and then return to the connector.
3. Determine when continuity should exist.
   a. Typically, whenever a switch or button is turned on, it closes the circuit, and the meter should indicate continuity.

b. When the switch or button is turned off, it opens the circuit, and the meter should not indicate continuity.

4. Trace the wires from the part to the nearest connector. Separate the connector.

5. Connect an ohmmeter to the connector half that leads to the part being checked. If the test is being made at the terminals on the part, remove all other wires connected to the terminals so they do not influence the meter reading.

6. Operate the switch/button and check for continuity.

ELECTRICAL CONNECTORS

The position of the connectors may have been changed during previous repairs. Always confirm the wire colors to and from the connector and follow the wiring harness to the various components when performing tests.

> *CAUTION*
> *Although connectors may appear rugged, the internal pins are easily damaged and dislodged, which may cause a malfunction. Exercise care when handling or testing the connectors.*

Under normal operating conditions the connectors are weather-tight. If continuous operation in adverse operating conditions such as off-road use is expected, the connectors may be packed with dielectric grease to prevent the intrusion of water or other contaminants. Do not use a substitute that may interfere with current flow. Dielectric grease is specifically-formulated to seal the connector and not increase current resistance.

An often overlooked area when troubleshooting are the ground connections. Make sure they are corrosion-free and tight. Apply dielectric grease to the terminals before reconnecting them.

BATTERY

Negative Battery Terminal

Some service procedures require disconnecting the battery cable from the negative battery terminal.

1. Turn the ignition switch off.

2. Remove the left side cover (Chapter Seventeen).

3. Remove the bolt and disconnect the cable from the negative battery terminal (A, **Figure 1**).

4. Move the cable out of the way and secure it so it cannot accidentally touch the negative battery terminal.

5. Reconnect the cable to the negative battery terminal (A, **Figure 1**), and then tighten the bolt securely.

6. Install the left side cover (Chapter Seventeen).

Battery Service

Refer to Chapter Three for battery replacement, inspection and charging procedures.

Battery Case
Removal/Installation

1. Remove the battery (Chapter Three).

2. Remove the starter relay switch (this chapter).

3. Remove the fuse box (A, **Figure 2**) from the battery case.

4. Extract the trim clip (B, **Figure 2**).

5. Remove the battery case mounting bolts (C, **Figure 2**). Move the EVAP purge control valve bracket (D, **Figure 2**) out of the way.

6. Remove the battery case (E, **Figure 2**).

7. Reverse the removal steps for installation. Tighten the battery case mounting bolts securely.

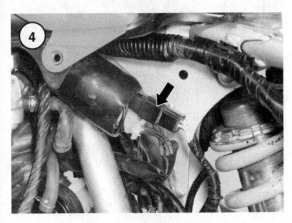

CHARGING SYSTEM

The charging system consists of the battery, the alternator and the voltage regulator/rectifier. Alternating current generated by the alternator is rectified to direct current. The voltage regulator maintains the correct voltage to the battery and additional electrical loads (lights, ignition, etc.) regardless of variations in engine speed and load. A 20-amp main fuse protects the circuit.

Testing

1. Remove the left side cover (Chapter Seventeen).
2. Start the engine and let it reach normal operating temperature. Turn off the engine.

CAUTION
Do not short either of the voltmeter test probes during this test.

3. Leave the battery cables connected to the battery and connect a DC voltmeter to both battery terminals (A and B, **Figure 1**). The no-load voltage should be greater than 13 volts. If the no-load voltage is less than specified (**Table 1**), the battery requires service as described in Chapter Three.
4. Start the engine and let it idle.

5. Gradually increase engine speed to 5000 rpm. At 5000 rpm, the voltmeter should read between 15.5 volts and the no-load battery voltage.
6. If the charging voltage is not within specifications, first check the alternator-to-battery wire harness for loose or damaged connectors. If the wire harness connectors are correct, check the alternator stator, and then check the voltage regulator/rectifier as described in this chapter.
7. Disconnect the voltmeter.
8. Install the left side cover (Chapter Seventeen).

ALTERNATOR

The alternator consists of the flywheel, which contains the rotor magnets and stator coil assembly. Flywheel removal and installation procedures are covered in Chapter Five.

Flywheel Testing

The flywheel is permanently magnetized and cannot be tested except by replacing it with a known good one. The rotor can lose magnetism over time or from a sharp blow. Replace the flywheel if defective or damaged.

Stator

The stator coil (A, **Figure 3**) is mounted inside the left crankcase cover. The stator coil can be tested with the left crankcase cover mounted on the engine. The stator coil is also referred to as the charge coil.

Testing

1. Remove the battery case (this chapter).
2. Disconnect the alternator stator connector (**Figure 4**).
3. Use an ohmmeter and measure resistance between each yellow wire at the stator end of the connector. **Table 1** lists the specified stator coil resistance.
4A. If the resistance is as specified, the stator coil is good.
4B. If the resistance is higher than specified, the coil is damaged. Replace the stator assembly.
5. Use an ohmmeter and check continuity from each yellow wire terminal in the alternator stator end of the connector and to ground. Replace the stator coil if any yellow terminal has continuity to ground. Continuity indicates a short within the stator coil winding.

11

NOTE
Before replacing the stator assembly, check the electrical wires to and within the electrical connector for any open or poor connections.

6. If the stator coil fails either of these tests, replace it (this section).

7. Reconnect the alternator stator connector (**Figure 4**).

Removal/installation

NOTE
The stator coil and crankshaft position sensor wire are bundled together and must be serviced as a unit assembly.

1. Remove the left crankcase cover (Chapter Five).

2. Remove the grommet (B, **Figure 3**) and wire clamp securing the wires to the cover.

3. Disconnect the crankshaft position (CKP) sensor connector (C, **Figure 3**).

4. Remove the crankshaft position (CKP) sensor mounting bolts (D, **Figure 3**).

5. If necessary, remove the crankshaft position (CKP) sensor (E, **Figure 3**).

6. Remove the bolts (F, **Figure 3**) securing the stator coil (A) to the left crankcase cover.

7. Carefully remove the stator coil and wire assembly from the left crankcase cover.

8. Install by reversing the removal steps. Note the following:
   a. Apply threadlock to the crankshaft position (CKP) sensor bolt threads.
   b. Tighten the CKP sensor mounting bolts to 5.0 N•m (44 in.-lb.).
   c. Tighten the stator coil mounting bolts securely.
   d. Connect the crankshaft position (CKP) sensor wire tightly to the sensor.

VOLTAGE REGULATOR/RECTIFIER

Wiring Harness Test

1. Remove the left side cover (Chapter Seventeen).

2. Disconnect the voltage regulator/rectifier electrical connector (A, **Figure 5**).

NOTE
Perform all of the tests at the wiring harness connectors, not at the regulator/rectifier.

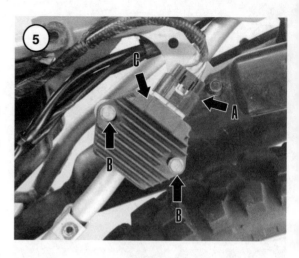

NOTE
When checking for faulty wiring also check for dirty or loose connector terminals.

3. Check the battery circuit lead as follows:
   a. Connect a voltmeter between the red/white wire terminal and green wire terminal.
   b. With the ignition switch off, the voltmeter should read battery voltage.
   c. If the measured voltage is less than battery voltage, verify the main fuse is good. Then, check the wires for damage.
   d. Disconnect the voltmeter leads.

4. Check the ground wire as follows:
   a. Connect an ohmmeter between the green wire connector terminal and a good engine ground.
   b. The ohmmeter must read continuity.
   c. If there is no continuity (zero or low resistance), check the green wire for damage.

5. Check the stator coil and wires (this chapter).

6. If the above tests do not indicate a fault, the regulator/rectifier may be defective. Substitute a known good unit or have the regulator/rectifier tested by a dealership.

Removal/Installation

1. Remove the left side cover (Chapter Seventeen).

2. Disconnect the voltage regulator/rectifier electrical connector (A, **Figure 5**).

3. Remove the bolts (B, **Figure 5**) securing the voltage regulator/rectifier and remove the voltage regulator/rectifier (C).

4. Install by reversing the removal steps. Note the following:
   a. Make sure the electrical connector is tight and free of corrosion.
   b. Tighten the voltage regulator/rectifier mounting bolts securely.

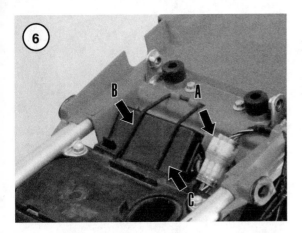

IGNITION SYSTEM

All models are equipped with an electronic ignition system.

Servicing Precautions

Take certain measures to protect the ignition system when working on it.

1. Never disconnect any of the electrical connections while the engine is running.

2. Apply dielectric grease to all electrical connectors before reconnecting them. This will help seal out moisture.

3. The electrical connectors must be free of corrosion and properly connected.

4. The ignition control module (ICM) is held in a rubber mount. If removed, be sure to reinstall it into the rubber mount.

Troubleshooting

Refer to Chapter Two for ignition system troubleshooting procedure and component tests.

IGNITION CONTROL MODULE (ICM)

Removal/Installation

1. Remove the seat (Chapter Seventeen).
2. Disconnect the negative battery lead (this chapter).

NOTE
Due to limited space, it may be difficult to disengage the connector from the mounting clip. If necessary, push the mounting clip out of the rear fender from the underside of the fender.

3. Disconnect the ICM electrical connector (A, **Figure 6**). Disengage the connector from the mounting clip.
4. Detach the rubber strap (B, **Figure 6**) securing the ICM in place.
5. Remove the ICM (C, **Figure 6**).
6. Reverse the removal steps for installation. Make sure the connector fully engages the mounting clip and is securely fastened.

CRANKSHAFT POSITION (CKP) SENSOR

Removal/Installation

NOTE
The stator coil and crankshaft position (CKP) sensor wire are bundled together and must be serviced as an assembly.

1. Remove the left crankcase cover (Chapter Five).
2. Disconnect the crankshaft position (CKP) sensor connector (C, **Figure 3**).
3. Remove the crankshaft position (CKP) sensor retaining bolts (D, **Figure 3**).
4. Remove the crankshaft position (CKP) sensor (E, **Figure 3**).
5. If necessary to remove the sensor wire, remove the stator coil (this chapter).
6. Install by reversing the removal steps. Note the following:
   a. Apply threadlock to the crankshaft position (CKP) sensor bolt threads.
   b. Tighten the sensor mounting bolts to 5.0 N•m (44 in.-lb.).

IGNITION COIL

Removal/Installation

1. Remove the fuel tank (Chapter Nine).
2. Disconnect the high voltage lead (**Figure 7**) from the spark plug.

11

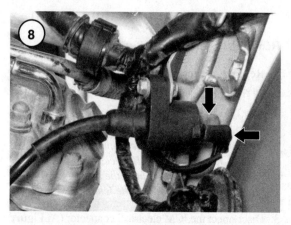

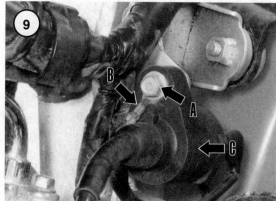

3. Disconnect the primary electrical wires (**Figure 8**) from the coil.

4. Remove the mounting bolt (A, **Figure 9**) and ground wire terminal (B).

5. Remove the ignition coil (C, **Figure 9**).

6. Install by reversing the removal steps. Note the following:

   a. Position the ground wire terminal (B, **Figure 9**) so it is 45° from vertical.

   b. Make sure all electrical connections are free of corrosion and tight.

   c. Tighten the ignition coil mounting bolt securely.

STARTING SYSTEM

> *CAUTION*
> *Operate the starter for no more than 5 seconds at a time. Do not operate it for approximately 10 seconds between starting periods.*

The starting system consists of the starter, starter gears, starter relay and starter switch.

When the starter switch is pressed, it engages the starter relay that completes the circuit allowing electricity to flow from the battery to the starter. The neutral switch and clutch switch complete the starter relay circuit when closed.

The starter gears are covered in Chapter Five.

Troubleshooting

Refer to Chapter Two.

ELECTRIC STARTER

Removal/Installation

1. Disconnect the negative battery lead (this chapter).

2. Remove the exhaust pipe (Chapter Four).

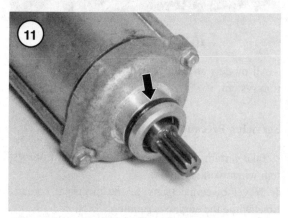

3. Slide back the rubber boot (A, **Figure 10**) on the electrical cable connector.

4. Disconnect the starter electrical cable from the starter terminal (B, **Figure 10**).

5. Remove the bolts (C, **Figure 10**) securing the starter and ground wire (D) to the crankcase.

> *NOTE*
> *Due to the tight fit of the O-ring (**Figure 11**) on the starter nose, the starter may be difficult to pull out of the mounting hole.*

6. Remove the starter from the top of the crankcase.

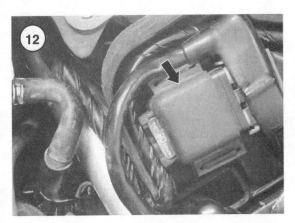

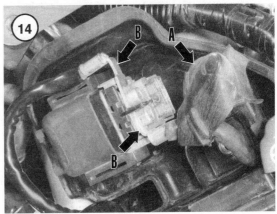

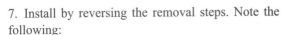

5. Move the rubber boot (A, **Figure 14**) off the two large cable leads.

6. Remove the bolts, and then disconnect the two large cables (B, **Figure 14**) from the starter relay switch.

7. Remove the starter relay switch.

8. Install by reversing the removal steps. Note the following:

   a. Transfer the 20-amp main fuse (and spare) to the new starter relay switch.

   b. Tighten the two large cable bolts leads securely.

7. Install by reversing the removal steps. Note the following:

   a. Lubricate the starter O-ring (**Figure 11**) with grease.

   b. Clean any rust or corrosion from the starter cable eyelet.

   c. Install the ground cable terminal (D, **Figure 10**) under the rear starter mounting bolt.

   d. Tighten the starter mounting bolts securely.

Disassembly/Inspection/Assembly

Refer to *Starter (2008-On Models)* in Chapter Ten for starter service procedures.

STARTER RELAY SWITCH

Removal/Installation

1. Remove the left side cover (Chapter Seventeen).

2. Disconnect the negative battery cable (this chapter).

3. Dislodge the starter relay holder (**Figure 12**) from the mounting bracket.

4. Disconnect the starter relay switch electrical connector (**Figure 13**).

Testing

Troubleshoot the starting circuit as described in Chapter Two. If the problem has been isolated to the starter relay switch, perform the following test:

1. Remove the left side cover (Chapter Seventeen).

2. Shift the transmission into neutral.

3. Turn the ignition switch on and press the starter button. The starter relay switch should click when the starter button is pressed. If a click is not heard, continue with the test procedure.

4. Test the starter relay switch ground circuit as follows:

NOTE
*It is not necessary to disconnect the two large cables (B, **Figure 14**) when removing the switch.*

   a. Remove the starter relay switch (this section) for access to the connector (**Figure 13**).

   b. Disconnect the starter relay switch electrical connector.

   c. Connect an ohmmeter to the light green/red starter relay wire terminal in the connector and a good engine ground.

   d. Shift the transmission into neutral and release the clutch lever.

e. The ohmmeter must read continuity.

f. Place the transmission in gear with the side-stand up, and pull in the clutch lever fully.

NOTE
If there is no continuity, also check the sidestand switch.

g. The ohmmeter must read continuity.

h. Disconnect the ohmmeter leads.

5. Check for voltage at the starter relay switch as follows:

a. Remove the starter relay switch (this section) for access to the connector (**Figure 13**).

b. Disconnect the starter relay switch electrical connector.

c. Reconnect the negative battery cable.

d. Connect the positive lead of a voltmeter to the starter relay switch connector yellow/red wire and the negative voltmeter lead to a good engine ground.

e. Turn the ignition switch on and press the starter button while reading the voltmeter.

f. The voltmeter must indicate battery voltage. If not, check the circuit.

g. Turn the ignition switch off and remove the voltmeter leads.

6. Check the starter relay switch operation as follows:

a. Remove the starter relay switch (this section).

b. Connect an ohmmeter to the two blade terminals nearest the fuse on the starter relay switch (**Figure 15**). The ohmmeter should show no continuity.

c. Connect a fully-charged 12-volt battery to the starter relay switch. Connect the positive battery terminal to the yellow/red wire relay terminal and the negative battery terminal to the green/red wire relay terminal. The ohmmeter should now read continuity.

d. Disconnect the battery and ohmmeter leads.

7. Replace the starter relay switch if it fails any part of this test.

CLUTCH DIODE

The clutch diode is part of the starter circuit and is wired between the clutch switch and neutral switch. The diode prevents the flow of current from the neutral switch back through the clutch switch.

Suspect a faulty clutch diode if the neutral light comes on when the transmission is in gear and the clutch is disengaged. Also, look for a dirty or loose clutch diode connection if the starter does not operate when the transmission is in neutral.

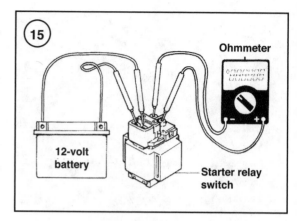

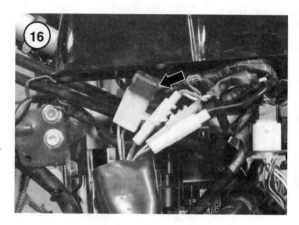

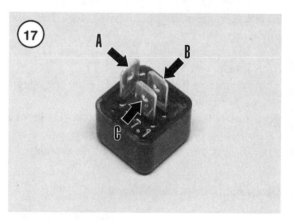

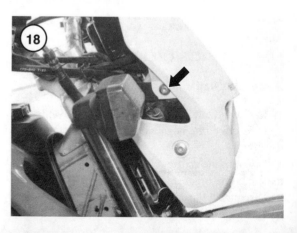

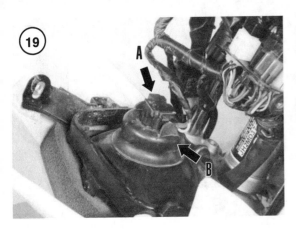

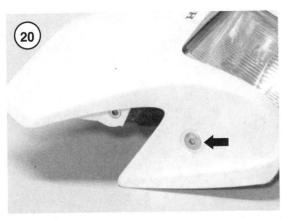

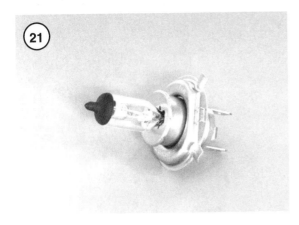

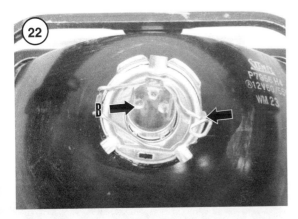

Testing/Replacement

1. Remove the headlight visor (this chapter).
2. Disconnect the diode (**Figure 16**) from the electrical connector.
3. Using an ohmmeter, connect a test lead to indicated terminal (A, **Figure 17**). Then, touch the remaining ohmmeter test lead to indicated terminal (B, **Figure 17**). Reverse the test leads and check continuity in the opposite direction. The ohmmeter should indicate continuity in one direction and no continuity when the test leads are reversed.
4. Repeat the test at indicated terminals (A and C, **Figure 17**).
5. Replace the diode if it fails any of these tests.

LIGHTING SYSTEM

Headlight Visor, Lens Assembly and Bulb Removal/Installation

1. Remove the bolts (**Figure 18**) on each side securing the headlight visor to the mounting brackets.
2. Disconnect the electrical connector (A, **Figure 19**) from the backside of the bulb.
3. Remove the rubber cover (B, **Figure 19**) from the back of the headlight.
4. Remove the bolt (**Figure 20**) on each side securing the headlight lens assembly to the mounting bracket and remove the assembly from the visor.

> *CAUTION*
> *The headlight is equipped with a quartz-halogen bulb (**Figure 21**). Do not touch the bulb glass. Skin oil can reduce bulb life. Clean the bulb with a cloth moistened in alcohol or lacquer thinner.*

5. Unhook the clip (A, **Figure 22**) and remove the light bulb (B). Replace with a new bulb.
6. Install by reversing the removal steps. Note the following:

11

a. Install the rubber bulb cover (B, **Figure 19**) so the TOP arrow points toward the top of the headlight.

b. Position the headlight visor so the lower prongs sit in the pockets (**Figure 23**) in the front fender.

c. Tighten the headlight visor and headlight assembly mounting bracket bolts securely.

d. Adjust the headlight (this section).

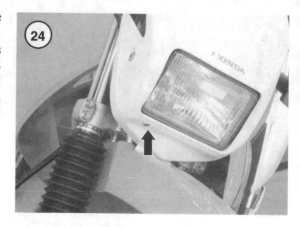

Headlight Adjustment

Adjust the headlight according to regulations in your area.

To adjust the headlight horizontally, turn the adjuster (**Figure 24**) located in the lower section of the visor. Turn the adjuster either clockwise or counterclockwise until the aim is correct.

To adjust the headlight vertically, proceed as follows:

1. Loosen the visor (A, **Figure 25**) and headlight retaining (B) bolts.

2. Move the headlight assembly either up or down until the aim is correct.

3. Tighten the visor and headlight retaining bolts securely.

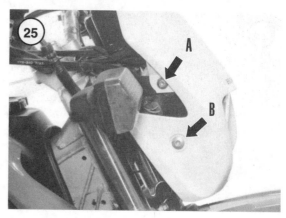

Taillight/Brake Light Bulb Replacement

1. Remove the lens retaining screws (A, **Figure 26**), and then remove the lens (B).

2. Push the defective bulb into the socket, turn it counterclockwise and remove it.

3. Carefully clean the lens and reflective surface on the bulb holder.

4. Install a new bulb.

5. Install the lens and gasket. Tighten the screws to 0.9 N•m (8 in.-lb.). Do not overtighten the screws; the lens may crack.

6. Check taillight and brake light operation.

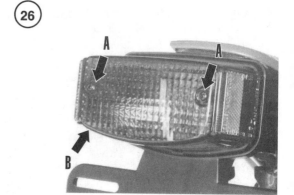

Turn Signal Bulb Replacement

1. Remove the lens retaining screw (A, **Figure 27**), and then remove the lens (B).

2. Push the defective bulb into the socket, turn it counterclockwise and remove it.

3. Carefully clean the lens and reflective surface on the bulb holder.

4. Install a new bulb.

5. Install the lens and gasket. Tighten the screws to 0.9 N•m (8 in.-lb.). Do not overtighten the screw; the lens may crack.

6. Check the turn signal light operation.

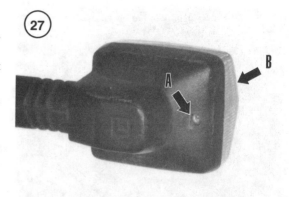

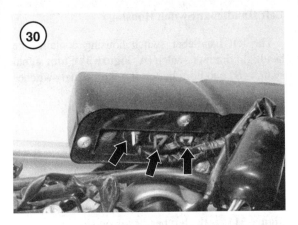

Turn Signal Relay Testing/Replacement

There is no specific test for the turn signal relay. Determine if the relay is causing a turn signal malfunction by testing and eliminating the other components in the turn signal system.

If all other turn signal components test good, perform the following:

1. Remove the headlight visor (this chapter).
2. Detach the turn signal relay (**Figure 28**) from the bracket.
3. Disconnect the electrical connector from the turn signal relay.
4. Connect a piece of wire between the terminals in the connector.
5. Operate the turn signals. If the turn signal light does not come on, check the turn signal components. If the turn signal light comes on, the turn signal relay is faulty.
6. Reverse the removal steps to reinstall or replace the relay. Tighten all fasteners securely.

Indicator Light Replacement

1. Remove the headlight visor (this chapter).
2. Free the large boot and connectors (**Figure 29**) from the clamp and move out of the way.
3. Remove the bulb socket (**Figure 30**) for the defective bulb from the meter indicator panel.
4. Pull the bulb out of the socket and replace it.
5. Reverse the removal steps for installation. Tighten all fasteners securely.

SWITCHES

Ignition Switch Removal/Installation

1. Remove the headlight visor (this chapter).
2. Disconnect the ignition switch connector (A, **Figure 31**).

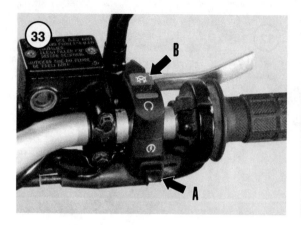

3. Remove the ignition switch mounting bolts (A, **Figure 32**).

4. Remove the ignition switch (B, **Figure 32**).

5. Install by reversing the removal steps. Tighten the ignition switch mounting bolts to 26.5 N•m (20 ft.-lb.). Tighten all other fasteners securely.

Right Handlebar Switch Housing

The right handlebar switch housing contains the start button (A, **Figure 33**) and engine stop switch (B). Individual switches are not available.

Replacement

1. Remove the headlight visor (this chapter).

2. Remove any clamps securing the switch wiring harness to the handlebar.

3. Disconnect the electrical connector (B, **Figure 31**) for the right handlebar switch.

> *NOTE*
> *The handlebar switch wiring harness also includes wiring for the front brake light switch. If complete removal is necessary, also disconnect the brake light switch connectors as described in this section.*

4. Remove the switch housing screws and separate the switch halves. Remove the switch and wiring harness from the frame.

5. Install the switch housing by reversing the removal steps. Align the lower switch housing pin with the hole in the handlebar, and then install the housing. Tighten all fasteners securely.

6. Start the engine and check both switches in their operating position.

Left Handlebar Switch Housing

The left handlebar switch housing contains the headlight dimmer switch (A, **Figure 34**), turn signal switch (B) and horn button (C). Individual switches are not available.

Replacement

1. Remove the headlight visor (this chapter).

2. Remove any clamps securing the switch wiring harness to the handlebar.

3. Disconnect the electrical connectors (C and D, **Figure 31**) for the left handlebar switch.

> *NOTE*
> *The handlebar switch wiring harness also includes wiring for the clutch switch. If complete removal is necessary, also disconnect the clutch switch connectors as described in this section.*

4. Remove the switch housing screws and separate the switch halves. Remove the switch and wiring harness from the frame.

5. Install the switch housing by reversing the removal steps. Align the lower switch housing pin with the

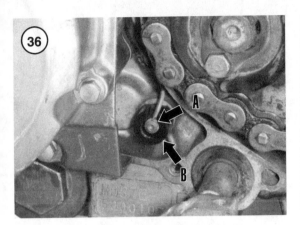

hole in the handlebar, and then install the housing. Tighten all fasteners securely.

6. Start the engine and check each of the switches in their operating position.

Neutral Switch

The neutral switch is mounted in the lower left side of the crankcase next to the gearshift shaft assembly.

Testing

1. Shift the transmission into neutral.
2. Remove the EVAP purge control valve (Chapter Nine).
3. Disconnect the connector (**Figure 35**).
4. Connect the leads of an ohmmeter or continuity tester between the light green/red wire terminal and green wire terminal. The tester should indicate continuity when the transmission is in neutral and infinity when the transmission is in gear.
5A. If the neutral switch fails either test, check the wiring harness for damaged, dirty or loose-fitting terminals.

5B. If the wiring harness is good, continue the test procedure.
6. Remove the drive sprocket cover (Chapter Twelve).
7. Repeat continuity test at the neutral switch terminal (A, **Figure 36**) and ground. If the neutral switch fails this test, replace the switch.

Replacement

1. Remove the drive sprocket cover (Chapter Twelve).
2. Remove the spacer (B, **Figure 36**).
3. Depress the washer (A, **Figure 37**) and disconnect the switch wire (B).
4. Remove the neutral switch (A, **Figure 38**) and O-ring (B).
5. Reverse the removal steps for installation. Note the following:
   a. Install a new O-ring (B, **Figure 38**) and lubricate it with oil.
   b. Make sure the switch is fully-seated.

Clutch/Front Brake Lever Switches

WARNING
Do not ride the motorcycle until the front brake light switch works correctly.

Testing

1. Disconnect the connector from the switch.
2. Connect an ohmmeter to the switch terminals.
3. Pull in the lever. There should be continuity.
4. If there is no continuity, replace the switch.

Removal/installation

1. Disconnect the connector from the switch.
2. Remove the switch mounting screw and remove the switch.
3. Install the switch and tighten the mounting screw securely.
4. Connect the connector to the switch.

11

5. Check operation.

Rear Brake Light Switch

WARNING
Do not ride the motorcycle until the rear
brake light switch works correctly.

Testing

1. Remove the battery case (this chapter).
2. Move back the boot. Then, disconnect the brake light switch wires at the electrical connector (**Figure 39**).
3. Connect the leads of an ohmmeter or continuity tester to the connector terminals. The tester should indicate continuity when the rear brake pedal is depressed and infinity when the pedal is released.
4. If necessary, replace the rear brake light switch (this section) if it fails this test.
5. Connect the switch connector.

Removal/installation

1. Remove the battery case (this chapter).
2. Move back the boot. Then, disconnect the brake light switch wires at the electrical connector (**Figure 39**).
3. Detach the spring (A, **Figure 40**) from the brake light switch.
4. Unscrew the brake light switch from the mounting nut (B, **Figure 40**).
5. Reverse the removal steps to install the brake light switch.
6. Adjust the rear brake light switch (Chapter Three).

Sidestand Switch Removal/Installation

Testing

1. Remove the battery case (this chapter).
2. Disconnect the sidestand switch electrical connector (**Figure 41**).
3. Connect the leads of an ohmmeter or continuity tester to the connector terminals. The tester should indicate continuity when the sidestand is up and infinity when the sidestand is down.
4. If necessary, replace the rear brake light switch (this section) if it fails this test.
5. Connect the switch connector.

Removal/installation

1. Remove the battery case (this chapter).
2. Disconnect the sidestand switch electrical connector (**Figure 41**).

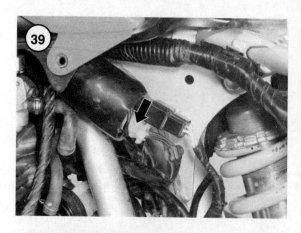

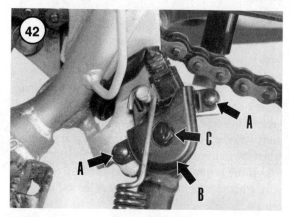

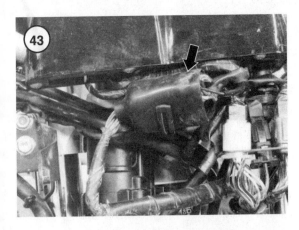

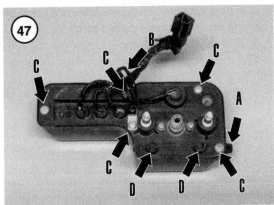

3. Release all clamps and bands securing the electrical wire from the connector to the sidestand.

4. Remove the bolts (A, **Figure 42**) securing the sidestand switch cover (B), and then remove the cover.

5. Remove the bolt (C, **Figure 42**) securing the switch to the sidestand pivot bolt.

6. Remove the switch and wiring harness from the frame.

7. Install by reversing the removal steps. Note the following:

    a. Align the switch pin with the sidestand hole.

    b. Align the switch groove with the sidestand return spring holding pin.

    c. Apply threadlock to the switch retaining bolt (C, **Figure 42**) threads, and then tighten the bolt securely.

11

METER/INDICATOR PANEL

Removal/Installation

1. Remove the headlight visor (this chapter).

2. Free the large boot and connectors (**Figure 43**) from the clamp and move out of the way.

3. Disconnect the meter/indicator panel electrical connector (**Figure 44**). If necessary, disconnect adjacent connector(s) for better access.

4. Unscrew the speedometer cable housing nut (**Figure 45**) from the speedometer.

5. Remove the retaining nut (**Figure 46**) on each side. These nuts secure the connector holder bracket and meter panel.

6. Lift off the meter/panel.

7. To remove the speedometer, perform the following:

    a. Remove the screw and reset knob (A, **Figure 47**) on the speedometer.

    b. Note the position of the wiring clamp (B, **Figure 47**). Then, remove the five screws (C, **Figure 47**) securing the housing to the base. Separate the housing from the base.

c. Remove the two screws (D., **Figure 47**) retaining the speedometer to the base.

d. Remove the speedometer.

8. Install by reversing the removal steps. Note the following:

a. Make sure all electrical connectors are free of corrosion and tight.

b. Tighten all screws, the retaining nuts and the speedometer cable housing nuts securely.

HORN

Testing

1. Disconnect the electrical connectors (A, **Figure 48**) from the horn.

2. Connect a 12-volt battery to the horn terminals. The horn should sound.

3. If it does not, replace the horn.

Removal/Installation

1. Disconnect the electrical connectors (A, **Figure 48**) from the horn.

2. Remove the bolt (B, **Figure 48**) securing the horn to the mounting bracket.

3. Remove the horn.

4. Install by reversing the removal steps. Note the following:

a. Tighten the mounting bolt (B, **Figure 48**) securely.

b. Test the horn to make sure it operates correctly.

FUSES

Whenever a fuse blows, determine the cause before replacing the fuse. Usually, the trouble is a short circuit in the wiring, but worn-through insulation or a short to ground due to a disconnected wire may also be a cause.

> *CAUTION*
> *If replacing a fuse, make sure the ignition switch is turned to the off position. This lessens the chance of a short circuit.*

> *CAUTION*
> *Never substitute any metal object for a fuse. Never use a higher amperage fuse than specified. An overload could cause a fire and the complete loss of the motorcycle.*

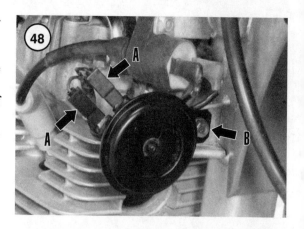

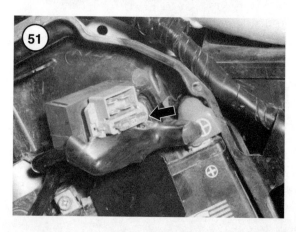

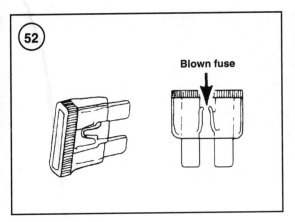

Blown fuse

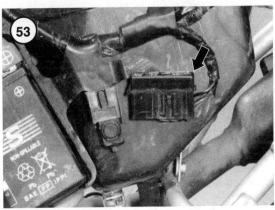

Main Fuse

The 20-amp main fuse is mounted on the starter relay switch. To check or replace the main fuse, perform the following:
1. Remove the left side cover (Chapter Seventeen).
2. Disconnect the negative battery cable (this chapter).
3. Pull out and disengage the starter relay (**Figure 49**) from the mounting bracket.
4. Disconnect the starter relay connector (**Figure 50**).
5. Remove the main fuse (**Figure 51**).
6. Inspect the fuse. Replace the fuse if it has blown (**Figure 52**).
7. Reverse the removal steps to install the main fuse.

Fuses

Fuses for the electrical circuits are located in the fuse box (**Figure 53**) attached to the left side of the air box. The current rating for each circuit fuse is 10 amps.

If a fuse in the fuse box blows, perform the following:
1. Turn the ignition switch off.
2. Remove the left side cover (Chapter Seventeen).

3. Open the fuse box cover.
4. Remove and inspect the fuse. Replace the fuse if it has blown (**Figure 52**).

NOTE
There is a spare fuse contained in the fuse box.

5. Close the fuse box cover.
6. Install the left side cover (Chapter Seventeen).

WIRING DIAGRAMS

The wiring diagrams are located at the end of this manual.

NOTE
Scan the QR code or search for "Clymer Manuals YouTube Tech Tips" to see an overview on electrical troubleshooting with a wiring diagram.

11

TABLES 1-5 ARE ON THE FOLLOWING PAGE.

Table 1 CHARGING SYSTEM SPECIFICATIONS

Alternator	
Capacity	188 W at 5000 rpm
Stator coil resistance*	0.1-1.0 ohms
Battery	
Capacity	12V, 6 A.h.
Charging current	
Normal	0.6 A/5-10 hour
Quick	3.0 A/1 hour
Current draw	0.1 mA max.
Regulator/rectifier	
Type	Triple phase/full-wave rectification
Regulated voltage	14.7-15.5 volts at 5000 rpm
Voltage @ 20° C/68° F	
Fully-charged	13.0-13.2V
Needs charging	Below 12.3V

*Perform test at 20° C (68° F). Do not test if the engine or component is hot.

Table 2 STARTER SERVICE SPECIFICATIONS

	New mm (in.)	Service limit mm (in.)
Starter brush length	12.0 (0.47)	6.5 (0.26)

Table 3 REPLACEMENT BULBS

	Voltage-wattage
Headlight	12V-60/55W
Indicator lights	
High beam	12V-1.7W
Neutral	12V-3.4W
Turn signal	12V-3.4W
Meter light	12V-3.4W
Taillight/brakelight	12V-8/27W
Turn signal	12V-23W

Table 4 FUSES

	Fuse rating
Main fuse	20 amp
Sub-fuses located in fuse box	10 amp

Table 5 ELECTRICAL SYSTEM TORQUE SPECIFICATIONS

	N•m	in.-lb.	ft.-lb.
Brake/taillight lens screw	0.9	8	–
Crankshaft position sensor			
mounting bolts	5.0	44	–
Ignition switch mounting bolts	26.5	–	20
Flywheel bolt	74	–	54
Turn signal lens screw	0.9	8	–

CHAPTER TWELVE

WHEELS, TIRES AND DRIVE CHAIN

This chapter describes service procedures for the wheels, wheel bearings, tires, drive chain and sprockets. Routine maintenance procedures for these components are found in Chapter Three.

Specifications are listed in **Tables 1-4** located at the end of this chapter.

FRONT WHEEL

Removal

1. Support the motorcycle with the front wheel off the ground.
2. On CRF230L and CRF230M models, remove the speedometer cable retaining screw (A, **Figure 1**). Then, withdraw the speedometer cable end (B, **Figure 1**) from the drive unit.
3. Loosen the axle holder nuts (A, **Figure 2**) sufficiently on the right fork leg to reduce the grip of the axle holder on the axle. Nut removal is not necessary.
4. Unscrew the front axle (B, **Figure 2**) and remove it from the right side. Then, roll the wheel forward.

CAUTION
To prevent damage to the brake disc, do not set the wheel down so it rests on the brake disc.

NOTE
Do not operate the front brake lever with the wheel removed. Insert a spacer block between the pads until the wheel is installed. This prevents the caliper pistons from extending if the lever is operated.

5. Inspect the front wheel (this section).

Installation

1. Clean the axle bearing surfaces on the fork tube and axle holder.
2. Remove the spacer block from between the brake pads.
3. If removed on CRF230F models, install the left-side spacer (**Figure 3**) with the flange side facing out. Lubricate the seal lips with grease prior to spacer insertion.
4. If removed on CRF230L and CRF230M models, install the speedometer gear unit by aligning the two drive tangs (A, **Figure 4**) with the slots (B) in the gear hub.
5. Carefully insert the disc between the brake pads. Then, install the front axle from the right side and finger-tighten the axle.

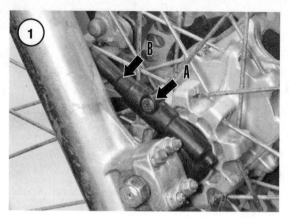

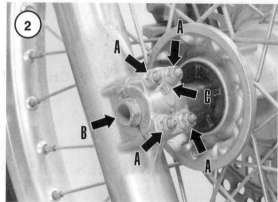

6. On CRF230L and CRF230M models, check that the boss (A, **Figure 5**) on the speedometer gear unit fits under the lug (B) on the fork tube.

7. If removed, install the axle holder so the UP mark (C, **Figure 2**) faces upward. Install the axle holder nuts and finger-tighten the nuts.

8. Tighten the front axle (B, **Figure 2**) to 74 N•m (55 ft.-lb.).

9. Tighten the axle holder nuts (A, **Figure 2**) to 12 N•m (106 in.-lb.).

NOTE
Be sure the cable end and drive unit tangs mesh when installing the cable end.

10. On CRF230L and CRF230M models, install the speedometer cable end into the gear unit. Then, install the retaining screw (A, **Figure 1**).

11. Remove the motorcycle from the stand so the front wheel is on the ground. Apply and hold the front brake. Then, compress and release the front suspension several times to reposition the pads against the disc.

12. Check that the wheel spins freely and the brake operates properly.

Inspection

1. Inspect the seals (A, **Figure 6**) for wear, hardness, cracks or other damage. If necessary, replace the seals (this chapter).

2. Inspect the bearings on both sides of the wheel for:

    a. Roughness. Turn each bearing inner race by hand and check for smooth movement and quiet operation.

    b. Radial and lateral play (**Figure 7**). Try to push the bearing in and out to check for lateral play. Slight play is normal. Try to push the bearing up and down to check for radial play. Any radial play should be difficult to feel. If play

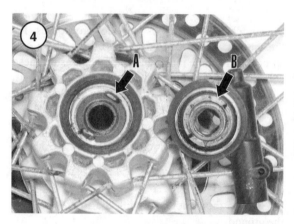

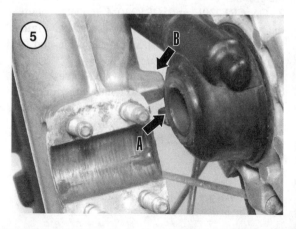

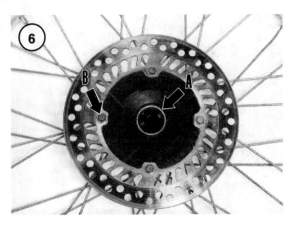

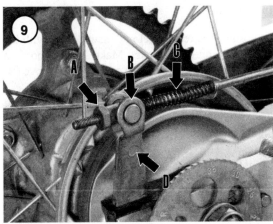

is easily felt, the bearing is worn out. If necessary, replace both bearings as a set (this chapter).

3. Clean the axle and spacers in solvent to remove all grease and dirt. Make sure the axle contact surfaces are clean.

4. Check the axle for straightness with a set of V-blocks and dial indicator (**Figure 8**). Refer to **Table 2** for maximum axle runout. Actual runout is one-half of the gauge reading. Do not attempt to straighten a bent axle.

5. Check the brake disc bolts (B, **Figure 6**) for tightness (**Table 4**). Refer to Chapter Sixteen for brake disc service.

6. On CRF230L and CRF230M models, inspect the speedometer gear unit. Inspect the plastic gear for damage. Inspect the seal for hardness, cracks and other damage. Replace the O-ring if damaged.

7. Refer to *Wheel Service* (this chapter) to inspect and true the rim.

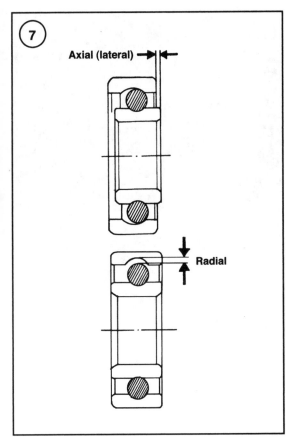

REAR WHEEL (CRF230F MODELS)

Removal

1. Support the motorcycle with the rear wheel off the ground.

2. Remove the rear brake adjuster nut (A, **Figure 9**), joint pin (B) and spring (C).

3. Loosen rear axle nut (A, **Figure 10**).

4. Rotate the drive chain adjuster (B, **Figure 10**) on each side to obtain maximum drive chain slack.

5. Move the rear wheel as far forward as possible.

6. Remove the axle (**Figure 11**) and allow the wheel to drop to the ground.

7. Remove the axle spacer (**Figure 12**).

8. Lift the drive chain off the sprocket and remove the rear wheel.

9. Inspect the rear wheel (this section).

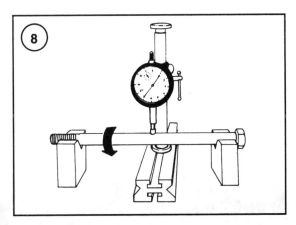

12

Installation

1. Position the rear wheel in the swing arm with the drive chain on the sprocket. Make sure the boss on the swing arm (A, **Figure 13**) engages the groove (B) on the brake panel.

2. Install the left-side spacer (**Figure 12**) with the flange side facing out. Lubricate the seal lips with grease prior to spacer insertion.

3. Install the axle bolt, drive chain adjusters and nut. Do not tighten the nut.

4. Install the spring (C, **Figure 9**) onto the brake rod.

5. Install the joint pin (B, **Figure 9**) into the brake arm (D). Then, insert the brake rod into the joint pin and install the brake adjuster (A).

6. Adjust the drive chain (Chapter Three). Tighten the rear axle nut to 108 N•m (80 ft.-lb.).

7. Adjust the rear brake (Chapter Three).

8. After the wheel is completely installed, rotate it several times to make sure that it rotates freely. Apply the rear brake several times to verify proper operation.

Inspection

1. Inspect the seal (**Figure 14**) for wear, hardness, cracks or other damage. If necessary, replace the seal (this chapter).

2. Inspect the bearings on both sides of the wheel for:

    a. Roughness. Turn each bearing inner race by hand and check for smooth movement and quiet operation.

    b. Radial and lateral play (**Figure 7**). Try to push the bearing in and out to check for lateral play. Slight play is normal. Try to push the bearing up and down to check for radial play. Any radial play should be difficult to feel. If play is easily felt, the bearing is worn out. If necessary, replace both bearings as a set (this chapter).

3. Clean the axle and spacer in solvent to remove all grease and dirt. Make sure the axle contact surfaces are clean.

4. Check the axle for straightness with a set of V-blocks and dial indicator (**Figure 8**). Refer to **Table 2** for maximum axle runout. Actual runout is one-half of the gauge reading. Do not attempt to straighten a bent axle.

> *CAUTION*
> *The driven sprocket is attached to the rear hub with Allen bolts and nuts. Do not loosen these fasteners by turning the Allen bolt. Instead, hold the Allen bolt and loosen the nut to avoid rounding out the Allen bolt heads.*

5. Check the driven sprocket bolts (**Figure 15**) for tightness. If loose, tighten the driven sprocket nuts to 32 N•m (24 ft.-lb.).

6. Refer to *Wheel Service* (this chapter) to inspect and true the rim.

REAR WHEEL
(CRF230L AND CRF230M MODELS)

Removal

1. Loosen the rear axle nut (A, **Figure 16**).

2. Rotate the drive chain adjuster (B, **Figure 16**) toward the front of the motorcycle so the wheel can be moved forward for maximum chain slack.

3. Remove the rear axle nut, washer and drive chain adjuster.

4. Support the motorcycle securely with the rear wheel off the ground.

5. Move the wheel forward and disegage the drive chain from the driven sprocket.

6. Withdraw the rear axle (A, **Figure 17**) and drive chain adjuster (B) from the wheel and swing arm.

7. Slide the wheel to the rear and remove it. Do not lose the spacer on each side of the wheel hub.

> *CAUTION*
> *To prevent damage to the brake disc, do not set the wheel down so it rests on the brake disc.*

8. Tie the caliper and bracket assembly to the frame.

> *NOTE*
> *Do not operate the rear brake pedal with the wheel removed. Insert a spacer block between the pads until the wheel is installed. This prevents the caliper pistons from extending if the pedal is operated.*

9. Inspect the rear wheel (this chapter).

Installation

1. Clean the axle bearing surfaces.

2. Remove the spacer block from between the brake pads.

3. Lubricate the seal lips with grease prior to spacer insertion.

4. Position the hub spacers (**Figure 18**) with the flange side facing out away from the bearings. Install the wide spacer onto the sprocket side of the wheel.

5. Install the caliper bracket onto the swing arm so the boss (A, **Figure 19**) on the swing arm engages the groove (B) on the brake caliper bracket.

12

6. Install the wheel while also engaging the drive chain around the drive sprocket.

7. Install the axle bolt, drive chain adjusters, washer and nut. Do not tighten the nut. Make sure the axle passes through the caliper mounting bracket.

8. Adjust the drive chain (Chapter Three). Tighten the axle nut to 93 N•m (69 ft.-lb.).

9. After the wheel is completely installed, rotate it several times to make sure that it rotates freely. Apply the rear brake several times to make sure the brake pads contact the brake disc correctly.

Inspection

1. Inspect the seals (A, **Figure 20**) for excessive wear, hardness, cracks or other damage. If necessary, replace the seals (this chapter).

2. Inspect the bearings on both sides of the wheel for:

   a. Roughness. Turn each bearing inner race by hand and check for smooth movement and quiet operation.

   b. Radial and lateral play (**Figure 7**). Try to push the bearing in and out to check for lateral play. Slight play is normal. Try to push the bearing up and down to check for radial play. Any radial play should be difficult to feel. If play is easily felt, the bearing is worn out. If necessary, replace the bearings as a set (this chapter).

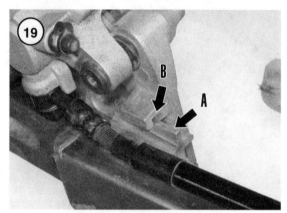

3. Clean the axle and spacers in solvent to remove all grease and dirt. Make sure all axle contact surfaces are clean.

4. Check the axle for straightness with a set of V-blocks and dial indicator (**Figure 8**). Refer to **Table 2** for maximum axle runout. Actual runout is one-half of the gauge reading. Do not attempt to straighten a bent axle.

5. Check the brake disc bolts (B, **Figure 20**) for tightness (**Table 4**). Refer to Chapter Sixteen for brake disc service.

> *CAUTION*
> *The driven sprocket is attached to the rear hub with Allen bolts and nuts. Do not loosen these fasteners by turning the Allen bolt. Instead, hold the Allen bolt and loosen the nut to avoid rounding out the Allen bolt heads.*

6. Check the driven sprocket bolts (**Figure 21**) for tightness. If loose, tighten the driven sprocket nuts to 32 N•m (24 ft.-lb.).

7. Refer to *Wheel Service* (this chapter) to inspect and true the rim.

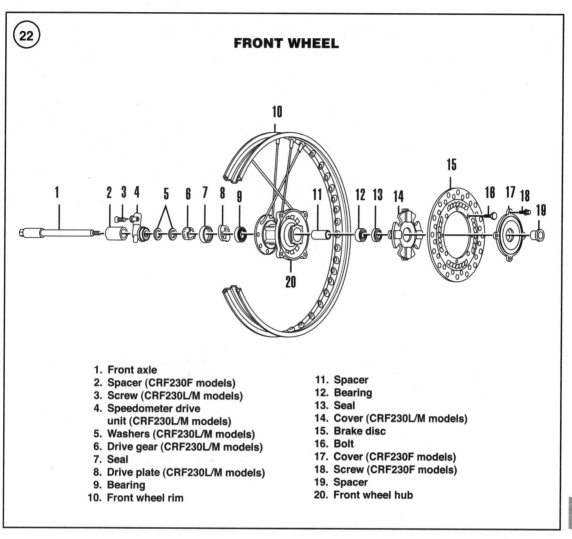

FRONT WHEEL

1. Front axle
2. Spacer (CRF230F models)
3. Screw (CRF230L/M models)
4. Speedometer drive
   unit (CRF230L/M models)
5. Washers (CRF230L/M models)
6. Drive gear (CRF230L/M models)
7. Seal
8. Drive plate (CRF230L/M models)
9. Bearing
10. Front wheel rim

11. Spacer
12. Bearing
13. Seal
14. Cover (CRF230L/M models)
15. Brake disc
16. Bolt
17. Cover (CRF230F models)
18. Screw (CRF230F models)
19. Spacer
20. Front wheel hub

12

FRONT
AND REAR HUBS

The front and rear hubs contain the seals, wheel bearings and a spacer. The front hub on all models supports a brake disc, and the rear hub carries the driven sprocket. The rear hub on CRF230L and CRF230M models also supports a brake disc. Refer to **Figures 22-24** when servicing the front and rear hubs in this section.

Procedures for servicing the front and rear hubs are essentially the same. Where differences occur, they are described in the procedure.

Inspection

The bearings can be inspected with the wheels installed on the motorcycle. With the wheels installed, leverage can be applied to the bearings to detect wear. In addition, the wheels can be spun to listen for roughness in the bearings. If the wheel has been removed, inspect the bearings as described in the wheel removal procedure (this chapter). If the wheel is still installed, inspect the bearings as follows:

1. Support the motorcycle with the wheel off the ground. The axle bolt or nut must be tight.

2. Grasp the wheel with both hands, 180° apart. Rock the wheel up and down, and side to side, to check for radial and lateral play. Have an assistant apply the brake while the test is repeated. Play will be detected in severely worn bearings, even though the wheel is locked.

3. Push the front or rear brake caliper, if so equipped, in by hand. This forces the caliper piston(s) away from the pads so that the wheel can spin without the brake pads contacting the brake disc.

NOTE
If the disc brake drags and the bearing cannot be heard, remove the wheel and support it on a truing stand.

23. REAR WHEEL (CRF230F MODELS)

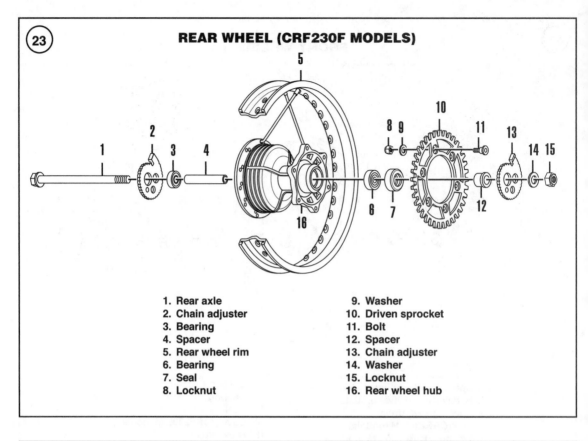

1. Rear axle
2. Chain adjuster
3. Bearing
4. Spacer
5. Rear wheel rim
6. Bearing
7. Seal
8. Locknut
9. Washer
10. Driven sprocket
11. Bolt
12. Spacer
13. Chain adjuster
14. Washer
15. Locknut
16. Rear wheel hub

24. REAR WHEEL (CRF230L AND CRF230M MODELS)

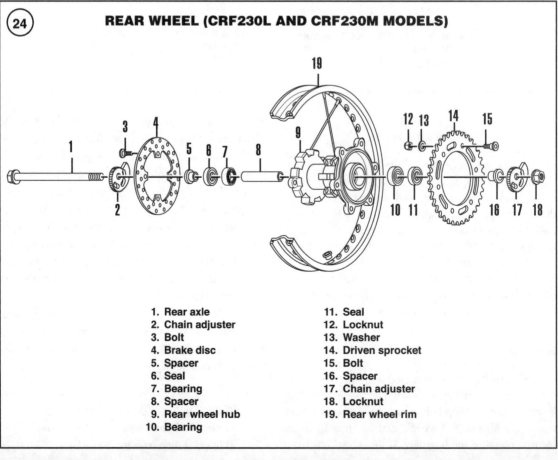

1. Rear axle
2. Chain adjuster
3. Bolt
4. Brake disc
5. Spacer
6. Seal
7. Bearing
8. Spacer
9. Rear wheel hub
10. Bearing
11. Seal
12. Locknut
13. Washer
14. Driven sprocket
15. Bolt
16. Spacer
17. Chain adjuster
18. Locknut
19. Rear wheel rim

4. Spin the wheel and listen for bearing noise. A grinding or catching noise indicates worn bearings.

CAUTION
Do not remove the wheel bearings to check their condition. If the bearings are removed, replace them.

5. If damage is evident, replace the bearings as a set (this section). Always install new seals.
6. Apply the front and rear brakes, if so equipped, to reposition the brake pads against the brake disc.

Seal Replacement

Seals protect the bearings from dirt and moisture contamination. Always install new seals when replacing bearings.

CAUTION
During seal replacement, do not set the wheel on the brake disc. Support the wheel on wooden blocks.

1. Pry the seals out of the hub with a seal puller, tire iron or wide-bladed screwdriver (**Figure 25**). Place a shop cloth under the tool to protect the hub from damage.
2. Clean the seal bore.

3. Inspect unshielded bearings for proper lubrication. If necessary, clean and repack the bearings while installed in the hub.

NOTE
If new bearings will be fitted, replace the bearings before installing the seals.

4. Pack grease into the lip of the new seal.
5. Place the seal in the bore with the closed side of the seal facing out. The seal must be square in the bore.

CAUTION
When driving seals, the edge of the driver must fit at the perimeter of the seal. If the driver outside diameter is appreciably smaller than that of the seal, the driver will press against the center of the seal and damage it.

6. Use a seal driver or socket (**Figure 26**) to install the seal in the bore. Install the seal so it is flush with the top (A, **Figure 27**, typical) of the hub bore surface.

Wheel Bearing Replacement

Wheel bearings are installed with a slight press fit and are not generally difficult to remove when the seals have been properly serviced. However, when damaged seals are not replaced, corrosion caused by water entering through the seals can seize or etch the bearings in the hub bore, making removal very difficult. Work carefully to avoid damaging the hub when replacing the bearings. Discard the bearings after removing them.

Tools

This section lists various tool possibilities to remove the front and rear wheel bearings.

The two methods available for removing the front and rear wheel bearings are:

12

1. Expanding wheel bearing collets (**Figure 28**)—Collets and driver rods can be purchased as a set or individually. For the front hub, use a 15-mm expanding collet. For the rear hub, use a 17-mm expanding collet. Bearing collets are available from specialty tool suppliers.

2. Common shop tools—The wheel bearings can also be removed with a propane torch, drift and hammer.

Removal

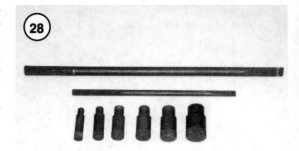

> *CAUTION*
> *During bearing removal, do not allow the wheel to rest on the brake disc. Support the wheel with wooden blocks.*

1. Remove the seals (A, **Figure 27**) as described in this section.

2. Examine the wheel bearings for excessive damage, especially the inner race (B, **Figure 27**). If the inner race of one bearing is damaged, remove the opposite bearing first. If both bearings are damaged, select the bearing with the least amount of damage and remove it first. On rusted and damaged bearings, applying pressure against the inner race can cause it to pop out, leaving the outer race pressed in the hub. Refer to *Damaged Bearings* (this section) for additional removal techniques.

3. On the front wheel of CRF230L and CRF230M models, remove the speedometer drive plate (**Figure 29**).

> *WARNING*
> *Wear safety glasses when removing the bearings in the following steps.*

4A. Remove the wheel bearings using expanding collets (**Figure 30**) as follows:
   a. Select the correct size collet and insert it into one of the hub bearings.
   b. From the opposite side of the hub, insert the remover shaft into the slot in the backside of the collet. Position the hub with the collet tool resting against a solid surface and strike the remover shaft so it wedges firmly into the collet.
   c. Position the hub so the remover head is free to move. Strike the end of the remover shaft, forcing the bearing out of the hub. Remove the bearing and tool. Release the collet from the bearing. Discard the bearing.
   d. Remove the spacer from the hub.
   e. Repeat the procedure to remove the remaining bearing.

4B. Remove the wheel bearings using a hammer, drift and propane torch as follows:

> *WARNING*
> *When using a propane torch to heat the hub, work in a well-ventilated area away from combustible materials. Wear protective clothing, including eye protection and insulated gloves.*

   a. Clean all lubricants from the wheel.
   b. Heat the hub around the bearing to be removed. Work the torch in a circular motion around the hub, taking care not to hold the torch in one area.

> *CAUTION*
> *Do not damage the spacer when removing the bearing. If necessary, grind a clearance groove in the drift to enable it to contact the bearing while clearing the spacer.*

   c. Turn the wheel over and tilt the spacer away from one side of the bearing using a long driver (**Figure 31**).
   d. Tap around the inner bearing race. Make several passes until the bearing exits the hub.
   e. Remove the spacer from the hub.
   f. Turn the hub over and heat the opposite side.

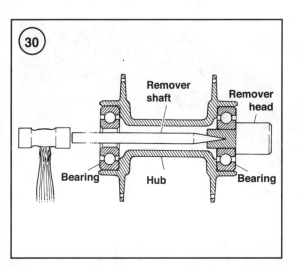

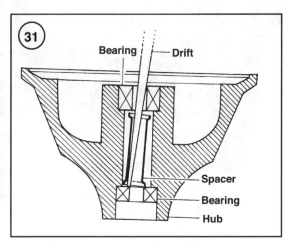

g. Drive out the opposite bearing using a large socket or bearing driver inserted through the hub.

h. Inspect the spacer for burrs created during removal. Remove burrs with a file.

5. Clean and dry the hub and spacer.

6. Check the hub mounting bore for cracks or other damage. If the bearings were a loose fit in the hub, the hub mounting bore and hub may be damaged.

CAUTION
The spacer contacts the wheel bearing inner races to prevent them from moving inward when the axle is tightened. If a spacer is too short, or if it is not installed, the inner bearing races will move inward and bind on the axle, causing bearing damage and seizure.

7. Inspect the spacer for flared ends. Check the ends for cracks or other damage. Do not try to repair the spacer by cutting or grinding its end surfaces as this will shorten the spacer. Replace the spacer if one or both ends are damaged.

Installation

1. Before installing the new bearings and seals, note the following:

a. Install bearings so the closed side faces out. If a bearing is sealed on both sides, install the bearing so the marks face out. If a shield is installed on one side of the bearing, the shield side must face out.

b. Apply grease (NLGI No. 2) to bearings that are open on one or both sides. Work the grease into the cavities between the balls and races.

c. Support the bottom side of the hub, near the bore, when installing bearings.

d. At the front hub, install the right bearing first. Then, install the left bearing.

e. At the rear hub, install the left bearing first. Then, install the right bearing.

2. Heat the hub evenly around the bearing bore.

3. Place the first bearing squarely against the bore opening with the closed side facing out. Select a driver with an outside diameter slightly smaller than the bearing outside diameter. Then, drive the bearing into the bore until it bottoms (**Figure 32**).

4. Turn the hub over. Install the spacer and center it against the center race.

5. Position the opposite bearing squarely against the bore opening with its closed side facing out. Drive the bearing partway into the bearing bore. Make sure the spacer is centered in the hub. If not, install the axle through the hub to align the spacer with the bearing. Then, remove the axle and continue installing the bearing until it bottoms.

NOTE
If the axle does not go in, the spacer is not aligned correctly with one of the bearings.

6. Insert the axle though the hub and turn it by hand. Check for any roughness or binding, indicating bearing damage.

12

7. On CRF230L and CRF230M models, install the speedometer drive plate (**Figure 29**). Make sure the drive tangs face out.

8. Install the seals (this section).

Damaged Bearings

If damaged wheel bearings remain in use, the inner race can break apart, leaving the outer race pressed in the hub. Removal is difficult because only a small part of the race is accessible above the hub shoulder, leaving little material to drive against. To remove an outer bearing race under these conditions, first heat the hub evenly with a propane torch. Drive out the outer race with a drift and hammer. It may be necessary to grind a clearance tip on the end of the drift, to avoid damaging the hub bore. Remove the race evenly by applying force at different points around the race. Do not allow the race to bind in its bore. After removing the race, inspect the hub mounting bore for cracks or other damage.

WHEEL SERVICE

To prevent wheel failure, inspect the wheels, bearings and tires at the intervals specified in Chapter Three.

Component Condition

Wheels used on off-road motorcycles receive a lot of abuse. It is important to inspect the wheel regularly for lateral (side-to-side) and radial (up-and-down) runout, spoke tension, and rim damage. When a wheel has a noticeable wobble, it is out of true. This is usually caused by loose spokes, but it can be caused by an impact-damaged rim.

Truing a wheel corrects the lateral and radial runout to bring the wheel back into specification.

The condition of the individual wheel components will affect the ability to successfully true the wheel. Note the following;

1. Spoke condition: Do not attempt to true a wheel with bent or damaged spokes. Doing so places an excessive amount of tension on the spoke, hub and rim. Overtightening the spoke may damage the spoke nipple hole in the hub or rim. Inspect for and replace damaged spokes.

> *NOTE*
> *When a properly trued wheel hits a sharp object, all the force of wheel impact is equally divided or transferred among all of the wheel spokes. The spokes are able to bend or bow slightly, thus absorbing the shock usually and*

preventing the rim and hub from damage. When the spokes are overtightened, they are unable to flex, causing all the impact to be absorbed by the hub or rim. When the spokes are too loose, the force of wheel impact is divided unequally between the spokes, with the tighter spokes receiving most of the force and isolating the impact in one area along the rim and hub. This eventually causes a cracked or broken hub or rim.

2. Nipple condition: When truing the wheels the nipples must turn freely on the spokes. However, corroded and rusted spoke threads are common and this makes them difficult to adjust. Spray a penetrating liquid onto the nipples and allow sufficient time for it to penetrate before trying to turn the nipples. Turn the spoke wrench in both directions and continue to apply penetrating liquid. If the spoke wrench rounds off the nipple, it is necessary to remove the tire from the rim, cut the spokes out of the wheel and install new spokes.

3. Rim condition: Minor rim runout can be corrected by truing the wheel; however, overtightening the spokes to correct a damaged rim may damage the hub and rim. Inspect the rims for cracks, flat spots or dents (**Figure 33**). Check the spoke holes for cracks or enlargement. Replace excessively damaged rims.

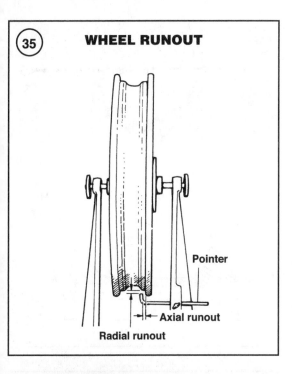

WHEEL RUNOUT

Pointer

Axial runout

Radial runout

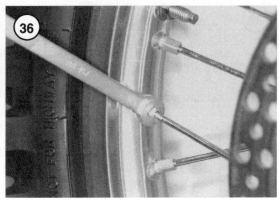

Wheel Truing Preliminaries

Before checking the runout and truing the wheel, note the following:

1. Clean the rim and spoke nipples.

2. Make sure the wheel bearings are in good condition. Refer to the front and rear wheel inspection procedures in this chapter.

3. Inspect the spoke holes in the rim for cracks, hole elongation and other damage. Replace the rim if damaged.

4. A small amount of wheel runout is acceptable. Attempting to true the wheel to a zero reading may damage the rim and hub from overtightened spokes. Also, considering the environment off-road motorcycles operate in, minor rim and spoke damage may make it more difficult to accurately true the wheel.

NOTE
A solid pointer works better than a dial indicator when truing rims with deep scratches, dents and other contact wear.

5. Check runout by mounting a pointer against the fork or swing arm and slowly rotating the wheel. When checking the rear wheel, it will be easier if the chain is first removed from the driven sprocket. If the wheel needs major tuning, remove the tire and mount the wheel on a truing stand (**Figure 34**). An adjustable pointer (**Figure 35**) or dial indicator mounted next to the rim allows runout to be measured in both directions.

6. Use the correct size of spoke wrench (**Figure 36**). Using the wrong type of tool or incorrect size spoke wrench may round off the spoke nipples, making adjustment difficult.

Tightening Loose Spokes

This section describes steps for checking and tightening loose spokes without affecting the wheel runout. When many spokes are loose and the wheel is running out of true, refer to *Wheel Truing Procedure* in this section.

1. Support the wheel so that it can turn freely. If the rear wheel is being checked while on the motorcycle, remove the chain from the driven sprocket.

2. Spokes can be checked for looseness by one of three ways:

   a. Spoke torque: Spoke torque wrenches are available from different tool companies. When using a spoke torque wrench, the correct torque specification is listed in **Table 4**.

   b. Hand check: Grasp and squeeze two spokes where they cross. Loose spokes can be flexed by hand. Tight spokes feel stiff with little noticeable movement. Tighten the spokes until the tension between the different spoke groups feels the same.

   c. Spoke tone: Tapping a spoke causes it to vibrate and produce sound waves. Loose and tight spokes produce different sounds or tones. A tight spoke will ring. A loose spoke has a soft or dull ring. Tap each spoke with a spoke wrench or screwdriver to identify loose spokes.

3. Check the spokes using one of the methods described (this section). If there are loose spokes, spin the wheel and note the following:

   a. If the wheel is running true, continue with the procedure to tighten the loose spokes.

   b. If the wheel is running out of true, go to *Wheel Truing Procedure* (this section) to measure runout and true the wheel.

12

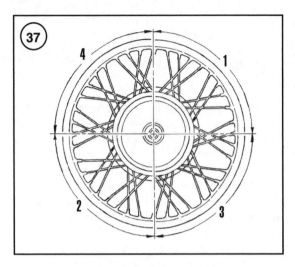

4. Use tape and divide the rim into four equally spaced sections. Number the sections as shown in **Figure 37**.

> *NOTE*
> *If the spokes are hard to turn, spray penetrating oil into the top of the nipple. Wipe excess oil from the rim.*

5. Start by tightening the loose spokes in Section 1. Then, tighten the spokes in sections 2, 3 and 4. Do not turn each spoke more than a fourth to a half turn at a time as this over-tightens the spokes and forces the wheel out of true. Work slowly while checking spoke tightness. Continue until all of the spokes are tightened evenly.

6. When all the spokes are tightened evenly, spin the wheel. If there is any noticeable runout, true the wheel as described (this section).

Wheel Truing Procedure

Table 2 lists axial (or lateral) (side-to-side) and radial (up-and-down) wheel runout specifications.

1. Clean the rim, spokes and nipples.

2. If the tire is mounted on the rim, position the pointer as shown in **Figure 34**. Otherwise, position a pointer (or dial indicator) against the rim as shown in **Figure 35**.

> *NOTE*
> *It is normal for the rim to jump at the point where the rim was welded together. Also small cuts and dings in the rim will affect the runout reading, especially when using a dial indicator.*

3. Spin the wheel slowly and check the lateral and radial runout. If the rim is out of adjustment, continue the procedure.

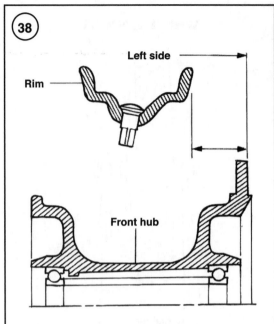

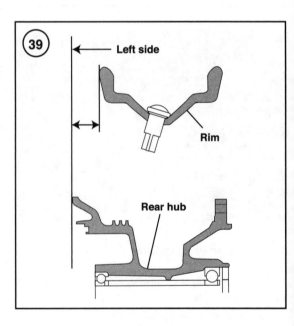

4. Spray penetrating oil into the top of each nipple. Wipe excess oil from the rim.

> *NOTE*
> *If the runout is minimal, the tire can be left on the rim. However, if the runout is excessive, or if the rim must be centered with the hub, remove the tire from the rim.*

5. If there are a large number of loose spokes, or if some or all of the spokes were replaced, measure the hub-to-rim offset as shown in **Figure 38** (front), **Figure 39** (rear, CRF230F models) or **Figure 40** (rear, CRF230L and CRF230M models) and com-

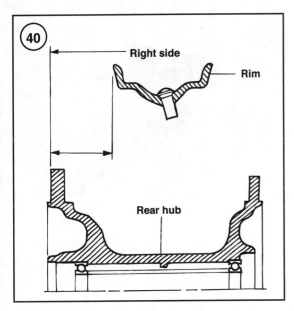

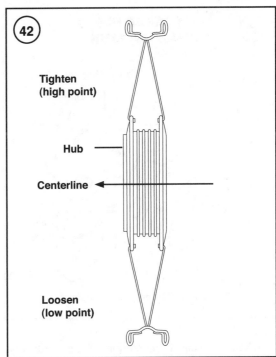

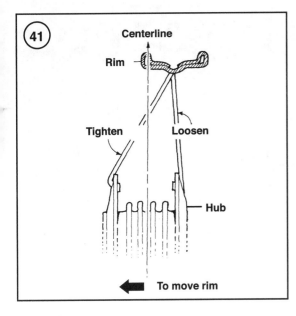

pare to the specifications in **Table 2**. If necessary, reposition the hub before truing the wheel.

NOTE
Determining the number of spokes to loosen and tighten depends on how far the runout is out of adjustment. Loosen two or three spokes, and then tighten the opposite two or three spokes. If the runout is excessive and affects a greater area along the rim, loosen and tighten a greater number of spokes.

NOTE
Alternate between checking and adjusting lateral and radial runout.

Remember, changing spoke tension on one side of the rim will affect the tension on the other side of the rim.

6A. Axial (lateral) runout adjustment: If the side-to-side runout is out of specification, adjust the wheel. For example, to pull the rim to the left side (**Figure 41**), tighten the spokes on the left side of the hub (at the runout point) and loosen the adjacent spokes on the right side of the hub. Always loosen and tighten the spokes in equal number of turns.

6B. Radial runout adjustment: If the up and down runout is out of specification, the hub is not centered in the rim. Draw the high point of the rim toward the centerline of the wheel by tightening the spokes in the area of the high point, and loosening the spokes on the side opposite the high point (**Figure 42**). Tighten the spokes in equal amounts to prevent distortion.

7. After truing the wheel, seat each spoke in the hub by tapping it with a flat nose punch and hammer. Then, recheck the spoke tension and wheel runout. Readjust spoke tension if necessary (this section).

8. Check the ends of the spokes where they are threaded in the nipples. Grind off any ends that protrude through the nipples to prevent them from puncturing the tube.

DRIVE CHAIN

Refer to **Table 3** for drive chain specifications. Refer to Chapter Three for routine drive chain inspection, adjustment and lubrication procedures.

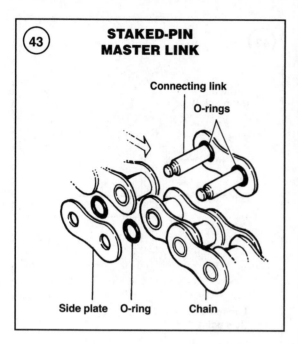

STAKED-PIN MASTER LINK

Connecting link

O-rings

Side plate   O-ring   Chain

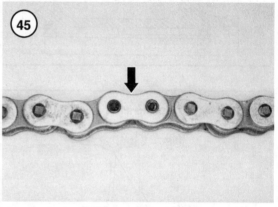

When checking the condition of the chain, also check the condition of the sprockets (Chapter Three). If either the chain or sprockets are worn, replace all drive components at the same time. Using new sprockets with a worn chain, or a new chain on worn sprockets will shorten the life of the new part.

A drive chain equipped with a staked-pin type master link (**Figure 43**) is standard equipment on all models.

> *NOTE*
> *Identify the chain type installed on the motorcycle. A different type of replacement chain may have been installed instead of the original equipment-type of chain.*

Removal/Installation

The drive chain uses a staked master link (**Figure 43**) and can be removed/replaced with the swing arm mounted on the motorcycle by breaking the chain at the master link. The following section describes chain removal and installation using a chain service tool (**Figure 44**, typical) available from many tool suppliers. This tool, or an equivalent, can be used to break roller chains up to No. 630 and can be used to rivet chain sizes up to No. 530. Always follow the tool manufacturer's instructions provided with the tool. Supplement the instructions provided with the chain tool by performing the following:

1. Support the motorcycle with the rear wheel off the ground.

2. Loosen the rear axle nut and the chain adjusters. Push the rear wheel forward until maximum chain slack is obtained.

3. Assemble the extractor bolt onto the body bolt. Then, turn the extractor bolt until its pin is withdrawn into the pin guide, following the chain tool manufacturer's instructions.

4. Turn the chain to locate the crimped pin ends (**Figure 45**) on the master link. Break the chain at this point.

> *WARNING*
> *Discard the connecting link, side plate and O-rings after removing them. Never reuse these parts as they could break and cause the chain to separate. Reusing a staked master link may cause the chain to come apart and lock the rear wheel, causing a serious accident.*

5. Install the chain tool across the master link. Then, operate the tool and push the connecting link out of the side plate to break the chain. Remove the side plate, connecting link and O-rings (**Figure 43**) and discard them.

6. If installing a new drive chain, count the links of the new chain, and if necessary, cut the chain to

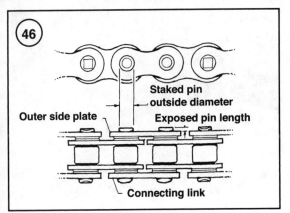

Staked pin outside diameter

Exposed pin length

Outer side plate

Connecting link

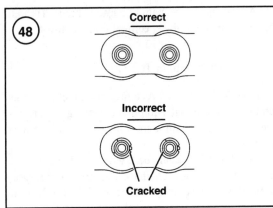

Correct

Incorrect

Cracked

length (this section). Refer to **Table 3** for the original equipment chain sizes and lengths.

NOTE
Always install the drive chain around the swing arm before connecting and staking the master link.

7. Install the chain around the drive sprocket, swing arm and driven sprocket.

8. Assemble the new master link as follows:
   a. Install an O-ring on each connecting link pin (**Figure 43**).
   b. Insert the connecting link through the inside of the chain and connect both chain ends together.
   c. Install the remaining two O-rings (**Figure 43**) onto the connecting link pins.
   d. Install the side plate (**Figure 43**) so the identification mark faces out (away from chain).

9. Stake each connecting link pin as follows:

NOTE
*The master link service specifications listed in **Table 3** are for the original equipment drive chain.*

   a. Measure the height of the connecting link from the outer side plate surface to the top of the

connecting link pin (**Figure 46**). If the height measurement (**Table 3**) is incorrect, confirm that the correct master link is being installed. If so, readjust the side plate height position on the connecting link.

NOTE
If the diameter of one pin end is out of specification, remove and discard the master link. Then, install a new master link assembly.

   b. Assemble the chain tool onto the master link and carefully stake each connecting link pin until its outside diameter is correct (**Figure 46**). Work carefully and do not exceed the specified outside diameter measurement (**Table 3**). Measure with a caliper in two places on each pin, 90° apart (**Figure 47**).

10. Remove the chain tool and inspect the master link for any cracks or other damage. Check the staked area for cracks (**Figure 48**). Then, make sure the master link O-rings were not crushed. If there are cracks on the staked link surfaces or other damage, remove the master link and install a new one.

WARNING
An incorrectly-installed master link may cause the chain to come apart and lock the rear wheel, causing a serious accident. If the tools to safely rivet the chain together are not available, take it to a dealership. Do not ride the motorcycle unless absolutely certain the master link is installed correctly.

11. If there are no cracks, pivot the chain ends where they hook onto the master link. Each chain end must pivot freely. Compare by pivoting other links of the chain. If one or both drive chain ends cannot pivot on the master link, the chain is too tight. Remove and install a new master link assembly.

12

12. Adjust the drive chain (Chapter Three). Tighten the rear axle nut to the specification in **Table 4**.

Cutting A Drive Chain To Length

Table 3 lists the correct number of chain links required for original equipment gearing. If the replacement drive chain is too long, cut it to length as follows.

1. Stretch the new chain on a workbench.

2. If installing a new chain over stock gearing, refer to **Table 3** for the correct number of links for the new chain. If sprocket sizes were changed, install the new chain over both sprockets, with the rear wheel moved forward, to determine the correct number of links to remove (**Figure 49**). Make a mark on the two chain pins to cut. Count the chain links one more time or check the chain length before cutting. Include the master link when counting the drive chain links.

3A. If using a chain breaker-type tool, use it to separate the drive chain.

> *WARNING*
> *Wear eye protection when operating a grinding tool.*

3B. To break the drive chain with a grinder, perform the following:

  a. Grind the head of two pins flush with the face of the side plate with a grinder or suitable grinding tool.

  b. Press the side plate out of the chain with a chain breaker; support the chain carefully while doing this. If the pins are still tight, grind more material from the end of the pins. Then, try to press the side plate out of the chain again.

  c. Remove the side plate and push out the connecting link.

4. Install the new drive chain (this chapter).

SPROCKETS

This section describes service procedures for replacing the drive (front) and driven (rear) sprockets. Refer to **Table 3** for original equipment sprocket sizes.

After replacing the chain and sprockets, check the drive chain sliders for worn or damaged parts (Chapter Three).

Drive Sprocket Removal/Installation

1. Increase drive chain slack (Chapter Three).

2. Remove the clamp bolt (A, **Figure 50**), and then remove the gear shift lever (B).

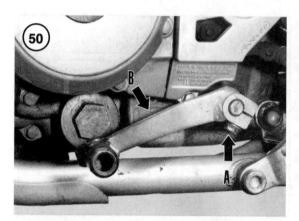

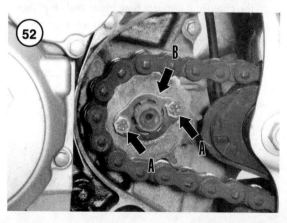

3. Remove the bolts securing the drive sprocket cover (**Figure 51**) and remove the cover.

4. Remove the bolts (A, **Figure 52**) securing the drive sprocket.

5. Rotate the drive sprocket holder (B, **Figure 52**) in either direction and slide it off the shaft. Then, remove the sproket.

6. Clean and inspect the parts.

7. Reverse the removal steps to install the drive sprocket. Note the following:

NOTE
The drive sprocket on CRF230L and CRF230M models may be installed in either direction.

a. On CRF230F models, install the drive sprocket so the raised side (**Figure 53**) is toward the engine.

b. Install the gearshift lever at the standard or desired height (Chapter Three). Tighten the clamp bolt (A, **Figure 50**) to the specification in **Table 4**.

c. Tighten the drive sprocket bolts (A, **Figure 52**) securely.

d. Adjust the drive chain (Chapter Three).

Driven Sprocket
Removal and Installation

1. Remove the rear wheel (this chapter).

CAUTION
The driven sprocket is attached to the rear hub with Allen bolts and nuts. Do not loosen these fasteners by turning the Allen bolt. Instead, hold the Allen bolt and loosen the nut to avoid rounding out the Allen bolt heads.

2. Remove the nuts, washers, Allen bolts (**Figure 54**) and driven sprocket from the rear hub.

3. Inspect the sprocket mounting tabs for cracks or other damage. Replace the hub if damaged.

4. Clean and dry the sprocket fasteners. Replace damaged fasteners.

5. Install the new sprocket onto the rear hub.

6. Install the Allen bolts, washers, and nuts and finger-tighten.

7. Install the rear wheel (this chapter).

8. Hold the Allen bolts (**Figure 54**). Following a crossing pattern, tighten the nuts in two or three steps to 32 N•m (24 ft.-lb.).

9. Adjust the drive chain (Chapter Three). Tighten the rear axle nut to the specification in **Table 4**.

TIRES AND WHEELS

Removal

1. Remove the valve core and deflate the tire. Remove the valve stem locknut.

2. On wheels so equipped, loosen the rim lock nut(s) (**Figure 55**).

NOTE
Warming the tire makes it softer and more pliable. Place the tire and wheel assembly in the sun or in a completely

12

*closed automobile. Place the new tire
in the same location.*

3. Press the entire bead on both sides of the tire into
the center of the rim.

4. Lubricate the beads with soapy water.

> *CAUTION*
> *Use tire irons without sharp edges. If
> necessary, file the ends of the tire irons
> to remove any rough edges.*

5. Insert the tire iron under the bead next to the valve
stem (**Figure 56**). Force the bead on the opposite
side of the tire into the center of the rim. Then, pry
the bead over the rim with the tire iron.

6. Insert a second tire iron next to the first to hold the
bead over the rim (**Figure 57**). While holding the tire
with one iron, work around the tire with the second
iron, prying the tire over the rim. Be careful not to
pinch the inner tube with the tire irons.

7. Remove the inner tube (**Figure 58**) from the tire.
If necessary, reach inside the tire and remove the
valve from the hole in the rim.

8. Remove the nut and washer and remove the rim
lock(s) from the rim.

9. Stand the tire upright and pry the second tire bead
(**Figure 59**) over the rim.

Inspection

1. Inspect the tire for any damage.

2. Fill the tube with air to check for leaks.

3. Check the rim locks and nuts (**Figure 55**). Replace
if damaged.

> *NOTE*
> *If water and dirt entered the rim, dis-
> card the rubber rim band. Wrap the
> center of the rim with two separate
> revolutions of duct tape. Punch holes
> through the tape at the rim lock and
> valve stem hole positions.*

4. Make sure the spoke ends do not protrude above
the nipple heads and into the center of the rim. Grind
or file off any protruding spoke ends.

Installation

> *NOTE*
> *Installation will be easier if the tire is
> pliable. This can be achieved by warm-
> ing the tire in the sun or in an enclosed
> vehicle.*

1. Sprinkle talcum powder around the interior of
the tire casing. Distribute the powder so it is on all

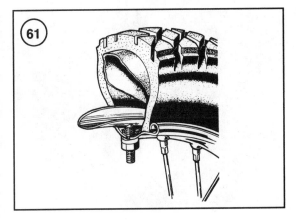

surfaces that will touch the inner tube. The powder minimizes chafing and helps the tube distribute itself when inflated.

NOTE
Depending on the make and type of tire installed, check the sidewall and determine if it must be installed in a specific direction. A directional arrow is often embossed in the sidewall.

2. If a rubber rim band is used, make sure the band is in place with the rough side toward the rim. Align the holes in the band with the holes in the rim.
3. Lubricate one bead and push it onto the rim (**Figure 60**). When necessary, work the tire from the opposite side of the rim.
4. Install the rim lock, lockwasher and nut (**Figure 55**). Do not tighten at this time. The rim lock must be over the edge of both tire beads when installation is completed (**Figure 61**).
5. Install the core into the valve stem, and then insert the tube into the tire. Check that the tube is not twisted as it is tucked into the tire. Put the locknut on the upper end of the valve stem to prevent the stem from falling out of the hole.
6. Inflate the tube until it is rounded and no longer wrinkled. Too much air makes tire installation diffi-

cult and too little air increases the chance of pinching the tube.
7. Lubricate the second tire bead, and then start installation opposite the valve stem. Fit the rim lock over the tire bead. Then, work around the rim, hand-fitting as much of the tire as possible. If necessary, relubricate the bead. Before final installation, check that the valve stem is straight and the inner tube is not pinched. Use the tire irons to pry the remaining section of bead onto the rim (**Figure 62**).
8. Check the bead for uniform fit, on both sides of the tire.

WARNING
If the tire does not seat at the recommended pressure, do not continue to overinflate the tire. Deflate the tire and reinflate to the recommended seating pressure. Relubricate the beads, if necessary.

9. Lubricate both beads and inflate the tire to seat the beads onto the rim. Inflate the tire to 1 1/2 times the recommended air pressure (**Table 1**).
10. If so equipped, tighten the rim lock nut(s) to specification (**Table 4**).
11. Adjust the tire pressure to the proper specification (**Table 1**).
12. Tighten the valve stem locknut, but do not overtighten or the valve system may be damaged. Then, install the cap.

WHEEL BALANCE

A wheel that is not balanced is unsafe because it seriously affects the steering and handling of the motorcycle. Depending on the degree of unbalance and the speed of the motorcycle, anything from a mild vibration to a violent shimmy may occur, which may result in loss of control. An imbalanced wheel also causes abnormal tire wear.

Motorcycle wheels can be checked for balance either statically (single-plane balance) or dynamically

12

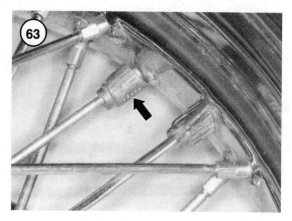

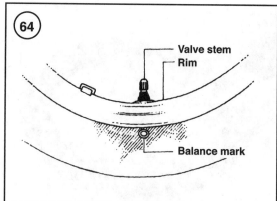

(dual-plane balance). This section describes how to static balance the wheels using a wheel balancing stand. To obtain a higher degree of accuracy, take both wheels to a dealership and have them balanced dynamically with a computerized dual-plane wheel balancer. This machine spins the wheel to accurately detect any imbalance.

Balance weights (**Figure 63**) are used to balance the wheel and are attached to the spokes. Weight kits are available from motorcycle dealerships.

The wheel must be able to rotate freely when checking wheel balance. Because excessively worn or damaged wheel bearings affect the accuracy of this procedure, check the wheel bearings as described in this chapter. Also, confirm that the tire balance mark, a paint mark on the tire, is aligned with the valve stem (**Figure 64**).

1. Remove the wheel (this chapter).
2. Clean the seals and inspect the wheel bearings (this chapter).
3. Clean the tire, rim and spokes. Remove any stones or pebbles stuck in the tire tread.

NOTE
Leave the brake disc mounted on the front wheel when checking and adjusting wheel balance.

4A. Mount the front wheel (with brake disc attached) on a balance stand.
4B. Mount the rear wheel (with sprocket, and brake disc on CRF230L and CRF230M models) on a balance stand (**Figure 65**).

NOTE
To check the original balance of the wheel, leave the original weights attached to the spokes.

5. Spin the wheel by hand and let it coast to a stop. Mark the tire at its bottom point with chalk.
6. Spin the wheel several more times. If the same spot on the tire stops at the bottom each time, the

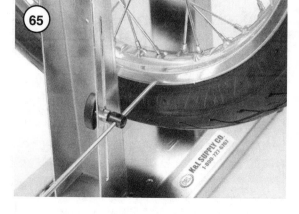

wheel is out of balance. This is the heaviest part of the tire. When an unbalanced wheel is spun, it always comes to rest with the heaviest spot at the bottom.

7. Attach a test weight to the wheel at the point opposite the heaviest spot and spin the wheel again.
8. Experiment with different weights until the wheel, when spun, comes to rest at a different position each time. When a wheel is correctly balanced, the weight of the tire and wheel assembly is distributed equally around the wheel.

NOTE
Do not exceed 60 grams (2.1 oz.) on the front wheel or 70 grams (2.5 oz.) on the rear wheel. If a wheel requires an excessive amount of weight, make sure the weight mark on the tire aligns with the valve stem.

9. Remove the test weight and install the correct size weight or weights onto the rim. Crimp the weight (**Figure 63**) tightly against the spoke and nipple.
10. Record the weight, number and position of the weights in the maintenance log at the end of the manual. Then, if the motorcycle experiences a handling or vibration problem in the future, use the log to check for any missing balance weights as previously recorded.
11. Install the wheel (this chapter).

Table 1 TIRE SPECIFICATIONS

Item	Front	Rear
Tire type	Tube	Tube
Size		
CRF230F models	80/100-21	100/100-18
CRF230L models	2.75-21 45P	120/80-18M/C 62P
CRF230M models	110/70-17M/C 54H	130/70-17M/C 62H
Manufacturer		
CRF230F models	Pirelli MT320H	Pirelli MT320H
CRF230L models	Bridgestone TW27	Bridgestone TW30
CRF230M models	Dunlop GT401FK	Dunlop GT401K
Minimum tread depth		
CRF230F, CRF230L models	3.0 mm (0.12 in.)	3.0 mm (0.12 in.)
CRF230M models	1.5 mm (0.06 in.)	2.0 mm (0.08 in.)
Inflation pressure (cold)[1]		
CRF230F models	103 kPa[2] (15 psi)	100 kPa[2] (15 psi)
CRF230L models	124 kPa[2] (18 psi)	152 kPa[2] (22 psi)
CRF230M models	200 kPa[2] (29 psi)	200 kPa[2] (29 psi)

1. Tire inflation pressure is for original equipment tires. Aftermarket tires may require different inflation pressure. Follow the tire manufacturer's instructions.
2. Up to maximum weight capacity.

Table 2 WHEEL SPECIFICATIONS

Item	Specification
Axle runout (max.)	0.2 mm (0.008 in.)
Wheel hub-to-rim offset distance	
CRF230F models	
Front	19.3-21.3 mm (0.76-0.84 in.)
Rear	21.3-23.3 mm (0.84-0.92 in.)
CRF230L models	
Front	22.25-24.25 mm (0.876-0.955 in.)
Rear	22.5-24.5 mm (0.89-0.97 in.)
CRF230M models	
Front	2.0-4.0 mm (0.08-0.16 in.)
Rear	3.0-5.0 mm (0.12-0.20 in.)
Wheel rim axial runout (max.)	2.0 mm (0.08 in.)
Wheel rim radial runout (max.)	2.0 mm (0.08 in.)

12

Table 3 DRIVE CHAIN AND SPROCKET SPECIFICATIONS

Item	Specification
Drive chain	
CRF230F models	DID 520V6 (110 links)
	RK 520SMOZ2 (110 links)
CRF230L models	DID 520VC5 (100 links)
	RK 520MOZ9 (100 links)
CRF230M models	DID 520V (100 links)
	RK 520MOZ9 (100 links)
Drive chain slack	
CRF230F models	20-30 mm (3/4-1 1/4 in.)
CRF230L and CRF230M models	25-35 mm (1.0-1 3/8 in.)
Drive chain master link	
CRF230F models	
Pin length	
DID	1.15-1.55 mm (0.045-0.061 in.)
RK	1.2-1.4 mm (0.47-0.55 in.)
Stake diameter	
DID	5.4-5.6 mm (0.21-0.22 in.)
RK	5.40-5.65 mm (0.213-0.222 in.)
CRF230L, CRF230M models	

(continued)

Table 3 DRIVE CHAIN AND SPROCKET SPECIFICATIONS (continued)

Item	Specification
Drive chain master link (continued)	
CRF230L, CRF230M models (continued)	
Pin length	
DID	1.3-1.5 mm (0.05-0.06 in.)
RK	1.2-1.4 mm (0.47-0.55 in.)
Stake diameter	
DID	5.4-5.6 mm (0.21-0.22 in.)
RK	5.4-5.6 mm (0.21-0.22 in.)
Sprocket sizes	
Drive sprocket(front)	13 teeth
Driven sprocket (rear)	
CRF230F models	50 teeth
CRF230L models	39 teeth
CRF230M models	38 teeth

Table 4 WHEELS, TIRES AND DRIVE CHAIN TORQUE SPECIFICATIONS

Item	N•m	in. lb.	ft.-lb.
Brake disc bolt			
Front	20	–	15
Rear (CRF230L and CRF230M models)	42	–	31
Driven sprocket nuts	32	–	24
Front axle	74	–	55
Front axle holder nuts	12	106	–
Gearshift lever clamp bolts			
CRF230F models	12	106	–
CRF230L and CRF230M models	16	144	–
Rear axle nut			
CRF230F models	108	–	80
CRF230L and CRF230M models	93	–	69
Rim lock nut			
CRF230F models	13	120	–
Wheel spoke nipple			
Front Wheel			
CRF230F models	4.0	35	–
CRF230L and CRF230M models	3.7	33	–
Rear wheel			
CRF230F models	4.0	35	–
CRF230L and CRF230M models	3.7	33	–

CHAPTER THIRTEEN

FRONT SUSPENSION AND STEERING

This chapter describes repair and maintenance procedures for the front fork and steering components. Refer to Chapter Twelve for front wheel and tire service. Front suspension specifications are listed in **Table 1** and **Table 2** at the end of this chapter.

HANDLEBAR (CRF230F MODELS)

Removal

1. Disengage the number plate loop (A, **Figure 1**) from the handlebar.
2. Pull the breather hose (B, **Figure 1**) out of the steering head.
3. Detach any clamps securing wires to the handlebar.
4. Remove the clamp screw (A, **Figure 2**). Then, remove the stop switch (B, **Figure 2**). Watch for the ground terminal under the switch screw.
5. Remove the bolts (A, **Figure 3**) securing the clutch lever assembly (B).
6. Lay the clutch lever assembly and cable over the frame or front fender. Be careful that the cables are not kinked.

> *CAUTION*
> *Cover the frame with a heavy cloth or plastic tarp to protect it from accidental brake fluid spills. Wash spilled brake fluid off any painted or plated surfaces immediately, as it will destroy the finish. Use soapy water and rinse thoroughly.*

7. Remove the bolts (A, **Figure 4**) securing the brake master cylinder and lay it over the frame. Keep the reservoir (B, **Figure 4**) in the upright position to minimize loss of brake fluid and to keep air from entering the brake system. It is not necessary to disconnect the brake line.
8. Remove the mounting screws. Then, remove the starter switch assembly (A, **Figure 5**).
9. Fold back the rubber boot and remove the screws (B, **Figure 5**) securing the throttle assembly (C, **Figure 5**). Then, carefully lay the throttle assembly and cables over the fender or back over the frame. Be careful that the cables are not kinked.
10. Remove the bolts securing the handlebar upper holders (A, **Figure 6**). Then, remove the upper holders.
11. Remove the handlebar (B, **Figure 6**).

Installation

1. To maintain a good grip on the handlebar and to prevent it from slipping down, clean the knurled section of the handlebar with a wire brush. It should be rough so it will be held securely by the holders. Also, clean the holders.
2. Position the handlebar on the lower handlebar holders so the punch mark (**Figure 7**) on the handle-

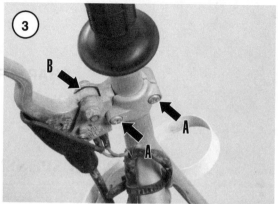

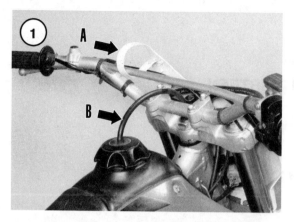

bar is aligned with the top surface of the handlebar holder.

3. Install the upper handlebar holders (A, **Figure 6**) so the punch mark (**Figure 8**) is to the front.

4. Tighten the front bolts first, and then the rear bolts. A gap should exist between the rear mating surfaces of the upper and lower holders. Tighten all handlebar holder bolts to 26 N•m (19 ft.-lb.).

5. Apply a light coat of multipurpose grease to the throttle grip area on the handlebar before installing the throttle grip assembly.

6. Install the throttle housing as follows:

   a. If removed, lubricate the ends of the throttle cables with lithium grease. Then, insert the cable ends into the handlebar throttle control.

   b. Reconnect the pull (A, **Figure 9**) and return (B) throttle cables. Route the cables into the cable guide (C, **Figure 9**) and position the cable guide into the throttle housing. Make sure the cables fit into the grooves in the guide.

   c. Install the throttle housing cover. Mate both housings together and install the mounting screws. Finger-tighten the screws at this time.

   d. Align the clamp mating surface on the throttle housing with the punch mark on the handlebar. Tighten the upper, and then the lower screw. Tighten the throttle housing screws securely.

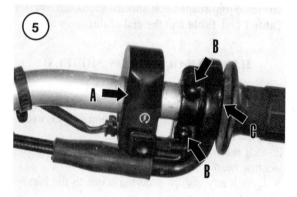

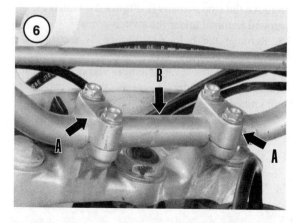

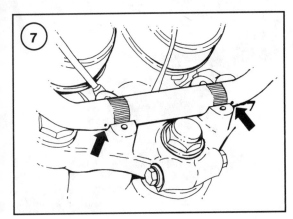

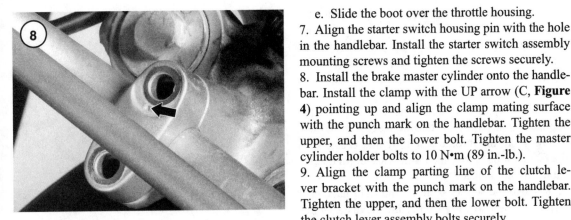

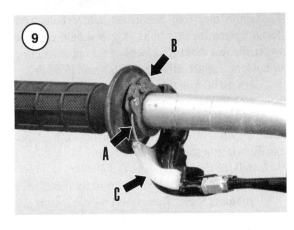

e. Slide the boot over the throttle housing.

7. Align the starter switch housing pin with the hole in the handlebar. Install the starter switch assembly mounting screws and tighten the screws securely.

8. Install the brake master cylinder onto the handlebar. Install the clamp with the UP arrow (C, **Figure 4**) pointing up and align the clamp mating surface with the punch mark on the handlebar. Tighten the upper, and then the lower bolt. Tighten the master cylinder holder bolts to 10 N•m (89 in.-lb.).

9. Align the clamp parting line of the clutch lever bracket with the punch mark on the handlebar. Tighten the upper, and then the lower bolt. Tighten the clutch lever assembly bolts securely.

10. Connect the ground wire terminal to the stop switch clamp screw (A, **Figure 2**). Align the gap at the bottom of the clamp straps with the punch mark on the handlebar. Install the clamp screw and tighten securely.

11. Operate the throttle grip and make sure it turns smoothly. Turn the handlebar and check the throttle operation in both lock positions.

12. Adjust the throttle operation (Chapter Three).

HANDLEBAR
(CRF230L AND CRF230M MODELS)

Removal

1. Remove the rear view mirrors.

2. Detach any clamps securing wires to the handlebar.

3. Disconnect the front brake light switch electrical connectors (**Figure 10**).

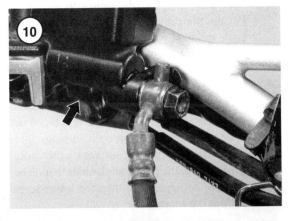

> *CAUTION*
> *Cover the frame with a heavy cloth or plastic tarp to protect it from accidental brake fluid spills. Wash any spilled brake fluid off painted or plated surfaces immediately, as it will destroy the finish. Use soapy water and rinse thoroughly.*

13

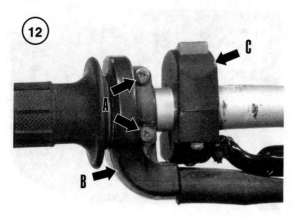

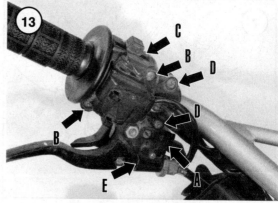

4. Remove the bolts (A, **Figure 11**) securing the brake master cylinder (B) and lay it over the frame. Keep the reservoir in the upright position to minimize loss of brake fluid and to keep air from entering the brake system. It is not necessary to disconnect the brake line.

5. Fold back the boot and remove the screws (A, **Figure 12**) securing the throttle assembly (B) and carefully lay the throttle assembly and cables over the fender or back over the frame. Be careful that the cables are not kinked.

6. Remove the screws securing the right handlebar switch assembly (C, **Figure 12**) and move the switch assembly out of the way.

7. Disconnect the connectors (A, **Figure 13**) from the clutch switch on the clutch lever bracket.

8. Remove the screws (B, **Figure 13**) securing the left handlebar switch assembly (C) and move the switch assembly out of the way.

9. Remove the screws (D, **Figure 13**) securing the clutch lever assembly (E).

10. Lay the clutch assembly over the frame or front fender. Be careful that the cables are not kinked.

11. Remove the bolts (A, **Figure 14**) securing the handlebar upper holders (B). Then, remove the handlebar upper holders.

12. Remove the handlebar (C, **Figure 14**).

Installation

1. To maintain a good grip on the handlebar and to prevent it from slipping down, clean the knurled section of the handlebar with a wire brush. It should be rough so it will be held securely by the holders. Also clean the holders.

2. Position the handlebar on the lower handlebar holders so the punch mark (**Figure 7**) on the handlebar is aligned with the top surface of the handlebar holder.

3. Install the upper handlebar holders so the punch mark (**Figure 15**) is to the front.

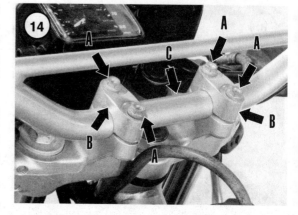

4. Tighten the front handlebar holder bolts first. Then, tighten the rear bolts. A gap should exist between the rear mating surfaces of the upper and lower holders. Tighten all bolts to 26 N•m (19 ft.-lb.).

5. Align the boss on the side of the right or left switch housing with the punch mark on the handlebar.

6. Apply a light coat of multipurpose grease to the throttle grip area on the handlebar before installing the throttle grip assembly.

7. Install the throttle housing as follows:

   a. Lubricate the ends of the throttle cables with lithium grease. Then, insert the cable ends into the handlebar throttle control.

   b. Reconnect the pull (A, **Figure 9**) and return (B) throttle cables. Route the cables into the cable guide (C) and position the cable guide into the throttle housing. Make sure the cables fit into the grooves in the guide.

   c. Install the throttle housing cover. Mate both housings together and install the mounting screws. Finger-tighten the screws at this time.

   d. Slide the boot over the throttle housing.

   e. Align the clamp mating surface on the throttle housing with the punch mark on the handlebar. Tighten the upper, and then the lower screw. Tighten the screw securely.

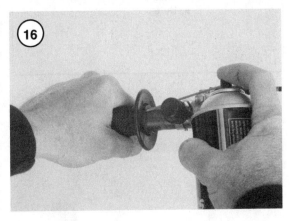

8. Install the brake master cylinder (B, **Figure 11**) onto the handlebar. Install the clamp with the UP arrow (C, **Figure 11**) pointing up and align the clamp mating surface with the punch mark on the handlebar. Tighten the upper bolt first. Then, tighten the lower bolt. Tighten the master cylinder clamp bolts securely.

9. Align the clamp parting line of the clutch lever bracket with the punch mark on the handlebar. Tighten the upper screw first, and then lower. Tighten both screws securely.

10. Operate the throttle grip and make sure it turns smoothly. Turn the handlebar and check the throttle operation in both lock positions.

11. Adjust the throttle operation (Chapter Three).

HANDLEBAR GRIPS

Replacement

Depending on the condition of the handlebar grips, different removal methods are available. Use contact cleaner and compressed air to remove the grips if they are to be reused. If the grips are torn and damaged, it may be possible to push them off by hand. This section lists different ways for removing grips. While some riders cut the grips off, the tool used in this method can score the throttle tube or the aluminum handlebar (if used), so use caution if using this method. Replace the grips with the handlebar installed on the motorcycle.

NOTE
When removing handlebar grips that are in good condition, it is best to use a technique that pushes or slides them off the handlebar. Trying to pull a grip off the handlebar stretches the grip and tightens it against the handlebar.

1. If the grips are to be reused, make alignment marks on the grips.

2. If the grips are torn and damaged, grab the inner grip flange and pull it off the handlebar or throttle tube, inside out.

3. If cutting the grips, carefully cut through the grip flange and pull it back to expose the handlebar or throttle tube. Continue to pull the grip away from the handlebar or throttle tube while cutting it lengthwise. Pulling the grip helps prevent the blade from contacting the handlebar or throttle tube. After cutting the grip, spread it and pull it off, inside out.

4. To remove the left grip so it can be reused, insert a thin screwdriver between the grip and handlebar. Work carefully to prevent tearing the grip or gouging the handlebar. Then, squirt contact cleaner into the open area under the grip (**Figure 16**). Immediately remove the screwdriver, turn the grip by hand to break the adhesive bond between the grip and handlebar. Then, push or slide the grip off. If necessary, repeat this step at different points around the grip until it slides off.

5. To remove the right grip from the throttle tube so it can be reused:

   a. Make sure the grip is in good condition. This technique does not work on cut or damaged grips.

   b. Disconnect the throttle cables and remove the throttle housing (this chapter). Separate the throttle tube from the throttle housing.

13

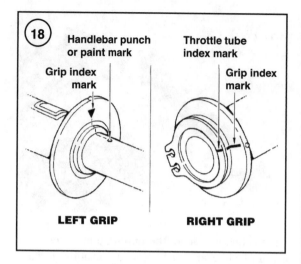

LEFT GRIP   RIGHT GRIP

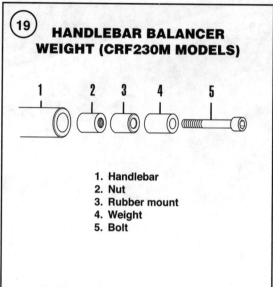

HANDLEBAR BALANCER WEIGHT (CRF230M MODELS)

1 2 3 4 5

1. Handlebar
2. Nut
3. Rubber mount
4. Weight
5. Bolt

c. Insert the nozzle from an air gun between the grip and throttle tube and carefully blow the grip slowly off the throttle tube (**Figure 17**).

6. Remove grip adhesive from the handlebar and throttle tube with solvent or WD-40. Then, clean with contact cleaner to remove any oil residue.

CAUTION
Do not install a new grip over a damaged or broken throttle tube. The glue will leak through and stick to the handlebar and the inner throttle tube surfaces.

7. Inspect the throttle tube for any cracks or damage. Replace the throttle tube if necessary.

8. Inspect the handlebar ends for scoring, grooves and other damage. Sand or file until the surface is smooth.

9. Reinstall the throttle tube (without the new grip) into the throttle housing. Install the throttle housing and the throttle cables (this chapter).

10A. If installing original equipment grips, note the following:

    a. Align the index mark on the throttle grip flange with the edge of the throttle tube (**Figure 18**).

    b. Align the index mark on the left grip flange with the punch or paint mark on the handlebar (**Figure 18**).

10B. On aftermarket grips, the grip may mount in a specific direction on the handlebar or throttle tube. Check the grip manufacturer's instructions before installing them.

11. Recheck the riding position and adjust the handlebar, if necessary.

12. Identify the left and right (throttle tube) grips.

13. Install the grips as follows:

    a. Cover the hole in the end of the throttle tube with duct tape to prevent the cement from con-

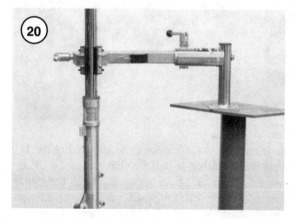

tacting the handlebar and inner throttle tube surface.

    b. If hidden end caps are to be used, install them into the handlebar ends before installing the grips.

NOTE
Make sure the grip cement is applicable for the grips being installed. A specific cement may be required when installing Gel grips and other soft compound grips. Always refer to the adhesive manufacturer's instructions for application and drying time.

    c. Apply grip cement to the inside surface of the grip and to the grip contact surface on the left side of the handlebar or on the throttle tube.

    d. Install the grip with a twisting motion to spread the cement evenly. Then, quickly align the grip with the handlebar or throttle tube. Squeeze the outer end of the left grip to make sure it

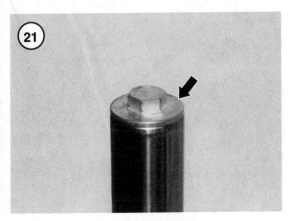

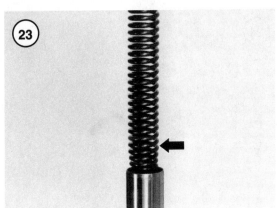

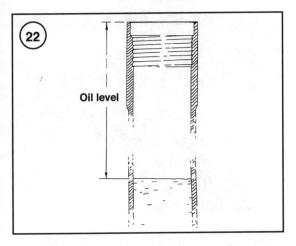

Oil level

FRONT FORK

Work stands (**Figure 20**, [www.parktool.com]) appropriate for holding the fork are available. Their quick adjustability and padded clamps make them ideal for many service procedures. If a vise is used, use soft jaw inserts.

Oil Change

1. Remove the fork leg (this chapter).

> *WARNING*
> *Spring pressure may propel the fork top*
> *cap out after release from the threads.*

2. If not loosened during the removal sequence, unscrew the fork top cap (**Figure 21**) from the fork tube.
3. Remove the fork top cap and the fork spring.
4. Remove the fork from the vise, pour out the fork oil and discard it. Pump the fork several times by hand to expel most of the remaining oil.
5. Fill the fork tube with fork oil. Refer to **Table 1** for the proper type of oil and the specified quantity for each fork leg.
6. Hold the fork assembly upright and slowly pump the fork several times.
7. Compress the fork completely and measure the fluid level (**Figure 22**) from the top of the fork tube after the fork oil settles. Refer to **Table 1** for the specified fork oil level.
8. Wipe the fork spring with a lint-free cloth.
9. Install the fork spring (**Figure 23**) with the close-wound coils toward the bottom.
10. Make sure the O-ring seal (**Figure 24**) is in place on the fork top cap and is in good condition; replace it if necessary.
11. Install the fork top cap into the fork tube while pushing down on the spring. Start screwing the cap in slowly; do not cross-thread it.

contacts the end of the handlebar. For the right grip, make sure there is a small gap between the grip and the throttle housing, and the grip contacts the end of the throttle tube.
14. Observe the grip cement manufacturer's drying time before riding the motorcycle.

BALANCER WEIGHTS (CRF230M MODELS)

A balancer weight (anti-vibration) assembly is located in both ends of the handlebar.

Removal/Installation

Refer to **Figure 19**.
1. Remove the left handlebar grip or throttle grip (this chapter).
2. Remove the balancer weight mounting bolt and remove the weight assembly.
3. Inspect the rubber center mount. Replace if deteriorated or otherwise damaged.
4. Assemble and install the weight assembly by reversing the preceding procedure. Tighten the balancer weight mounting bolt to 10 N•m (89 in.-lb.).

13

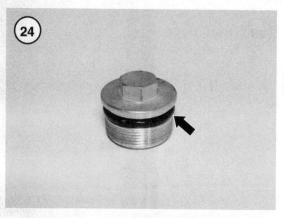

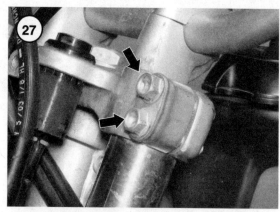

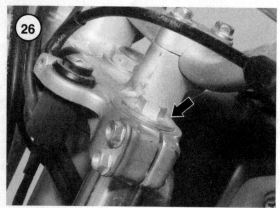

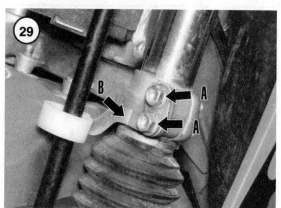

12. To tighten the fork cap, place the fork tube in a vise or holder, or install the fork tube on the motorcycle (this section). Tighten the fork top cap to the specification listed in **Table 1**.

13. Install the fork leg (this section).

14. Repeat for the other fork leg.

Removal/Installation

1. On CRF230F models, remove the number plate (Chapter Seventeen).

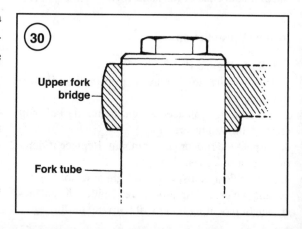

Upper fork bridge

Fork tube

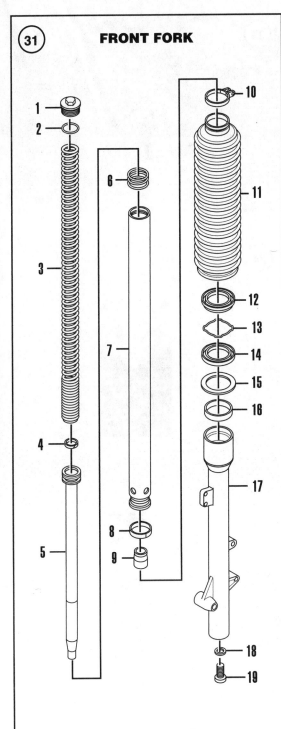

FRONT FORK ③①

1. Top cap
2. O-ring
3. Fork spring
4. Piston ring
5. Damper rod
6. Rebound spring
7. Fork tube
8. Fork tube bushing
9. Oil lock piece
10. Clamp
11. Cover
12. Dust seal
13. Stopper ring
14. Oil seal
15. Backup ring
16. Slider bushing
17. Slider
18. Seal washer
19. Bolt

2. If the fork is going to be disassembled, perform the following:
   a. Loosen the Allen bolt (**Figure 25**) at the bottom of the fork leg just enough to break it loose, otherwise, fork oil may flow out of the slider.
   b. Loosen, but do not remove, the fork top cap (**Figure 26**).

3. Remove the front wheel (Chapter Twelve).

4. If removing the left fork leg, detach the brake hose bracket from the fork leg.

CAUTION
Do not allow the front brake caliper to hang from the brake hose.

5. If removing the left fork leg, remove the brake caliper (Chapter Sixteen).

6. If removing the right fork leg on CRF230L and CRF230M models, detach the speedometer cable clamp from the fork leg.

7A. On CRF230F models, if not already loosened, loosen the top fork bridge bolts (**Figure 27**).

7B. On CRF230L and CRF230M models, if not already loosened, loosen the top fork bridge bolts (**Figure 28**).

8. Loosen the lower fork bridge bolts (A, **Figure 29**).

9. Slide the fork leg from the upper and lower fork bridge. It may be necessary to slightly rotate the fork leg while pulling it down and out.

10. Install the fork leg by reversing the removal steps. Note the following:
   a. Install the fork legs so that the top of the fork tube aligns with the top surface of the top fork bridge (**Figure 30**).
   b. If the fork leg was disassembled, tighten the fork top cap to the specification listed in **Table 2**.
   c. Tighten the lower fork bridge bolts to 32 N•m (24 ft.-lb.).
   d. Tighten the top fork bridge bolts to 27 N•m (20 ft.-lb.).
   e. Apply threadlock to the threads of the Allen bolt at the bottom of the fork leg. Install the Allen bolt with a new sealing washer and tighten the Allen bolt to 20 N•m (15 ft.-lb.).
   f. Install the brake caliper (Chapter Sixteen). Tighten the caliper mounting bolts to 30 N•m (22 ft.-lb.).
   g. On CRF230F models, tighten the brake hose bracket bolts to 10 N•m (89 in.-lb.). On CRF230L and CRF230M models, tighten the brake hose bracket bolts securely.

13

Disassembly

Refer to **Figure 31**.

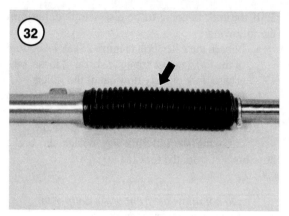

1. Remove the front fork legs (this chapter).

2. Loosen the retaining clamps, and then remove the fork cover (**Figure 32**).

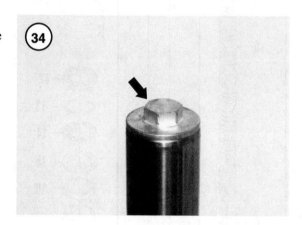

> *NOTE*
> *When loosening the Allen bolt in the bottom of the fork leg, leave the fork top cap and fork spring installed until the Allen bolt is loosened and removed. The internal spring pressure against the damper rod assembly will help hold it in place as the Allen bolt is loosened and removed.*

3. If the Allen bolt in the bottom of the fork leg was not loosened prior to fork removal, use the following procedure:

   a. Install the fork in a workstand or vise with soft jaws.

   b. Have an assistant compress the fork tube assembly as much as possible and hold it compressed against the damper rod.

   c. Loosen the Allen bolt (**Figure 33**) at the base of the slider with an Allen wrench and an impact tool. Do not remove the Allen bolt at this time.

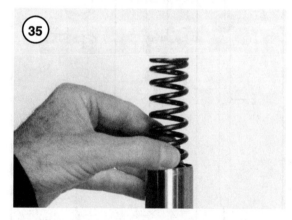

> *WARNING*
> *Be careful when removing the top cap as the spring is under pressure. Protect your eyes accordingly.*

> *NOTE*
> *Keep the fork leg upright after removing the top cap to prevent oil spillage.*

4. Slowly unscrew and remove the top cap (**Figure 34**).

5. Remove the spring (**Figure 35**).

6. Turn the fork assembly upside down over a drain pan and stroke the fork several times to drain the oil.

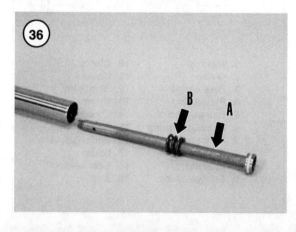

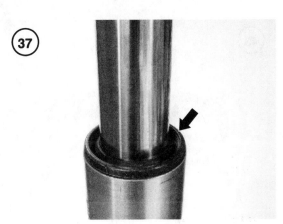

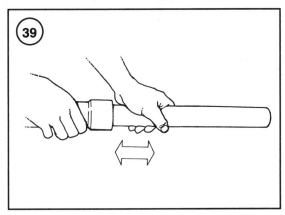

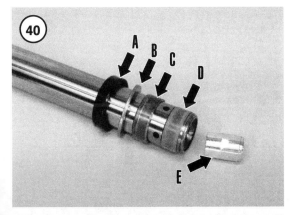

7. Remove the Allen bolt and seal washer from the bottom of the slider. Discard the seal washer. Discard the Allen bolt if the flats are starting to round out.

8. Slide out the damper rod (A, **Figure 36**) and rebound spring (B).

9. Remove the dust seal (**Figure 37**) from the slider.

10. Remove the stopper ring (**Figure 38**) from the slider.

> *NOTE*
> *On this type of fork, force is needed to remove the fork tube from the slider.*

11. There is an interference fit between the bushing in the fork slider and bushing in the fork tube. To remove the fork tube from the slider, pull hard on the fork tube using quick in-and-out strokes (**Figure 39**). Doing so will withdraw the oil seal (A, **Figure 40**), backup ring (B) and slider bushing (C).

12. Withdraw the fork tube from the slider.

> *NOTE*
> *Do not remove the fork tube bushing (D, **Figure 40**) unless it is going to be replaced. Inspect it as described in this section.*

13. Remove the oil lock piece (E, **Figure 40**) if it did not come out with the fork tube.

14. Slide off the oil seal, backup ring and slider bushing from the fork tube.

15. Inspect all parts (this section).

Inspection

1. Thoroughly clean all parts in solvent and dry them. Check the fork tube for signs of wear or scratches.

2. Check the damper rod for straightness (**Figure 41**). Replace a bent damper rod.

3. Make sure the oil holes in the damper rod are clear. Clean out if necessary.

4. Inspect the damper rod (A, **Figure 42**) and piston ring (B) for wear or damage. Replace if necessary.

13

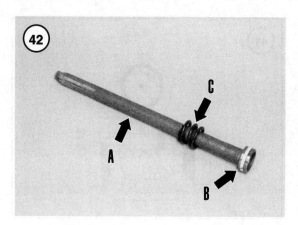

5. Check the fork tube for straightness. If bent or severely scratched, replace it.

6. Inspect the slider for dents or exterior damage that may cause the fork tube to stick. Replace if necessary.

7. Inspect the brake caliper mounting bosses on the slider for cracks or other damage. If damaged, replace the slider.

8. Inspect the fork tube (A, **Figure 43**) and slider (B) bushings. If either is scratched or scored, replace them. If the Teflon coating is worn off so that the copper base material is showing on approximately 3/4 of the total surface, replace the bushing.

9. Check the backup ring for distortion or damage; replace if necessary.

10. Inspect the fork top cap threads in the fork tube for wear or damage.

11. Inspect the fork top cap threads for wear or damage.

12. Inspect the oil seal seating area in the slider for damage or burrs. Clean up if necessary.

13. Clean the threads of the Allen bolt thoroughly with cleaning solvent or spray contact cleaner.

14. Measure the free length of the fork spring (**Figure 44**). If the spring free length is less than the service limit listed in **Table 1**, replace the spring.

15. Replace parts that are worn or damaged. Simply cleaning and reinstalling unserviceable components will not improve performance of the front suspension.

Assembly

1. Coat all parts with fresh fork oil prior to installation.

2. Carefully install the bushing onto the fork tube. Make sure the fork bushing fits properly in the groove on the fork tube (**Figure 45**).

3. If removed, install the piston ring (B, **Figure 42**) onto the damper rod (A).

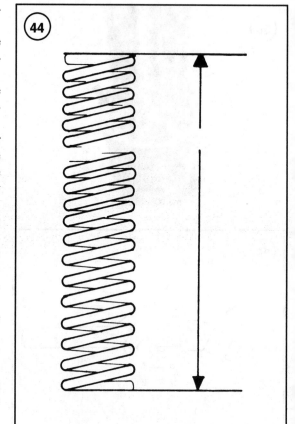

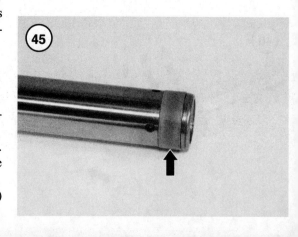

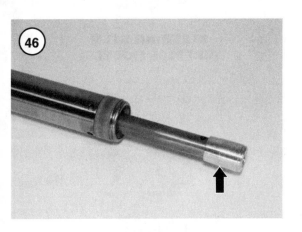

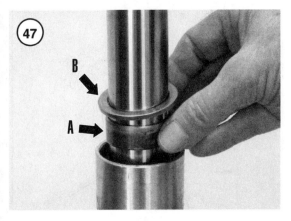

4. Install the rebound spring (C, **Figure 42**) onto the damper rod (A). Lubricate the piston ring, and then insert this assembly into the fork tube (**Figure 36**). Do not scratch the piston ring on the tube threads.

5. Temporarily install the fork spring to hold the damper rod in place.

6. Temporarily install the fork cap and tighten securely.

7. Install the oil lock piece (**Figure 46**) onto the damper rod.

8. Install the fork leg into the slider.

9. Install a new seal washer on the Allen bolt.

10. Apply a small amount of threadlock to the damper rod Allen bolt threads prior to installation. Install the Allen bolt and tighten to 20 N•m (15 ft.-lb.).

11. Unscrew the fork top cap and remove the fork spring from the fork tube.

12. Slide the fork slider bushing (A, **Figure 47**) and the backup ring (B) down the fork tube and rest them on top of the fork slider.

NOTE
*Place a plastic bag over the end of the fork tube (**Figure 48**) and coat it with fork oil. This will prevent damage to the dust seal and the oil seal lips when installing them over the top of the fork tube.*

13. Install the new oil seal as follows:
   a. Coat the new seal with fresh fork oil.
   b. Position the oil seal with the open groove facing upward and slide the seal (**Figure 49**) down onto the fork tube.

NOTE
*A fork seal driver (**Figure 50**) is required to install the fork slider bushing and fork seal into the slider. A number of different aftermarket fork seal drivers are available that can be used for this purpose. Another method is to use a piece of pipe or metal collar with the*

13

correct dimensions to slide over the fork tube and seat against the seal. When selecting or fabricating a driver tool, it must have sufficient weight to drive the bushing and oil seal into the slider.

c. Slide the fork seal driver, or its eqivalent, down the fork tube and seat it against the seal.

d. Operate the driver tool to drive the fork slider bushing and fork seal into the slider. Continue until the stopper ring groove in the slider is visible above the fork seal.

14. Slide the stopper ring down the fork tube.

15. Install the stopper ring and make sure it is completely seated in the groove in the fork slider.

16. Install the dust seal (**Figure 51**) into the slider. Press it in until it is completely seated.

17. Fill the fork leg with oil (this section).

18. Install the fork cover and clamps. Position the cover so the vent holes are toward the rear.

19. Repeat the assembly procedure for the other fork leg.

20. Install the fork leg (this section).

STEERING HEAD (CRF230F MODELS)

The steering stem pivots on tapered roller bearings contained in the steering head (**Figure 52**). The bearing outer races (mounted in the frame) and the lower bearing (mounted on the steering stem) should not be removed unless they require replacement.

Remove the steering stem and lubricate the bearings at the intervals specified (Chapter Three).

Special Tools

A special wrench must be used to turn the notched ring nut on the steering stem for bearing adjustment, disassembly and assembly. The following tools are available.

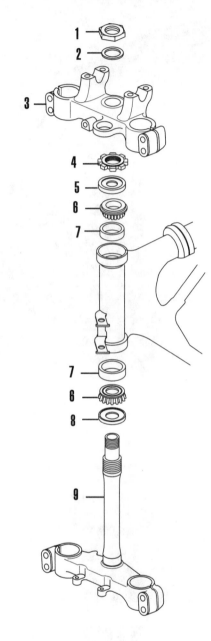

STEERING STEM (CRF230F MODELS)

1. Stem nut
2. Washer
3. Upper fork bridge
4. Steering adjust nut
5. Dust seal
6. Bearing
7. Outer bearing race
8. Dust seal
9. Steering stem

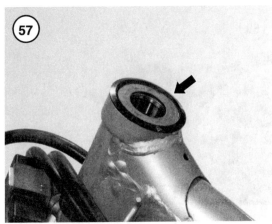

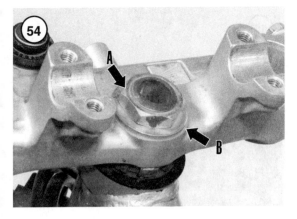

1. T-stem Nut Wrench and Bearing Adjustment Spanner (Motion Pro part No. 08-0232).
2. Steering stem socket (Honda part No. 07916-KA50100).
3. Universal spanner wrench (**Figure 53**) that can be used as a torque adapter.

Disassembly

> *NOTE*
> *The front brake system is completely detached in this procedure. Suspend the master cylinder and caliper so there is no tension on the brake hose.*

1. Disconnect the ignition switch connectors (Chapter Ten).
2. Remove the front wheel (Chapter Twelve).
3. Remove the front fender (Chapter Seventeen).
4. Remove the handlebar (this chapter).
5. Remove the front fork legs (this chapter).
6. Remove the fork clamp bolts (**Figure 27** and **Figure 28**) on each side of the top fork bridge.
7. Loosen the steering stem nut (A, **Figure 54**).
8. Remove the brake hose guide (B, **Figure 29**) on the left side of the lower fork bridge.
9. Remove the steering stem nut (A, **Figure 54**) and washer (B).
10. Remove the top fork bridge (**Figure 55**).

> *CAUTION*
> *Hold the steering stem so it cannot fall out of the steering head.*

11. Remove the steering adjust nut (**Figure 56**) using a spanner wrench.
12. Remove the steering stem.
13. Remove the dust seal (**Figure 57**) and upper bearing (**Figure 58**).

13

Inspection

Replace worn or damaged parts as described in this section. If impact damage has occurred, check the frame, steering stem and top fork bridge.

CAUTION
Steering bearings are usually damaged from a lack of lubrication or incorrect adjustment. A loose steering adjustment increases clearance between bearings and races. Pounding from off-road use damages the bearings. Over-tightening the bearing adjustment will also damage the bearings.

NOTE
Do not remove the lower bearing (Figure 59) for cleaning or lubrication. If the bearing can be reused, service it while it is mounted on the steering stem. Remove the bearing only to replace it.

1. Clean the bearings and races in solvent.
2. Clean the steering stem, steering adjust nut and steering stem nut threads thoroughly to ensure accurate torque readings and steering adjustment during reassembly.
3. Check the steering head frame welds for cracks and fractures. Refer repair to a qualified frame shop or welding service.
4. Check the steering stem nut and steering adjust nut for damage.
5. Check the steering stem and top fork bridge for cracks and damage. Check the steering stem for straightness.
6. Check the bearing races (**Figure 60**) in the frame for dimples, pitting, galling and impact damage. If a race is worn or damaged, replace both races and bearings (this chapter).

7. Check the tapered roller bearings for flat spots, pitting, wear and other damage. If a bearing is damaged, replace both races and bearings (this chapter).
8. When reusing bearings, clean them thoroughly with a degreaser. Pack the bearings with waterproof bearing grease before reinstalling them.

Assembly and Steering Adjustment

Refer to **Figure 52**.
1. Make sure the upper and lower bearing races are properly seated in the frame.
2. Lubricate the bearings and races with a waterproof bearing grease.
3. Install the steering stem (A, **Figure 61**) through the bottom of the frame and hold it in place.
4. Install the upper bearing (B, **Figure 61**) over the steering stem and seat it into its race.
5. Install the dust seal and the steering adjust nut (**Figure 56**). Tighten the nut finger-tight.

NOTE
During adjustment, the steering adjust nut must be tight enough to remove play, both horizontal and vertical, yet loose enough so the steering assembly

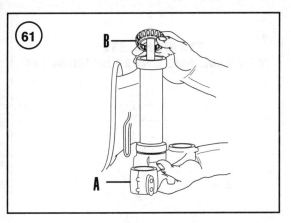

will turn to both lock positions without binding.

6A. To seat the bearings using a spanner wrench/torque adapter and torque wrench tool combination (**Figure 62**), perform the following:

a. Tighten the steering adjust nut (**Figure 62**) to 25 N•m (18 ft.-lb.).

Note:
Place the tool at right angles to the torque wrench as shown.

b. Turn the steering stem from lock-to-lock several times to seat the bearings.

c. Loosen the steering adjust nut.

d. Tighten the steering adjust nut to 4 N•m (35 in.-lb.).

e. Check bearing play by turning the steering stem from lock-to-lock several times. The steering stem must pivot smoothly with no binding or roughness.

6B. If the spanner wrench/torque adapter and torque wrench tool combination is not available, tighten the steering adjust nut as follows:

a. Tighten the steering adjust nut (**Figure 56**) to seat the bearings. Turn the steering stem several times to seat the bearings. Then, tighten the nut again.

b. Loosen the steering adjust nut.

c. Tighten the steering adjust nut while checking bearing play.

7. Install the top fork bridge, washer and steering stem nut. Tighten the steering stem nut finger-tight.

8. Slide both fork tubes into position and tighten the upper and lower fork tube clamp bolts so the forks cannot slide out.

9. Tighten the steering stem nut (A, **Figure 54**) to 108 N•m (80 ft.-lb.).

NOTE
Because tightening the steering stem nut affects the steering bearing pre-load, it may be necessary to repeat the adjustment procedure several times until the steering adjustment is correct.

10. Check bearing play by turning the steering stem from side to side. The steering stem must pivot smoothly. If the steering stem adjustment is incorrect, readjust the bearing play as follows:

a. Loosen the steering stem nut (A, **Figure 54**).

b. Loosen or tighten the steering adjust nut as required to adjust the steering play.

c. Retighten the steering stem nut (A, **Figure 54**) to 108 N•m (80 ft.-lb.).

d. Recheck bearing play by turning the steering stem from side to side. If the play feels correct, turn the steering stem so the front fork is facing straight ahead. While an assistant steadies the motorcycle, grasp the fork tubes, and try to move them front to back. If there is play and the bearing adjustment feels correct, the bearings and races are probably worn and require replacement.

11. Install the handlebar (this chapter).

12. Install the front fender (Chapter Seventeen).

13. Install the front wheel (Chapter Twelve).

14. Connect the ignition switch connectors (Chapter Ten).

15. After 30 minutes to 1 hour of riding time, check the steering adjustment. If necessary, adjust the steering as described in this chapter.

STEERING HEAD (CRF230L AND CRF230M MODELS)

The steering head (**Figure 63**) is equipped with caged ball bearings. The bearing outer races (mounted in the frame) and the lower bearing inner race (mounted on the steering stem) should not be removed unless they require replacement.

Remove the steering stem and lubricate the bearings at the intervals specified in Chapter Three.

13

Special Tools

A special wrench must be used to turn the notched ring nut on the steering stem for bearing adjustment, disassembly and assembly. The following tools are available.

1. T-stem Nut Wrench and Bearing Adjustment Spanner (Motion Pro part No. 08-0232).
2. Steering stem socket (Honda part No. 07916-KA50100).
3. Universal spanner wrench (**Figure 62**) that can be used as a torque adapter.

Disassembly

1. Remove the front wheel (Chapter Twelve).
2. Remove the front fender (Chapter Seventeen).
3. Remove the handlebar (this chapter).
4. Remove the headlight (Chapter Eleven).
5. Slide back the boot (**Figure 64**) and disconnect the wiring connectors from the meter/headlight panel.
6. Remove the connectors from the panel mounting bracket (**Figure 65**).
7. Remove the meter/headlight panel (Chapter Eleven).
8. Remove the turn signal relay (Chapter Eleven).
9. Detach the front brake hose guide (**Figure 66**) from the steering stem.
10. Remove the front fork (this chapter).
11. Remove the turn signal bracket on each side of the upper fork bridge.
12. Remove the steering stem cap (A, **Figure 67**).
13. Loosen the steering stem nut (B, **Figure 67**).
14. Remove the stem nut (B, **Figure 67**) and washer (C).
15. Remove the upper fork bridge (**Figure 68**).

CAUTION
Hold the steering stem so it cannot fall out of the steering head.

16. Remove the steering adjust nut (**Figure 69**) using a spanner wrench.
17. Remove the steering stem.
18. Remove the upper dust seal (**Figure 70**).
19. Remove the upper bearing race (**Figure 71**)
20. Remove the bearing ball assembly (**Figure 72**).
21. Remove the bearing ball assembly (**Figure 73**) from the steering stem.

Inspection

Replace worn or damaged parts as described in this section. If impact damage has occurred, check the frame, steering stem and top fork bridge.

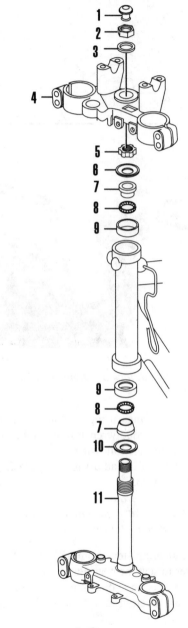

**STEERING STEM
(CRF230L AND CRF230M MODELS)**

1. Cap
2. Stem nut
3. Washer
4. Upper fork bridge
5. Steering adjust nut
6. Dust seal
7. Inner bearing race
8. Bearing
9. Outer bearing race
10. Dust seal
11. Steering stem

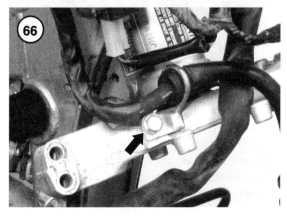

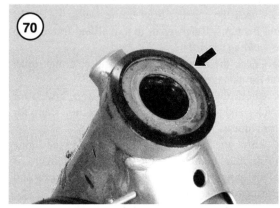

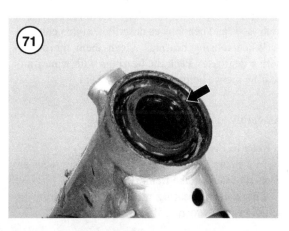

13

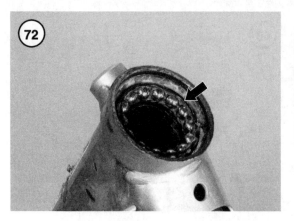

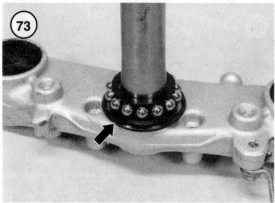

CAUTION
Steering bearings are usually damaged from a lack of lubrication or incorrect adjustment. A loose steering adjustment increases clearance between bearings and races. Pounding from off-road use damages the bearings. Over-tightening the bearing adjustment will also damage the bearings.

1. Clean the bearings and races in solvent.
2. Clean the steering stem, steering adjust nut and steering stem nut threads thoroughly to ensure accurate torque readings and steering adjustment during reassembly.
3. Check the steering head frame welds for cracks and fractures. Refer repair to a qualified frame shop or welding service.
4. Check the steering stem nut and steering adjust nut for damage.
5. Check the steering stem and top fork bridge for cracks and damage. Check the steering stem for straightness.
6. Check the bearing races (**Figure 74**) in the frame for dimples, pitting, galling and impact damage. If a race is worn or damaged, replace both races and bearings as described in this section.
7. Check the ball bearings for flat spots, pitting, wear and other damage. If a bearing is damaged, replace both races and bearings as described in this chapter.
8. When reusing bearings, clean them thoroughly with a degreaser. Pack the bearings with waterproof bearing grease before reinstallling them.

Assembly and Steering Adjustment

Refer to **Figure 63**.
1. Make sure the upper and lower bearing races are properly seated in the frame.
2. Lubricate all bearing races and ball bearing assemblies with waterproof bearing grease.

3. Install the ball bearing assembly (**Figure 73**) onto the steering stem.
4. Install the steering stem into the steering head and hold it in place.
5. Install the upper ball bearing assembly (**Figure 72**) and bearing race (**Figure 71**).
6. Apply grease to the seal lip. Then, install the upper dust seal (**Figure 70**).
7. Install the steering adjust nut so the stepped side is (**Figure 75**) down and tighten fingertight.
8. Using a suitable tool, tighten the steering adjust nut (**Figure 76**) to 5 N•m (44 in.-lb.).
9. Loosen the steering adjust nut, and turn the steering stem from lock-to-lock several times to seat the bearings.
10. Retighten the steering adjust nut to 4 N•m (35 in.-lb.).
11. Check bearing play by turning the steering stem from lock-to-lock. The steering stem must pivot smoothly.
12. Install the upper fork bridge (**Figure 68**).
13. Temporarily install the fork legs to align the upper fork bridge and the steering stem.
14. Install the washer (C, **Figure 67**) and steering stem nut (B). Tighten the steering stem nut to 103 N•m (76 ft.-lb.).

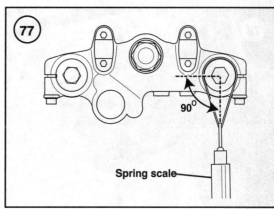

15. Check bearing play by turning the steering stem from side to side. The steering stem must pivot smoothly with no play. If the steering stem does not turn freely, readjust the bearing play.

16. Install the steering stem cap (A, **Figure 67**).

17. Install the turn signal bracket on each side of the upper fork bridge.

18. Install the front fork legs (this chapter).

19. Reattach the front brake hose guide (**Figure 66**) to the steering stem.

20. Install the turn signal relay (Chapter Eleven).

21. Install the meter/headlight panel (Chapter Eleven).

22. Install the panel connectors in the mounting bracket (**Figure 65**).

23. Connect the meter/headlight panel wiring connectors and replace the boot (**Figure 64**).

24. Install the headlight (Chapter Eleven).

25. Install the handlebar (this chapter).

26. Install the front fender (Chapter Seventeen).

27. Install the front wheel (Chapter Twelve).

STEERING PLAY CHECK AND ADJUSTMENT

Steering adjustment removes free play in the steering stem and bearings while allowing free steering stem ro-

tation. Excessive play or roughness in the steering stem produces imprecise steering and possible bearing damage. Improper bearing lubrication or an incorrect steering adjustment (too loose or tight) usually causes these conditions. Incorrect clutch and throttle cable routing can also affect steering operation.

1. Support the motorcycle with the front wheel off the ground. Have an assistant steady the motorcycle.

2. Turn the handlebar from side to side. The steering stem should move freely and without any binding or roughness. If it feels as if the bearings are catching, the bearing races are probably damaged.

3. Turn the handlebar so the front wheel points straight ahead. Alternately push (slightly) one end of the handlebar, and then the other. The front end should turn to each side from the center under its own weight. Note the following:

   a. If the steering stem moved roughly or stopped before hitting the frame stop, check the clutch and throttle cable routing. Reroute the cable(s) if necessary.

   b. If the cable routing is correct and the steering is tight, the steering adjustment is too tight or the bearings require lubrication or replacement.

   c. If the steering stem moved from side to side correctly, continue the procedure to check for excessive looseness.

4A On CRF230F models, grasp the fork tubes firmly (near the axle) and attempt to move the wheel front to back. Note the following:

   a. If movement can be felt at the steering stem, the steering adjustment is probably loose. Continue the procedure to adjust the steering.

   b. If there is no movement and the front end turns correctly as described in this procedure, the steering adjustment is correct.

4B. On CRF230L and CRF230M models, proceed as follows:

   a. Attach a spring scale to the fork tube between the top and lower fork bridges.

13

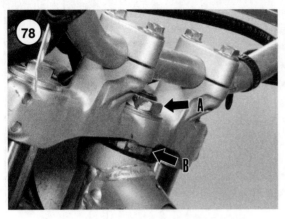

b. Pull the spring scale while keeping the scale at a right angle to the steering head (**Figure 77**).

c. The spring scale should read 10.8-16.7 N (2.4-3.8 lb.) just as the fork tube starts to move. Make sure no cables, wires or other objects prevent the movement.

d. If the scale reading is incorrect, continue the procedure to adjust the steering.

5A. On CRF230F models, adjust the steering as follows:

a. Loosen the steering stem nut (A, **Figure 78**).

b. If the steering is too loose, tighten the steering adjust nut (B, **Figure 78**).

c. If the steering is too tight, loosen the steering adjust nut.

d. Tighten the steering stem nut (A, **Figure 78**) to 108 N•m (80 ft.-lb.).

5B. On CRF230L and CRF230M models, adjust the steering as follows:

a. Loosen the steering stem nut (A, **Figure 79**).

b. If the steering is too loose, tighten the steering adjust nut (B, **Figure 79**).

c. If the steering is too tight, loosen the steering adjust nut.

d. Tighten the steering stem nut (A, **Figure 79**) to 103 N•m (76 ft.-lb.).

6. Recheck the steering adjustment as described in this procedure.

STEERING HEAD BEARING RACES

The steering head bearing races (**Figure 52** and **Figure 63**) are pressed into the frame steering head. Do not remove the bearing races unless they require replacement.

Steering Head Bearing Race Replacement

Do not remove the upper and lower (**Figure 74**) outer bearing races in the steering head unless they

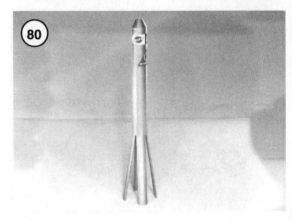

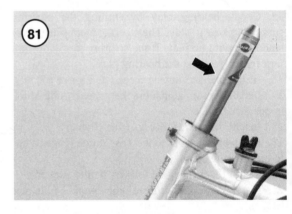

require replacement. Replace a bearing race and bearing as a set.

Special tools are available for bearing removal and installation.

1A. Use a bearing race removal tool (**Figure 80**, [www.parktool.com]) as follows:

a. Insert the tool through the steering head.

b. Position the tool (**Figure 81**, typical) so the legs contact the bearing race edge.

c. Strike the end of the tool to force the bearing race out of the steering head.

1B. Use hand tools as follows:

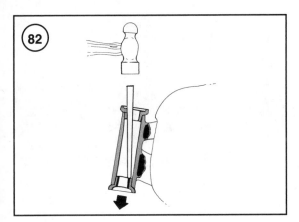

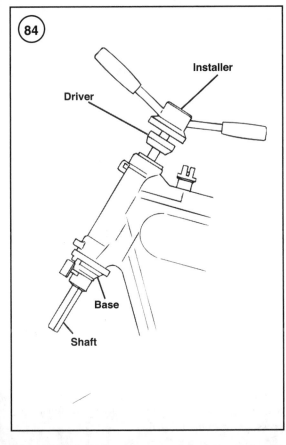

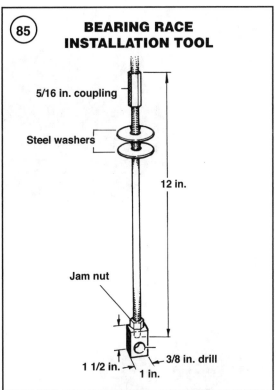

a. Insert an aluminum drift into the steering head (**Figure 82**).

b. Carefully drive the race out from the inside. Strike at different spots around the race to prevent it from binding in the mounting bore.

2. Repeat the procedure for the other race.

3. Clean the race bore and check for cracks or other damage.

4. Place the new race squarely into the mounting bore opening with its tapered side facing out (**Figure 83**).

CAUTION
When using a tool to install the bearing races, do not allow the rod or tool to contact the face of the bearing race as it may damage it.

5A. Use a bearing race installation tool (**Figure 84**, [www.parktool.com]) as follows:

a. Place the correct size race installer on the tool shaft.

b. Insert the tool shaft into the steering head so the installer contacts the bearing race.

c. Install the clamp on the shaft end.

d. Turn the tool handle until the bearing race is seated in the steering head.

e. Disassemble the tool. Verify that the race is properly seated.

5B. Use a fabricated bearing race installation tool (**Figure 85**). The tool shown consists of a thread-

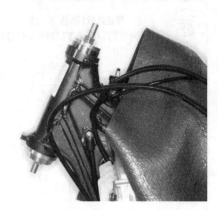

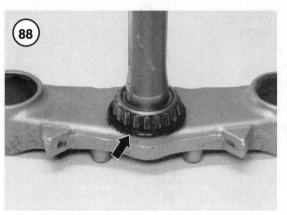

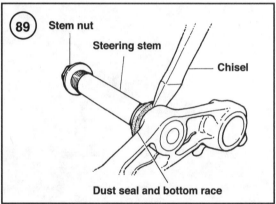

ed rod and appropriately sized discs. One disc fits the outer diameter of the race, while the other disc is slightly larger than the diameter of the steering head.

    a. Assemble the tool as shown in **Figure 86**.
    b. Tighten the nut to pull in and seat the race **Figure 87**.
    c. Remove the tool and verify that the race is properly seated.

6. Reverse tool and repeat procedure to install the other race, if necessary.

7. Lubricate the bearing races with grease.

Steering Stem Bearing Replacement (CRF230F Models)

On CRD230F models, replace the steering stem bearing (**Figure 88**) as described in this section.

1. Install the steering stem nut onto the steering stem to protect the threads.

WARNING
Wear safety glasses when removing the steering stem bearing.

2. Remove the steering stem bearing and dust seal using a hammer and chisel (**Figure 89**). Strike at dif-

ferent spots underneath the bearing to prevent it from binding on the steering stem.

3. Clean the steering stem with solvent and dry thoroughly.

4. Inspect the steering stem and replace if damaged.

5. Install a new dust seal onto the steering stem. Lubricate the seal lip with grease.

6. Pack the new bearing with waterproof bearing grease.

7. Slide the new bearing onto the steering stem until it stops.

8A. To install the new steering stem bearing with a press, perform the following:

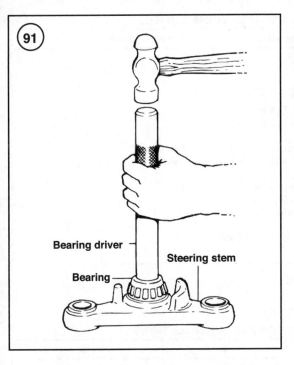

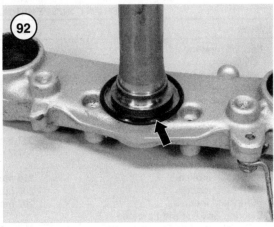

a. Install the steering stem and the new bearing in a press and support it with two bearing drivers (**Figure 90**). Make sure the bearing driver presses against the inner bearing race and does not contact the bearing rollers.

b. Press the bearing onto the steering stem until it bottoms (**Figure 88**).

8B. To install the new steering stem bearing using a bearing driver, perform the following:

a. Slide a bearing driver or long pipe over the steering stem until it seats against the bearing inner race (**Figure 91**).

b. Drive the bearing onto the steering stem until it bottoms (**Figure 88**).

Steering Stem Inner Bearing Race Replacement (CRF230L And CRF230M Models)

Perform the following steps to replace the steering stem inner bearing race (**Figure 92**).

1. Install the steering stem nut onto the steering stem to protect the threads.

WARNING
Wear safety glasses when removing the steering stem bearing race in Step 3.

2. To remove the steering stem lower race, try twisting and pulling it up by hand. If it will not come off, proceed to Step 3.

3. Use a hammer and chisel to drive off the race (**Figure 89**). Strike at different spots underneath the race to prevent it from binding on the steering stem.

4. Remove the lower dust seal.

5. Clean the steering stem with solvent and dry thoroughly.

6. Inspect the steering stem and replace if damaged.

7. Install the dust seal. Lubricate the dust seal lips with grease.

8. Slide the lower race over the steering stem with the bearing surface pointing up.

9. Drive or press the race onto the steering stem following the procedure described in CRF230F models (this section). Make sure the race is bottomed and seated squarely.

13

Table 1 FRONT SUSPENSION SPECIFICATIONS

Item	Specification	Service Limit
Fork oil		
Type	Pro Honda Suspension Fluid SS-8 or an equivalent	
Capacity		
CRF230F models		
2003-2007 models	380 ml (12.85 U.S. oz.)	
2008-on models	382 ml (12.91 U.S. oz.)	
CRF230L, CRF230M models	407 ml (13.8 U.S. oz.)	

(continued)

Table 1 FRONT SUSPENSION SPECIFICATIONS (continued)

Item	Specification	Service Limit
Fork oil (continued)		
Oil level		
CRF230F models		
2003-2007 models	144 mm (5.7 in.)	
2008-on models	142 mm (5.6 in.)	
CRF230L, CRF230M models	121 mm (4.8 in.)	
Fork spring free length		
CRF230F models	597.6 mm (23.53 in.)	586 mm (23.1 in.)
CRF230L, CRF230M models	557.7 mm (21.96 in.)	546.5 mm (21.52 in.)
Front fork travel		
CRF230F models	216 mm (8.50 in.)	–
CRF230L models	205 mm (8.07 in.)	–
CRF230M models	207 mm (8.15 in.)	–
Steering head bearing preload		
(CRF230L and CRF230M models)	10.8-16.7 N (2.4-3.8 lbf)	–

Table 2 FRONT SUSPENSION TORQUE SPECIFICATIONS

Item	N•m	in. lb.	ft.-lb.
Balancer weight mounting bolt			
(CRF230M models)	10	89	–
Brake caliper mounting bolts	30	–	22
Brake hose bracket bolts			
(CRF230F models)	10	89	–
Brake master cylinder clamp bolts	10	89	–
Clutch lever pivot bolt			
2004-on CRF230F models	1	9	–
Clutch lever pivot nut			
2004-on CRF230F models	6	53	–
Damper rod bolt	20	–	15
Fork bridge bolts			
Lower	32	–	24
Top	27	–	20
Fork leg Allen bolt	20	–	15
Fork top cap			
CRF230F models	23	–	17
CRF230L and CRF230M models	22	–	16
Handlebar holder bolts	26	–	19
Steering adjust nut		Refer to text	
Steering stem nut			
CRF230F models	108	–	80
CRF230L, CRF230M models	103	–	76

CHAPTER FOURTEEN

REAR SUSPENSION (CRF230F MODELS)

This chapter describes repair and replacement procedures for the rear shock absorber, shock linkage assembly and swing arm. Refer to Chapter Twelve for rear wheel, rear axle and tire service information.

Rear suspension specifications are listed in **Table 1** and **Table 2** located at the end of this chapter.

SHOCK ABSORBER

The single shock absorber is a spring-loaded, hydraulically-damped unit with an integral oil/nitrogen reservoir. To adjust the rear shock absorber, refer to Chapter Three.

Removal/Installation

1. Support the motorcycle with the rear wheel off the ground.
2. Remove the rear shock link bolt (A, **Figure 1**) and allow the rear wheel to drop to the ground.
3. Remove the front shock link bolt (B, **Figure 1**).
4. Remove the shock link (C, **Figure 1**).
5. Remove the lower shock absorber bolt (A, **Figure 2**).
6. Remove the upper shock absorber bolt (**Figure 3**).
7. Remove the shock absorber.
8. Inspect the shock absorber (this section).

9. Installation is the reverse of removal. Note the following:
   a. Clean and dry the fasteners. Inspect and replace damaged fasteners.
   b. Install the shock absorber mounting bolts from the left side. Tighten the upper and lower bolts to 44 N•m (32 ft.-lb.).
   c. Install the front shock link bolt (B, **Figure 1**) from the right side. Tighten the bolt to 44 N•m (32 ft.-lb.).
   d. Install the rear shock link bolt (A, **Figure 1**) from the left side. Tighten the bolt to 44 N•m (32 ft.-lb.).

Inspection

Individual parts are not available from the manufacturer. If the shock absorber is damaged, replace the complete shock absorber, or take the unit to a shop that services motorcycle shock absorbers.

1. Inspect the upper bushing (A, **Figure 4**) and mounting bolt for wear or damage. The bolt must be a firm fit in the bushing bore. The bushing must be tight in the rubber mounting.
2. Check the shock absorber for signs of oil leaks. If the shock absorber is leaking, replace it.
3. Check the damper rod (B, **Figure 4**) for bending, rust or other damage.
4. Inspect the spring for cracks.

5. Inspect the lower clevis (C, **Figure 4**) and mounting bolt for wear or damage. The bolt must be a firm fit in the bore.

SHOCK LINKAGE

The shock linkage consists of the shock arm, shock links, pivot bolts, seals and bearings. Service the assembly at the intervals specified in Chapter Three, or more frequently if operated in extreme conditions.

Removal/Installation

Refer to **Figure 5**.
1. Clean the shock linkage assembly to prevent dirt from contaminating the bearings when removing the linkage components.
2. Support the motorcycle with the rear wheel off the ground.
3. Remove the rear shock link bolt (A, **Figure 1**) and allow the rear wheel to drop to the ground.
4. Remove the front shock link bolt (B, **Figure 1**).
5. Remove the shock link (C, **Figure 1**).
6. Remove the lower shock absorber bolt (A, **Figure 2**).
7. Detach the lower portion of the drive chain slider (**Figure 6**) for access to the pivot bolt.
8. Remove the pivot bolt (B, **Figure 2**) securing the shock arm to the swing arm.
9. Remove the shock arm (C, **Figure 2**).
10. Inspect the components (this section).
11. Reverse the removal steps for installation. Note the following:
   a. If a dust seal is dislodged, apply multipurpose lithium paste grease to the dust seal lips and install the dust seal (**Figure 7**) with the flat side out.
   b. Install the shock arm-to-swing arm pivot bolt from the left side. Tighten the bolt to 78 N•m (58 ft.-lb.).
   c. Install the lower shock absorber mounting bolt from the left side. Tighten the bolt to 44 N•m (32 ft.-lb.).
   d. Install the front shock link bolt (B, **Figure 1**) from the right side. Tighten the bolt to 44 N•m (32 ft.-lb.).
   e. Install the rear shock link bolt (A, **Figure 1**) from the left side. Tighten the bolt to 44 N•m (32 ft.-lb.).

Inspection

1. Inspect the shock link (C, **Figure 1**) and shock arm (C, **Figure 2**) for cracks or damage; replace if necessary.

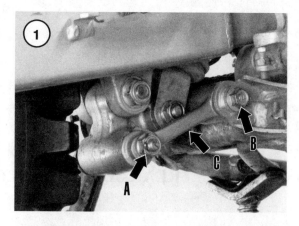

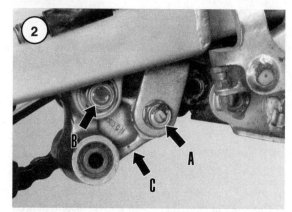

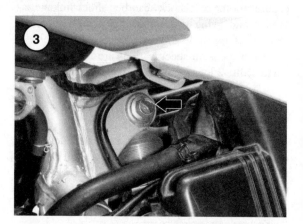

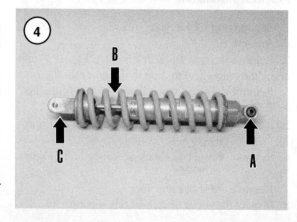

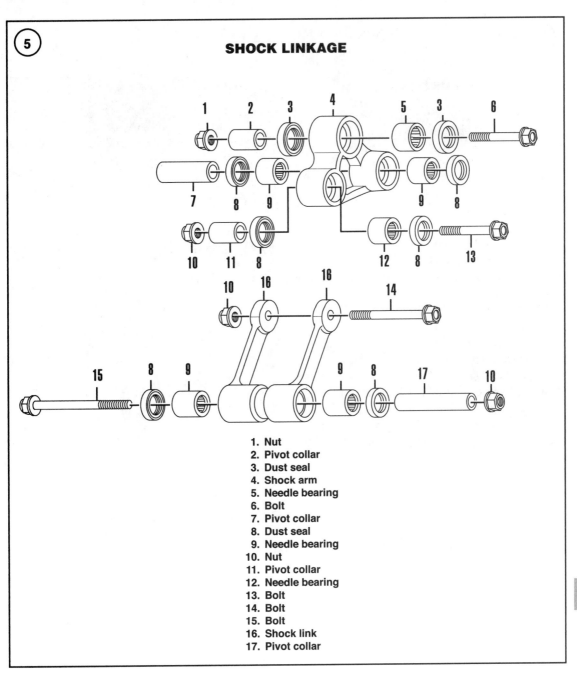

SHOCK LINKAGE

1. Nut
2. Pivot collar
3. Dust seal
4. Shock arm
5. Needle bearing
6. Bolt
7. Pivot collar
8. Dust seal
9. Needle bearing
10. Nut
11. Pivot collar
12. Needle bearing
13. Bolt
14. Bolt
15. Bolt
16. Shock link
17. Pivot collar

14

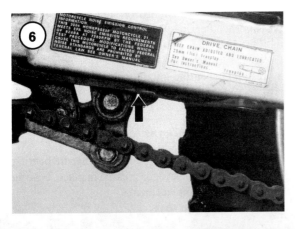

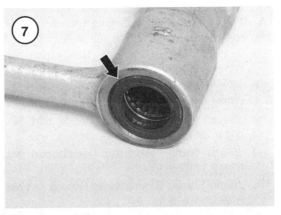

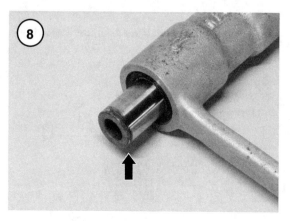

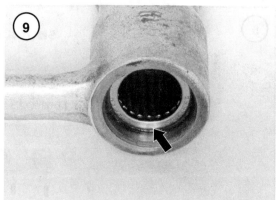

2. Remove the dust seals (**Figure 7**) and push out the pivot collars (**Figure 8**).

3. Clean all parts in solvent and thoroughly dry with compressed air.

4. Inspect the pivot collars for scratches, abrasion or abnormal wear; replace if necessary.

5. Inspect the bearings (**Figure 9**). If damaged or worn, replace as described in this section.

6. Inspect the dust seals. Replace all of them as a set if any are worn or starting to deteriorate. If the dust seals are in poor condition, they will allow dirt to enter into the pivot areas and cause bearing wear.

7. Coat all bearings, pivot collars and the inside of the dust seals with multipurpose lithium paste grease.

8. Insert the pivot collars into the bearings.

NOTE
Make sure the dust seal lips seat correctly. If not, they will allow dirt and moisture into the bearings and cause wear.

9. Install the dust seals (**Figure 7**) with the flat side out.

Bearing Replacement

Shock arm needle bearing replacement

1A. If available, use the following special tools, or their equvialents, to remove the needle bearings:

   a. 17-mm bearing ID driver (Honda part No. 07749-3710001).

   b. 17-mm bearing ID attachment (Honda part No. 07746-0010800).

   c. 17-mm bearing ID pilot (Honda part No. 07746-0040400).

   d. 20-mm bearing ID driver (Honda part No. 07949-3710001).

   e. 20-mm bearing ID attachment (Honda part No. 07746-0010700).

   f. 20-mm bearing ID pilot (Honda part No. 07746-0040500).

1B. If these special tools are not available, use a suitable socket or driver and a hydraulic press (**Figure 10**) to remove the needle bearings.

2. Discard the needle bearings.

3. Thoroughly clean the shock arm in solvent and blow dry with compressed air.

4. Apply a light coat of oil to the inner surface of the shock arm prior to installation of the needle bearings.

5. Position the needle bearings with the marks facing toward the driver tool.

6. Correctly position the needle bearing onto the shock arm.

7. Using the special tools, or suitable equivalents, press in each bearing. Press the bearing into the bore until the bearing is 5.8-6.2 mm (0.23-0.24 in.) below the outer surface of the bore.

8. Install the bearing into the other side of the shock arm.

Shock link needle bearing replacement

The shock link is equipped with a needle bearing on each side. The bearing is pressed in place; bearing removal requires replacement.

1. Remove the dust seals.

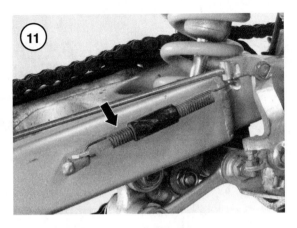

2. Using a blind bearing puller (Chapter One), withdraw the needle bearing (**Figure 9**) from the shock link. Discard the needle bearing.

3. Remove the remaining needle bearing on the other side of the shock link.

4. Thoroughly clean out the inside of the shock link with solvent and dry with compressed air.

NOTE
Either bearing may be installed first.

5. Apply a light coat of multipurpose lithium grease to all parts prior to installation.

CAUTION
Make sure the bearing is square with the shock link bore during installation. If installed incorrectly, the needle bearing can be damaged during installation and may not be aligned correctly.

6. Position the new needle bearing with the marks facing toward the outside.

7A. If available, use the following special tools, or their equivalent, to install the needle bearings:
   a. Driver (Honda part No. 07749-0010000).
   b. Attachment (Honda part No. 07746-0010800).
   c. Pilot (Honda part No. 07746-0040400).

7B. If these special tools are not available, use a suitable socket or driver and a hydraulic press to install the needle bearings.

8. Using the special tools, or suitable equivalents, press in each bearing. Press the bearing into the bore until the bearing is 5.8-6.2 mm (0.23-0.24 in.) below the outer surface of the bore.

9. Install the bearing into the other side of the shock link.

SWING ARM

The swing arm is supported by needle bearings that ride on the pivot bolt. The condition of the bearings can greatly affect handling performance. If worn parts are not replaced, they can produce erratic and dangerous handling. Common symptoms are wheel hop, pulling to one side during acceleration and pulling to the other side during braking.

Removal

1. Detach the rear brake return spring (**Figure 11**).
2. Remove the rear wheel (Chapter Twelve).
3. Remove the shock linkage (this chapter).
4. Grasp the rear end of the swing arm and try to move it from side to side in a horizontal arc. There should be no noticeable side play. If play is evident and the pivot bolt is tightened correctly, the bearings or pivot collar should be replaced.
5. Remove the locknut (**Figure 12**) and withdraw the pivot bolt from the left side.

NOTE
The dust seals on each side of the pivot hubs may fall off during swing arm removal.

6. Pull back on the swing arm, free it from the drive chain, and then remove the swing arm from the frame. Account for the seals on each side of the swing arm pivot bore.
7. Inspect the swing arm (this section).
8. Reverse the removal steps for installation. Note the following:
   a. Pack the bearings with multipurpose lithium grease.
   b. Lubricate the dust seal lips with grease.
   c. Tighten the swing arm pivot bolt to 88 N•m (65 ft.-lb.).

Disassembly/Inspection/Assembly

1. Remove the swing arm (this section).
2. Remove both dust seals (A, **Figure 13**).

14

3. Remove the drive chain slider (B, **Figure 13**) from the swing arm.

> *NOTE*
> *The pivot collar serves as the inner race for the needle bearings.*

4. Remove the pivot collar (**Figure 14**), clean in solvent and dry thoroughly.

5. Inspect the pivot collar for scoring, excessive wear, corrosion or other damage.

6. Inspect the needle bearings (**Figure 15**) as follows:

    a. Wipe off any excess grease from the needle bearing at each end of the swing arm.

    b. Turn each bearing and make sure they rotate smoothly. The needle bearings wear very slowly and wear is very difficult to measure.

    c. Check the rollers for evidence of wear, pitting or color change (bluish tint) indicating heat from lack of lubrication.

> *NOTE*
> *Always replace both needle bearings even though only one may be worn.*

7. Lubricate the needle bearings with multipurpose lithium grease.

8. Lubricate the pivot collar (**Figure 14**) with multipurpose lithium grease, and then insert it into the swing arm.

9. Install the drive chain slider (B, **Figure 13**). Make sure the pin on the upper slider leg fits into the hole in the swing arm. Do not install the fastener that secures the lower slider leg; it is installed after the shock linkage is installed.

10. Coat the inside of both dust caps with multipurpose lithium grease and install them onto the hubs of the swing arm.

11. Install the swing arm (this chapter).

Bearing Replacement

The swing arm is equipped with a needle bearing on each side. The bearing is pressed in place; bearing removal requires replacement.

1. Remove the dust seals, chain slider and pivot collar (this section).

2. Using a blind bearing puller (Chapter One), withdraw the needle bearing (**Figure 15**) from the swing arm. Discard the needle bearing.

3. Remove the remaining needle bearing on the other side of the swing arm.

4. Thoroughly clean out the inside of the swing arm with solvent and dry with compressed air.

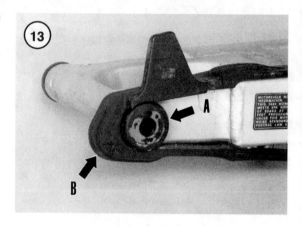

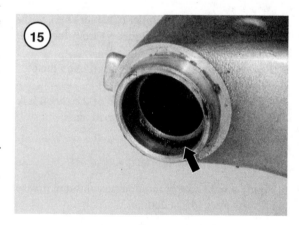

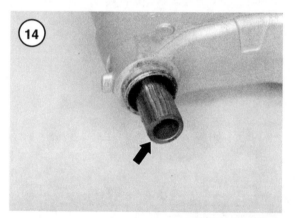

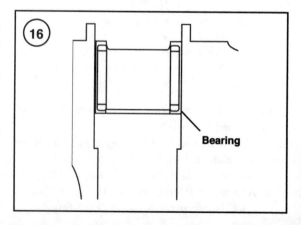

Bearing

NOTE
Either bearing may be installed first.

5. Apply a light coat of multipurpose lithium grease to all parts prior to installation.

CAUTION
Make sure the bearing is square with the swing arm bore during installation. If installed incorrectly, the needle bearing can be damaged during installation and may not be aligned correctly.

6. Position the new needle bearing with the end marks facing toward the outside.

7A. If available, use the following special tools, or their equivalents, to install the needle bearings:
    a. Driver (Honda part No. 07749-0010000).
    b. Attachment (Honda part No. 07746-0010700).
    c. Pilot (Honda part No. 07746-0040500).

7B. If these special tools are not available, use a suitable driver and a hydraulic press to press in the needle bearings.

8. Press the bearing into the swing arm so the outer end of the bearing is recessed 8 mm (0.32 in.) into the swing arm (**Figure 16**).

9. Install the bearing into the other side of the swing arm.

10. Install the pivot collar, chain slider and dust seals (this section).

Table 1 REAR SUSPENSION SPECIFICATIONS

Item	Specification
Bearing depth	
Shock arm	5.8-6.2 mm (0.23-0.24 in.)
Shock link	5.8-6.2 mm (0.23-0.24 in.)
Swing arm	8.0 mm (0.32 in.)

Table 2 REAR SUSPENSION TORQUE SPECIFICATIONS

Item	N•m	in. lb.	ft.-lb.
Shock absorber mounting bolts	44	–	32
Shock link-to-frame pivot bolt (front)	44	–	32
Shock arm-to-swing arm pivot bolt	78	–	58
Shock link-to-shock arm pivot bolt (rear)	44	–	32
Swing arm pivot bolt	88	–	65

14

CHAPTER FIFTEEN

REAR SUSPENSION (CRF230L AND CRF230M MODELS)

This chapter describes repair and replacement procedures for the rear shock absorber, shock linkage assembly and swing arm. Refer to Chapter Twelve for rear wheel, rear axle and tire service information.

Rear suspension specifications are listed in **Table 1 and Table 2** located at the end of this chapter.

SHOCK ABSORBER

The single shock absorber is a spring-loaded hydraulically damped unit with an integral oil/nitrogen reservoir. To adjust the rear shock absorber, refer to Chapter Three.

Removal/Installation

1. Remove the seat (Chapter Seventeen).
2. Remove the mudguard from the bottom of the rear fender.
3. Remove the battery case (Chapter Eleven).
4. On CRF230L models, remove the chain cover above the rear sprocket.
5. Support the motorcycle with the rear wheel off the ground.
6. Remove the rear shock link bolt (**Figure 1**) and allow the rear wheel to drop to the ground.
7. Remove the lower shock absorber bolt (**Figure 2**).
8. Remove the upper shock absorber bolt (**Figure 3**) and remove the shock absorber.
9. Installation is the reverse of removal. Note the following:

a. Clean and dry the shock absorber fasteners. Inspect fasteners and replace if damaged.
b. Install the shock mounting bolts from the left side. Tighten the bolts to 44 N•m (32 ft.-lb.).
c. Install the rear shock link bolt from the left side. Tighten the nut to 44 N•m (32 ft.-lb.).
d. On CRF230L models, install the chain cover so the flange (**Figure 4**) on the front of the cover engages the bracket on the swing arm.

Inspection

Individual parts are not available from the manufacturer. If the shock absorber is damaged, replace the complete shock absorber, or take the unit to a shop that services motorcycle shock absorbers.
1. Inspect the upper bushing (A, **Figure 5**) and mounting bolt for wear or damage. The bolt must be a firm fit in the bore. The bushing must be tight in the rubber mounting.
2. Check the shock absorber for signs of oil leaks. If the shock absorber is leaking, replace it.
3. Check the damper rod (B, **Figure 5**) for bending, rust or other damage.
4. Inspect the spring for cracks.
5. Inspect the lower clevis (C, **Figure 5**) and mounting bolt for wear or damage. The bolt must be a firm fit in the bore.

SHOCK LINKAGE

The shock linkage consists of the shock arm, shock link, pivot bolts, seals and bearings. Service

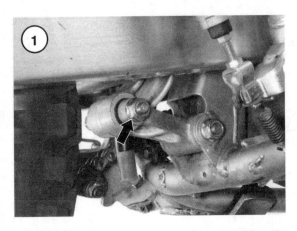

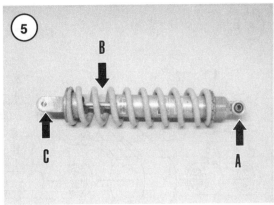

the assembly at the intervals specified in Chapter Three, or more frequently if operated in extreme conditions.

Removal/Installation

Refer to **Figure 6**.

1. Detach the drive chain cover from the swing arm.

2. Remove the mud guard from the front of the rear fender.

3. Clean the shock linkage assembly carefully to prevent dirt from contaminating the bearings when removing the linkage components.

4. Support the motorcycle with the rear wheel off the ground.

5. Remove the pivot bolt (A, **Figure 7**) securing the shock arm to the shock link.

6. Remove pivot bolt (B, **Figure 7**) securing the shock link to the frame.

7. Remove the shock link (C, **Figure 7**).

8. Remove the pivot bolt (A, **Figure 8**) securing the shock arm to the swing arm.

9. Remove the lower shock absorber mounting bolt (B, **Figure 8**).

10. Remove the shock arm (C, **Figure 8**).

11. Inspect the components (this section).

12. Reverse the removal steps for installation. Note the following:

   a. If removed, make sure the dust seals seat correctly. If not, they will allow dirt and moisture into the bearings and cause wear.

   b. Apply multipurpose lithium paste grease to the dust seal lips prior to installation.

   c. Install all bolts from the left side.

   d. Tighten the shock link-to-frame pivot bolt (front) to 44 N•m (32 ft.-lb.).

   e. Tighten the shock arm-to-swing arm pivot bolt to 68 N•m (50 ft.-lb.).

   f. Tighten the lower shock absorber mounting bolt to 44 N•m (32 ft.-lb.).

15

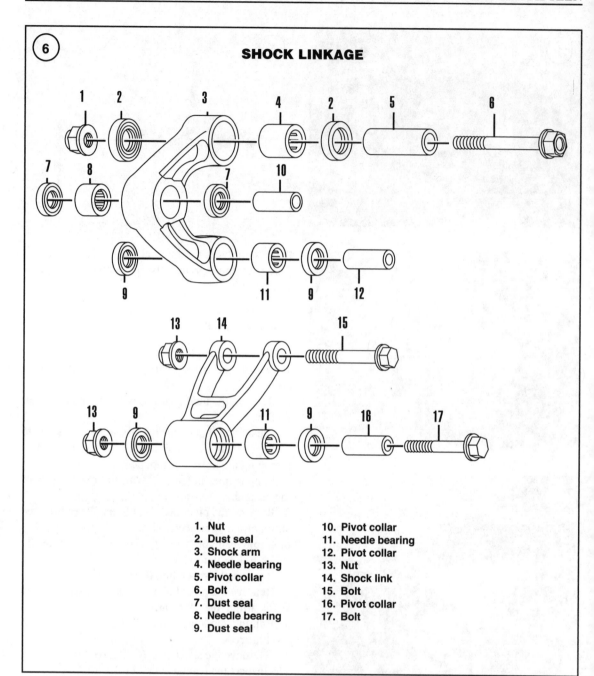

SHOCK LINKAGE

1. Nut
2. Dust seal
3. Shock arm
4. Needle bearing
5. Pivot collar
6. Bolt
7. Dust seal
8. Needle bearing
9. Dust seal
10. Pivot collar
11. Needle bearing
12. Pivot collar
13. Nut
14. Shock link
15. Bolt
16. Pivot collar
17. Bolt

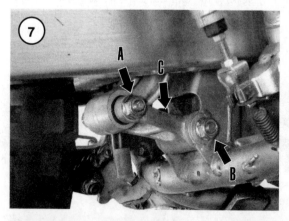

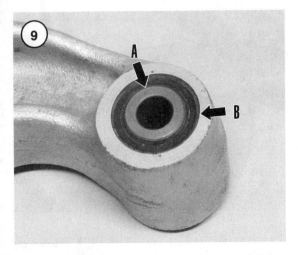

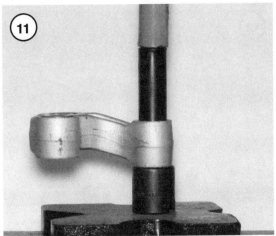

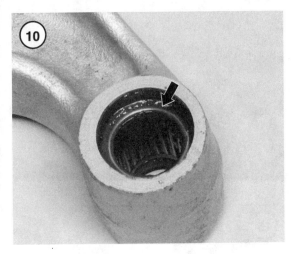

g. Tighten the shock link-to-shock arm pivot bolt (rear) to 44 N•m (32 ft.-lb.).

Inspection

1. Inspect the shock link and shock arm for cracks or damage; replace if necessary.
2. Push out the pivot collar (A, **Figure 9**) and remove the dust seal (B) at each pivot location.
3. Clean all parts in solvent and thoroughly dry with compressed air.
4. Inspect the pivot collars for scratches, abrasion or abnormal wear; replace if necessary.
5. Inspect the bearings (**Figure 10**). If damaged or worn, replace as described in this section.
6. Inspect the dust seals. Replace all of them as a set if any are worn or starting to deteriorate. If the dust seals are in poor condition, they will allow dirt to enter into the pivot areas and cause bearing wear.
7. Coat all bearings, pivot collars and the inside of the dust seals with multipurpose lithium paste grease.
8. Insert the pivot collars into the bearings.
9. Install the dust seals with the flat side out.

Bearing Replacement

Shock arm needle bearing

1A. If available, use the following special tools, or their equivalents, to remove the needle bearings.
    a. Driver (Honda part No. 07946-MJ00100 or 07956-MJ1A100).
    b. Attachment (Honda part No. 07746-0010700).
1B. If these special tools are not available, use a suitable socket or driver and a hydraulic press to remove the needle bearings (**Figure 11**).
2. Discard the needle bearings.
3. Thoroughly clean the shock arm in solvent and blow dry with compressed air.
4. Apply a light coat of oil to the inner surface of the shock arm prior to installation of the needle bearings.
5. Position the needle bearings with the marks facing toward the driver tool.
6. Correctly position the needle bearing onto the shock arm.
7A. If available, use the following special tools, or their equivalents, to install in the needle bearings:
    a. 17-mm bearing ID driver (Honda part No. 07749-0010000).
    b. 17-mm bearing ID attachment (Honda part No. 07746-0010700).
    c. 17-mm bearing ID pilot (Honda part No. 07746-0040400).
    d. 20-mm bearing ID driver (Honda part No. 07749-0010000).
    e. 20-mm bearing ID attachment (Honda part No. 07746-0010700).
    f. 20-mm bearing ID pilot (Honda part No. 07746-0040500).
7B. If these special tools are not available, use a suitable socket or driver and a hydraulic press to install the needle bearings.

15

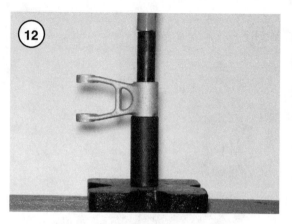

8. Press the bearing into the bore until the bearing is 5.8-6.2 mm (0.23-0.24 in.) below the outer surface of the bore.

Shock link needle bearing

1A. If available, use the following special tools, or their equivalents, to remove the needle bearings:
    a. Driver (Honda part No. 07946-MJ00100 or 07946-MJ0A100).
    b. Attachment (Honda part No. 07746-0010700).
1B. If these special tools are not available, use a suitable socket or driver and a hydraulic press to remove the needle bearing (**Figure 12**).
2. Discard the needle bearing.
3. Thoroughly clean the shock link in solvent and blow dry with compressed air.
4. Apply a light coat of oil to the inner surface of the shock link prior to installation of the needle bearing.
5. Correctly position the needle bearing onto the shock link. Apply force to the end of the bearing with the marks.
6A. If available, use the following special tools, or their equivalents, to install the needle bearings:
    a. Driver (Honda part No. 07749-0010000).
    b. Attachment (Honda part No. 07746-0010700).
    c. Pilot (Honda part No. 07746-0040400).
6B. If these special tools are not available, use a suitable socket or driver and a hydraulic press to install the needle bearing.
7. Press the bearing into the bore until the bearing is 8.8-9.2 mm (0.35-0.36 in.) below the outer surface of the bore.

SWING ARM

The swing arm is supported by needle bearings that ride on the pivot bolt. The condition of the bearings can greatly affect handling performance. If worn parts are not replaced, they can produce erratic and dangerous handling. Common symptoms are wheel

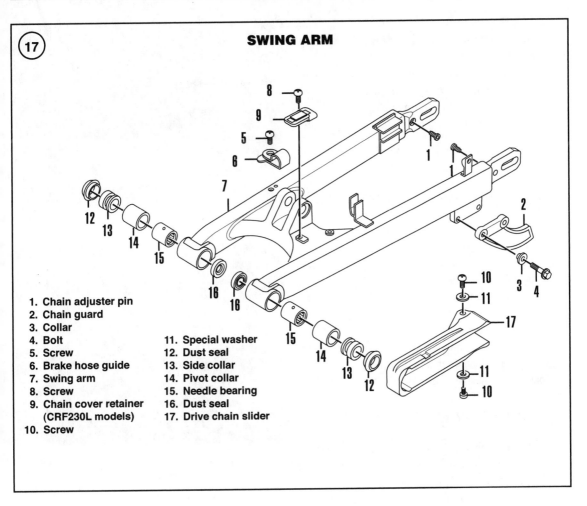

SWING ARM

1. Chain adjuster pin
2. Chain guard
3. Collar
4. Bolt
5. Screw
6. Brake hose guide
7. Swing arm
8. Screw
9. Chain cover retainer
   (CRF230L models)
10. Screw
11. Special washer
12. Dust seal
13. Side collar
14. Pivot collar
15. Needle bearing
16. Dust seal
17. Drive chain slider

hop, pulling to one side during acceleration and pulling to the other side during braking.

Removal

1. Remove the mudguard from the bottom of the rear fender.
2. Remove the drive chain guard (A, **Figure 13**).
3. Remove the drive chain cover (B, **Figure 13**).
4. Remove the rear wheel (Chapter Twelve).
5. Remove the shock link-to-shock arm bolt (**Figure 14**).

> *CAUTION*
> *Do not allow the rear brake caliper to hang from the brake hose. Suspend or support the caliper so it is out of the way.*

6. Detach the rear brake hose from the guide (A, **Figure 15**) on the swing arm.
7. Remove the shock arm-to-swing arm bolt (B, **Figure 15**).
8. Grasp the rear end of the swing arm and try to move it from side to side in a horizontal arc. There

should be no noticeable side play. If play is evident and the pivot bolt is tightened correctly, the bearings or pivot collar should be replaced.
9. Remove the locknut on the left side. Then, withdraw the pivot bolt (**Figure 16**) from the right side.
10. Pull back on the swing arm, free it from the drive chain and remove the swing arm from the frame.
11. Inspect the swing arm (this chapter).
12. Reverse the removal steps for installation. Note the following:
   a. Apply a light coat of multipurpose lithium grease to the pivot bolt.
   b. Tighten the swing arm pivot bolt to 68 N•m (50 ft.-lb.).
   c. Tighten the shock arm-to-swing arm pivot bolt to 68 N•m (50 ft.-lb.).
   d. Tighten the shock link-to-shock arm pivot bolt to 44 N•m (32 ft.-lb.).
   e. Tighten the rear brake hose guide screw to 1.5 N•m (13 in.-lb.).

Disassembly/Inspection/Assembly

Refer to **Figure 17**.

15

1. Remove the swing arm (this section).
2. Remove the drive chain slider (**Figure 18**) from the swing arm.
3. On CRF230L models, remove the drive chain cover retainer (**Figure 19**), if necessary.
4. Remove the side collar (**Figure 20**).

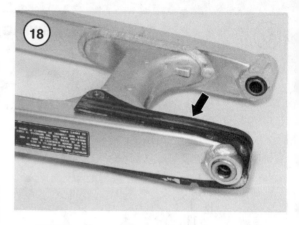

NOTE
The pivot collar serves as the inner race for the needle bearing.

5. Remove the pivot collar (A, **Figure 21**), clean in solvent and dry thoroughly.
6. Remove the dust seals (B, **Figure 21**) on the inner sides of the swing arm leg.
7. Inspect the pivot collar for scoring, excessive wear, corrosion or other damage.
8. Disassemble the components in the remaining swing arm leg.
9. Inspect the chain slider. Replace the slider if excessively worn or damaged. Damage to the swing arm can occur if the slider wears through.
10. Inspect the needle bearings (**Figure 22**) as follows:

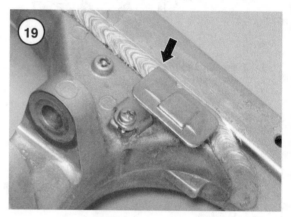

   a. Wipe off any excess grease from the needle bearing.
   b. Turn the bearing and make sure it rotates smoothly. The needle bearings wear very slowly and wear is very difficult to measure.
   c. Check the rollers for evidence of wear, pitting or color change (bluish tint) indicating heat from lack of lubrication.
   d. Pack the bearings with multipurpose lithium grease.
11. Lubricate the pivot collar with multipurpose lithium grease, and then insert it into the swing arm.
12. If removed, install the dust seal (A, **Figure 23**) onto the side collar so the flat side of the seal faces the wide end (B) of the collar.
13. Coat the dust seals with multipurpose lithium grease.

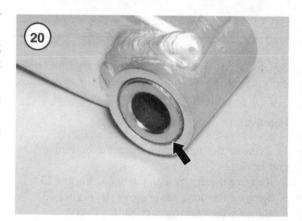

14. Install each side collar so the wide end of the collar (B, **Figure 23**) is toward the outside of the swing arm.
15. On CRF230L models, install the drive chain cover retainer (**Figure 19**) if removed. Apply threadlock to the screw threads. Install and tighten the retainer screw to 6 N•m (53 in.-lb.).
16. Install the drive chain slider (**Figure 18**). Make sure the bosses on the slider enter the holes in the swing arm. Tighten the drive chain slider screw to 4.2 N•m (37 in.-lb.).
17. Install the swing arm (this section).

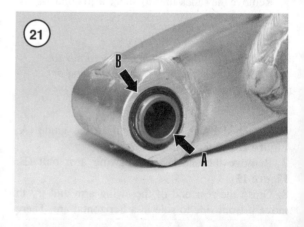

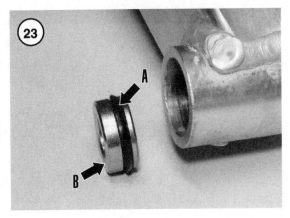

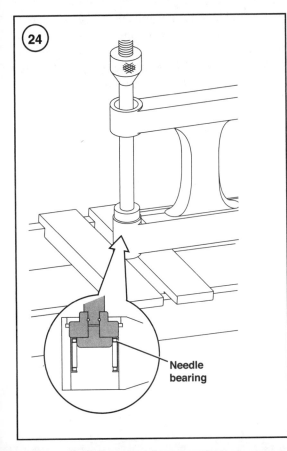

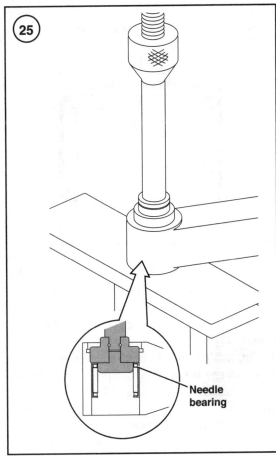

Bearing Replacement

The swing arm is equipped with a needle bearing in each leg. The bearing is pressed in place; bearing removal requires replacement.

The following procedures describe bearing removal and installation using either a press or hand tools.

Press method

To replace either side needle bearing, perform the following:

1. Support the swing arm in a press (**Figure 24**).

2. Using suitable tools such as a suitable socket or driver, press the needle bearing out of the swing arm and discard it.

3. Check the bearing mounting bore for cracks or other damage.

4. Support the swing arm in a press with the inner side of the leg facing down (**Figure 25**).

5. Position the needle bearing with the marks facing out.

6A. If available, use the following special tools, or their equivalents, to install the needle bearings:

   a. Driver (Honda part No. 07749-0010000).

15

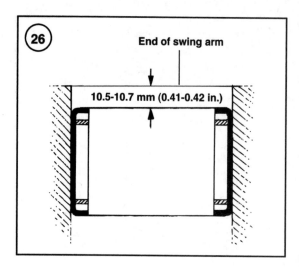

End of swing arm

10.5-10.7 mm (0.41-0.42 in.)

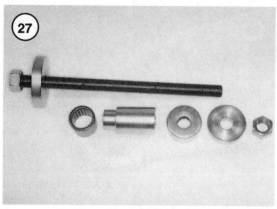

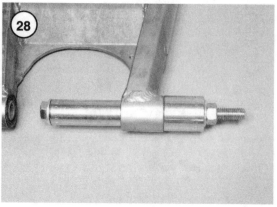

b. Attachment (Honda part No. 07746-0010700).

c. Pilot (Honda part No. 07746-0040500).

6B. If these special tools are not available, use a suitable socket or driver to install the needle bearings (**Figure 22**).

7. Correctly position the bearing and press it into the swing arm so the outer end of the bearing (**Figure 26**) is recessed 10.5-10.7 mm (0.41-0.42 in.) into the swing arm.

8. Install the remaining bearing.

Hand tool method

The following procedure requires a drawbolt-type of bearing removal/installation tool (**Figure 27**). An equivalent tool can be made from a bolt, nut, washers and sockets. The driver is a socket that is capable of passing through the bore, yet is longer than the bore depth. The larger socket fits on the perimeter of the bore, but is also large enough to accept the removed bearing(s).

1. Apply penetrating oil to the bearing(s) and bore.

2. If necessary, heat the immediate area around the bearing(s) to be removed.

3. Assemble the tool as shown in **Figure 28**, typical.

4. Hand-tighten the nut until the assembly is squarely positioned against the bearing and swing arm contact points.

5. Turn the nut and drive the bearing(s) into the large socket. Dispose of the old bearings.

6. Clean and inspect the bearing bore.

7. Lubricate the new bearings with grease.

8. Align the bearing squarely on the outside face of the bore. The marks on the bearing must face out.

9. Reverse the direction of the tool and hand-tighten the nut until the tool and bearing are squarely positioned with the bore. Note that a large-diameter, thick washer can be substituted for the large socket to make handling easier.

10. Press the bearing into the swing arm so the outer end of the bearing is recessed 10.5-10.7 mm (0.41-

Table 1 REAR SUSPENSION SPECIFICATIONS

Item	Specification
Bearing depth	
Shock arm	5.8-6.2 mm (0.23-0.24 in.)
Shock link	8.8-9.2 mm (0.35-0.36 in
Swing arm	10.5-10.7 mm (0.41-0.42 in.)

Table 2 REAR SUSPENSION TORQUE SPECIFICATIONS

Item	N•m	in. lb.	ft.-lb.
Drive chain cover retainer screw (CRF230L models)	6.0	53	–
Drive chain slider screw	4.2	37	–
Rear brake hose guide screw	1.5	13	–
Shock absorber mounting bolts	44	–	32
Shock link-to-frame pivot bolt (front)	44	–	32
Shock arm-to-swing arm pivot bolt	68	–	50
Shock link-to-shock arm pivot bolt (rear)	44	–	32
Swing arm pivot bolt	68	–	50

15

BRAKES

This chapter covers service, repair and replacement procedures for the front and rear brake systems. Brake specifications are listed in **Tables 1-6** located at the end of this chapter.

All models are equipped with a hydraulically-actuated, single-disc brake at the front wheel. The CRF230F model is equipped with a mechanically-actuated drum brake at the rear wheel. CRF230L and CRF230M models are equipped with a hydraulically-actuated, single-disc brake at the rear wheel.

BRAKE FLUID SELECTION

WARNING
Do not intermix silicone-based (DOT 5) brake fluid with glycol-based (DOT 4) brake fluid as it can cause brake system failure.

When adding brake fluid, use DOT 4 brake fluid from a sealed container. DOT 4 brake fluid is glycol-based and draws moisture, which greatly reduces its ability to perform correctly. Purchase brake fluid in small containers and discard small leftover quantities. Do not store a container of brake fluid with less than 1/4 of the fluid remaining.

Do not reuse drained fluid. Discard old fluid properly.

BRAKE SERVICE

WARNING
The proper operation of the brake system depends on a supply of clean brake fluid (DOT 4) and a clean work environment when any service is being performed. Any debris that enters the system can damage the components and cause poor brake performance.

WARNING
When working on the brake system, do not inhale brake dust. It may contain asbestos, which is a known carcinogen. Do not use compressed air to blow off brake dust. Use an aerosol brake cleaner. Wear a face mask that meets OSHA requirements. Wash hands and forearms thoroughly after completing the work. Wet down the brake dust on brake components before working on the brake system. Dispose of all brake dust and cleaning materials properly.

WARNING
Do not ride the motorcycle unless the brakes work correctly.

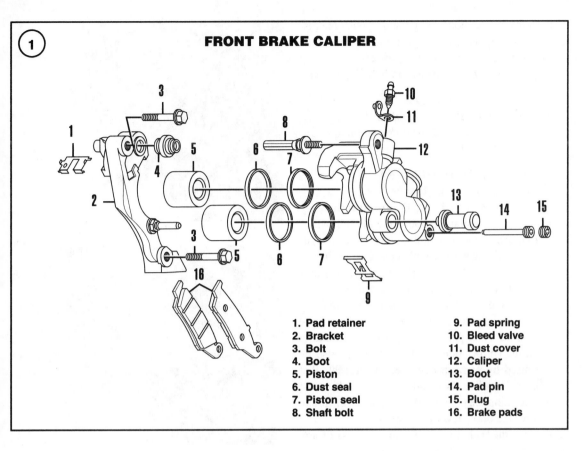

FRONT BRAKE CALIPER

1. Pad retainer
2. Bracket
3. Bolt
4. Boot
5. Piston
6. Dust seal
7. Piston seal
8. Shaft bolt
9. Pad spring
10. Bleed valve
11. Dust cover
12. Caliper
13. Boot
14. Pad pin
15. Plug
16. Brake pads

Consider the following when servicing the brake system:

1. The hydraulic components rarely require disassembly. Make sure it is necessary.

2. Keep the front brake master cylinder reservoir cover in place to prevent the entry of moisture and debris.

3. Clean parts with an aerosol brake parts cleaner or denatured alcohol. Never use petroleum-based solvents on internal brake system components. They cause seals to swell and distort, which can lead to system failure.

4. Do not allow brake fluid to contact plastic, painted or plated parts. It will damage the surface.

5. If brake fluid contacts the motorcycle, wash the area with soapy water and rinse thoroughly.

6. Do not reuse brake fluid. Dispose of it properly.

7. If the hydraulic system, not including the reservoir cover, has been opened the system must be bled to remove air from the system. Refer to *Brake Bleeding* (this chapter).

FRONT BRAKE PADS

There is no recommended time interval for changing the pads in the front brake caliper. Pad wear depends greatly on riding habits and conditions. The brake pads have wear grooves that allow inspection without removal. Refer to *Brakes* in Chapter Three for inspection procedures. Always replace brake pads as a set.

Replacement

Refer to **Figure 1**.

1. Read *Brake Service* (this chapter).

CAUTION
Do not allow the master cylinder reservoir to overflow when pushing the pistons. If the fluid level is too high, remove the cover and withdraw some of the fluid from the reservoir with a syringe.

CAUTION
Before pushing the pistons into the caliper to make room for the new pads, check for debris buildup on the end of the pistons. When the pistons are pushed back into the caliper, this material can damage the caliper seals. If there is pad residue built up on the ends of the pistons, try to clean the pistons with a soft brush and denatured alcohol while the caliper is assembled or remove and disassemble the caliper to clean the pistons.

16

2. Push the caliper body in by hand to push the pistons into the caliper to make room for the new pads.

3. Remove the pad pin plug (**Figure 2**).

4. Loosen and remove the pad pin bolt (**Figure 3**).

CAUTION
If the pads will be reinstalled, handle them carefully to prevent damage and contamination.

5. Remove the brake pads (**Figure 4**).

6. Remove the pad spring (**Figure 5**).

7. Inspect the brake pads (A, **Figure 6**) for uneven wear, damage or contamination. Note the following:

   a. Remove surface contamination by lightly sanding the lining surface with a piece of sandpaper placed on a flat surface. If the lining material is contaminated, replace both brake pads.

   b. Wear should be approximately the same for both brake pads. If the inner pad is worn more than the outer pad, the caliper may be binding on the caliper bracket. This wear can also be caused by worn or damaged piston seals that have lost their flex and ability to self-adjust (returning the piston and disengaging the brake after the brake lever is released).

8. Replace the pads as a set if the thickness of any one pad has worn down to its wear groove.

9. Check the caliper for signs of leaks around the pistons. If brake fluid is leaking from the caliper bores, overhaul the front brake caliper (this chapter).

10. Clean the pad pin (B, **Figure 6**) and plug (C). Remove rust and corrosion from the pad pin and inspect for excessive wear, grooves or other damage. Replace if damaged.

11. Inspect the pad spring (D, **Figure 6**) and replace if damaged.

12. Inspect the brake disc for oil contamination (especially if the fork seal was leaking). Spray both sides of the brake disc with a brake or contact cleaner. Inspect the brake disc for wear (this chapter).

13. Install the pad spring (**Figure 7**) so it grips the brake caliper tightly. Replace the pad spring if it does not stay in position.

14. Install the inner and outer brake pads (**Figure 4**). Push them in place so the upper end of each pad seats against the pad retainer (**Figure 8**) in the caliper bracket.

15. Push both pads against the pad spring and install the pad pin bolt (**Figure 3**) into the caliper and through the hole in the bottom of each brake pad.

16. Tighten the pad pin bolt (**Figure 3**) to 18 N•m (156 in.-lb.).

17. Install and tighten the pad pin plug (**Figure 2**) to specification in **Table 5** or **Table 6**.

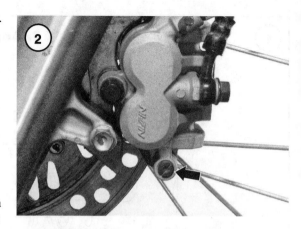

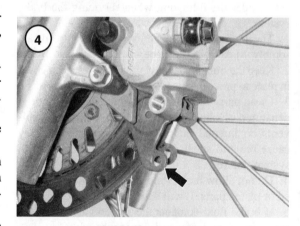

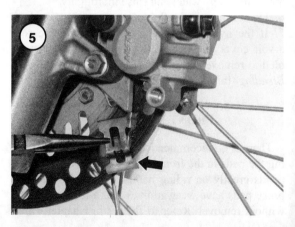

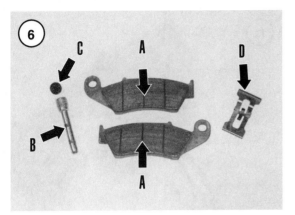

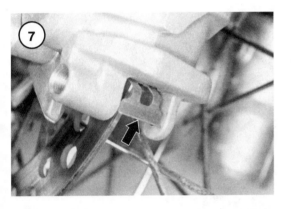

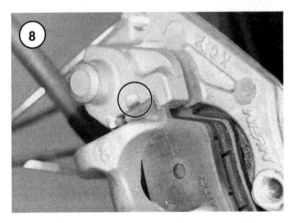

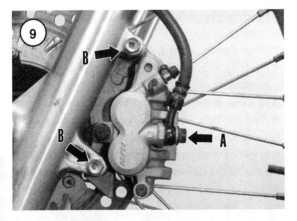

18. Operate the brake lever to seat the pads against the disc. The brake lever should feel firm when applied.

19. Check the brake fluid level in the reservoir. If necessary, add new DOT 4 brake fluid.

20. Raise the front wheel and check that the wheel spins freely and the brake operates properly.

> *WARNING*
> *Do not ride the motorcycle until the front brake operates correctly. Make sure the brake lever travel is not excessive and the lever does not feel spongy. Either condition indicates the front brake must be bled as described in this chapter.*

21. Break in the pads by braking slowly at first, and then increase braking pressure. Do not overheat new brake pads.

FRONT BRAKE CALIPER

Removal/Installation

1. If the caliper will be disconnected from the brake hose, drain the brake system as described in this chapter. After draining, remove the brake hose union bolt (A, **Figure 9**) and both sealing washers while the caliper is mounted on the fork. Tie a plastic bag over the end of the hose.

2A. If the caliper will be removed from the motorcycle, remove the caliper mounting bolts (B, **Figure 9**).

2B. If the caliper will be left attached to the brake hose:

    a. Remove the caliper mounting bolts (B, **Figure 9**) and secure the caliper with a length of wire. Do not allow the caliper to hang by the brake hose.

> *NOTE*
> *A spacer block will prevent the pistons from being forced out of the caliper if the front brake lever is applied with the brake caliper removed.*

    b. Insert a spacer block between the brake pads.

3. Service the caliper (this section).

4. Installation is the reverse of removal. Note the following:

    a. If the pads are installed in the caliper, press the caliper pistons back into the caliper so the pads will clear the disc.

    b. Apply a medium-strength threadlock onto the front brake caliper mounting bolts (B, **Figure 9**). Install and tighten the bolts to 30 N•m (22 ft.-lb.).

16

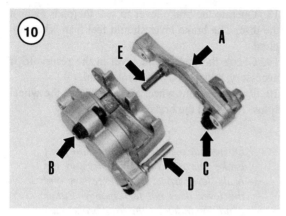

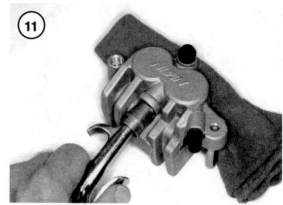

c. Check the brake fluid level in the reservoir and fill or remove fluid as necessary.

d. After installing the brake caliper, operate the brake lever several times to seat the pads against the brake disc.

e. If the brake hose was disconnected from the caliper, install a new sealing washer on each side of the brake hose and tighten the union bolt to 34 N•m (25 ft.-lb.). Fill and bleed the brake system as described in this chapter.

f. With the front wheel raised, check that the wheel spins freely and the brake operates properly.

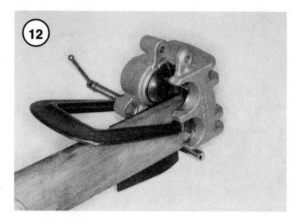

Disassembly

Refer to **Figure 1**.

Removing the pistons hydraulically

If the piston and dust seals are in good condition and there are no signs of brake fluid leaking from the bores, it may be possible to remove the pistons hydraulically. However, note that brake fluid will spill from the caliper once the pistons are free.

Read this procedure through to understand the steps and tools required.

1. Remove the front brake caliper (this section). Do not loosen or remove the brake hose.

2. Remove the caliper bracket from the caliper. Have a supply of paper towels and a pan available to catch and wipe up spilled brake fluid.

3. Hold the caliper with the pistons facing down and slowly operate the brake lever to push the pistons out of their bores.

4A. If both pistons move evenly, continue until they extend far enough to be removed by hand.

4B. If the pistons do not move evenly, perform the following:

   a. Stop and push the extended piston back into its bore by hand so that both pistons are even.

   b. Then, repeat the procedure until the pistons can be removed by hand.

   c. If the results are the same, reposition the extended piston again.

   d. Install a strip of wood across the caliper to block the piston.

   e. Then, operate the brake lever while preventing the moving piston from extending.

   f. If the other piston now starts to move, continue with this technique until both pistons move evenly and can be gripped and removed by hand.

5. After removing the pistons, hold the caliper over the drain pan to catch the brake fluid draining through the caliper.

6. Remove the union bolt with an impact gun (air or electric), if available. Otherwise, hold the caliper in a secure manner and remove the union bolt with hand tools. If the caliper cannot be held securely to remove the bolt, stuff paper towels into the caliper bores to absorb brake fluid leaking from the hose and reservoir. Temporarily reinstall the caliper bracket and mount the caliper onto the slider with its mounting bolts to hold it in place. Then, remove the union bolt and both washers.

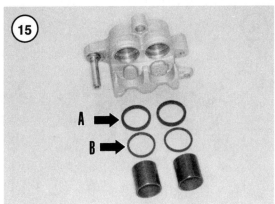

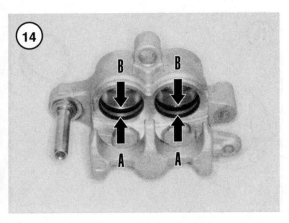

7. Continue caliper disassembly to remove remaining components as described in *Removing the pistons with compressed air* (this section),

Removing the pistons with compressed air

1. Remove the brake caliper (this section).
2. Slide the caliper bracket (A, **Figure 10**) out of the caliper.
3. Remove the rubber boot (B, **Figure 10**) from the caliper by grasping its thick outer edge and pulling it out of its mounting hole. Then, remove the rubber boot (C, **Figure 10**) from the caliper bracket.
4. Remove the pad retainer (**Figure 8**) from the caliper bracket.
5. Close the bleed valve so air cannot escape.

> *WARNING*
> *Wear eye protection when using compressed air to remove the pistons, and keep your fingers away from the piston.*

> *CAUTION*
> *Do not try to pry out the piston. This will damage the piston and caliper bore.*

6. Cushion the caliper pistons with a shop rag and position the caliper with the piston bores facing down. Apply compressed air through the brake hose port (**Figure 11**) to pop the pistons out. If only one piston came out, block its bore opening with a piece of thick rubber (old inner tube), wooden block and clamp as shown in **Figure 12**. Apply compressed air again and remove the remaining piston. Refer to **Figure 13**.
7. Use a small wooden or plastic tool and remove the dust seals (A, **Figure 14**) and piston seals (B) from the caliper bore grooves and discard them.
8. Remove the bleed valve and dust cover from the caliper.
9. Clean and inspect the brake caliper assembly (this section).

Assembly

> *NOTE*
> *Use new DOT 4 brake fluid when lubricating the piston seals, pistons and caliper bores in the following steps.*

1. Install the bleed valve and dust cover on the caliper.
2. Soak the new piston and dust seals in brake fluid.
3. Lubricate the cylinder bores with brake fluid.

> *NOTE*
> *The piston seals (A, **Figure 15**) are thicker than the dust seals (B).*

> *NOTE*
> *Make sure each seal fits squarely inside its bore groove.*

4. Install a new piston seal into each rear bore groove (B, **Figure 14**).
5. Install a new dust seal into each front bore groove (A, **Figure 14**).
6. Lubricate the pistons with brake fluid.

16

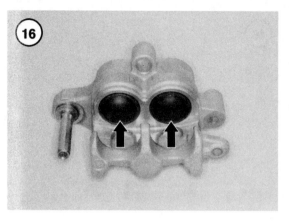

CAUTION
The tight piston-to-seal fit can make pis-
ton installation difficult. Do not install
the pistons by pushing them straight in
as they may bind in their bores and tear
the seals.

7. With the open side facing out, align a piston with the caliper bore. Rock the piston slightly to center it in the bore while at the same time pushing the lower end past the seals. When the lower end of the piston passes through both seals, push and bottom the piston (**Figure 16**) in the bore. After installing the other piston, clean spilled brake fluid from the area in front of the pistons to prevent brake pad contamination.

8. Pinch the open end of the large rubber boot and push this end through the mounting hole in the caliper until its outer shoulder bottoms (B, **Figure 10**). Make sure the boot opening faces toward the inside of the caliper. Partially fill the boot with silicone brake grease.

9. Install the small boot into the groove in the caliper bracket (A, **Figure 17**). Partially fill the boot with silicone brake grease.

10. Hook the pad retainer (B, **Figure 17**) onto the caliper bracket.

11. Lubricate the fixed shafts on the caliper (D, **Figure 10**) and caliper bracket (E) with silicone brake grease.

12. Align and slide the mounting bracket (A, **Figure 10**) onto the caliper body. Hold the caliper and slide the caliper bracket in and out by hand. Make sure there is no roughness or binding.

13. Install the brake caliper assembly (this section) and brake pads (this chapter).

Inspection

WARNING
Do not allow oil or grease on any of
the brake components. Do not clean the
parts with kerosene or other petroleum-

based products. These chemicals cause
the rubber brake system components to
swell, which may cause brake failure.

All models use a floating caliper design, in which the caliper slides or floats on shafts mounted parallel with each other on the caliper and caliper bracket. Rubber boots around each shaft prevent dirt from damaging the shafts. If the shafts are worn or damaged the caliper can move out of alignment on the caliper bracket. This will cause brake drag, uneven pad wear and overheating. Inspect the rubber boots and shafts during caliper inspection as they play a vital role in brake performance.

Refer to **Figure 1** when servicing the front brake caliper assembly. Replace parts that are out of specification (**Table 1** or **Table 2**) or show damage (this section).

CAUTION
The caliper bore and seal grooves can
be difficult to clean, especially if brake
fluid was leaking past the seals. Clean
the grooves carefully to avoid damag-
ing the grooves and bore surfaces.

1. Clean and dry the caliper and the other metal parts. Clean the seal grooves carefully. If the con-

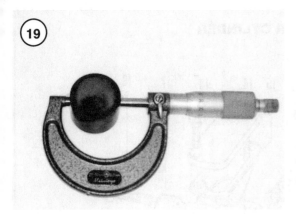

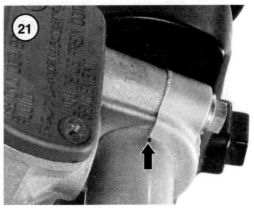

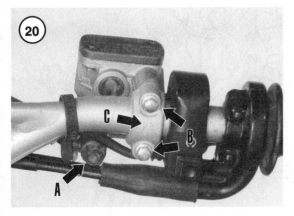

5. Check the pistons for wear marks, scoring, cracks or other damage.

6. Measure the outside diameter of the pistons (**Figure 19**).

7. Check the bleed valve and dust cap for wear or damage. Make sure air can pass through the bleed valve.

8. Check the union bolt for wear or damage. Discard the washers.

9. Inspect the brake pads, pad spring, pad pin plug and pad pin bolt as described in this chapter.

FRONT MASTER CYLINDER (CRF230F MODELS)

Removal/Installation

1. Remove the master cylinder cover and diaphragm assembly. Use a syringe to withdraw brake fluid from the master cylinder reservoir. Discard the brake fluid. Reinstall the diaphragm and master cylinder cover.

2. Remove the union bolt (A, **Figure 20**) and washers securing the brake hose to the master cylinder. Seal the brake hose in a plastic bag to prevent brake fluid drips.

3. Remove the bolts (B, **Figure 20**) and clamp holding the master cylinder to the handlebar, and then remove the master cylinder.

4. If necessary, service the master cylinder (this section).

5. Clean the handlebar, master cylinder and clamp mating surfaces.

6. Install the master cylinder holder with the UP mark (C, **Figure 20**) on the holder facing up. Align the edge of the master cylinder clamp surface with the punch mark on the handlebar (**Figure 21**).

7. Install and tighten the master cylinder mounting bolts. Tighten the upper bolt first. Then, tighten the lower bolt. Tighten both mounting clamp bolts to 10 N•m (89 in.-lb.).

tamination is difficult to remove, soak the caliper in a suitable solvent, and then reclean. If any of the rubber parts are to be reused, clean them with denatured alcohol or new DOT 4 brake fluid. Do not use a petroleum-based solvent.

2. Inspect the caliper bracket (A, **Figure 10**), fixed shafts and rubber boots as follows:

  a. Inspect the rubber boots (B and C, **Figure 10**) for cracks, tearing, weakness or other damage.

  b. Inspect the fixed shafts (D and E, **Figure 10**) on the caliper housing and caliper bracket for excessive or uneven wear. If the fixed shaft is damaged, remove and discard the shaft. Apply threadlock to a new fixed shaft. Install and tighten the shaft to the specification in **Table 5** or **Table 6**.

  c. If the caliper bracket fixed shaft is damaged, replace the caliper bracket assembly. However, if the fixed shaft on the caliper body is loose, remove the shaft and clean the threads on the shaft and the caliper bracket of all threadlock residue. Apply threadlock to the shaft threads and tighten to specification **Table 5** or **Table 6.**

3. Check each cylinder bore for corrosion, pitting, deep scratches or other wear.

4. Measure the inside diameter of the caliper bores (**Figure 18**).

16

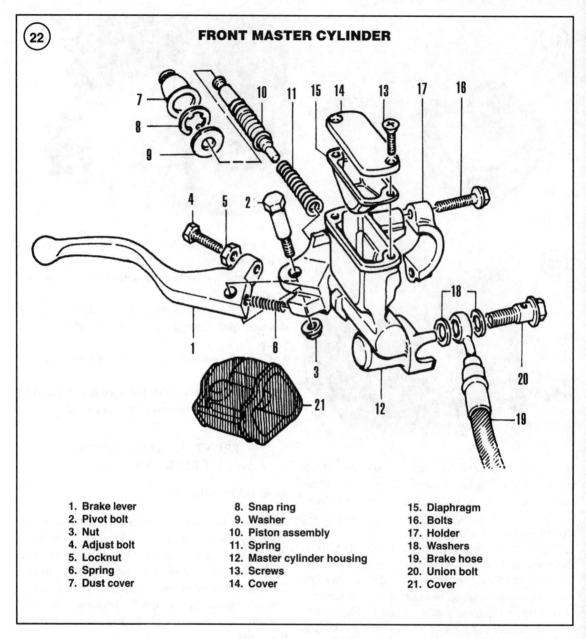

FRONT MASTER CYLINDER

22

1. Brake lever
2. Pivot bolt
3. Nut
4. Adjust bolt
5. Locknut
6. Spring
7. Dust cover
8. Snap ring
9. Washer
10. Piston assembly
11. Spring
12. Master cylinder housing
13. Screws
14. Cover
15. Diaphragm
16. Bolts
17. Holder
18. Washers
19. Brake hose
20. Union bolt
21. Cover

8. Secure the brake hose to the master cylinder with the union bolt (A, **Figure 20**) and two new washers. Install a washer on each side of the brake hose. Center the brake hose between the arms on the master cylinder and tighten the union bolt to 34 N•m (25 ft.-lb.).

9. Bleed the front brake (this chapter).

Disassembly

Refer to **Figure 22**.

1. Remove the master cylinder (this section).

2. Remove the lever cover.

3. Remove the nut (A, **Figure 23**), pivot bolt, brake lever (B) and spring (**Figure 24**).

4. To hold the master cylinder, thread a bolt and nut into the master cylinder. Tighten the nut against the master cylinder. Then, clamp the bolt and nut in a vise (**Figure 25**).

5. Remove the dust cover from the master cylinder and piston.

WARNING
If brake fluid is leaking from the piston bore, the piston cups are worn or damaged. Replace the piston assembly.

NOTE
Long-arm snap ring pliers that enable easy extraction of the snap ring are

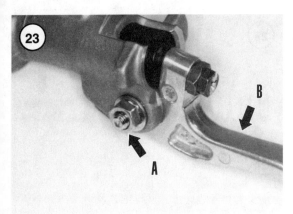

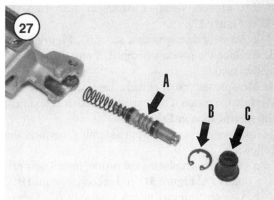

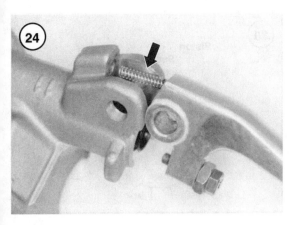

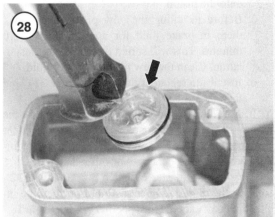

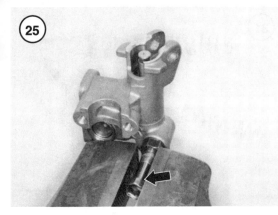

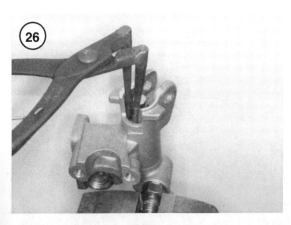

*available from several tool manufac-
turers.*

6. Compress the piston and remove the snap ring
(**Figure 26**) with snap ring pliers.

7. Remove the piston and spring assembly (A,
Figure 27) from the master cylinder bore.

8. Remove the separator (**Figure 28**) and O-ring
from the reservoir.

Inspection

1. Wash the piston and cylinder with brake fluid.
Refer to *Brake Fluid Selection* (this chapter).

> *CAUTION*
> *Do not remove the primary and second-
> ary cups from the piston assembly.*

2. Check the piston assembly for the following defects:

    a. Broken, distorted or collapsed piston return
       spring (A, **Figure 29**).

    b. Worn, cracked, damaged or swollen primary
       (B, **Figure 29**) and secondary (C) cups.

    c. Scratched, scored or damaged piston (D,
       Figure 29).

16

d. Corroded, weak or damaged snap ring (B, **Figure 27**).

e. Worn or damaged dust cover (C, **Figure 27**).

3. Replace the piston assembly, if any part is worn or damaged.

4. Measure the piston outside diameter (**Figure 30**). Replace the piston if the outside diameter is less than the specification in **Table 1**.

5. To assemble a new piston assembly, perform the following:

a. When you replacing the piston, install new primary (A, **Figure 31**) and secondary cups (B).

b. Use the original piston assembly (C, **Figure 31**) as a reference when installing the new cups onto the piston.

c. Before installing the new piston cups, soak them in brake fluid for approximately 5-10 minutes. This will soften them and ease installation. Clean the new piston in brake fluid.

d. Install the secondary cup (B, **Figure 31**), and then the primary cup (A) onto the piston.

6. Inspect the master cylinder bore. Replace the master cylinder if the bore is corroded, scored or damaged in any way. Do not hone the master cylinder bore to remove scratches or other damage.

7. Measure the master cylinder bore (**Figure 32**). Replace the master cylinder assembly if the bore inside diameter exceeds the specification in **Table 1**.

8. Check for plugged supply (A, **Figure 33**) and relief (B) ports in the master cylinder. Clean with compressed air.

9. Inspect the brake lever and pivot bolt; replace if worn or damaged.

10. Inspect the reservoir cap, diaphragm plate and diaphragm for damage. Inspect the diaphragm for cracks or deterioration. Replace damaged parts as required.

Assembly

Refer to **Figure 22**. Lubricate the parts with DOT 4 brake fluid.

1. If installing a new piston, assemble it as described in this section.

2. Lubricate the piston assembly and cylinder bore with brake fluid.

3. Install the spring—small end first—onto the piston as shown in A, **Figure 29**.

> *CAUTION*
> *Do not allow the piston cups to tear or turn inside out when installing the piston into the master cylinder bore. Both cups are larger than the bore. To ease installation, lubricate the cups and piston with brake fluid*

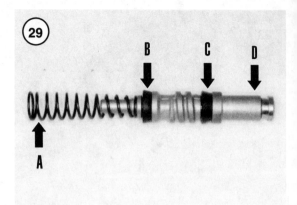

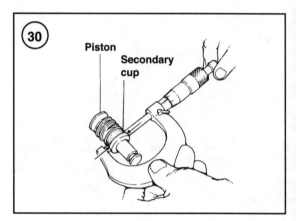

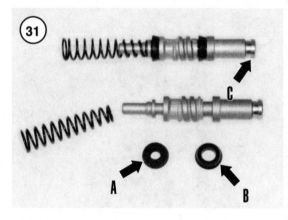

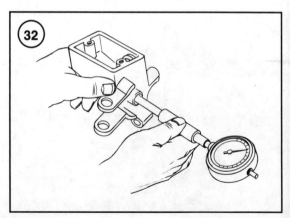

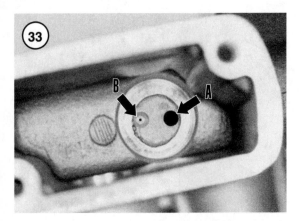

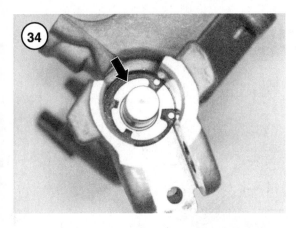

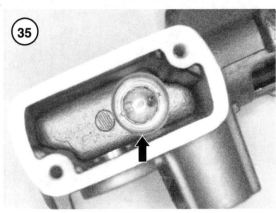

4. Insert the piston assembly—spring end first—into the master cylinder bore (**Figure 27**).

5. Mount the master cylinder in a vise (**Figure 25**).

6. Install the washer over the pushrod and set it on the piston.

7. Compress the piston assembly and install the snap ring. Make sure the snap ring seats in the groove completely (**Figure 34**). Push and release the piston a few times to make sure it moves smoothly and that the snap ring does not pop out.

8. Slide the dust cover (C, **Figure 27**) over the piston. Seat the dust cover's large end against the push rod ring, and install the small end into the push rod groove.

9. Lubricate the separator O-ring with brake fluid. Install the separator (**Figure 35**) into the master cylinder.

10. Install the diaphragm, master cylinder cover and screws. Tighten the master cylinder cover screws to 2 N•m (18 in.-lb.).

11. Install the brake lever as follows:

    a. Lubricate the pivot bolt with silicone brake grease.

    b. Install the spring (**Figure 24**) into the brake lever.

    c. Insert the spring into the master cylinder hole and install the brake lever into position.

    d. Install the pivot bolt and tighten to specification (**Table 5**).

    e. Install the pivot nut (**Figure 23**) and tighten to 6 N•m (53 in.-lb.),

    f. Operate the brake lever and make sure it moves freely with no binding or roughness.

12. Install the master cylinder (this chapter).

FRONT BRAKE MASTER CYLINDER (CRF230L AND CRF230M MODELS)

Removal/Installation

1. Remove the right rear view mirror.

2. Disconnect the front brake light switch electrical connectors (A, **Figure 36**).

3. Remove the master cylinder cover (**Figure 37**) and diaphragm. Use a syringe to withdraw brake fluid from the master cylinder reservoir. Discard the brake fluid. Reinstall the diaphragm and master cylinder cover.

4. Remove the union bolt (B, **Figure 36**) and washers securing the brake hose to the master cylinder. Seal the brake hose in a plastic bag to prevent brake fluid drips.

5. Remove the bolts (A, **Figure 38**) and clamp holding the master cylinder to the handlebar, and then remove the master cylinder.

6. If necessary, service the master cylinder (this section).

7. Clean the handlebar, master cylinder and clamp mating surfaces.

16

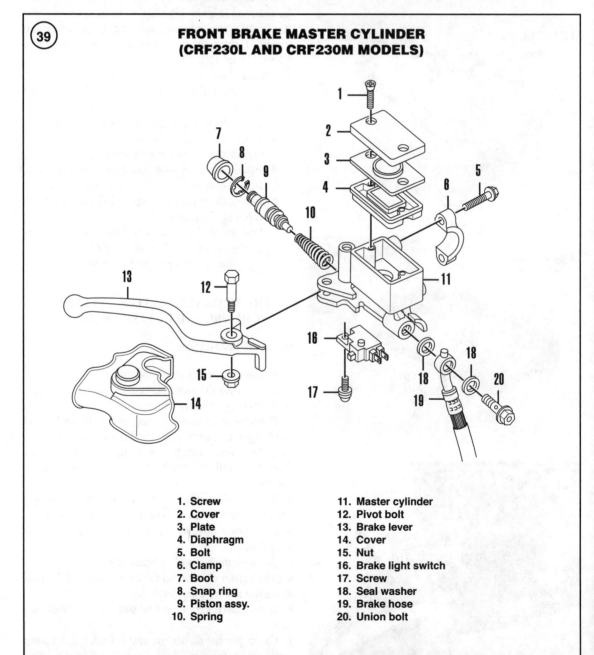

**FRONT BRAKE MASTER CYLINDER
(CRF230L AND CRF230M MODELS)**

1. Screw
2. Cover
3. Plate
4. Diaphragm
5. Bolt
6. Clamp
7. Boot
8. Snap ring
9. Piston assy.
10. Spring
11. Master cylinder
12. Pivot bolt
13. Brake lever
14. Cover
15. Nut
16. Brake light switch
17. Screw
18. Seal washer
19. Brake hose
20. Union bolt

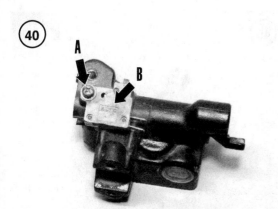

40

A

B

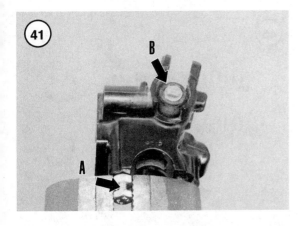

41

B

A

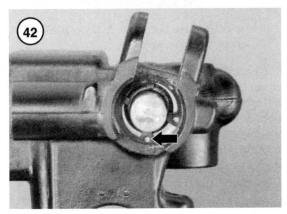

42

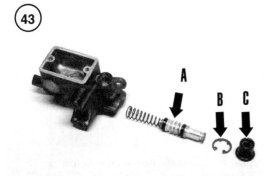

43

A

B C

8. Mount the master cylinder onto the handlebar. Then, install the clamp and both mounting bolts. Install the clamp with the UP mark (B, **Figure 38**) facing up. Align the clamp mating surface with the punch mark on the handlebar.

9. Tighten the upper clamp bolt first. Then, tighten the lower bolt. Tighten the bolts securely.

10. Attach the brake hose to the master cylinder with the union bolt and two new washers. Install a washer on each side of the fitting. Position the fitting against the master cylinder boss. Install the union bolt and tighten to 34 N•m (25 ft.-lb.).

11. Bleed the front brake (this chapter).

Disassembly

Refer to **Figure 39**.

1. Remove the master cylinder (this chapter).

2. Remove the brake lever pivot bolt and nut. Then, remove the brake lever from the master cylinder.

3. Remove the brake light switch retaining screw (A, **Figure 40**), and then remove the switch (B).

4. Remove the master cylinder cover screws and remove the cover, diaphragm plate and diaphragm from the master cylinder.

5. To hold the master cylinder, thread a bolt and nut into the master cylinder. Tighten the nut against the master cylinder. Then, clamp the bolt (A, **Figure 41**) and nut in a vise as shown in.

6. Remove the dust cover (B, **Figure 41**) from the groove in the end of the piston.

WARNING
If brake fluid is leaking from the piston bore, the piston cups are worn or damaged. Replace the piston assembly.

NOTE
Long-arm snap ring pliers that enable easy extraction of the snap ring are available from several tool manufacturers.

7. Compress the piston and remove the snap ring (**Figure 42**) from the groove in the master cylinder.

8. Remove the snap ring and piston assembly (A, **Figure 43**) from the master cylinder bore.

Inspection

1. Wash the piston and cylinder with clean brake fluid.

CAUTION
Do not remove the primary and secondary cups from the piston assembly.

16

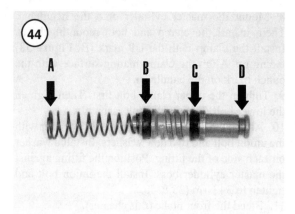

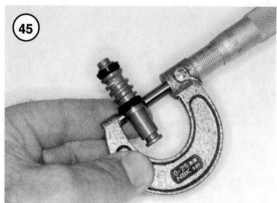

2. Check the piston assembly for the following defects:

    a. Broken, distorted or collapsed piston return spring (A, **Figure 44**).

    b. Worn, cracked, damaged or swollen primary (B, **Figure 44**) and secondary cups (C).

    c. Scratched, scored or damaged piston (D, **Figure 44**).

    d. Corroded, weak or damaged snap ring (B, **Figure 43**).

    e. Worn or damaged dust cover (C, **Figure 43**).

3. Replace the piston assembly if any part is worn or damaged.

4. Measure the piston outside diameter (**Figure 45**). Replace the piston if its diameter is less than the service limit in **Table 2**.

5. To assemble a new piston assembly, perform the following:

    a. When replacing the piston, install new primary (A, **Figure 46**) and secondary (B) cups.

    b. Use the original piston assembly (C, **Figure 46**) as a reference when installing the new cups onto the piston.

    c. Before installing the new piston cups, soak them in brake fluid for approximately 5-10 minutes. This will soften them and ease installation. Clean the new piston in brake fluid.

    d. Install the secondary cup (B, **Figure 46**), and then the primary cup (A) onto the piston.

6. Inspect the master cylinder bore. Replace the master cylinder if the bore is corroded, scored or damaged in any way. Do not hone the master cylinder bore to remove scratches or other damage.

7. Measure the master cylinder bore (**Figure 47**). Replace the master cylinder assembly if the bore inside diameter exceeds the service limit in **Table 2**.

NOTE
*The master cylinder reservoir ports are covered by a clear plastic disc (**Figure 48**) to prevent debris from entering the*

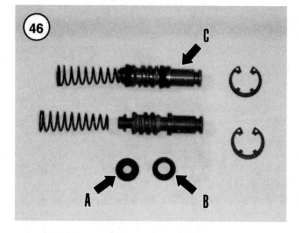

ports. Remove the disc only if it is necessary to clean the ports.

8. Check for plugged supply and relief ports in the master cylinder reservoir. Clean with compressed air.

9. Inspect the brake lever and pivot bolt; replace if worn or damaged.

10. Inspect the reservoir cap, diaphragm plate and diaphragm for damage. Inspect the diaphragm for cracks or deterioration. Replace damaged parts as required.

Assembly

Refer to **Figure 39**. Lubricate the parts with fresh DOT 4 brake fluid.

1. If installing a new piston, assemble it as described in this section.

2. Lubricate the piston assembly and cylinder bore with clean brake fluid.

3. Install the spring—small end first—onto the piston (A, **Figure 44**).

CAUTION
Do not allow the piston cups to tear or turn inside out when installing the piston into the master cylinder bore. Both

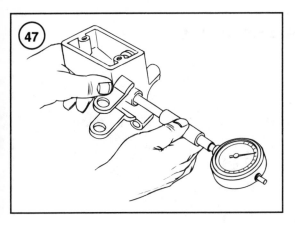

*cups are larger than the bore. To ease
installation, lubricate the cups and piston with brake fluid*

4. Insert the piston assembly—spring end first—
into the master cylinder bore (**Figure 43**).

5. Using a bolt (A, **Figure 41**), mount the master
cylinder in a vise.

6. Compress the piston assembly and install the snap
ring (**Figure 42**). Make sure the snap ring seats in the
groove completely. Push and release the piston a few
times to make sure it moves smoothly and that the
snap ring does not pop out.

7. Slide the dust cover (B, **Figure 41**) onto the piston. Seat the cover in the cylinder bore and in the
piston groove.

8. Install the diaphragm, master cylinder cover and
screws. Tighten the master cylinder cover screws to
1.5 N•m (13 in.-lb.).

9. Install the brake lever, pivot bolt and nut. Tighten
the pivot bolt and nut to the specification in **Table 6**.
Then, operate the hand lever and make sure it moves
freely with no binding or roughness.

10. Install the master cylinder (this section).

REAR DRUM BRAKE (CRF230F MODELS)

> *WARNING*
> *When working on the brake system, do
> not inhale brake dust. It may contain
> asbestos, which can cause lung injury
> and cancer. Wear a face mask that
> meets OSHA requirements for trapping
> asbestos particles. Wash your hands
> and forearms thoroughly after com-
> pleting the work.*

Refer to Chapter Three for complete rear brake adjustment procedure.

Disassembly

Refer to **Figure 49** when performing this procedure.

1. Remove the rear wheel (Chapter Twelve).

2. Pull the brake assembly straight up and out of the
brake drum.

3. Carefully pull up on both brake shoes in a
V-formation (**Figure 50**) and remove the brake shoes
and return springs as an assembly.

4. Disconnect the return springs from the brake
shoes.

5. To remove the brake arm and cam, perform the
following:
 a. Remove the cover (A, **Figure 51**).
 b. Remove the bolt (B, **Figure 51**).
 c. Remove the arm (C, **Figure 51**).
 d. Remove the wear indicator (**Figure 52**).
 e. Remove the cam (A, **Figure 53**) and lockwasher (B).

Inspection

1. Thoroughly clean and dry all parts except the
brake linings.

2. Check the contact surface (**Figure 54**) of the
drum for corrosion and damage. If necessary, clean
the drum using 120 sandpaper.

3. Measure the inside diameter of the brake drum
(**Figure 55**). If the measurement is greater than the
service limit listed in **Table 3**, or the drum is out-of-
round, replace the rear hub.

4. Inspect the linings (**Figure 56**) for imbedded foreign material. Dirt can be removed with a stiff wire
brush. Check for any traces of oil or grease. If the
linings are contaminated, they must be replaced.

5. Measure the brake linings with a set of calipers
(**Figure 57**). Replace the brake shoes if the lining
thickness is less than 2 mm (0.08 in.).

16

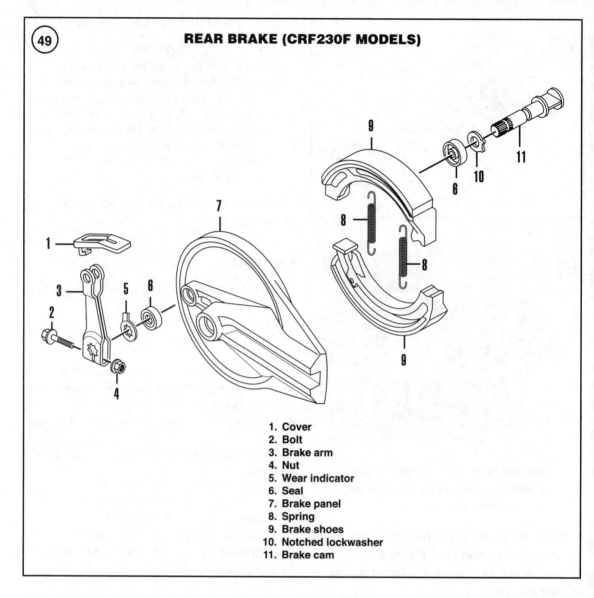

(49) REAR BRAKE (CRF230F MODELS)

1. Cover
2. Bolt
3. Brake arm
4. Nut
5. Wear indicator
6. Seal
7. Brake panel
8. Spring
9. Brake shoes
10. Notched lockwasher
11. Brake cam

6. Inspect the cam lobe and the pivot pin area of the shaft (**Figure 58**) for wear and corrosion. Minor roughness can be removed with fine emery cloth.

7. Inspect the bearing surface for the cam in the backing plate (A, **Figure 59**). If it is worn or damaged, replace the backing plate. The cam should also be replaced at the same time.

8. Inspect the brake shoe return springs for wear. If they are stretched, they will not fully retract the brake shoes from the drum, resulting in a power-robbing drag on the drum and premature wear of the linings. Replace if necessary; always replace the springs as a pair.

9. Inspect the dust seal. Replace if damaged. Install the dust seal so the flat side is out. Apply grease to the seal lip.

10. Inspect the rear axle bore (B, **Figure 59**) in the backing plate for wear, scoring or other damage. If necessary, replace the backing plate.

Assembly

1. If the cam was removed, lubricate it with a light coat of molybdenum-disulfide grease.

2. Install the notched lockwasher so the notch (A, **Figure 60**) fits around the lug (B).

3. Install the cam into the backing plate from the backside.

4. Install the wear indicator ring onto the cam while aligning the ring tab with the cam groove (**Figure 61**).

5. Install the brake arm. Make sure to align the punch marks on the brake arm (A, **Figure 62**) and shaft end.

6. Install the brake arm bolt (B, **Figure 62**). Tighten the bolt to 10 N•m (89 in.-lb.).

7. Install the arm cover (C, **Figure 62**).

8. Lubricate the cam and pivot post with a light coat of molybdenum-disulfide grease; avoid getting any

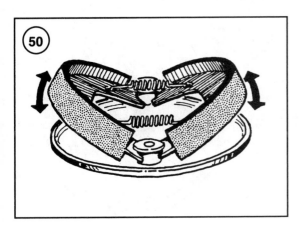

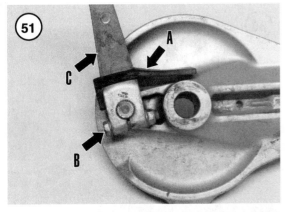

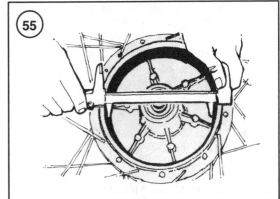

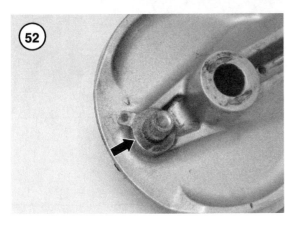

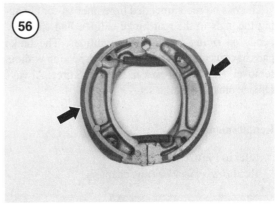

16

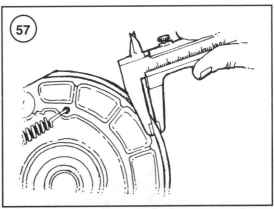

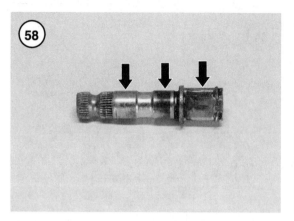

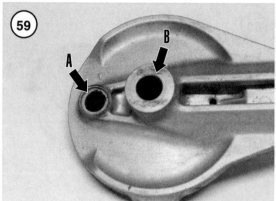

grease on the brake backing plate where the brake linings may come in contact with it.

9. Assemble the return springs onto the brake shoes.

10. Hold the brake shoes in a "V" formation with the return springs attached (**Figure 50**) and snap them into place on the brake backing plate.

11. Install the brake panel assembly into the brake drum.

12. Install the rear wheel (Chapter Twelve).

13. Adjust the rear brake (Chapter Three).

REAR BRAKE PADS
(CRF230L AND CRF230M MODELS)

There is no recommended time interval for changing the pads in the rear brake caliper. Pad wear depends on riding habits and conditions. The brake pads have wear grooves that allow inspection without removal. Refer to *Brakes* in Chapter Three. Always replace brake pads as a set.

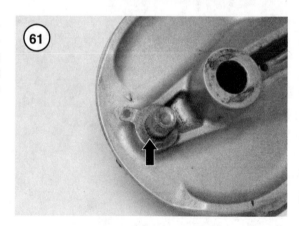

Replacement

Refer to **Figure 63**.

1. Read *Brake Service* (this chapter).

> *CAUTION*
> *Do not allow the master cylinder reservoir to overflow when pushing in the pistons. If the fluid level is high, remove the cover and withdraw some of the fluid from the reservoir with a syringe.*

> *CAUTION*
> *Before pushing the piston into the caliper to make room for the new pads, check for debris buildup on the end of the piston. When the piston is pushed back into the caliper, this material can damage the caliper seals. If there is debris buildup on the end of the piston,*

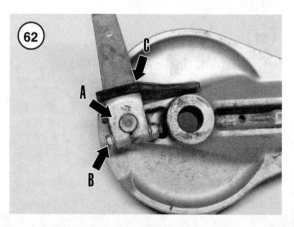

63   REAR BRAKE CALIPER (CRF230L AND CRF230M MODELS)

1. Pad retainer
2. Bracket
3. Bracket fixed shaft
4. Boot
5. Piston
6. Boot
7. Dust seal
8. Piston seal
9. Caliper
10. Bleed valve
11. Cover
12. Caliper fixed shaft
13. Pad pin
14. Plug
15. Brake pads
16. Pad spring

try to clean the end of the piston with a soft brush and denatured alcohol while the caliper is assembled or remove and disassemble the caliper to clean the piston.

2. Push the caliper body in by hand to push the piston into the caliper to make room for the new pads.

3. Unscrew the pad pin plug (**Figure 64**).

4. Remove the pad pin retainer bolt (A, **Figure 65**).

5. Remove the inboard and outboard brake pads (B, **Figure 65**) from the caliper.

6. If necessary, remove the pad spring (C, **Figure 65**).

7. Inspect the brake pads (B, **Figure 65**) for uneven wear, damage or contamination. Note the following:

   a. Remove surface contamination by lightly sanding the lining surface with a piece of sandpaper placed on a flat surface. If lining material is contaminated, replace both brake pads.

   b. Wear should be approximately the same for both brake pads. If the inner pad is worn more than the outer pad, the caliper may be binding on the caliper bracket. This wear can also be caused by worn or damaged piston seals that have lost their flex and ability to self-adjust (returning the pistons and disengaging the brakes after the brake lever is released).

8. Replace the pads as a set if the thickness of any one pad has worn down to its wear groove.

9. Check the caliper for signs of leaks around the pistons. If brake fluid is leaking from the caliper bores, overhaul the brake caliper (this section).

16

10. Clean the pad pin and plug. Remove rust and corrosion from the pad pin. Then, inspect it for excessive wear, grooves or other damage. Replace the pin if damaged.

11. Inspect the pad spring (C, **Figure 65**) and replace if damaged.

12. Inspect the brake disc for oil contamination. Spray both sides of the brake disc with brake cleaner. Inspect the brake disc for wear (this chapter).

13. When new pads are installed in the caliper, the master cylinder brake fluid will rise as the caliper piston is repositioned. Perform the following:

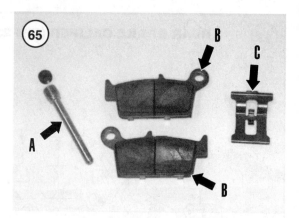

   a. Remove the right side cover (Chapter Fifteen).
   b. Clean the top of the master cylinder of all dirt and foreign matter.
   c. Unscrew and remove the top cover (**Figure 66**), set plate and diaphragm from the master cylinder reservoir.
   d. Slowly push the caliper piston into the caliper. Constantly check the reservoir to make sure brake fluid does not overflow. Remove fluid, if necessary, before it overflows.
   e. The piston should move freely. If it does not and there is evidence of it sticking in the cylinder, remove and service the caliper (this chapter).

14. Push the caliper piston in all the way to allow room for the new pads.

15. If removed, install the pad spring (**Figure 67**).

16. Insert the inboard brake pad (**Figure 68**) into the caliper and hook the front edge onto the caliper boss.

17. Insert the outboard brake pad (**Figure 69**) into the caliper and hook the front edge onto the caliper boss.

18. Align the outboard pad pin hole with the bore of the caliper and push the pad pin (A, **Figure 70**) through the outboard pad (B).

19. Continue to push the pad pin through the inboard pad (C, **Figure 70**) and caliper (D). Push the pin in until it bottoms out.

20. Tighten the pad pin bolt to 18 N•m (13 ft.-lb.).

21. Install the pad pin plug (**Figure 64**) and tighten to 2.4 N•m (21 in.-lb.).

22. Operate the brake pedal to seat the pads against the disc. The brake pedal should feel firm when applied.

23. Check the brake fluid level in the reservoir. If necessary, add new DOT 4 brake fluid.

24. Raise the rear wheel and check that the wheel spins freely and the brake operates properly.

25. Break in the pads by braking slowly at first, and then increase braking pressure. Do not overheat new brake pads.

REAR BRAKE CALIPER
(CRF230L AND CRF230M MODELS)

Read *Brake Service* (this chapter).

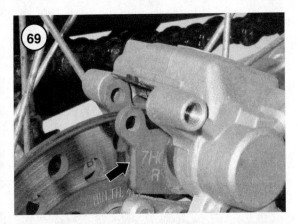

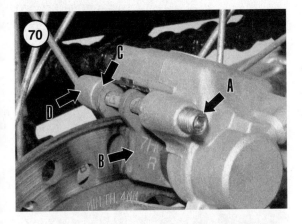

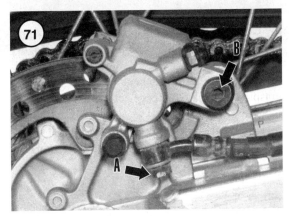

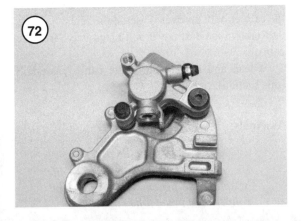

Removal/Installation

NOTE
If hydraulic pressure will be used to dislodge the piston during disassembly, do not disconnect the brake line yet.

1. If caliper disassembly is required, perform the following:
   a. Place a container under the brake line at the caliper.
   b. Remove the union bolt (A, **Figure 71**) and sealing washers securing the brake line fitting to the caliper assembly. Remove the brake line and let the brake fluid drain into the container.
   c. To prevent the entry of moisture and dirt, cover the end of the brake line and tie the loose end up to the frame.
2. Remove the rear wheel (Chapter Twelve).
3. If necessary, remove the brake pads (this chapter).

NOTE
If the caliper will not be disconnected from the brake hose during the removal procedure, insert a small wooden block between the brake pads. This prevents the caliper piston from extending out of the caliper if the brake pedal is actuated.

4. If the caliper will be disassembled using hydraulic force to expel the piston, refer to *Disassembly* in this section.
5. If the caliper fixed shaft (B, **Figure 71**) will be removed, loosen the pin.
6. Remove the caliper and bracket assembly (**Figure 72**).
7. Remove the caliper bracket from the caliper, if necessary.
8. Install the brake caliper by reversing the removal steps. Note the following:
   a. If necessary, tighten the brake caliper fixed shaft (B, **Figure 71**) to 27 N•m (20 ft.-lb.).
   b. If the brake hose was not disconnected, remove the spacer block from between the brake pads and slide the caliper bracket onto the swing arm. Make sure the brake pads were not contaminated with brake fluid.
   c. If the brake hose was disconnected, install the brake hose with a new sealing washer on each side of the fitting onto the caliper. Install the union bolt and tighten to 34 N•m (25 ft.-lb.).
   d. If the brake hose was disconnected, refill the master cylinder and bleed the rear brake (this chapter).
   e. Operate the rear brake pedal to seat the pads against the brake disc.

16

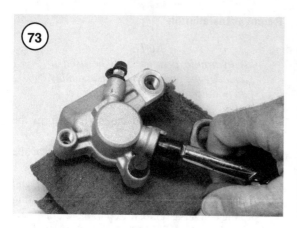

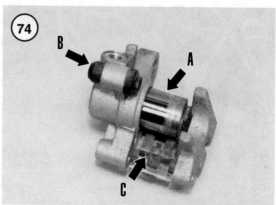

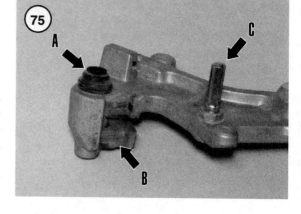

Disassembly

Refer to **Figure 63**.

Removing the piston hydraulically

If the piston and dust seals are in good condition and there are no signs of brake fluid leaking from the bore, it may be possible to remove the piston hydraulically. However, note that brake fluid will spill from the caliper once the piston becomes free.

1. Remove the rear brake caliper (this section). Do not loosen or remove the brake hose.
2. Remove the caliper bracket from the caliper. Have a supply of paper towels and a pan available to wipe up and catch spilled brake fluid.
3. Hold the caliper with the piston facing out and operate the brake pedal to push the piston out of the caliper bore.
4. Remove the union bolt with an impact gun (air or electric), if available. Otherwise, hold the caliper and caliper bracket against the swing arm with an adjustable wrench and remove the union bolt with hand tools.
5. Continue caliper disassembly to remove the remaining components as described in *Removing the piston with compressed air* (this section).

Removing the piston with compressed air

1. Remove the rear brake caliper (this section).
2. Slide the caliper bracket out of the caliper.

> *WARNING*
> *Wear eye protection when using compressed air to remove the piston. Keep your fingers away from the piston.*

> *CAUTION*
> *Do not try to pry out the piston. This will damage the piston and caliper bore.*

3. Cushion the piston with a shop rag and position the caliper with the piston bore facing down. Apply compressed air through the brake hose port (**Figure 73**) to force out the piston (A, **Figure 74**).
4. Remove the caliper rubber boot (B, **Figure 74**) by grasping its thick outer edge and pulling it out of its mounting hole.
5. Remove the pad spring (C, **Figure 74**).
6. Remove the rubber boot (A, **Figure 75**) from the caliper bracket.
7. Remove the pad retainer (B, **Figure 75**) from the caliper bracket.
8. Use a small wooden or plastic tool and remove the dust seal (A, **Figure 76**) and piston seal (B) from the caliper bore grooves. Discard the seals.
9. Remove the dust cover and bleed valve from the caliper.
10. Clean and inspect the brake caliper assembly (this section).

Assembly

> *NOTE*
> *Use new DOT 4 brake fluid when lubricating the piston seals, piston and caliper bore in the following steps.*

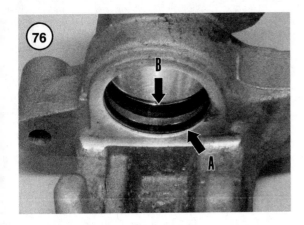

4. Install a new piston seal into the rear bore groove (B, **Figure 76**).

5. Install a new dust seal into the front bore groove (A, **Figure 76**).

6. Lubricate the piston with brake fluid.

> *CAUTION*
> *The tight piston-to-seal fit can make piston installation difficult. Do not install the piston by pushing it straight in as it may bind in the bore and tear the seals.*

7. Align the piston with the caliper bore so the open side faces out. Rock the piston slightly to center it in the bore while at the same time pushing its lower end past the seals. When the lower end of the piston clears both seals, push and bottom the piston (**Figure 78**) into the bore. Clean spilled brake fluid from the area in front of the piston to prevent brake pad contamination.

8. Install the rubber boot (B, **Figure 74**) through the mounting hole in the caliper. Make sure the boot opening faces toward the inside of the caliper. Partially fill the boot with silicone brake grease.

9. Install the bleed valve and tighten fingertight.

10. Install the pad spring onto the caliper.

11. Install the boot (A, **Figure 75**) into the caliper bracket. Partially fill the boot with silicone brake grease.

12. Install the pad retainer (B, **Figure 75**) onto the caliper bracket.

13. If removed, install the fixed shaft (C, **Figure 75**) into the caliper and tighten to 27 N•m (20 ft.-lb.)

14. Lubricate the caliper fixed shaft and caliper bracket fixed shaft with silicone brake grease.

15. Align and slide the caliper bracket onto the caliper body (**Figure 79**). Hold the caliper and slide the caliper bracket in and out by hand. Make sure there is no roughness or binding.

16. Install the brake caliper assembly (this section) and brake pads (this chapter).

Inspection

All models use a floating caliper design, in which the caliper slides or floats on shafts mounted parallel with each other on the caliper and caliper bracket. Rubber boots around each shaft prevent dirt from damaging the shafts. If the shafts are worn or damaged, the caliper can move out of alignment on the caliper bracket. This causes brake drag, uneven pad wear and overheating. Inspect the rubber boots and shafts during caliper inspection as they play a vital role in brake performance. Replace parts that are out of specification (**Table 4**) or show damage (this section).

16

1. Install the bleed valve and dust cap into the caliper.

2. Soak the new piston and dust seals in brake fluid.

3. Lubricate the cylinder bore with brake fluid.

> *NOTE*
> *The piston seal (A, **Figure 77**) is thicker than the dust seal (B).*

> *NOTE*
> *Make sure each seal fits squarely inside its bore groove.*

WARNING
Do not allow oil or grease on any of the brake components. Do not clean the parts with kerosene or other petroleum products. These chemicals cause the rubber brake system components to swell, which may cause brake failure.

1. Clean and dry the caliper and the other metal parts. Clean the seal grooves carefully. If the contamination is difficult to remove, soak the caliper in a suitable solvent, and then reclean. If any of the rubber parts are to be reused, clean them with denatured alcohol or new DOT 4 brake fluid. Do not use a petroleum-based solvent.

2. Inspect the caliper bracket, fixed shafts and rubber boots as follows:
   a. Inspect the rubber boots for cracks, tearing, weakness or other damage.
   b. Inspect the fixed shafts on the caliper and caliper bracket for excessive or uneven wear. If the caliper fixed shaft is damaged, remove and discard the shaft. Install a new caliper fixed shaft and tighten to 27 N•m (20 ft.-lb.). If the caliper bracket fixed shaft is damaged, remove and discard the shaft. Apply threadlock and install a new caliper bracket fixed shaft. Tighten shaft to 12 N•m (106 in.-lb.).

3. Check the caliper bore for corrosion, pitting, deep scratches or other wear.

4. Measure the inside diameter of the caliper bore (**Figure 80**). Replace caliper if bore diameter exceeds service limit in **Table 4**.

5. Check the piston for wear marks, scoring, cracks or other damage.

6. Measure the outside diameter of the piston (**Figure 81**). Replace piston if diameter is less than service limit in **Table 4**.

7. Check the bleed valve and dust cap for wear or damage. Make sure air can pass through the bleed valve.

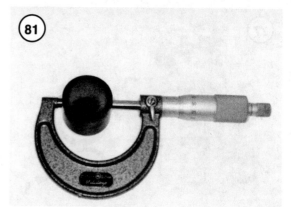

8. Check the union bolt for wear or damage. Discard the washers.

9. Inspect the brake pads, pad spring and pad pin bolt (this chapter).

REAR MASTER CYLINDER AND RESERVOIR (CRF230L AND CRF230M MODELS)

Removal/Installation

Refer to **Figure 82**.

1. Remove the right side cover (Chapter Seventeen).

2. Clean the top of the master cylinder of all dirt and foreign matter.

3. Perform the following:
   a. Remove the mounting bolt and bracket (A, **Figure 83**).
   b. Reposition the reservoir on the frame and reinstall the mounting bolt without the bracket.
   c. Unscrew the top cap (B, **Figure 83**). Pull up and loosen the top cap and the diaphragm. This will allow air to enter the reservoir so the brake fluid can drain out more quickly.

4. Remove the dust cap (**Figure 84**) and place a tight fitting hose onto the rear caliper bleed screw. Then,

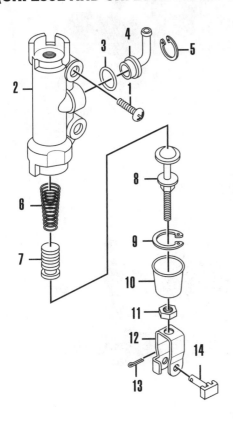

82 **REAR MASTER CYLINDER (CRF230L AND CRF230M MODELS)**

1. Bolt
2. Master cylinder
3. O-ring
4. Fitting
5. Snap ring
6. Spring
7. Piston assembly
8. Push rod
9. Snap ring
10. Boot
11. Nut
12. Clevis
13. Cotter pin
14. Clevis pin

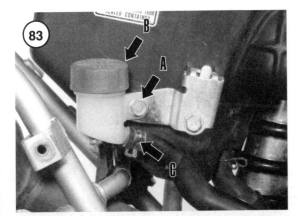

83

84

85

loosen the bleed screw. Place the other end of the hose in a container to catch the brake fluid.

5. Apply the rear brake pedal as many times as necessary to pump the fluid out of the rear hydraulic brake lines. Dispose of this brake fluid—never reuse brake fluid. Remove the hose and tighten the bleed screw securely.

6. Remove the union bolt and sealing washers (A, **Figure 85**) from the top of the master cylinder. Discard the sealing washers.

7. Remove the hose from the top of the master cylinder and cover the end of the hose to prevent the entry of foreign matter.

8. Remove the cotter pin and withdraw the clevis pin (B, **Figure 85**) securing the push rod to the brake pedal. Discard the cotter pin.

9. Detach the supply hose (C, **Figure 83**) from the reservoir fitting.

10. Remove the bolts (C, **Figure 85**) securing the master cylinder to the frame.

11. Be prepared to catch brake fluid from the hose or master cylinder. Remove the master cylinder.

12. If necessary, service the master cylinder (this section).

13. Reverse the removal procedure to install the master cylinder. Note the following:

16

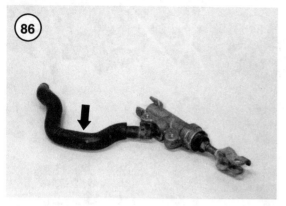

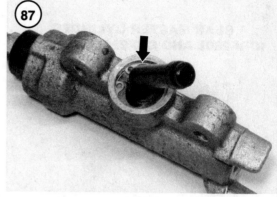

a. Tighten the master cylinder mounting bolts to 14 N•m (120 in.-lb.).

b. Install new seal washers on the union bolt. Tighten the union bolt to 34 N•m (25 ft.-lb.).

c. Fill the brake fluid reservoir and bleed the brake system (this chapter).

Disassembly

Refer to **Figure 82**.

1. Remove the rear master cylinder (this chapter).

2. Detach the supply hose (**Figure 86**) from the master cylinder fitting.

3. Remove the snap ring (**Figure 87**) that retains the hose and fitting against the master cylinder. Remove the fitting and O-ring.

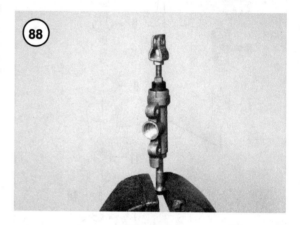

4. To hold the master cylinder during servicing, screw a bolt into the union bolt hole in the master cylinder. Clamp the bolt (not the master cylinder) in a vise (**Figure 88**).

5. Pull the rubber boot away from the master cylinder. Then, remove the snap ring (**Figure 89**).

> *CAUTION*
> *Do not remove the primary cup from the piston.*

6. Remove the pushrod and piston assemblies (**Figure 90**) from the cylinder.

Inspection

If any internal parts are damaged they must be replaced as a set. The repair kit contains the primary cup (A, **Figure 91**), secondary cup (B), piston (C), spring (D), snap ring and rubber boot.

1. Wash the piston and cylinder with brake fluid. Refer to *Brake Fluid Selection* in this chapter.

2. Inspect the master cylinder bore surface for signs of wear and damage. If there is any scoring or pitting in the bore, replace the master cylinder assembly. The body cannot be replaced separately.

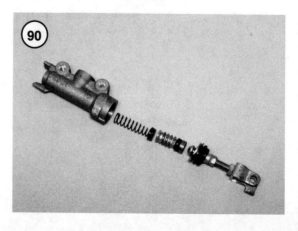

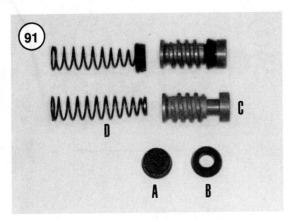

91

92

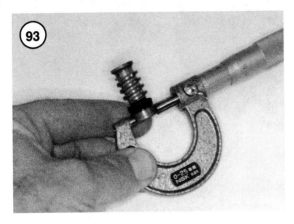

93

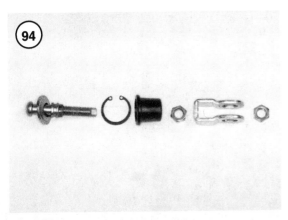

94

3. Inspect the piston contact surfaces for signs of wear and damage. If less than perfect, replace the piston assembly.

4. Check the end of the piston for wear caused by the pushrod. If worn, replace the piston assembly.

5. Measure the master cylinder bore inside diameter (**Figure 92**). Replace the master cylinder if the bore inside diameter exceeds the service limit listed in **Table 4.**

6. Measure the outside diameter of the piston (**Figure 93**) with a micrometer. Replace the piston assembly if the outside diameter is less than the service limit listed in **Table 4.**

7. Make sure the passages in the body of the master cylinder are clear. Clean with compressed air.

8. Inspect the pushrod assembly (**Figure 94**). Check for stripped threads and inspect the rubber boot for tears or deterioration; replace if necessary.

9. Inspect the snap ring grooves in the master cylinder body for damage; replace the master cylinder if necessary.

10. Check the spring for cracks or other damage; replace if necessary.

Assembly

1. Soak the new piston assembly and cups in fresh brake fluid for at least 15 minutes to make the cups pliable. Coat the inside of the cylinder bore with fresh brake fluid prior to the assembly of parts.

2. Assemble the piston (A, **Figure 95**), cups (B) and spring (C) as follows.

    a. Apply brake fluid to the piston so the cups will slide over the ends.

    b. Identify the wide (open) side of the primary cup (A, **Figure 91**). When installed, the wide side of the cup must face in the direction of the arrow (**Figure 95**). Install the primary cup onto the small end of the spring.

    c. Identify the wide (open) side of the secondary cup (B, **Figure 91**). When installed, the wide side of the cup must face in the direction of the arrow (**Figure 95**). Install the secondary cup onto the piston (C, **Figure 91**).

    d. The assembled piston should appear as shown in **Figure 95**.

3. Lubricate the cylinder bore, piston and cups with brake fluid.

CAUTION
When installing the piston assembly, do not allow the cups to turn inside out.

4. Install the spring and piston assembly into the cylinder as a unit (**Figure 90**).

16

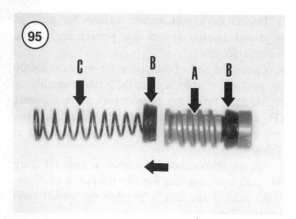

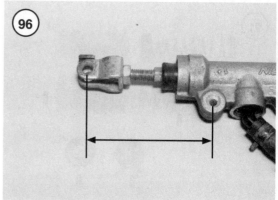

5. Install the pushrod assembly into the body (**Figure 96**).

NOTE
Install the snap ring so the flat side is out.

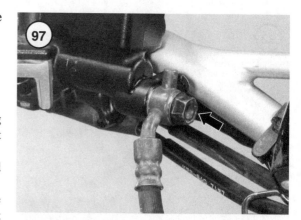

6. Compress the pushrod and install the snap ring (**Figure 89**) into the groove in the body. Make sure it seats completely.

7. Slide on the rubber boot so it seals the lower end of the body.

8. Measure the pushrod length (**Figure 96**) from the center of the bottom master cylinder mounting bolt hole to the center of the hole in the clevis. The correct pushrod length is listed in **Table 4**. To adjust, loosen the nut securing the clevis and turn the clevis to the correct position. Retighten the nut to 17.2 N•m (13 ft.-lb.).

9. Install the master cylinder (this chapter).

BRAKE HOSE REPLACEMENT

1. Drain the appropriate brake system (this chapter) for the hose to be replaced.

2. Before disconnecting the brake hoses, note how they are routed and mounted onto the master cylinder and brake caliper. Install the new hoses so they face in the same direction. Note also how the ends of the brake hoses are routed through guides or positioned next to a stop at the master cylinders and brake calipers. These hold the brake hoses in position when the union bolts (**Figure 97** and **Figure 98**, typical) are tightened.

3. Remove the union bolts and washers for the brake hose requiring replacement. Discard the washers.

4. Install the new brake hose in the reverse order of removal. Perform the following:

    a. On CRF230F models, position the front brake hose so the outer sheath end is 10 mm (0.39 in.) above the clamp on the fork leg (**Figure 99**).

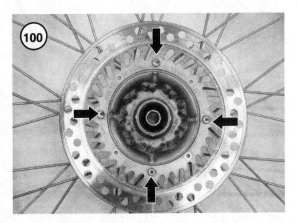

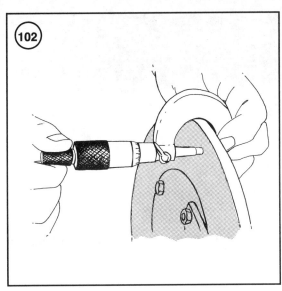

BRAKE DISC

CRF230F models are equipped with a front wheel brake disc. CRF230L and CRF230M models are equipped with a brake disc (**Figure 100**, typical) on both wheels. Each brake disc is separate from the wheel hub and can be removed after removing the wheel from the motorcycle, and then removing the mounting bolts.

Inspection

The brake disc can be inspected while mounted on the motorcycle. Small marks on the disc are not important, but radial scratches that run all the way around the disc surface and are deep enough to snag a fingernail can reduce braking effectiveness and increase brake pad wear. If these grooves are evident, and the brake pads are wearing rapidly, replace the brake disc.

Do not machine a deeply scored or warped disc. Removing disc material causes the disc to overheat rapidly and warp. Maintain the discs by keeping them clean and corrosion-free. Clean the discs with a non-petroleum solvent.

Refer **Table 1**, **Table 2** and **Table 4** for standard and service limit specifications for the brake discs. The minimum thickness dimension (**Figure 101**) is also stamped on the outside of the disc.

1. Support the motorcycle on a workstand.

2. Measure the thickness around the disc at several locations with a micrometer (**Figure 102**). Replace the disc if its thickness at any point is less than the service limit (**Table 1**, **Table 2** or **Table 4**) or less than the dimension stamped on the disc.

NOTE
Before checking disc runout, make sure the wheel bearings are in good condition and the wheel is running true (Chapter Twelve).

3. Measure disc runout with a dial indicator (**Figure 103**). Replace the disc if the runout exceeds the service limit (**Table 1**, **Table 2** or **Table 4**).

Removal/Installation

1. Remove the wheel (Chapter Twelve).

2. Remove the bolts (**Figure 100**, typical) securing the brake disc to the wheel hub. Remove the brake disc.

3. Inspect the brake disc flanges on the hub for cracks or other damage. Replace the hub if damage is evident.

b. Install new sealing washers when installing the union bolts.

c. Tighten the union bolt to 34 N•m (25 ft.-lb.).

d. Fill the master cylinder and bleed the brake (this chapter).

e. Operate the brake lever or brake pedal while observing the brake hose connections. Check for a loose connection or other damage.

16

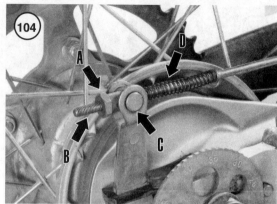

4. Clean the nuts and bolts of all threadlock residue. Replace the bolts if the hex drive end has started to round out.

5. Install the brake disc onto the hub with the stamped side of the disc facing out.

CAUTION
The brake disc mounting bolts are self locking. Discard the old bolts and install new bolts.

6. On the front wheel, install the hub cover (if removed). On CRF230F models, tighten the hub cover screws to 2 N•m (18 in.-lb.).

7. Install new brake disc mounting bolts. Tighten the bolts to 20 N•m (15 ft.-lb.).

8. On the rear wheel of CRF230L and CRF230M models, install new brake disc mounting bolts. Tighten the bolts to 42 N•m (31 ft.-lb.).

9. Install the wheel (Chapter Twelve).

REAR BRAKE PEDAL (CRF230F MODELS)

Removal/Installation

1. Remove the brake adjusting nut (A, **Figure 104**).

2. Disengage the brake rod (B, **Figure 104**) from the joint pin (C). Remove the spring (D, **Figure 104**).

3. Detach the brake return spring (**Figure 105**) from the pedal.

4. Remove the cotter pin (A, **Figure 106**) and washer (B).

5. Remove the rear brake pedal.

6. Inspect the grease seals in the frame. Replace if necessary.

7. Clean the pivot bore in the frame and the pedal pivot shaft. Inspect the bore and pivot shaft for damage and excessive wear.

8. Install the brake pedal by reversing the removal steps. Apply lithium-based multipurpose grease to the pivot shaft.

9. Adjust brake pedal freeplay (Chapter Three).

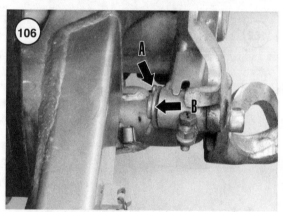

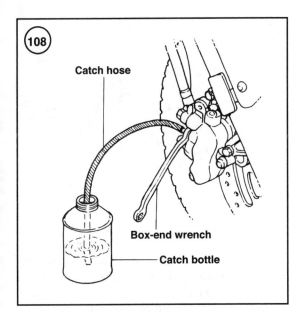

Catch hose

Box-end wrench

Catch bottle

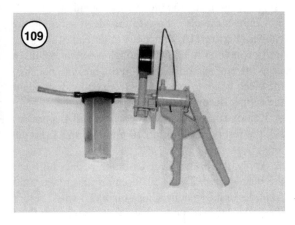

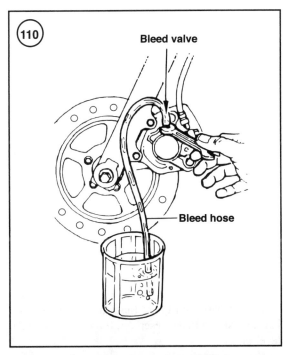

Bleed valve

Bleed hose

REAR BRAKE PEDAL
(CRF230L AND CRF230M MODELS)

Removal/Installation

1. Remove the cotter pin from the clevis pin (A, **Figure 107**). Then, remove the clevis pin.
2. Disconnect the brake switch spring (B, **Figure 107**) and return spring (C) from the pedal.
3. Remove the cotter pin and washer from the pedal pivot pin.
4. Remove the brake pedal.
5. Inspect the grease seals in the frame. Replace if necessary.
6. Clean the pivot bore in the frame and the pedal pivot shaft. Inspect the bore and pivot shaft for damage and excessive wear.
7. Install the brake pedal by reversing the removal steps. Apply lithium-based multipurpose grease to the pivot shaft.
8. Operate the rear brake pedal, making sure it pivots and returns correctly.

BRAKE SYSTEM DRAINING

Refer to *Brake Service* in this chapter.

The brake system can be drained either manually or with a vacuum pump. When draining the system manually, the master cylinder is used as a pump to expel brake fluid from the system. An empty bottle, a length of clear hose that fits tightly onto the caliper bleed valve and a box-end wrench (**Figure 108**) are required. When using vacuum to drain the system, a hand-operated vacuum pump (**Figure 109**) is required.

1. Remove the diaphragm from the reservoir.
2A. When draining the system manually, perform the following:
    a. Connect the hose to the caliper bleed valve (**Figure 110**). Then, insert the other end of the hose into a clean bottle.
    b. Apply (do not pump) the brake lever or brake pedal until it stops, and then hold it in this position.
    c. Open the bleed valve with a wrench. Then, continue to apply the brake lever or brake pedal until it reaches the end of its travel. This expels some of the brake fluid from the system.
    d. Hold the lever or pedal in this position and close the bleed valve. Then, slowly release the lever or pedal.
    e. Repeat this sequence to remove as much brake fluid as possible.
2B. When using a vacuum pump, perform the following:

16

a. Assemble the pump and connect it to the caliper bleed valve (**Figure 111**) following the tool manufacturer's instructions.

b. Operate the pump lever five to ten times to create a vacuum in the line. Then, open the bleed valve with a wrench. Brake fluid will begin to flow into the bottle connected to the vacuum pump.

c. When the fluid draining from the system begins to slow down and before the gauge on the pump (if so equipped) reads 0 HG of vacuum, close the bleed valve.

d. Repeat this sequence to remove as much brake fluid as possible.

3. Close the bleed valve and disconnect the hose or vacuum pump.

4. If necessary, use a syringe to remove brake fluid remaining in the bottom of the master cylinder reservoir.

5. Reinstall the diaphragm cover.

6. Discard the brake fluid removed from the system.

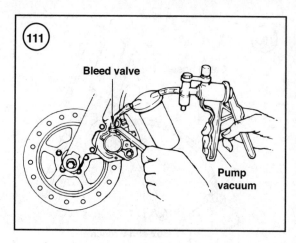

Bleed valve

Pump vacuum

BRAKE BLEEDING

Refer to *Brake Service* in this chapter.

Whenever air enters the brake system, bleed the system to remove the air. Air can enter the system when the brake fluid level drops too low, after flushing the system or when a union bolt or brake hose is loosened or removed. Air in the brake system will increase lever or pedal travel while causing it to feel spongy and less responsive. Under excessive conditions, it can cause complete loss of brake pressure.

Bleed the brakes manually or with a vacuum pump. Both methods are described in this section.

When adding brake fluid during the bleeding process, use new DOT 4 brake fluid. Do not reuse brake fluid drained from the system or use a silicone based DOT 5 brake fluid. Because brake fluid is very harmful to most surfaces, wipe up any spills immediately with soapy water.

When bleeding the brakes, check the fluid level in the master cylinder frequently. If the reservoir runs dry, air will enter the system and the system will need to be bled again.

Manual Bleeding

This procedure describes how to bleed the brake system manually by using the master cylinder as a pump. An empty bottle, a length of clear hose and a box-end wrench (**Figure 108**) are required.

1. Make sure both brake system union bolts are tight.

2. Remove the dust cap from the brake bleed valve and clean the valve and its opening of all dirt and debris. If a dust cap was not used, use a thin screwdriver or similar tool and compressed air to remove all dirt from inside the bleed valve opening.

3. Connect the clear hose to the bleed valve on the caliper (**Figure 110**). Place the other end of the hose into a container filled with enough new brake fluid to keep the end submerged. Loop the hose higher than the bleed valve to prevent air from being drawn into the caliper during bleeding.

4. Remove the master cylinder cover and diaphragm. Fill the reservoir to within 10 mm (3/8 in.) from the top.

5. Apply the brake lever or brake pedal and open the bleed valve. This will force air and brake fluid from the brake system. Close the bleed valve before the brake lever or pedal reaches its maximum limit or before brake fluid stops flowing from the bleed valve. Do not release the brake lever or pedal while the bleed valve is open. If the system was previously drained or new parts installed, brake fluid will not start draining from the system until after several repeated attempts are made. This is normal.

NOTE
Check the fluid level in the reservoir frequently. Do not let it run dry or additional bleeding will be needed.

6. Repeat this process until the brake fluid exiting the system is clear, with no air bubbles. If the system is difficult to bleed, tap the master cylinder and caliper housing with a soft-faced mallet to dislodge internal air bubbles so they can be released.

7. The system is bled when the brake lever or pedal feels firm, and there are no air bubbles exiting the system. Close the bleed valve and remove the bleed hose.

8. If necessary, add brake fluid to correct the level in the master cylinder reservoir. It must be above the level line.

Vacuum Bleeding

This procedure describes how to bleed the brake system with a vacuum pump (**Figure 109**).

1. Make sure both brake system union bolts are tight.
2. Remove the dust cap from the bleed valve and clean the valve and its opening of all dirt and other debris. If a dust cap was not used, use a thin screwdriver or similar tool and compressed air to remove all dirt from inside the bleed valve opening.
3. Remove the master cylinder cover and diaphragm. Fill the reservoir to within 10 mm (3/8 in.) from the top.
4. Assemble the vacuum pump according to the tool manufacturer's instructions.
5. Attach the pump hose to the bleed valve (**Figure 111**).
6. Operate the pump handle five to ten times to create a vacuum in the line between the pump and caliper. Then, open the bleed valve with a wrench. Doing so forces air and brake fluid from the system. Close the bleed valve before the brake fluid stops flowing from the valve or before the master cylinder reservoir runs empty. If the vacuum pump is equipped with a vacuum gauge, close the bleed valve before the vacuum reading on the gauge reaches 0 HG of vacuum.

7. Repeat this process until the brake fluid exiting the system is clear, with no air bubbles. If the system is difficult to bleed, tap the master cylinder and caliper housing with a soft-faced mallet to dislodge the internal air bubbles so they can be released.

NOTE
If the brake lever or pedal feel firm, indicating that air has been bled from the system, but air bubbles are still visible in the hose connected to the bleed valve, air may be entering the hose from its connection around the bleed valve.

8. The system is bled when the brake lever or pedal feels firm, and there are no air bubbles exiting the system. Tighten the bleed valve and disconnect the pump hose.
9. If necessary, add fluid to correct the level in the master cylinder reservoir. It must be above the level line.

Table 1 FRONT BRAKE SERVICE SPECIFICATIONS (CRF230F MODELS)

	New mm (in.)	Service limit mm (in.)
Brake disc thickness	2.8-3.2 (0.11-0.13)	2.5 (0.10)
Brake disc runout	–	0.1 (0.004)
Brake pad thickness*		
Caliper bore inside diameter	27.000 (1.0630)	–
Caliper piston outside diameter	26.968 (1.0617)	–
Master cylinder bore inside diameter	12.700 (0.5000)	–
Master cylinder piston outside diameter	12.684 (0.4994)	–

*Minimum pad thickness is determined by wear limit groove. Refer to Chapter Three.

16

Table 2 FRONT BRAKE SERVICE SPECIFICATIONS (CRF230L AND CRF230M MODELS)

	New mm (in.)	Service limit mm (in.)
Brake disc thickness	3.3-3.7 (0.13-0.15)	3.0 (0.12)
Brake disc runout	–	0.3 (0.012)
Brake pad thickness*		
Caliper bore inside diameter	25.400-25.450 (1.0000-1.0020)	25.460 (1.0024)
Caliper piston outside diameter	25.318-25.368 (0.9968-0.9987)	25.310 (0.9965)
Master cylinder bore inside diameter	12.700-12.743 (0.5000-0.5017)	12.755 (0.5022)
Master cylinder piston outside diameter	12.657-12.684 (0.4983-0.4994)	12.645 (0.4978)

*Minimum pad thickness is determined by wear limit groove. Refer to Chapter Three.

Table 3 REAR BRAKE SERVICE SPECIFICATIONS (CRF230F MODELS)

	New mm (in.)	Service limit mm (in.)
Brake drum inside diameter	110.0-110.2 (4.33-4.34)	111.0 (4.37)
Brake lining thickness	4.2 (0.17)	2.0 (0.08)

Table 4 REAR BRAKE SERVICE SPECIFICATIONS (CRF230L AND CRF230M MODELS)

	New mm (in.)	Service limit mm (in.)
Brake disc thickness	4.3-4.7 (0.17-0.19)	4.0 (0.16)
Brake disc runout	–	0.3 (0.01)
Brake pad thickness*		
Caliper bore inside diameter	27.000-27.050 (1.0630-1.0650)	27.06 (1.065)
Caliper piston outside diameter	26.918-26.968 (1.0598-1.0617)	26.91 (1.059)
Master cylinder bore inside diameter	14.000-14.043 (0.5512-0.5529)	14.055 (0.5533)
Master cylinder piston outside diameter	13.957-13.984 (0.5495-0.5506)	13.945 (0.5490)
Master cylinder pushrod length	69.5 (2.74)	–

*Minimum pad thickness is determined by wear limit groove. Refer to Chapter Three.

Table 5 BRAKE TORQUE SPECIFICATIONS (CRF230F MODELS)

	N•m	in.-lb.	ft.-lb.
Brake bleed valve	5.4	48	–
Front brake caliper fixed shaft	23	–	17
Front brake caliper mounting bolts	30	–	22
Front brake caliper pad pin bolt	18	156	–
Front brake caliper pad pin plug	3	27	–
Front brake disc bolts	20	–	15

(continued)

Table 5 BRAKE TORQUE SPECIFICATIONS (CRF230F MODELS) (continued)

	N•m	in.-lb.	ft.-lb.
Front brake lever pivot bolt			
2003-2005 models	6	53	–
2006-on models	1	9	–
Front brake lever pivot nut	6	53	–
Front brake master cylinder clamp bolt	10	89	–
Front brake master cylinder cover screws	2	18	–
Rear brake arm bolt	10	89	–
Union bolt	34	–	25

Table 6 BRAKE TORQUE SPECIFICATIONS (CRF230L AND CRF230M MODELS)

	N•m	in.-lb.	ft.-lb.
Brake bleed valve	6	53	–
Brake disc			
Front	20	–	15
Rear	42	–	31
Front brake caliper fixed shaft	22	–	16
Front brake caliper mounting bolts	30	–	22
Front brake caliper pad pin bolt	18	156	–
Front brake caliper pad pin plug	2.4	21	–
Front brake lever pivot bolt	1	9	–
Front brake lever pivot nut	5.9	52	–
Front brake master cylinder cover screws	1.5	13	–
Rear brake caliper bracket fixed shaft	12	106	–
Rear brake caliper fixed shaft	27	–	20
Rear brake caliper pad pin bolt	18	156	–
Rear brake caliper pad pin plug	2.4	21	–
Rear brake master cylinder mounting bolts	14	120	–
Rear brake pushrod clevis locknut	17.2	156	–
Union bolt	34	–	25

16

CHAPTER SEVENTEEN

BODY

LEFT SIDE COVER

Removal/Installation (CRF230F Models)

1. Remove the upper retaining bolt (A, **Figure 1**) and collar.
2. Remove the lower bolt (B, **Figure 1**).
3. Remove the retaining screw (C, **Figure 1**).
4. Pull the cover (D, **Figure 1**) out of the rear grommet.
5. Detach the front of the cover from the front grommet, and then remove the cover.
6. Reverse the removal steps for installation. Tighten the bolts and retaining screw securely.

Removal/Installation (CRF230L and CRF230M Models)

1. Remove the trim clip (A, **Figure 2**).
2. Remove the bolts (B, **Figure 2**).
3. Pull the cover (C, **Figure 2**) out of the upper grommet, and then remove the cover.
4. Reverse the removal steps for installation. Note the following:
   a. Tighten the bolts to 1 N•m (9 in.-lb.).
   b. Make sure the trim clip is securely installed.

RIGHT SIDE COVER

Removal/Installation (CRF230F Models)

1. Remove the retaining screw (A, **Figure 3**).
2. Pull the cover (B, **Figure 3**) out of the rear grommet.
3. Detach the front of the cover from the front grommet, and then remove the cover.
4. Reverse the removal steps for installation. Tighten the retaining screw securely.

Removal/Installation (CRF230L and CRF230M Models)

1. Remove the bolts (A, **Figure 4**).
2. Pull the cover (B, **Figure 4**) out of the upper grommet and remove the cover.
3. Reverse the removal steps for installation. Tighten the bolts to 1 N•m (9 in.-lb.).

SEAT

Removal/Installation (CRF230F Models)

1. Remove the side covers as described in this chapter.
2. Remove the seat retaining bolt (**Figure 5**), collar and nut on each side.
3. Lift up the rear of the seat. Then, remove the seat by pulling it rearward.
4. Reverse the removal steps to install the seat. Note the following:
   a. Make sure the notch (A, **Figure 6**) on the seat engages the post (B) on the fuel tank.
   b. Make sure the tab (C, **Figure 6**) on the seat engages the bracket (D) on the frame.
   c. Tighten the bolts securely.

Removal/Installation (CRF230L and CRF230M Models)

1. Remove the side covers (this chapter).
2. Remove the seat retaining bolt (**Figure 7**) on each side.
3. Lift up the rear of the seat. Then, remove the seat by pulling it rearward.
4. Reverse the removal steps to install the seat. Note the following:

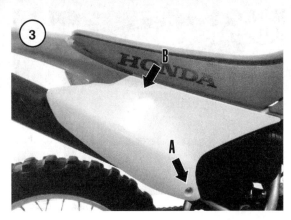

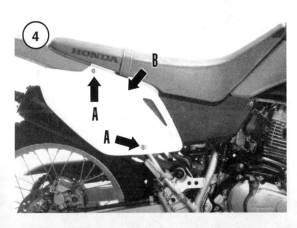

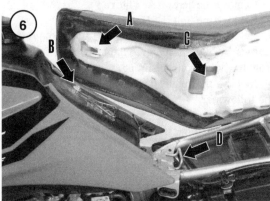

a. Make sure the notch (A, **Figure 8**) on the seat engages the post (B) on the fuel tank.
b. Make sure the tab (C, **Figure 8**) on the seat engages the bracket (D) on the frame.
c. Tighten the seat retaining bolts to 21.5 N•m (16 ft.-lb.).

FUEL TANK SHROUDS
(CRF230L AND CRF230M MODELS)

Removal/Installation

1. Remove the seat (this chapter).

17

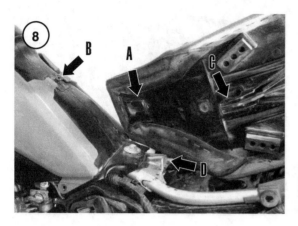

2. Remove the screw (A, **Figure 9**).

3. Remove the bolt (B, **Figure 9**).

4. Remove the shroud (C, **Figure 9**) by moving it rearward while disengaging the tab on the fuel tank from the holder on the shroud.

5. Reverse the removal steps for installation. Note the following:

    a. Make sure the tab on the fuel tank engages the holder on the shroud.

    b. Tighten the screw (A, **Figure 9**) and bolt (B) securely.

NUMBER PLATE (CRF230F MODELS)

Removal/Installation

1. Detach the number plate strap (**Figure 10**).

2. Remove the retaining bolt (**Figure 11**).

3. Remove the number plate.

4. Reverse the removal steps for installation. Note the following:

    a. Position the bottom of the number plate so the locating holes (A, **Figure 12**) fit around the tops of the front fender retaining bolts (B).

    b. Tighten the retaining bolt securely.

HEADLIGHT VISOR
(CRF230L AND CRF230M MODELS)

The headlight visor and headlight lens assembly must be removed as a unit. Refer to Chapter Eleven.

FRONT FENDER

Removal/Installation (CRF230F Models)

1. Remove the number plate (this chapter).

2. Remove the mounting bolts (A, **Figure 13**) and washers. Then, remove the front fender (B, **Figure 13**).

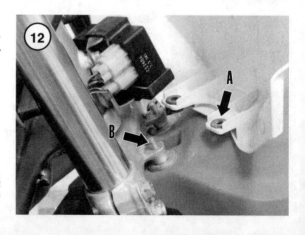

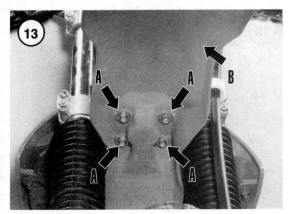

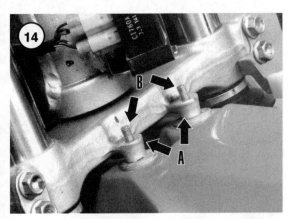

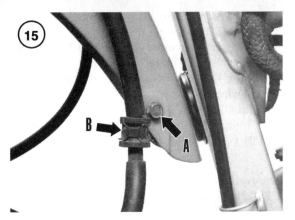

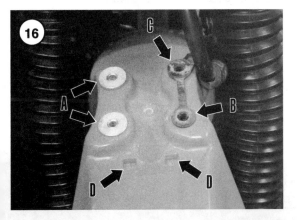

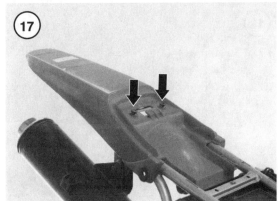

3. Reverse the removal step to install the front fender. Note the following:
   a. Install the flange collars (A, **Figure 14**) on the top side of the fender.
   b. Install the long bolts in the front mounting holes. The bolts (B, **Figure 14**) protrude through the mounting flange and fit into the mounting holes on the number plate.
   c. Tighten the mounting bolts securely.

**Removal/Installation
(CRF230L And CRF230M Models)**

1. Remove the bolt (A, **Figure 15**) and clamp (B) securing the front brake hose to the fender.
2. Remove the mounting bolts (A, **Figure 13**) and washers. Then, remove the front fender (B, **Figure 13**).
3. Reverse the removal steps to install the front fender. Note the following:
   a. Place the flange collars (A, **Figure 16**) in the holes on the right side of the fender.
   b. Place the brake hose bracket (B, **Figure 16**) in the holes on the left side of the fender.
   c. Place the flat washer (C, **Figure 16**) on the rear hole of the brake hose bracket.
   d. The lower prongs on the headlight visor fit into the pockets (D, **Figure 16**) in the front fender.
   e. Tighten the clamp bolt (A, **Figure 15**) and the mounting bolts (A, **Figure 13**) securely.

REAR FENDER

Removal/Installation (CRF230F Models)

1. Remove the seat as described in this chapter.
2. Remove the rear fender mounting bolts (**Figure 17**).
3. Remove the rear fender.
4. Reverse the removal steps to install the rear fender. Tighten the mounting bolts (**Figure 17**) securely.

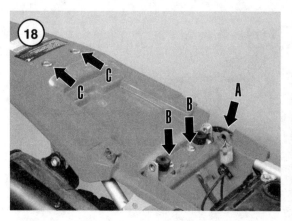

Removal/Installation
(CRF230L And CRF230M Models)

1. Remove the seat (this chapter).
2. Remove the ICM (Chapter Eleven).
3. Disengage the ICM connector lead from the guide (A, **Figure 18**) in the rear fender.
4. Remove the 6-mm (B, **Figure 18**) and 8-mm (C) mounting bolts.
5. Remove the rear fender.
6. Reverse the removal steps to install the rear fender. Note the following:
   a. Make sure the ICM connector lead engages the guide (A, **Figure 18**) in the rear fender.
   b. Tighten the mounting bolts securely.

SKID PLATE (CRF230F MODELS)

Removal/Installation

1. Remove the front bolt (A, **Figure 19**).
2. Remove the side bolts (B, **Figure 19**), and then remove the skid plate.
3. Reverse the removal steps for installation. Tighten the bolts securely.

FOOT PEGS

Removal/Installation (CRF230F Models)

1. Remove the cotter pin and washer.

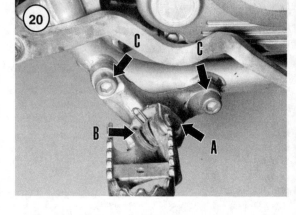

2. Remove the pivot pin (A, **Figure 20**) and spring (B).
3. Remove the foot peg.
4. If necessary to remove the foot peg bracket, remove the bolts (C, **Figure 20**).
5. Reverse the removal steps for installation. Note the following:
   a. Install new bracket bolts.
   b. Tighten the foot peg bolts to 59 N•m (44 ft.-lb.).

Removal/Installation
(CRF230L And CRF230M Models)

1. Remove the cotter pin and washer.
2. Remove the pivot pin and spring.
3. Remove the foot peg.
4. Reverse the removal steps for installation.

Table 1 BODY TORQUE SPECIFICATIONS

	N•m	in.-lb.	ft.-lb.
Foot peg bolt (CRF230F models)	59	–	44
Seat mounting bolts			
(CRF230L and CRF230M models)	21.5	–	16
Side cover assembly mounting bolts	1.0	9	–

INDEX

I

I

WIRING DIAGRAMS

Scan the QR code or search for "Clymer Manuals YouTube Tech Tips" to see an overview on electrical troubleshooting with a wiring diagram.

2003-ON CRF230F MODELS

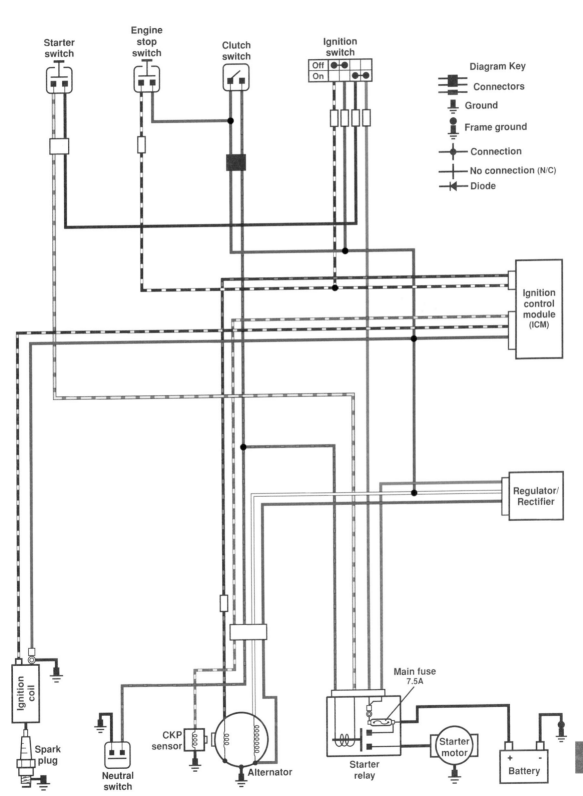

2008-2009 CRF230L/M MODELS

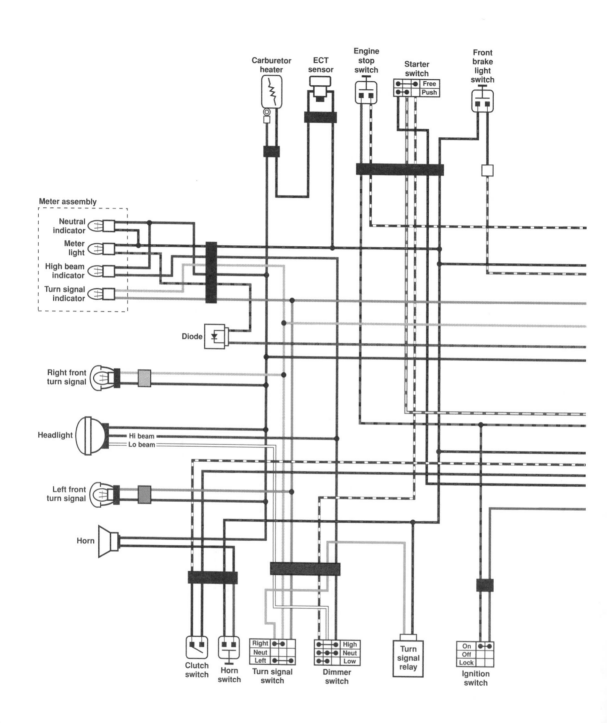

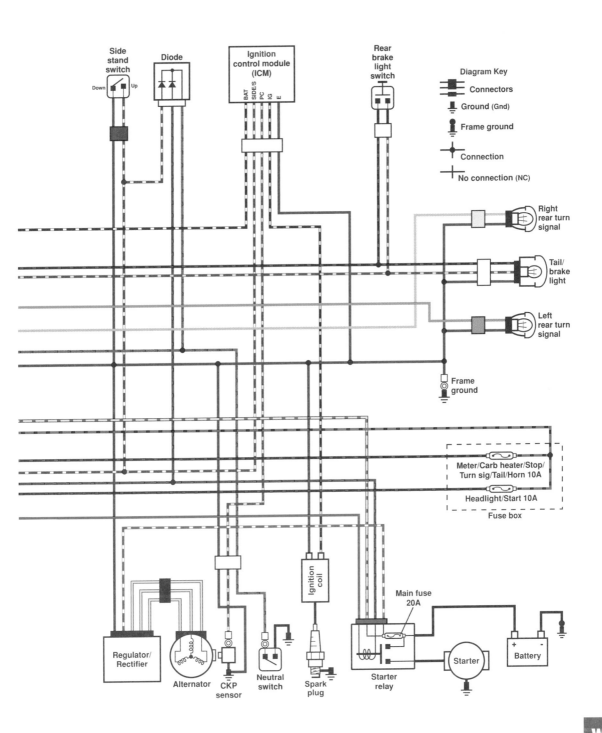

NOTES

NOTES

NOTES

NOTES

NOTES

MAINTENANCE LOG

Date	Miles	Type of Service

BMW

M308	500 & 600cc Twins, 55-69
M502-3	BMW R50/5-R100GS PD, 70-96
M500-3	BMW K-Series, 85-97
M501-3	K1200RS, GT & LT, 98-10
M503-3	R850, R1100, R1150 & R1200C, 93-05
M309	F650, 1994-2000

HARLEY-DAVIDSON

M419	Sportsters, 59-85
M429-5	XL/XLH Sportster, 86-03
M427-4	XL Sportster, 04-13
M418	Panheads, 48-65
M420	Shovelheads,66-84
M421-3	FLS/FXS Evolution,84-99
M423-2	FLS/FXS Twin Cam, 00-05
M250	FLS/FXS/FXC Softail, 06-09
M422-3	FLH/FLT/FXR Evolution, 84-98
M430-4	FLH/FLT Twin Cam, 99-05
M252	FLH/FLT, 06-09
M426	VRSC Series, 02-07
M424-2	FXD Evolution, 91-98
M425-3	FXD Twin Cam, 99-05
M254	Dyna Series, 06-11

HONDA

ATVs

M316	Odyssey FL250, 77-84
M311	ATC, TRX & Fourtrax 70-125, 70-87
M433	Fourtrax 90, 93-00
M326	ATC185 & 200, 80-86
M347	ATC200X & Fourtrax 200SX, 86-88
M455	ATC250 & Fourtrax 200/250, 84-87
M342	ATC250R, 81-84
M348	TRX250R/Fourtrax 250R & ATC250R, 85-89
M456-4	TRX250X 87-92; TRX300EX 93-06
M446-3	TRX250 Recon & Recon ES, 97-07
M215-2	TTRX250EX Sportrax and TRX250X, 01-12
M346-3	TRX300/Fourtrax 300 & TRX300FW/Fourtrax 4x4, 88-00
M200-2	TRX350 Rancher, 00-06
M459-3	TRX400 Foreman 95-03
M454-5	TRX400EX Fourtrax & Sportrax 99-13
M201	TRX450R & TRX450ER, 04-09
M205	TRX450 Foreman, 98-04
M210	TRX500 Rubicon, 01-04
M206	TRX500 Foreman, 05-11

Singles

M310-13	50-110cc OHC Singles, 65-99
M315	100-350cc OHC, 69-82
M317	125-250cc Elsinore, 73-80
M442	CR60-125R Pro-Link, 81-88
M431-2	CR80R, 89-95, CR125R, 89-91
M435	CR80R &CR80RB, 96-02
M457-2	CR125R, 92-97; CR250R, 92-96
M464	CR125R, 1998-2002
M443	CR250R-500R Pro-Link, 81-87
M432-3	CR250R, 88-91 & CR500R, 88-01
M437	CR250R, 97-01
M352	CRF250R, CRF250X, CRF450R & CRF450X, 02-05
M319-3	XR50R, CRF50F, XR70R & CRF70F, 97-09
M312-14	XL/XR75-100, 75-91
M222	XR80R, CRF80F, XR100R, & CRF100F, 92-09
M318-4	XL/XR/TLR 125-200, 79-03
M328-4	XL/XR250, 78-00; XL/XR350R 83-85; XR200R, 84-85; XR250L, 91-96
M320-2	XR400R, 96-04
M221	XR600R, 91-07; XR650L, 93-07
M339-8	XL/XR 500-600, 79-90
M225	XR650R, 00-07

Twins

M321	125-200cc Twins, 65-78
M322	250-350cc Twins, 64-74
M323	250-360cc Twins, 74-77
M324-5	Twinstar, Rebel 250 & Nighthawk 250, 78-03
M334	400-450cc Twins, 78-87
M333	450 & 500cc Twins, 65-76
M335	CX & GL500/650, 78-83
M344	VT500, 83-88
M313	VT700 & 750, 83-87
M314-3	VT750 Shadow Chain Drive, 98-06
M440	VT1100C Shadow, 85-96
M460-4	VT1100 Series, 95-07
M230	VTX1800 Series, 02-08
M231	VTX1300 Series, 03-09

Fours

M332	CB350-550, SOHC, 71-78
M345	CB550 & 650, 83-85
M336	CB650,79-82
M341	CB750 SOHC, 69-78
M337	CB750 DOHC, 79-82
M436	CB750 Nighthawk, 91-93 & 95-99
M325	CB900, 1000 & 1100, 80-83
M439	600 Hurricane, 87-90
M441-2	CBR600F2 & F3, 91-98
M445-2	CBR600F4, 99-06
M220	CBR600RR, 03-06
M434-2	CBR900RR Fireblade, 93-99
M329	500cc V-Fours, 84-86
M349	700-1000cc Interceptor, 83-85
M458-2	VFR700F-750F, 86-97
M438	VFR800FI Interceptor, 98-00
M327	700-1100cc V-Fours, 82-88
M508	ST1100/Pan European, 90-02
M340	GL1000 & 1100, 75-83
M504	GL1200, 84-87

Sixes

M505	GL1500 Gold Wing, 88-92
M506-2	GL1500 Gold Wing, 93-00
M507-3	GL1800 Gold Wing, 01-10
M462-2	GL1500C Valkyrie, 97-03

KAWASAKI

ATVs

M465-3	Bayou KLF220 & KLF250, 88-10
M466-4	Bayou KLF300, 86-04
M467	Bayou KLF400, 93-99
M470	Lakota KEF300, 95-99
M385-2	Mojave KSF250, 87-04

Singles

M350-9	80-350cc Rotary Valve, 66-01
M444-2	KX60, 83-02; KX80 83-90
M448-2	KX80, 91-00; KX85, 01-10 & KX100, 89-09
M351	KDX200, 83-88
M447-3	KX125 & KX250, 82-91; KX500, 83-04
M472-2	KX125, 92-00
M473-2	KX250, 92-00
M474-3	KLR650, 87-07
M240-2	KLR650, 08-12

Twins

M355	KZ400, KZ/Z440, EN450 & EN500, 74-95
M241	Ninja 250R (EX250), 88-12
M360-3	EX500, GPZ500S, & Ninja 500R, 87-02
M356-5	Vulcan 700 & 750, 85-06
M354-3	Vulcan 800, 95-05
M246	Vulcan 900, 06-12
M357-2	Vulcan 1500, 87-99
M471-3	Vulcan 1500 Series, 96-08
M245	Vulcan 1600 Series, 03-08

Fours

M449	KZ500/550 & ZX550, 79-85
M450	KZ, Z & ZX750, 80-85
M358	KZ650, 77-83
M359-3	Z & KZ 900-1000cc, 73-81
M451-3	KZ, ZX & ZN 1000 &1100cc, 81-02
M452-3	ZX500 & Ninja ZX600, 85-97
M468-2	Ninja ZX-6, 90-04
M469	Ninja ZX-7, ZX7R & ZX7RR, 91-98
M453-3	Ninja ZX900, ZX1000 & ZX1100, 84-01
M409-2	Concours, 86-06

POLARIS

ATVs

M496	3-, 4- and 6-Wheel Models w/250-425cc Engines, 85-95
M362-2	Magnum & Big Boss, 96-99
M363	Scrambler 500 4X4, 97-00
M365-5	Sportsman/Xplorer, 96-13
M366	Sportsman 600/700/800 Twins, 02-10
M367	Predator 500, 03-07

SUZUKI

ATVs

M381	ALT/LT 125 & 185, 83-87
M475	LT230 & LT250, 85-90
M380-2	LT250R Quad Racer, 85-92
M483-2	LT-4WD, LT-F4WDX & LT-F250, 87-98
M270-2	LT-Z400, 03-08
M343-2	LT-F500F Quadrunner, 98-02

Singles

M369	125-400cc, 64-81
M371	RM50-400 Twin Shock, 75-81
M379	RM125-500 Single Shock, 81-88
M386	RM80-250, 89-95
M400	RM125, 96-00
M401	RM250, 96-02
M476	DR250-350, 90-94
M477-4	DR-Z400E, S & SM, 00-12
M272	DR650, 96-12
M384-5	LS650 Savage/S40, 86-12

Twins

M372	GS400-450 Chain Drive, 77-87
M484-3	GS500E Twins, 89-02
M361	SV650, 1999-2002
M481-6	VS700-800 Intruder/S50, 85-09
M261-2	1500 Intruder/C90, 98-09
M260-3	Volusia/Boulevard C50, 01-11
M482-3	VS1400 Intruder/S83, 87-07

Triple

M368	GT380, 550 & 750, 72-77

Fours

M373	GS550, 77-86
M364	GS650, 81-83
M370	GS750, 77-82
M376	GS850-1100 Shaft Drive, 79-84
M378	GS1100 Chain Drive, 80-81
M383-3	Katana 600, 88-96
	GSX-R750-1100, 86-87
M331	GSX-R600, 97-00
M264	GSX-R600, 01-05
M478-2	GSX-R750, 88-92; GSX750F Katana, 89-96
M485	GSX-R750, 96-99
M377	GSX-R1000, 01-04
M266	GSX-R1000, 05-06
M265	GSX1300R Hayabusa, 99-07
M338	Bandit 600, 95-00
M353	GSF1200 Bandit, 96-03

YAMAHA

ATVs

M499-2	YFM80 Moto-4, Badger & Raptor, 85-08
M394	YTM200, 225 & YFM200, 83-86
M488-5	Blaster, 88-05
M489-2	Timberwolf, 89-00
M487-5	Warrior, 87-04
M486-6	Banshee, 87-06
M490-3	Moto-4 & Big Bear, 87-04
M493	Kodiak, 93-98
M287-2	YFZ450, 04-13
M285-2	Grizzly 660, 02-08
M280-2	Raptor 660R, 01-05
M290	Raptor 700R, 06-09
M291	Rhino 700, 2008-2012

Singles

M492-2	PW50 & 80 Y-Zinger & BW80 Big Wheel 80, 81-02
M410	80-175 Piston Port, 68-76
M415	250-400 Piston Port, 68-76
M412	DT & MX Series, 77-83
M414	IT125-490, 76-86
M393	YZ50-80 Monoshock, 78-90
M413	YZ100-490 Monoshock, 76-84
M390	YZ125-250, 85-87 YZ490, 85-90
M391	YZ125-250, 88-93 & WR250Z, 91-93
M497-2	YZ125, 94-01
M498	YZ250, 94-98; WR250Z, 94-97
M406	YZ250F & WR250F, 01-03
M491-2	YZ400F, 98-99 & 426F, 00-02; WR400F, 98-00 & 426F, 00-01
M417	XT125-250, 80-84
M480-3	XT350, 85-00; TT350, 86-87
M405	XT/TT 500, 76-81
M416	XT/TT 600, 83-89

Twins

M403	650cc Twins, 70-82
M395-10	XV535-1100 Virago, 81-03
M495-7	V-Star 650, 98-11
M284	V-Star 950, 09-12
M281-4	V-Star 1100, 99-09
M283	V-Star 1300, 07-10
M282-2	Road Star, 99-07

Triple

M404	XS750 & XS850, 77-81

Fours

M387	XJ550, XJ600 & FJ600, 81-92
M494	XJ600 Seca II/Diversion, 92-98
M388	XJ600 Radian & FZ600, 86-90
M396	FZR600, 89-93
M392	FZ700-750 & Fazer, 85-87
M411	XS1100, 78-81
M461	YZF-R6, 99-04
M398	YZF-R1, 98-03
M399	FZ1, 01-05
M397	FJ1100 & 1200, 84-93
M375-2	V-Max, 85-07
M374-2	Royal Star, 96-10

VINTAGE MOTORCYCLES

Clymer® Collection Series

M330	Vintage British Street Bikes, BSA 500-650cc Unit Twins; Norton 750 & 850cc Commandos; Triumph 500-750cc Twins
M300	Vintage Dirt Bikes, V. 1 Bultaco, 125-370cc Singles; Montesa, 123-360cc Singles; Ossa, 125-250cc Singles
M305	Vintage Japanese Street Bikes Honda, 250 & 305cc Twins; Kawasaki, 250-750cc Triples; Kawasaki, 900 & 1000cc Fours